IvyPrep

SAT: The Ultimate Guide Fall Supplement

Table of Contents

Essential Vocabulary

Sentence Completion

Critical Reading

Writing & Grammar

Mathematics

"It is a great nuisance that knowledge can be acquired only by hard work."

W. Somerset Maugham

Essential Vocabulary
16 word lists

Vocabulary Review 01

abate	v	to lessen; to subside
abdicate	v	to renounce one's throne
aberrant	adj	departing from an accepted standard
aberration	n	straying away from what is normal
abhorrent	adj	inspiring disgust; repugnant
abjure	v	to promise or swear to give up
abominable	adj	very unpleasant
abrasiveness	n	showing little concern for the feelings of others
absolve	v	to declare free from blame, guilt, or responsibility
abstruse	adj	difficult to comprehend obscure
abundant	adj	having plenty of
abut	v	to be net to or have a common boundary with
abysmal	adj	1. extremely bad 2. very deep
acclimate	v	to become accustomed to a new climate or to a new condition
accolade	n	praise approval
acerbic	adj	1. sharp and forthright 2. tasting sour or bitter
acidity	n	the bitterness or sharpness of a person's remark or tone
acme	n	the point at which someone or something is best or most successful
acquiescence	v	to accept something reluctantly but without protest
acquit	v	to free from a criminal charge by a verdict of not guilty
acumen	n	the ability to make good judgments and quick decisions
adept	adj	very skilled or proficient at something
adhere	v	to stick fast to
admonitory	adj	conveying a warning or reprimand
adoration	n	love and respect
adroit	adj	clever or skillful in using the hands or mind
adulation	n	excessive admiration or praise
adulterate	v	to render something poorer in quality by adding another substance
advice	n	guidance or recommendation
advocate	v	to publicly recommend or support
aerate	v	to introduce air into a material
affable	adj	polite and friendly

affiliation	n	the state or process of being associated with someone or something
affirmation	n	the act of asserting strongly and publicly
affluent	adj	having a great deal of money; wealthy
aggressive	adj	ready or likely to attack or confront
agnostic	n	a person who claims neither faith nor disbelief in God
ailment	n	a minor illness
alacrity	n	eager and cheerful readiness
allege	v	to claim or assert that someone has dome something wrong or illegal
alleviate	v	to make pain easier to bear
alliance	n	a union formed for mutual benefit
allure	v	to powerfully attract or charm
aloof	adj	not friendly or forthcoming; cool and distant
altercation	n	a noisy argument or disagreement
amalgamate	v	to combine or unite to form one organization or structure
ambitious	adj	showing a strong desire and determination to succeed
ameliorate	v	to improve; make better
amiable	adj	displaying a friendly and pleasant manner
anachronistic	adj	belonging to a time period other than the one in which it exists
anarchy	n	a state of disorder due to absence or lack of government authority
ancient	adj	having been in existence for a very long time
anesthetic	n	a substance that induces insensitivity to pain
animated	adj	full of life or excitement; lively
animosity	n	strong dislike
animus	n	1. hostility or ill feeling 2. motivation to do something
anomaly	n	something that deviated from what is standard
anonymous	adj	of unknown name
antagonism	n	active hostility or opposition
antediluvian	adj	ridiculously old-fashioned
antipathy	n	a deep-seated feeling of dislike; aversion
antiquated	adj	old-fashioned or outdated

Vocabulary Review 02

apathy	n	lack of interest, enthusiasm, or concern
apex	n	the top or highest part of something
apocryphal	adj	of doubtful authenticity, although widely circulated as being true
apogee	n	the highest point in the development of something
apolitical	adj	not interested or involved in politics
appease	v	to make quiet or calm
apprentice	n	a person who is learning a trade from a skilled employer
approbate	v	to approve formally; sanction
appurtenance	n	an accessory or other item associated with a particular activity or style of living
apropos	adj	very appropriate to a particular situation
arable	adj	used or suitable for growing crops
arbitrator	n	an independent person or body officially appointed to settle a dispute
arboreal	adj	of or relating to trees
arcane	adj	understood by few; mysterious or secret
archaic	adj	very old or old-fashioned
ardent	adj	enthusiastic or passionate
arduous	adj	involving or requiring strenuous effort
arid	adj	having little or no rain; too dry or barren to support vegetation
arrhythmic	adj	not rhythmic; without rhythm or regularity
articulate	adj	having or showing the ability to speak fluently and coherently
ascend	v	to go up or climb
ascertain	v	to find out for certain
ascetic	adj	characterize by the practice of severe self-discipline for religious reasons
asperity	n	harshness of tone or manner
aspersion	n	an attack on the reputation or integrity of someone or something
assault	v	to make a physical attack
assiduous	adj	showing great care and perseverance
assimilate	v	to take in information, ideas, or culture and understand fully
assuage	v	to make an unpleasant feeling less intense
astute	adj	having or showing an ability to accurately assess situations or people
atrocious	adj	of a very poor quality; extremely bad or unpleasant
atrophy	v	waste away, typically due to the degeneration of cells

audacious	adj	showing a willingness to take surprisingly bold risks
augment	v	to make something greater by adding to it; increase
augury	n	a sign of what will happen in the future; an omen
aural	adj	of or relating to the ear or the sense of hearing
austere	adj	severe or strict in manner, attitude, or appearance
autocratic	adj	of or relating to a ruler who has absolute power
autonomous	adj	have self-government, at least to a significant degree
autonomy	n	a self-governing country or region
aversion	n	strong dislike
avert	v	1. to turn away 2. to prevent or ward off
avid	adj	having or showing a keen interest in or enthusiasm for something
badinage	n	humorous or witty conversation
banal	adj	so lacking in originality as to be obvious and boring
banish	v	to send someone away from a country or place as a official punishment
banter	n	playful and friendly exchange of teasing remarks
barefaced	adj	shameless; undisguised
barrage	n	a concentrated outpouring, as of questions or blows
barter	v	to exchange goods or services for other goods or services without money
bath	n	the act of immersing and washing one's body in a large container of water
bawdy	adj	humorously indecent
beget	v	to give rise to,; bring about
beguile	v	to charm or enchant someone, sometimes in a deceptive way
belabor	v	to argue or elaborate in excessive detail
belies	v	to fail to give a true notion or impression of something
belittle	v	to make someone or something seem unimportant
bellicose	adj	demonstrating aggression and willingness to fight; warlike
bemuse	adj	puzzled, confused, or bewildered
benefactor	n	a person who gives money or other help to a person or cause
beneficent	adj	generous or doing good
benevolent	adj	well meaning and kindly

Vocabulary Review 03

benign	adj	1. mild and favorable 2. not harmful
bequeath	v	to leave a personal estate to a beneficiary by a will
berserk	adj	out of control with anger or excitement
beseech	v	to ask someone urgently to do something
besiege	v	to surround with armed forces in order to capture it
besmirch	v	to damage the reputation of someone or something
bewitch	v	to enchant or delight someone
bigot	n	a stubborn narrow-minded person
bilious	adj	spiteful; bad-tempered
blasphemous	adj	sacrilegious against God or sacred things; profane
blaze	n	a very large or fiercely burning fire
blight	n	a thing that spoils or damages something
blithe	adj	happy or joyous
bolster	v	to support or strengthen; to prop up
bombastic	adj	high-sounding but with little meaning; inflated
boor	n	an unrefined, ill-mannered person
boorish	adj	crude; offensive; rude
bountiful	adj	large in quantity, abundant
bounty	adj	abundance, plenty
boycott	v	to withdraw from commercial or social relations with
brazen	adj	bold and without shame
breadth	n	width range or extent
brevity	n	concise use of words
bulwark	n	a person, institution, or principle that acts as a defense
burlesque	n	humor that depends on comic imitation and exaggeration; absurdity
buttress	n	a source of defense or support
bypass	v	to go past or around
byzantine	adj	characterized by deviousness or underhanded procedures
cacophony	n	a harsh, discordant mixture of sounds
cajole	v	to use flattery or deceit to persuade
callous	adj	showing or having an insensitive and cruel disregard for others
calumny	n	the making of false and defamatory statements

candor	n	the quality of being open and honest in expression; frankness
capricious	adj	given to sudden and unaccountable changes of mood or behavior
carillon	n	a set of bells in a tower
castigate	v	to reprimand severely
cataclysmic	adj	relating to or denoting a violent natural event
catastrophic	adj	involving or causing sudden great damage or suffering
caucus	n	a group of people with shared concerns
caustic	adj	sarcastic in a scathing and bitter way
cavalier	n	a courtly gentleman
censure	v	to express severe disapproval of someone or something
centurion	n	commander of a unit of 100 soldiers
cerebral	adj	of the cerebrum of the brain
certitude	n	absolute certainty
chaffing	n	lighthearted joking; banter
chaos	n	complete disorder and confusion
charlatan	n	a person falsely claiming to have a special knowledge or skill; a fraud
chauvinistic	adj	feeling or displaying aggressive or exaggerated patriotism
cherubic	adj	having childlike innocence
chimera	n	a thing that is hoped or wished for but in fact is impossible to achieve
chorale	n	a choir or choral society
churlish	adj	rude in a mean-spirited and surly way
circuitous	adj	longer than the most direct way
circumlocution	n	the use of many words where fewer would do
circumscribe	v	to restrict something within limits
circumvent	v	to find a way around an obstacle
civility	n	formal politeness and courtesy in behavior or speech
cliché	n	a phrase or opinion that is overused
cloistered	adj	kept away from the outside world; shelter
coalition	n	an alliance for combined action
coax	v	to persuade gradually or by flattery to do something

Vocabulary Review 04

coerce	v	to persuade an unwilling person to do something by using force
cogent	adj	clear, logical, and convincing, usually describing an argument
comatose	adj	of or in a state of deep unconsciousness for a prolonged or indefinite period
commend	v	to praise formally or officially
commendable	adj	deserving praise
commensurate	adj	corresponding in size or degree; in proportion
commotion	n	a state of confused and noisy disturbance
compassionate	adj	feeling or showing sympathy and concern for others
compendious	adj	presenting the essential facts in a comprehensive but concise way
complement	v	to add to something in a way that enhances or improves it; make perfect
compliment	n	a polite expression of praise or respect
comply	v	to act in accordance with a wise or command
compulsive	adj	resulting form or relating to an irresistible urge
conciliatory	adj	intended or likely to placate or pacify
concord	n	agreement or harmony
concordant	adj	in agreement; consistent
concur	v	1. to agree with 2. to happen as the same time
condemn	v	to express complete of disapproval of, typically in public
condone	v	accept and allow behavior that is considered offensive to continue
conduct	n	the manner in which a person behaves in a particular occasion or context
conflagration	n	an extensive fire that destroys a great deal of land or property
conformity	n	compliance with standards, rules, or laws
congeal	v	solidify or coagulate, especially by cooling
congenial	adj	pleasant or agreeable because suited to one's taste or inclination
conglomerate	n	individual things or parts that are put together to form a whole
conniving	adj	given to or involved in conspiring to do something immoral or harmful
connoisseur	n	an expert judge in matters of taste
conscientious	adj	wishing to do what is right, especially in one's work or duty
consecrate	v	to make or declare something sacred
consensus	n	a general agreement
console	v	to comfort someone at a time of grief or disappointment
consolidate	v	to make something stronger or more solid or to combine a number of things

consortium	n	an association, typically of several business companies
consternation	n	feelings of anxiety or dismay, typically at something unexpected
consummate	v	to complete or make perfect
contagion	n	the communication of disease or ideas from one person to another
contempt	n	the feeling that a person or thing is beneath consideration or worthless
contentious	adj	causing or likely to cause an argument; controversial
contest	v	to oppose an action, decision, or theory as mistaken or wrong
contiguous	adj	sharing a common border with; touching
conviction	n	a firmly held belief or opinion
convivial	adj	friendly and lively; jovial
convoluted	adj	extremely complex and difficult to follow
copious	adj	abundant in supply or quantity
coquette	n	a woman who flirts
corollary	n	a direct or natural consequence or result
corporeal	adj	of or relating to a person's body
corpulence	n	the state of being fat; obesity
corroborate	v	to confirm or give support to
coterie	n	a small group of people with shared interests or tastes
cowardice	n	lack of bravery
cower	v	to crouch down in fear
cozen	v	to trick or deceive
craven	adj	contemptibly lacking in courage; cowardly
crest	n	the top of something, typically a mountain or hill
cryptic	adj	having a meaning that is mysterious or obscure
culpability	n	responsibility for a fault or wrong; blame
culpable	adj	deserving blame
curative	adj	able to cure something, typically a disease
cursory	adj	hasty and therefore not thorough or detailed
curtail	v	to reduce in extent or quantity; to impose a restriction on
dainty	adj	delicately small and pretty

Vocabulary Review 05

dalliance	n	a brief or casual involvement with something
dally	v	to act or move slowly
dapple	v	to mark with spots or round patches
dauntless	adj	showing fearlessness and bravery
dearth	n	a scarcity or lack of something; shortage
debacle	n	a sudden and ignominious failure; a fiasco
debased	adj	reduced in quality or value
debilitating	adj	tending to weaken something
debility	n	physical weakness, especially from an illness
debunk	v	to expose the falseness or hollowness of an idea
deceit	n	the action or practice of deceiving someone by concealing the truth
deceitful	adj	guilty of deceiving or misleading others
decorum	n	behavior in keeping with good taste and propriety
decoy	n	a person or thing that is used to mislead someone into a trap
decry	v	publicly denounce
defamation	n	the action of damaging the good reputation of someone; slander or libel
defect	v	to abandon one's cause in favor of an opposing one
defer	v	to submit humbly
deference	n	respect; putting another's interests before one's own
defiance	n	open resistance
deficit	n	the amount by which something, especially a sum of money, is too small
defile	v	to sully, mar, or spoil
deft	adj	demonstrating skill and cleverness
degenerate	adj	having lost the physical, mental, or moral qualities considered desirable
dehydrate	v	to lose a large amount of water from a body
deleterious	adj	causing harm or damage
delineate	v	to describe or portray precisely
demur	v	to raise doubts or rejections
denounce	v	to publicly declare to be wrong or evil
deplorable	adj	deserving strong condemnation; shockingly bad in quality
deprave	v	to make someone immoral or wicked
depreciate	v	to diminish in value over a period of time

deride	v	to express contempt for; to ridicule
derision	n	contemptuous ridicule or mockery
descry	v	to catch sight of
desiccate	v	to remove moisture from
despondent	adj	in low spirits from loss of hope or courage
despot	n	a cruel or oppressive ruler who holds absolute power
devious	adj	showing a skillful use of underhanded tactics to achieve goals
devoid	adj	entirely lacking or free from
dexterous	adj	demonstrating neat skill, especially with the hands
diatribe	n	a forceful and bitter verbal attack against someone or something
didactic	adj	in the manner of a teacher, or treating someone in a patronizing way
diffidence	n	modesty or shyness resulting from a lack of self-confidence
diffuse	v	to spread or cause to spread over a wide area
digest	n	a compilation or summary of material or information
dire	adj	extremely serious or urgent
dirge	n	a lament for the dead
discern	v	to perceive or recognize something
disclose	v	to make secret or new information known
discombobulate	v	to discount or confuse someone
disconsolate	adj	without consolation or comfort; unhappy
discord	n	disagreement between people
discredit	v	to harm the good reputation of someone or something
discrepancy	n	a lack of compatibility or similarity between two or more
disgraceful	adj	shockingly unacceptable
disillusioned	adj	disappointment in the discovery that something is less good than once believed
disown	v	to refuse to acknowledge or maintain and connection with
disparage	v	to regard or represent as being of little worth
dispense	v	to manage without; get rid of
disseminate	v	to spread or disperse something widely
dissident	adj	in opposition to official policy

Vocabulary Review 06

distend	v	to swell or cause to swell by pressure from inside
divulge	v	to make known
docile	adj	ready to accept control or instruction; submissive
dogmatic	adj	inclined to lay down principles as incontrovertibly true; stubborn
doleful	adj	expressing sorrow; mournful
dote	v	to be extremely and uncritically fond of
dowdy	adj	unfashionable and without style in appearance
drab	adj	lacking brightness or interest, drearily dull
dubious	adj	hesitating or doubting
dyslexia	n	having difficulty in reading and interpreting symbols
dyspeptic	adj	of or having indigestion or consequent irritability or depression
ebullient	adj	cheerful and full of energy
eccentric	adj	unconventional and slightly strange
eclectic	adj	deriving ideas, style, or taste from broad and diverse range
efface	v	to erase from a surface
egress	n	the action of going out of or leaving a place
elegy	n	a poem of serious reflection, typically a lament for the dead
elitist	n	a person who believes that a society should be ruled by an elite class
emancipate	v	to set free, especially from legal, social, or political restrictions
embellish	v	to make something more attractive by adding decorative details or features
embitter	v	to cause someone to feel bitter or resentful
embodiment	n	a tangible and visible form of an idea, quality, or feeling
emend	v	to make corrections and improvements to
empathy	n	the ability to understand and share the feelings of another
empirical	adj	based on verifiable by observation or experience rather than theory or logic
enamored	v	to be filled with a feeling of love for
enchant	v	to fill someone with great delight; charm
encompass	v	to surround and have or hold within
endear	v	to cause to be lived or liked
endorse	v	to declare one's public approval or support of
enervate	v	to cause someone to feel drained of energy or vitality; weaken
enigma	n	a person or thing that is mysterious, puzzling, or difficult to understand

enmity	n	the state or feeling of being actively opposed or hostile to someone
enrapture	v	to give intense pleasure or joy to
enterprise	n	a project or undertaking, typically one that is difficult or requires effort
enthrall	v	to capture the fascinated attention of
entice	v	to attract or tempt by offering pleasure or advantage
entourage	n	a group of people attending or surrounding an important person
entreat	v	to ask someone earnestly or anxiously to do something
enumerate	v	to mention a number of things one by one
ephemeral	adj	lasting for a very long time
epidemic	n	a widespread occurrence of an infectious disease
epigram	n	a pithy saying or remark expressing an idea in a clever and amusing way
epitome	n	a person or thing that is a perfect example of a particular quality or type
equanimity	n	mental calmness and evenness of temper, especially in a difficult situation
equitable	adj	fair and impartial
equivocal	adj	open to more than one interpretation; ambiguous
equivocation	n	the use of ambiguous language to conceal the truth or to avoid commitment
eradicate	v	to destroy completely; to put an end to
err	v	to be mistaken or incorrect; to make a mistake
erratic	adj	not even or regular in pattern or movement; unpredictable
erroneous	adj	wrong; incorrect
erudite	adj	having or showing great knowledge or learning
escort	v	to accompany someone or something for protection or security
esoteric	adj	intended to be understood by a few people with specialized knowledge
estrangement	n	the fact of no longer being on friendly terms or part of a social group
eulogize	v	to praise highly in speech or writing
eulogy	n	speech or writing that praises someone or something after death
euphemism	n	a mild or indirect expression substituted for one considered unpleasant
euphoria	n	a feeling or state of intense excitement and happiness
evanescent	adj	soon passing out of sight, memory, or existence
evoke	v	to call up bring out

Vocabulary Review 07

exacerbate	v	to make (a problem, bad situation, or negative feeling) worse
exasperate	v	to irritate intensely; infuriate
excised	v	to remove or cut out
exculpate	v	to clear from a charge of guilt
execrable	adj	extremely bad or unpleasant
execute	v	to carry out or put into effect
exhilarating	adj	making one feel very happy, animated or elated
exigent	adj	pressing; demanding
exile	v	to expel bar (someone) from their native country
exonerate	v	to clear from blame for a fault or wrongdoing
exorbitant	adj	much too high or great
expiate	v	to atone for guilt or sin
explicit	adj	stated clearly and in detail, leaving no room for confusion or doubt
exploit	v	to make full use of and derive benefit from a resource
extant	adj	still in existence
extemporized	v	to compose, perform or produce something without preparation; improvise
extenuate	v	to reduce the strength of, lessen seriousness, partially excuse
extirpate	v	to root out and destroy completely
extol	v	to praise highly
extort	v	to obtain by threats violence
extrapolate	v	to extend a conclusion from known facts to an unknown situation
extravagant	adj	lacking restraint in spending money or using resources
exuberant	adj	filled with or characterized by lively energy and excitement
fabricate	v	to invent or concoct something, typically with deceitful intent
facetious	adj	treating serious issues with deliberately inappropriate humor; flippant
facilitate	v	to make an action or process easy or easier
faction	n	a small, organized, dissenting group within a larger one
fallacious	adj	based on a mistaken belief
fallacy	n	a mistaken belief, especially one based on unsound argument
fallow	adj	inactive but with the possibility of activity in the future
falter	v	to start to lose strength or momentum
famished	adj	extremely hungry

fastidious	adj	very attentive to and concerned about accuracy and detail
fatuous	adj	silly and pointless
faultfinder	n	a person who is given to petty criticism and constant complaint
feckless	adj	lacking initiative or strength of character; irresponsible
feign	v	to pretend to be affect by a feeling, state, or injury
felicitous	adj	well chosen or suited to the circumstances
fervid	adj	intensely enthusiastic or passionate, especially to an excessive degree
feud	n	a state of prolonged mutual hostility
fickle	adj	changing frequently, especially regarding one's loyalties, interests, or affection
fidelity	n	faithfulness to a person, cause, or belief
fidget	v	to make small movements through nervousness or impatience
finagle	v	to obtain something by devious or dishonest means
finesse	n	intricate and refined delicacy
finicky	adj	fussy about one's needs or requirements
fitful	adj	active or occurring spasmodically or intermittently
flabbergasted	v	to surprise someone greatly; astonish
flagrant	adj	conspicuously or obviously offensive
flamboyant	adj	tending to attract attention because of their exuberance and confidence
fleeting	adj	lasting for a very short time; temporary
flirt	v	to behave as though attracted to someone or to deliberately expose oneself to harm
florid	adj	having a red or flushed complexion
flounder	v	struggle or stagger helplessly or clumsily in water or mud
flouting	v	openly disregard for a rule, law, or convention
flummox	v	perplex someone greatly, bewilder
foil	v	to prevent something considered wrong or undesirable from succeeding
foment	v	instigate or stir up an undesirable or violent sentiment or course of action
foolhardy	adj	recklessly bold or rash
foreseen	v	to be aware of beforehand; predict
foreshadow	v	to be a warning or indication of a future event
fortuitous	adj	happening by accident or chance rather than design

Vocabulary Review 08

foster	v	encourage or promote the development of
fracas	n	a noisy disturbance or quarrel
fractious	adj	irritable and quarrelsome, typically of children
fragile	adj	easily broken or damaged
fringe	n	an ornamental border of threads left loose or formed into tassels or twists
frugal	adj	sparing or economical with regard to money or food
furtive	adj	attempting to avoid notice or attention, typically because of guilt
fusillade	v	a series of shots fired at the same time or in quick succession
futility	n	pointlessness or uselessness
gaiety	n	the state or quality of being lighthearted or cheerful
garrulous	adj	excessively talkative
gaucherie	n	awkward, embarrassing or unsophisticated ways
gaunt	adj	lean and haggard, especially because of suffering
genealogy	n	a line of descent traced continuously from an ancestor
genial	adj	friendly and cheerful
germane	adj	relevant to a subject under consideration
glib	adj	fluent and voluble, but insincere and shallow
gloat	v	contemplate or dwell on one's own success or another's misfortune
glutton	n	an excessively greedy eater
grandiloquent	adj	pompous or extravagant in language, style or manner, often to impress
grating	adj	sounding harsh and unpleasant
greenhorn	n	a person who is new and inexperienced
gregarious	adj	fond of company; sociable
grief	n	deep sorrow, especially that caused by someone's death
grievous	adj	very severe or serious
grimy	adj	covered with or characterized by grime
grovel	verb	lie or move abjectly on the ground with one's face downward
guile	n	sly or cunning intelligence
guise	n	an outer appearance or mannerism to conceal an inner nature
hackneyed	adj	lacking significance through having been overused; unoriginal and trite
haggard	adj	looking exhausted and unwell, especially from fatigue, worry or suffering
halting	adj	slow and hesitant, especially through lack of self confidence, faltering

hamper	v	to hinder or impede the movement or progress of
harangue	n	a lengthy and aggressive speech
harbinger	n	a person or thing that announces or signals the approach of another
haughty	adj	arrogantly superior and disdainful
heinous	adj	utterly odious or wicked
herculean	adj	requiring great strength or effort
heresy	n	belief or opinion contrary to orthodox religious doctrine
heretic	n	a person believing in or practicing religious heresy
heterodox	adj	not conforming with accepted or orthodox standards or belief
heterogeneous	adj	diverse in character or content
hinder	v	to create difficulties for someone or something, resulting in delay
histrionic	adj	overly theatrical or melodramatic in character or style
hoax	n	a humorous or malicious deception
holistic	adj	characterized by comprehension of the parts that make the whole
honorable	adj	bringing or worthy of honor
hubris	n	excessive pride or self-confidence
humane	adj	having or showing compassion or benevolence
humdrum	adj	lacking in excitement or variety; dull; monotonous
hyperbole	n	exaggerated statements or claims not meant to be taken literally
iconoclast	n	a person who attacks cherished beliefs or institutions
idiosyncrasy	n	a mode of behavior or way of thought peculiar to an individual
ignominious	adj	deserving or causing public shame and disgrace
illicit	adj	forbidden by law, rules, or customs
illusory	adj	based on illusion; not real
impair	v	weaken or damage something, especially a human faculty or function
impassioned	adj	filled with or showing great emotion
impeccable	adj	in accordance with the highest standards of propriety; faultless
impecunious	adj	having little or no money
impede	v	to delay or prevent someone or something by obstructing them; hinder
impenetrable	adj	impossible to pass through or enter

Vocabulary Review 09

imperative	adj	of vital importance; crucial
imperious	adj	assuming power or authority without justification; arrogant and domineering
impersonal	adj	not influenced by, showing, or involving personal feelings
impetuous	adj	acting or done quickly without thought or care
impiety	n	lack of piety or reverence, especially for a god
impious	adj	not showing respect or reverence, especially for a god
implicit	adj	implied though not plainly expressed
impose	v	to force something unwelcome or unfamiliar to be accepted or put in place
impregnable	adj	unable to be defeated or destroyed; unassailable
impromptu	adj	done without being planned, organized, or rehearsed
impudent	adj	not showing due respect for another person; impertinent
impunity	n	exemption from punishment or freedom from the consequences of an action
inane	adj	silly; stupid
inattention	n	lack of attention; distraction
incentive	n	a thing that motivates or encourages one to do something
incite	v	to encourage or stir up violent or unlawful behavior
incognito	adj	having one's true identity concealed
incoherent	adj	expressed in an incomprehensible or confusing way; unclear
incongruous	adj	not in harmony with the surroundings or other aspects of something
inconspicuous	adj	not clearly visible or attracting attention; not conspicuous
indefatigable	adj	persisting tirelessly
indictment	n	evidence to illustrate that a situation is bad and deserves condemnation
indifference	n	lack of interest, concern, or sympathy
indigenous	adj	originating or occurring naturally in a particular place; native
indolent	adj	wanting to avoid activity or exertion; lazy
indomitable	adj	impossible to subdue or defeat
induce	v	to succeed in persuading or influencing someone to do something
indulgent	adj	having or indicating a tendency to be overly generous to or lenient
ineffable	adj	too great or extreme to be expressed or described in words
inefficacious	adj	not producing the desired effect
inert	adj	lacking the ability or strength to move
inexorable	adj	impossible to stop or prevent

infelicitous	adj	unfortunate; inappropriate
infelicity	n	a thing that is inappropriate, especially a remark or expression
infernal	adj	of, relating to, or characteristic of hell or the underworld
infest	v	to be present in a place or site in large numbers
inflammable	adj	easily set on fire
infuse	v	to fill; pervade
ingenious	adj	clever, original, and inventive
inimical	adj	tending to obstruct or harm
inimitable	adj	so good or unusual as to be impossible to copy; unique
innate	adj	inborn; natural
innocuous	adj	not harmful or offensive
inscrutable	adj	impossible to understand or interpret
insipid	adj	lacking flavor
insolence	n	rude and disrespectful behavior
insufferable	adj	too extreme to bear; intolerable
insular	adj	ignorant of or uninterested in ideas or people outside one's own experience
insult	v	to speak to or treat with disrespect or scornful abuse
insurrection	n	a violent uprising against an authority or government
integrity	n	honesty and strong moral principles
intemperance	n	lack of moderation or restraint
intemperate	adj	having or showing a lack of self-control; immoderate
intermittent	adj	occurring at irregular intervals; not continuous or steady
intersperse	v	to scatter among or between other things; place here and there
intonation	n	the rise and fall of the voice in speaking
intransigent	adj	unwilling or refusing to change one's view or to agree about something
intrepid	adj	fearless; adventurous, often used for rhetorical or humorous effect
introspect	v	to examine one's own thoughts or feelings
intuition	n	the ability to understand something quickly and without conscious reasoning
invective	n	insulting, abusive, or highly critical language
inveigh	v	to speak or write about something with great hostility

Vocabulary Review 10

inveterate	adj	having a particular habit, activity, or interest that is unlikely to change
inviolate	adj	free or safe from injury or violation
invocation	n	the action of invoking something or someone for assistance or as an authority
invulnerable	adj	impossible to harm or damage
irascible	adj	having or showing a tendency to be easily angered
irksome	adj	irritating; annoying
irrepressible	adj	not able to be controlled or restrained
irreproachable	adj	beyond criticism; faultless
irrevocable	adj	not able to be changed, reversed, or recovered; final
jaded	adj	tired, bored, or lacking enthusiasm after having too much of something
jaundiced	adj	affected by bitterness, resentment, or envy
jest	v	to speak or act in a joking manner
jilt	v	to suddenly reject or abandon a lover
jocular	adj	fond of or characterized by joking; humorous or playful
juxtapose	v	to place or deal with close together for contrasting effect
knack	n	an acquired or natural skill at performing a task
knell	n	the sound of a bell, especially when rung solemnly for a death or funeral
kudos	n	praise and honor received for an achievement
labyrinth	n	a complicated and irregular maze
lackadaisical	adj	lacking enthusiasm and determination; carelessly lazy
laconic	adj	using very few words
lag	v	to fall behind in movement, progress, or development
lament	v	to mourn a person's loss or death
lampoon	v	to publicly criticize through ridicule, irony, or sarcasm
languid	adj	displaying or having a disinclination for physical exertion or effort
languor	n	the state or feeling, often pleasant, or tiredness or inertia
largesse	n	generosity in bestowing money or gifts upon others
lassitude	n	a state of physical or mental weariness; lack of energy
latent	adj	existing but not yet developed or manifest; hidden; concealed
laudable	adj	deserving praise and commendation
laudatory	adj	expressing praise and commendation
lavish	adj	sumptuously rich, elaborate, or luxurious

laxative	adj	tending to stimulate or facilitate evacuation of the bowels
lecherous	adj	having or showing excessive or offensive sexual desires
lethargic	adj	sluggish and apathetic
lethargy	n	a lack of energy and enthusiasm
lewd	adj	crude and offensive in a sexual way
liable	adj	responsible by law; legally answerable
libel	n	a published false statement against another's reputation
libelous	adj	containing or constituting a libel
listless	adj	lacking energy or enthusiasm
lithe	adj	thin, supple, graceful
litigious	adj	concerned with lawsuits or litigations
loiter	v	to stand or wait around idly without apparent purpose
loquacious	adj	tending to take a great deal; talkative
lucid	adj	expressed clearly; easy to understand
lugubrious	adj	looking or sounding sad and dismal
luminary	n	a person who inspires or influences others
luxuriant	adj	rich and profuse in growth; lush
maestro	n	a distinguished musician, especially a conductor of classical music
magistrate	n	a civil officer or lay judge who administers the law
magnanimous	adj	very generous or forgiving
maladroit	adj	ineffective or bungling; clumsy
malignant	adj	1. very virulent or infectious 2. malevolent
malinger	v	to exaggerate or feign illness in order to escape duty or work
mandate	n	an official order or commission to do something
mandatory	adj	required by law or rules; compulsory
maniac	n	a person exhibiting extreme symptoms of wild behavior
manifest	v	to display or show a quality or feeling by one's actions or appearance
mar	v	to impair the appearance of; disfigure
marauding	adj	going about in search of things to steal or people to attack
maroon	v	to leave someone trapped and isolated in an inaccessible place

Vocabulary Review 11

massacre	n	an indiscriminate and brutal slaughter of people
meandering	adj	following a winding or indirect course
meddle	v	to interfere unduly with something that is not one's concern
melancholy	adj	having a feeling of pensive sadness, typically with no obvious case
melodramatic	adj	behavior that is more dramatic or emotional than the situation demands
mercenary	n	a professional soldier hired to serve in a foreign army
meretricious	adj	apparently attractive but having in reality no value or integrity
meritorious	adj	deserving reward or praise
mesmerize	v	hold the attention of someone to the exclusion of all else
meticulous	adj	showing great attention to detail; very careful and precise
miffed	adj	annoyed
militant	adj	aggressively supporting a cause favoring extreme, or confrontational methods
misanthrope	n	a person who dislikes humankind and avoids human society
misconstrue	v	to interpret something, especially a person's words or actions wrongly
miserly	adj	of, relating, or characteristic of someone who hoards wealth and spends little
misogynist	adj	reflecting or inspired by a hatred of women
misrepresentation	n	a false or misleading account of the nature of something
mitigate	v	to make less severe, serious, or painful
modicum	n	a small quantity of a particular thing that is desirable or valuable
modish	adj	conforming to or following what is currently popular and fashionable
mollify	v	to appease the anger or anxiety of someone
monotonous	adj	dull, tedious, and repetitious; lacking in variety and interest
morbid	adj	abnormal and unhealthy interest in disturbing and unpleasant subjects
morose	adj	sullen and ill-tempered
motley	adj	incongruously varied in appearance or character; disparate
multifarious	adj	many and of various types
mundane	adj	lacking interest or excitement; dull
munificent	adj	larger or more generous is usual or necessary
mutter	v	to say something in a low or barely audible voice with dissatisfaction
myopic	adj	lacking imagination, foresight, or intellectual insight
mystify	v	utterly bewilder or perplex someone
nefarious	adj	wicked or criminal, typically of an action or activity

neophyte	n	a person who is new to a subject, skill, or belief
nonchalant	adj	feeling or appearing casually calm and relaxed; not displaying anxiety
nondescript	adj	lacking distinctive or interesting features or characteristics
nonplussed	adj	surprised and confused so much that one is unsure how to react
notoriety	n	the state of being famous or well known for some bad quality or deed
noxious	adj	harmful, poisonous, or very unpleasant
nuance	n	a subtle difference in or shade of meaning, expression, or sound
obdurate	adj	stubbornly refusing to change one's opinion or course of action
obligatory	adj	required by a legal, moral, or other rule, compulsory
oblique	adj	not explicit or direct in addressing point
obloquy	n	strong public opinion or verbal abuse
obscure	adj	not discovered or known about; uncertain
obsequious	adj	obedient or attentive to an excessive or servile degree
obstinate	adj	stubbornly refusing to change one's opinion or chosen course of action
obstreperous	adj	noisy and difficult to control
obtuse	adj	annoyingly insensitive or slow to understand
odious	adj	extremely unpleasant; repulsive
odium	n	general or widespread hatred or disgust for a person
offhand	adj	ungraciously or offensively nonchalant or cool in manner
officious	adj	assertive of authority in an annoyingly domineering way
offset	v	to counteract something by having an opposing force or effect
ominous	adj	giving the impression that something bad or unpleasant is going to happen
onerous	adj	involving an amount of effort and difficulty that is oppressively burdensome
onset	n	the beginning of something, especially something unpleasant
onslaught	n	a fierce or destructive attack
opacity	n	the condition of lacking transparency or translucence
opaque	adj	not able to be seen through; not transparent
opportune	adj	well-chosen or particularly favorable or appropriate
opprobrious	adj	expressing harsh criticism or censure
opt	v	to make a choice from a range of possibilities

Vocabulary Review 12

opulence	n	great wealth or luxuriousness
ornate	adj	made in an intricate shape or decorated with complex patterns
ossified	adj	be stagnant or rigid
ostracism	n	exclusion from a society or group
oust	v	to drive out or expel someone from a position or place
outlandish	adj	looking or sounding bizarre or unfamiliar
outmoded	adj	old-fashioned
ovation	n	a sustained and enthusiastic show of appreciation from an audience
pacify	v	to quell the anger, agitation, or excitement of
palliate	v	to make disease symptoms less severe without removing the cause
palpable	adj	able to be touched or felt
pandemic	adj	prevalent over a whole country or the world
pandemonium	n	wild and noisy disorder or confusion; uproar
paradox	n	several statements that seem reasonable but lead to an illogical conclusion
paraphernalia	n	miscellaneous articles, especially the equipment needed for an activity
parody	n	an imitation with exaggeration for comic effect
parsimonious	adj	unwilling to spend money or use resources; stingy or frugal
parsimony	n	extreme unwillingness to spend money or use resources
partisan	n	a strong support of a party, cause, or person
passé	adj	no longer fashionable; out of date
pastiche	n	an artistic work in style that imitates that of another work, artist, or period
pathos	n	a quality that evokes pity or sadness
patronage	n	the support given by a patron
patronize	v	to treat with an apparent kindness that betrays a feeling of superiority
paucity	n	the presence of something only in small or insufficient quantities or amounts
pedantic	adj	of or like a person who is excessively concerned with minor details and rules
pedigree	n	the background or history of a person or thing
peevish	adj	easily irritated, especially by unimportant things
penchant	n	a strong or habitual liking for something or tendency to do something
penitent	adj	feeling or showing sorrow and regret for having done something wrong
penurious	adj	extremely poor; poverty-stricken
peremptory	adj	insisting on immediate attention or obedience, especially in an imperious way

perfidy	n	deceitfulness, untrustworthiness
perfunctory	adj	carried out with a minimum of effort or reflection
perjury	n	willfully telling an untruth in a court after having taken an oath
pernicious	adj	having a harmful effect, especially in a gradual or subtle way
perpetuate	v	to make an undesirable situation or an unfounded belief continue indefinitely
perplexing	adj	completely baffling; very puzzling
pertain	v	to be appropriate, related, or applicable
perturb	v	to make someone anxious or settled
peruse	v	to read something, typically in a thorough or careful way
petty	adj	of little importance; trivial
petulant	adj	childishly sulky or bad-tempered
philanderer	n	a man who readily or frequently enters into casual relationships with women
philanthropy	n	the desire to promote the welfare of others, often the donation of money
phlegmatic	adj	having an unemotional and stolidly calm disposition
phobia	n	an extreme or irrational fear of or aversion to something
pied	adj	having two or more different colors
pilfer	v	to steal, typically things of relatively low value
pillage	v	to rob a place using violence, especially in wartime
pinnacle	n	the most successful point; the culmination
pious	adj	devoutly religious
pique	n	a feeling of irritation or resentment resulting from slight to one's pride
pithy	adj	concise and forcefully expressive
placate	v	to make someone less angry or hostile
plaintive	adj	sounding sad and mournful
platitude	n	a moral remark or statement that has been used too often to be interesting
platitudinous	adj	used too often to be interesting or thoughtful; hackneyed
plaudits	n	(used as a plural noun) praise
pliant	adj	easily bent or twisted; pliable
polarize	v	to divide or cause to divide into two sharply contrasting sets of opinions
polemical	adj	involving strongly critical, or disputatious writing or speech

Vocabulary Review 13

pragmatic	adj	concerned with practical results rather than theories or principles
preamble	n	a preliminary or preparatory statement; an introduction
precipitate	v	to cause a bad or undesirable event or situation to happen suddenly
preclude	v	prevent from happening; make impossible
precursor	n	a person or thing that comes before another of the same kind
predator	n	an animal that naturally preys on others
predilection	n	a preference or special liking for something; a bias in favor of something
predispose	v	to make someone liable or inclined to a specified attitude, action, or condition
preempt	v	to take action in order to prevent an anticipated event from happening
preponderance	n	the quality or fact of being greater in number, quantity, or importance
preside	v	to be in charge of
presumptive	adj	of the nature of a presumed in the absence of further information
prevaricate	v	to speak or act in an evasive way
primordial	adj	existing at or from the beginning of time; primeval
pristine	adj	in its original condition; unspoiled
proclivity	n	an inclination or predisposition toward a particular thing
procure	v	to obtain something, especially with care or effort
prodigal	adj	spending money or resources freely and recklessly; wastefully extravagant
prodigy	n	a person, especially a young one, endowed with exceptional qualities
profane	adj	relating or devoted to that which is not sacred or biblical
profligate	adj	recklessly extravagant or wasteful in the use of resources
profound	adj	having or showing great knowledge
profundity	n	deep insight; great depth of knowledge or thought
prohibitive	adj	forbidding or restricting something
proliferate	v	to increase rapidly in numbers; multiply
prolix	adj	using or containing too many words; tediously lengthy
prolong	v	to extend the duration of
prominent	adj	important; famous
propensity	n	an inclination or natural tendency to behave in a particular way
prophecy	n	a prediction
propitiate	v	to win or regain the favor of a god, spirit, or person
proponent	n	a person who advocates a theory, proposal, or project

prosaic	adj	having the style or diction of prose; lacking poetic beauty
protocol	n	the accepted or established code of procedure or behavior in any group
provincial	adj	unsophisticated and narrow-minded
prudent	adj	acting with or showing care and thought for the future
pseudonym	n	a fictitious name, especially one used by an author
psychosis	n	a severe mental disorder in which contact is lost with external reality
pugnacious	adj	eager or quick to argue, quarrel, or fight
quack	n	a person who dishonestly claims to have specialized knowledge
quagmire	n	a soft boggy area of land that gives way underfoot
qualm	n	an uneasy feeling of doubt, worry, or fear, especially about one's own
quandary	n	a state of perplexity or uncertainty over what to do in a difficult situation
quarrelsome	adj	given to or characterized by an angry argument or disagreement
quell	v	to put an end to a rebellion or other disorder, typically by the use of force
quibble	n	a slight objection or criticism
quiescent	adj	in a state or period of inactivity or dormancy
quixotic	adj	exceedingly idealistic; unrealistic and impractical
quorum	n	the minimum number of members required to make a meeting valid
ramification	n	a consequence of an action or event, especially when complex or unwelcome
rampart	n	a defensive or protective barrier
rancor	n	bitterness or resentfulness, especially when long-standing
ransack	v	to go hurriedly through a place stealing things and causing damage
rant	v	to speak or shout at length in a wild, impassioned way
rapacious	adj	aggressively greedy or grasping
rash	adj	displaying a lack of careful consideration and disregard for consequences
ratify	v	to sign or give formal consent to a treaty, contract, or agreement
raze	v	to completely destroy a building, town, or other site
recant	v	to say that one no longer holds an opinion or belief
recast	v	to present or organize in a different form or style
receptive	adj	able or willing to receive something, especially signals or stimuli
recluse	n	a person who lives a solitary life and tends to avoid other people

Vocabulary Review 14

recondite	adj	little known; abstruse
recrimination	n	an accusation in response to one from someone else
recuperate	v	to recover from illness or exertion
redolent	adj	strongly reminiscent or suggestive of something
redouble	v	to make or become much greater, more intense, or more numerous
redundant	adj	not or no longer needed or useful; superfluous
refulgent	adj	shining brightly
regime	n	a system or planned way of doing things, especially one imposed from above
rehash	v	to put old ideas into a new form without significant change or improvement
rejuvenation	v	to make someone or something look or feel younger, fresher, or more lively
relapse	v	to return to a less active or a worse state
reminisce	v	to indulge in enjoyable recollection of past events
remiss	adj	lacking care or attention to duty; negligent
repartee	n	conversation or speech characterized by quick, witty comments or replies
repellent	adj	able to repel a particular thing; impervious to a particular substance
repine	v	to feel or express discontent; fret
replete	adj	filled or well-supplied with something
reprehensible	adj	deserving censure or condemnation
reprieve	v	to cancel or postpone the punishment of someone condemned to death
reprimand	v	to rebuke someone
reproach	v	to address someone in such a way as to express disapproval or disappointment
reproof	n	an expression of blame or disapproval
requiem	n	an act or token of remembrance
resentment	n	bitter indignation at having been treated unfairly
resolute	adj	admirably purposeful, determined, and unwavering
resplendent	adj	attractive and impressive through being richly colorful or sumptuous
resurrect	v	to bring a person back to life or an idea back in to favor
retard	v	to delay or hold back in terms of progress, development, or accomplishment
revert	v	to return to a previous state, condition, practice, etc.
revitalize	v	to imbue something with new life and vitality
rhetoric	n	the art of effective or persuasive speaking or writing
rhetorical	adj	of, relating to, or concerned with the art of rhetoric

rift	n	a crack, split, or break in something
riveting	adj	completely engrossing, compelling
rueful	adj	expressing sorrow or regret, especially when in a slightly humorous way
rustic	adj	of or relating to the countryside; rural
rusticate	v	to go to, live in, or spend time in the country
sacrilegious	adj	involving a violation or misuse of what is regarded as sacred
salubrious	adj	health-giving; healthy
sanctimonious	adj	making a show of being morally superior to other people
saturate	v	to cause something to be thoroughly soaked or filled to the limit
scope	n	the extent of the area or subject matter that something deals with
scour	v	to subject to a thorough search in order to locate something
scuttle	v	to run hurriedly or furtively with short quick steps
seasonable	adj	usual for or appropriate to a particular season of the year
sedative	adj	promoting calm or inducing sleep
sedentary	adj	tending to spend much time seated; somewhat inactive
seditious	adj	inciting or causing people to rebel against the authority of a state or monarch
sedulous	adj	showing dedication and diligence
serene	adj	calm, peaceful, and untroubled; tranquil
sermonized	v	to compose or deliver a sermon
serpentine	adj	winding and twisting like a snake
servile	adj	having or showing an excessive willingness to serve or please others
shameless	adj	characterized by or showing a lack of shame
shirk	v	to avoid or neglect a duty or responsibility
skeptical	adj	not easily convinced; having doubts or reservation
skimp	v	expend or use less time or money than is necessary in an attempt to economize
slake	v	to quench or satisfy one's thirst
slander	n	false spoken statement damaging to a person's reputation
slipshod	adj	characterized by a lack of care, thought, or organization
slouch	v	to stand, move, or sit in a lazy, drooping way
sluggish	adj	slow-moving or inactive

Vocabulary Review 15

sneer	n	a contemptuous or mocking smile, remark, or tone
snobbish	adj	like a person with an exaggerated respect for high social position
solace	n	comfort or consolation in a time of distress or sadness
solicitous	adj	characterized by or showing interest or concern
sophistry	n	the use of fallacious arguments, especially with the intention of deceiving
soporific	adj	tending to induce drowsiness or sleep
Spartan	adj	indifference to comfort or luxury traditionally associated with ancient Sparta
specious	adj	superficially plausible, but actually wrong
sporadic	adj	occurring at irregular intervals or only in a few places; scattered or isolated
spurious	adj	not being what it purports to be; false or fake
spurn	v	to reject with disdain or contempt
squalid	adj	extremely dirty and unpleasant, especially as a result of poverty or neglect
squeamish	adj	easily made to feel sick, or disgusted, especially by unpleasant images
squelch	v	to make a soft sucking sound as that made by walking heavily through mud
steadfast	adj	resolutely or dutifully firm and unwavering
stereotype	n	a widely held but fixed and oversimplified image or idea
stimulant	n	a substance that raises levels of physiological or nervous activity in the body
stingy	adj	unwilling to give or spend; ungenerous
stipulate	v	to specify a requirement, typically as part of a bargain or agreement
stratify	v	to arrange or classify
strident	adj	loud and harsh; grating
stupefy	v	to make someone unable to think or feel properly
stygian	adj	very dark
subdue	v	to overcome, quiet, or bring under control
subsidiary	adj	less important than but related or supplementary to
substance	n	a particular kind of matter with uniform properties
subversive	adj	seeking or intended to undermine an established system or institution
succulent	adj	tender, juicy, and tasty
sully	v	to damage the purity or integrity of; defile
supercilious	adj	behaving or looking as though one thinks is superior to others
superfluous	adj	unnecessary, especially through being more than enough
supersede	v	to take the place of a person or thing previously in authority or use; supplant

supine	adj	lying face upward
supplant	v	supersede and replace
supplicate	v	to ask or beg for something earnestly or humbly
surfeit	n	an excessive amount of something
surrogate	n	a substitute, especially a person deputizing for another in a specific role or office
swagger	v	to walk or behave in a very confident and typically arrogant or aggressive way
sycophant	n	a person who acts obsequiously toward someone important
taciturn	adj	reserved or uncommunicative in speech; saying little
tactful	adj	having or showing tact
tactile	adj	of or connected with the sense of touch
tangential	adj	diverging from a previous course or line; erratic
tangible	adj	perceptible by touch
tantamount	adj	equivalent in seriousness to; virtually the same as
tarnish	v	to make or become less valuable or respected
tedious	adj	too long, slow, or dull; tiresome or monotonous
temper	v	to serve as a neutralizing or counterbalancing force to something
temporize	v	to avoid making a decision or committing oneself in order to gain time
tenacious	adj	tending to keep a firm hold of something, clinging or adhering closely
tentative	adj	not certain or fixed; provisional
tenuous	adj	very weak or slight
terminate	v	to bring to an end
therapeutic	adj	of or relating to the healing of disease
thrive	v	to grow or develop well or vigorously
thwart	v	to prevent someone from accomplishing something
timeworn	adj	damaged or impaired, or made less attractive, as a result of age or use
tirade	n	a long, angry speech or criticism or accusation
toil	v	to work extremely hard or incessantly
tonic	adj	giving a feeling of vigor or well-being; invigorating
torpid	adj	mentally or physically inactive; lethargic
tortuous	adj	full of twists and tunes

Vocabulary Review 16

totalitarian	adj	of or relating to a system of centralized and all-powerful government
tractable	adj	easy to control or influence
tranquil	adj	free from disturbance; calm
transitory	adj	not permanent
transmute	v	to change in form, nature, or substance
travesty	n	a false, absurd, or distorted representation of something
treacle	n	cloying sentimentality or flattery
treaty	n	a formally concluded and ratifies agreement between countries
trendy	adj	very fashionable or up to date in style or influence
trepidation	n	a feeling of fear or agitation about something that may happen
trite	adj	overused and consequently of little importance; lacking originality
truce	n	an agreement between enemies or opponents to stop hostilities for a time
truculent	adj	eager or quick to argue or fight; aggressively defiant
tumult	n	a loud, confusing noise, especially one cause by a large mass of people
tyrant	n	a cruel and oppressive ruler
unanimity	n	agreement by all people involved; consensus
unconquerable	adj	not conquerable
undermine	v	to damage or weaken someone or something
unkempt	adj	having an untidy or disheveled appearance
unorthodox	adj	contrary to what is usual, traditional, or accepted; not orthodox
unprecedented	adj	never done or known before
unscathed	adj	without suffering and injury, damage, or harm
untoward	adj	unexpected and inappropriate or inconvenient
upbraid	v	to find fault with someone; to scold
uproar	n	a loud and impassioned noise or disturbance
vacillate	v	to alternate or waver between different opinions or actions; to be indecisive
vainglory	n	inordinate pride in oneself or one's achievement; excessive vanity
valor	n	great courage in the face of danger, especially in battle
vaporize	v	to convert or be converted into vapor
variegated	adj	exhibiting different colors, especially as irregular patches or streaks
veil	n	a thing that conceals, disguises, or obscures something
veneration	n	great respect; reverence

venture	n	a risky or daring journey or undertaking
veracious	adj	speaking or representing the truth
verbatim	adj	in exactly the same words as were used originally
verbose	adj	using or expressed in more words than are needed
veritable	adj	used as an intensifier, often to qualify a metaphor
vex	v	to make someone feel annoyed or worried, especially with trivial matters
vicarious	adj	acting or done for another
vilify	v	to speak or write in an abusive disparaging manner
vindicate	v	to clear someone of blame or suspicion
vindictive	adj	having or showing a strong or unreasoning desire for revenge
virtuosity	n	great skill in music or another artistic pursuit
virtuoso	n	a person highly skilled in music or another artistic pursuit
vituperate	v	to blame or insult someone in strong or violent language
vivacious	adj	attractively lively and animated
vogue	n	general acceptance or favor; popularity
voluble	adj	speaking or spoken incessantly and fluently
voracious	adj	wanting or devouring great quantities of food
wanderlust	n	a strong desire to travel
wane	v	to decrease in vigor, power, or extent; to become weaker
ward	v	to guard; protect
wary	adj	feeling or showing caution about possible dangers or problems
waver	v	to shake with a quivering motion
wheedle	v	to persuade through endearments or flattery
whim	n	a sudden desire or change of mind that is unusual or unexplained
winnow	v	to remove people or things from a group until only the best ones are left
wistful	adj	having or showing a feeling of vague or regretful longing
witticism	n	a witty remark
witty	adj	showing or characterized by quick and inventive verbal humor
wrath	n	extreme anger, chiefly used for humorous or rhetorical effect
zealot	n	a person who is fanatical and uncompromising in pursuit of their ideals

Sentence Completion

16 practice exercises

SAT Sentence Completion Exercise #01

38 Questions

DIRECTIONS

Each sentence below has one or two blanks, each blank indicating that something has been omitted. Beneath the sentence are five words or sets of words labeled A through E. Choose the word or set of words that, when inserted in the sentence, best fits the meaning of the sentence as a whole.

EXAMPLE:

Though the first moon landing took place half a century ago, its legacy is far from -------; today's astronauts, scientists and engineers continue to be inspired by its -------.

(A) over . . brevity
(B) flawless . . aftermath
(C) forgotten . . achievements
(D) accurate . . clarity
(E) secure . . obscurity

  Ⓒ

1. Ryan was neither brusque nor cunning but was as ------- and as ------- a man as I have ever met.

(A) cordial . . arrogant
(B) gentle . . candid
(C) suave . . wily
(D) insolent . . tolerant
(E) treacherous . . straightforward

2. The reporters' behavior was certainly -------, but they believed that such infringement on personal privacy was necessary to their work.

(A) dependable
(B) inconsequential
(C) predestined
(D) scintillating
(E) invasive

3. During the Middle Ages, plague and other ------- decimated the populations of entire towns.

(A) pestilences
(B) immunizations
(C) proclivities
(D) indispositions
(E) demises

4. When Harvard astronomer Cecilia Payne was ------- professor in 1956, it marked an important step in the reduction of ------- practices within the scientific establishment.

(A) accepted for . . disciplinary
(B) promoted to . . discriminatory
(C) honored as . . unbiased
(D) denounced as . . critical
(E) considered for . . hierarchical

5. Unlike most of their solitary relatives, arctic hares are -------, clumping into herds that can include as many as several thousand individuals.

(A) reserved   (B) boisterous (C) exclusive
    (D) meritorious   (E) gregarious

6. Carolyn Bennett, a maker of kaleidoscopes, attributes the current of ------- intact nineteenth-century kaleidoscopes to the normal human desire to ------- a mysterious object in order to discover how it works.

(A) complexity . . study
(B) uniqueness . . acquire
(C) exorbitance . . distribute
(D) paucity . . disassemble
(E) fragility . . discontinue

GO ON TO THE NEXT PAGE

7. Like a parasitic organism, the most detested character in the play depended on others for ------- and ------- nothing.

(A) ideas . . required
(B) diversion . . spared
(C) assistance . . destroyed
(D) survival . . consumed
(E) sustenance . . returned

8. Although refuse and ashes may seem ------- to some individuals, archaeologists can use such materials to draw conclusions about the daily lives of ancient people.

(A) undetectable
(B) fabricated
(C) insignificant
(D) historical
(E) abundant

9. By nature he was -------, usually confining his remarks to ------- expression.

(A) acerbic . . friendly
(B) laconic . . concise
(C) garrulous . . voluminous
(D) shrill . . complimentary
(E) vague . . emphatic

10. These studies will necessarily take several years because the ------- of the new drug involved in the project is not -------.

(A) availability . . tested
(B) virulence . . doubted
(C) effect . . immediate
(D) background . . practical
(E) value . . expendable

11. Although he was ------- by nature, he had to be ------- at work because of the need to slash costs.

(A) prudent . . profligate
(B) ferocious . . indefensible
(C) industrious . . productive
(D) extravagant . . parsimonious
(E) pleasant . . amiable

12. Like a martinet, Charles deals with all people in manner that implies they must ------- him.

(A) a haughty . . thwart
(B) an imperious . . obey
(C) an egalitarian . . salute
(D) a timorous . . cheat
(E) a cowardly . . understand

13. Tarantulas apparently have little sense of -------, for a hungry one will ignore a loudly chirping cricket placed in its cage unless the cricket happens to get in its way.

(A) touch   (B) time   (C) hearing
    (D) self-confidence   (E) temperature

14. Because of their ------- to expand their share of the credit card market, banks may be ------- credit to customers who are poor risks.

(A) reluctance . . increasing
(B) rush . . decreasing
(C) inability . . denying
(D) mandate . . limiting
(E) eagerness . . extending

GO ON TO THE NEXT PAGE

15. Though she claimed to be portraying the human figure, her paintings were entirely -------, characterized by simple geometric shapes.

(A) lifelike
(B) emotional
(C) naturalistic
(D) formless
(E) abstract

16. The Roman soldiers who invaded Britain had little respect for the Britons, usually referring to them in ------- terms.

(A) pejorative
(B) hypocritical
(C) impressive
(D) irrational
(E) ambiguous

17. Dr. Estella Jiménez believed that the experimental therapy would create new problems, some of them predictable but others totally -------.

(A) benign
(B) ineffective
(C) suggestive
(D) unexpected
(E) formal

18. Many contemporary novelists have forsaken a traditional intricacy of plot and detailed depiction of character for a distinctly ------- presentation of both.

(A) convoluted   (B) derivative
   (C) conventional   (D) conservative
   (E) unadorned

19. Even more ------- in gesture than in words, the characters in the movie achieve their greatest------- in pure silence.

(A) awkward . . success
(B) expressive . . eloquence
(C) trite . . originality
(D) incompetent . . performance
(E) skilled . . repose

20. Teachers are, in effect, encouraging ------- when they fail to enforce rules governing the time allowed to students for completion of their assignments.

(A) conformity   (B) procrastination
   (C) impartiality   (D) scholarship
   (E) plagiarism

21. Although surfing is often ------- as merely a modern pastime, it is actually ------- practice, invented long ago by the Hawaiians to maneuver through the surf.

(A) touted . . a universal
(B) depicted . . an impractical
(C) incorporated . . a leisurely
(D) overestimated . . a high-spirited
(E) dismissed . . a time-honored

22. The spacecraft has two ------- sets of electronic components; if one fails, its duplicate will still function.

(A) divergent   (B) identical   (C) simulated
   (D) mutual   (E) prohibitive

GO ON TO THE NEXT PAGE

23. Only if business continues to expand can it ------- enough new jobs to make up for those that will be ------- by automation.

(A) produce . . required
(B) invent . . introduced
(C) create . . eliminated
(D) repeal . . reduced
(E) formulate . . engendered

24. Trinkets intended to have only ------- appeal can exist virtually forever in landfills because of the ------- of some plastics.

(A) arbitrary . . scarcity
(B) theoretical . . resilience
(C) ephemeral . . durability
(D) obsessive . . fragility
(E) impetuous . . cheapness

25. Despite years of poverty and -------, the poet Ruth Fitter produced work that is now ------- by a range of literary critics.

(A) security . . hailed
(B) depression . . criticized
(C) celebrity . . publicized
(D) inactivity . . undermined
(E) adversity . . acclaimed

26. Fungus beetles are quite -------: they seldom move more than the few yards between fungi, their primary food.

(A) pugnacious (B) sedentary (C) gregarious
(D) capricious   (E) carnivorous

27. Many linguists believe that our ability to learn language is at least in part -------, that it is somehow woven into our genetic makeup.

(A) innate   (B) accidental   (C) empirical
(D) transitory   (E) incremental

28. An apparently gratuitous gesture, whether it is spiteful or solicitous, arouses our suspicion, while a gesture recognized to be ------- gives no reason for surprise.

(A) warranted   (B) dubious   (C) affected
(D) benevolent   (E) rancorous

29. The student's feelings about presenting the commencement address were -------; although visibly happy to have been chosen, he was nonetheless ------- about speaking in public.

(A) positive . . insecure
(B) euphoric . . hopeful
(C) unknown . . modest
(D) ambivalent . . anxious
(E) restrained . . confident

30. In sharp contrast to the previous night's revelry, the wedding was ------- affair.

(A) a fervent
(B) a dignified
(C) a chaotic
(D) an ingenious
(E) a jubilant

GO ON TO THE NEXT PAGE

31. The theory of the ------- of cultures argues that all societies with highly developed technologies will evolve similar social institutions.

(A) isolation
(B) aesthetics
(C) convergence
(D) fragmentation
(E) longevity

32. Fearing excessive publicity, the patient refused to discuss her situation without a promise of ------- from the interviewer.

(A) empathy
(B) abstinence
(C) attribution
(D) confidentiality
(E) candor

33. Ed's great skills as a basketball player ------- his ------- stature, enabling him to compete successfully against much taller opponents.

(A) reveal . . gargantuan
(B) emphasize . . modest
(C) detract from . . lofty
(D) compensate for . . diminutive
(E) contrast with . . towering

34. The biologist's discovery was truly -------: it occurred not because of any new thinking or diligent effort but because he mistakenly left a few test tubes out of the refrigerator overnight.

(A) Assiduous (B) insightful (C) fortuitous
  (D) exemplary (E) ominous

35. Alice Walker's The Temple of My Familiar, far from being a tight, ------- narrative, is instead ------- novel that roams freely and imaginatively over a half-million years.

(A) traditional . . a chronological
(B) provocative . . an insensitive
(C) forceful . . a concise
(D) focused . . an expansive
(E) circuitous . . a discursive

36. Both by ------- and by gender, American painter Mary Cassatt was an -------, because her artistic peers were French men.

(A) background . . amateur
(B) citizenship . . intellectual
(C) nationality . . anomaly
(D) style . . advocate
(E) skill . . expert

37. She told the conference that, far from having to be ------- subjects of an ------- technology, human beings can actually control the system to improve their collective future.

(A) loyal . . inconsequential
(B) passive . . ungovernable
(C) diligent . . experimental
(D) reluctant . . impeccable
(E) zealous . . incompatible

38. Like a charlatan, Harry tried to ------- the audience with ------- evidence.

(A) confuse . . cogent
(B) persuade . . incontrovertible
(C) dupe . . spurious
(D) educate . . devious
(E) enthrall . . substantiated

STOP

this is the end of the exercise

SAT Sentence Completion Exercise #02

38 Questions

DIRECTIONS

Each sentence below has one or two blanks, each blank indicating that something has been omitted. Beneath the sentence are five words or sets of words labeled A through E. Choose the word or set of words that, when inserted in the sentence, best fits the meaning of the sentence as a whole.

EXAMPLE:

Though the first moon landing took place half a century ago, its legacy is far from -------; today's astronauts, scientists and engineers continue to be inspired by its -------.

(A) over . . brevity
(B) flawless . . aftermath
(C) forgotten . . achievements
(D) accurate . . clarity
(E) secure . . obscurity

Ⓐ Ⓑ Ⓒ Ⓓ Ⓔ

---

1. It is ironic that the ------- insights of the great thinkers are voiced so often that they have become mere -------.

(A) original . . clichés
(B) banal . . beliefs
(C) dubious . . habits
(D) philosophical . . questions
(E) abstract . . ideas

2. Since the island soil has been barren for so many years, the natives must now ------- much of their food.

(A) deliver   (B) import   (C) produce
(D) develop   (E) utilize

3. Because Jenkins neither ------- nor defends either management or the striking workers, both sides admire his journalistic -------.

(A) criticizes . . acumen
(B) attacks . . neutrality
(C) confronts . . aptitude
(D) dismisses. ,flair
(E) promotes . . integrity

4. Some anthropologists claim that a few apes have been taught a rudimentary sign language, but skeptics argue that the apes are only ------- their trainers.

(A) imitating
(B) condoning
(C) instructing
(D) acknowledging
(E) belaboring

5. The most frustrating periods of any diet are the inevitable -------, when weight loss ------- if not stops.

(A) moods . . accelerates
(B) feasts . . halts
(C) holidays . . contracts
(D) plateaus . . slows
(E) meals . . ceases

6. Since the author's unflattering references to her friends were so -------, she was surprised that her ------- were recognized.

(A) laudatory . . styles
(B) obvious . . anecdotes
(C) oblique . . allusions
(D) critical . . eulogies
(E) apparent . . motives

GO ON TO THE NEXT PAGE

SC2　　SC2　　www.ivyprepschool.com　　SC2　　SC2

7. Mark was intent on maintaining his status as first in his class; because even the smallest mistakes infuriated him, he reviewed all his papers ------- before submitting them to his teacher.

(A) explicitly (B) perfunctorily (C) honestly (D) mechanically (E) assiduously

8. Since many disadvantaged individuals view their situations as ------- as well as intolerable, their attitudes are best described as -------.

(A) squalid . . obscure
(B) unpleasant . . bellicose
(C) acute . . sanguine
(D) immutable . . resigned
(E) political . . perplexed

9. The subtleties of this novel are evident not so much in the character ------- as they are in its profoundly ------- plot structure.

(A) assessment . . eclectic
(B) development . . trite
(C) portrayal . . aesthetic
(D) delineation . . intricate
(E) illustration . . superficial

10. If it is true that morality cannot exist without religion, then does not the erosion of religion herald the ------- of morality?

(A) regulation　(B) basis　(C) belief
(D) collapse　(E) value

11. Certain animal behaviors, such as mating rituals seem to be -------, and therefore ------- external factors such as climate changes, food supply, or the presence of other animals of the same species.

(A) learned . . immune to
(B) innate . . unaffected by
(C) intricate . . belong to
(D) specific. confused with
(E) memorized .controlled by

12. Her shrewd campaign managers were responsible for the fact that her political slogans were actually forgotten clichés revived and ------- with new meaning.

(A) fathomed
(B) instilled
(C) foreclosed
(D) instigated
(E) foreshadowed

13. The stoic former general led his civilian life as he had his military life, with simplicity and ------- dignity.

(A) benevolent
(B) informal
(C) austere
(D) aggressive
(E) succinct

14. Shaken by two decades of virtual anarchy. the majority of people were ready to buy ------- at any price.

(A) order
(B) emancipation
(C) hope
(D) liberty
(E) enfranchisement

GO ON TO THE NEXT PAGE

15. As a person who combines care with -------, Marisa completed her duties with ------- as well as zeal.

(A) levity . . resignation
(B) geniality . . ardor
(C) vitality . . willingness
(D) empathy. rigor
(E) enthusiasm . . meticulousness

16. Although bound to impose the law, a judge is free to use his discretion to ------- the anachronistic barbarity of some criminal penalties.

(A) mitigate   (B) understand   (C) condone
(D) provoke   (E) enforce

17. Dr. Schwartz's lecture on art, while detailed and scholarly, focused ------- on the pre-modern; some students may have appreciated his specialized knowledge, but those with more ------- interests may have been disappointed.

(A) literally . . medieval
(B) completely . . pedantic
(C) expansively . . technical
(D) voluminously . . creative
(E) exclusively . . comprehensive

18. Henry viewed Melissa as -------; she seemed to be against any position regardless of its merits.

(A) heretical   (B) disobedient   (C) contrary
(D) inattentive   (E) harried

19. Only when one actually visits the ancient ruins of marvelous bygone civilizations does one truly appreciate the sad ------- of human greatness.

(A) perspicacity (B) magnitude (C) artistry
(D) transience   (E) quiescence

20. Because his paintings represented the Midwest of the mid-1800s as a serene and settled landscape, Robert Ouncanson ------- Easterners hesitant about moving westward that relocation was indeed -------.

(A) convinced . . ridiculous
(B) contradicted. necessary
(C) reminded . . rash
(D) assured . . safe
(E) persuaded . . risky

21. Rachel Carson's book Silent Spring, which described a world made lifeless by the accumulation of hazardous pesticides, ------- a grass-roots campaign to ------- the indiscriminate use of such substances.

(A) catalyzed . . propagate
(B) protested . . limit
(C) conceived . . encourage
(D) inspired . . control
(E) allowed . . recommend

22. Florida Congresswoman Ileana Ros-Lehtinen chose to focus on how national issues affect her own -------, those voters she represents.

(A) opponents
(B) constituents
(C) successors
(D) mentors
(E) colleagues

GO ON TO THE NEXT PAGE

23. In a society that abhors -------, the nonconformist is persistently -------.

   (A) creativity . . glorified
   (B) rebelliousness . . suppressed
   (C) insurgency . . heeded
   (D) smugness . . persecuted
   (E) stagnation . . denigrated

24. Instead of presenting a balanced view of both sides of the issue, the speaker became increasingly -------, insisting on the correctness of his position.

   (A) inarticulate   (B) dogmatic   (C) elliptical
   (D) tactful   (E) ambiguous

25. Astronomers who suspected that the sunspot cycle is not eleven years long have been ------- by studies ------- their belief that the entire cycle is actually twice that long.

   (A) vindicated . . confirming
   (B) exonerated . . refuting
   (C) discredited . . substantiating
   (D) encouraged . . rejecting
   (E) humiliated . . proving

26. He ------- the practices of aggressive autograph seekers, arguing that anyone distinguished enough to merit such ------- also deserved to be treated courteously.

   (A) decried . . adulation
   (B) defended . . adoration
   (C) endorsed . . brusqueness
   (D) ignored . . effrontery
   (E) vilified . . disdain

27. Andrew has enrolled in a specialized culinary arts program as a way of indulging his ------- French cuisine.

   (A) abstinence from
   (B) tenacity over
   (C) moral qualms against
   (D) acquisition of
   (E) predilection for

28. Someday technology may make door-to-door mail delivery seem -------, that is, as incongruous as pony express delivery would seem now.

   (A) recursive
   (B) contemporaneous
   (C) predictable
   (D) anachronistic
   (E) revered

29. The novelist brings out the ------- of human beings time and time again by ------- their lives to the permanence of the vast landscape.

   (A) absurdity . . relating
   (B) transience . . likening
   (C) evanescence . . contrasting
   (D) complexity . . comparing
   (E) uniqueness . . opposing

30. The commissioner is an irreproachable public servant, trying to ------- integrity and honor to a department that, while not totally corrupt, has nonetheless been ------- by greed and corruption.

   (A) deny . . overrun
   (B) impute . . tainted
   (C) attribute . . purified
   (D) entrust . . invigorated
   (E) restore . . undermined

GO ON TO THE NEXT PAGE

31. Emily Dickinson was ------- poet, making few concessions to ordinary grammar or to conventions of meter and rhyme.

(A) a sensitive   (B) an imitative
(C) an idiosyncratic   (D) a realistic
(E) a decorous

32. 3. Some lizards display the characteristic of -------: if their tails are broken off during predatory encounters, the tails will eventually grow back.

(A) adaptation   (B) mimicry
(C) regeneration   (D) aggression
(E) mutability

33. The two travelers may have chosen ------- routes across the continent, but the starting point was the same for each.

(A) coinciding   (B) divergent   (C) direct
(D) charted   (E) intersecting

34. The author's use of copious detail, though intended to ------- the reader's appreciation of a tumultuous era, was instead regarded by many as a barrage of ------- information.

(A) excite . . illuminating
(B) reverse . . accurate
(C) curtail . . boring
(D) deepen . . trivial
(E) deter . . historical

35. Seemingly permeated by natural light, Rufino Tamayo's painting looks as If it bad been created with ------- hues.

(A) luminous   (B) florid   (C) ominous
(D) varnished   (E) fading

36. Conflicting standards for allowable radiation levels in foods made ------- appraisals of the damage to crops following the reactor meltdown extremely difficult.

(A) reliable   (B) private   (C) intrusive
(D) conscious   (E) inflated

37. In earlier ages, a dilettante was someone who delighted in the arts; the term bad none of the ------- connotations of superficiality that it has today and, in fact, was considered -------.

(A) implicit . . disreputable
(B) romantic . . threatening
(C) patronizing . . complimentary
(D) irritating . . presumptuous
(E) entertaining . . prestigious

38. The historian noted irony in the fact that developments once considered ------- by people of that era are now viewed as -------.

(A) inspirational . . impetuous
(B) bizarre . . irrational
(C) intuitive . . uncertain
(D) actual . . grandiose
(E) improbable . . inevitable

STOP

this is the end of the exercise

SAT Sentence Completion Exercise #03
38 Questions

DIRECTIONS
Each sentence below has one or two blanks, each blank indicating that something has been omitted. Beneath the sentence are five words or sets of words labeled A through E. Choose the word or set of words that, when inserted in the sentence, best fits the meaning of the sentence as a whole.

EXAMPLE:
Though the first moon landing took place half a century ago, its legacy is far from -------; today's astronauts, scientists and engineers continue to be inspired by its -------.

(A) over . . brevity
(B) flawless . . aftermath
(C) forgotten . . achievements
(D) accurate . . clarity
(E) secure . . obscurity

(A)   (B)   (C)   (D)   (E)

1. Her naturally optimistic outlook rapidly restored her -------, but he, because of his ------- disposition, continued to foresee nothing but a series of pains and regrets.

    (A) humor . . adventurous
    (B) bitterness . . cheerful
    (C) confidence . . resilient
    (D) contentiousness . . callous
    (E) exuberance . . gloomy

2. Due to complexities in the life cycle of malaria parasites, scientists have been consistently ------- in their attempts to develop an effective vaccine.

    (A) thwarted   (B) prepared   (C) conditional
    (D) secretive   (E) encouraged

3. Some potatoes of the Andes contain ------- known as glycoalkaloids, poisons that induce stomach pains, vomiting, and even death.

    (A) nutrients   (B) secretions   (C) inversions
       (D) toxins   (E) preservatives

4. The chamber orchestra refuses to identify its members; it is this insistence on ------- that sets this ensemble apart.

    (A) longevity   (B) disparity   (C) anonymity
       (D) mediocrity (E) dissonance

5. Gwendolyn Brooks's character Maud Martha appears ------- but feels great rage: she ------- her emotions with a mask of compliance.

    (A) responsive . . echoes
    (B) nonchalant . . exposes
    (C) docile . . camouflages
    (D) uncontrolled . . belies
    (E) invincible . . catapults

6. He maintains that ethnic and cultural ------- are generalizations no more related to what an individual is actually like than are the ------- representations of constellations to the actual nature of a star.

    (A) traditions . . chemical
    (B) stereotypes . . pictorial
    (C) details . . figurative
    (D) heritages . . prophetic
    (E) specimens . . graphic

GO ON TO THE NEXT PAGE

7. Understandably, it is the ------- among theater critics who become most incensed when producers insist on ------- celebrated classic plays.

(A) strategists . . discussing
(B) mediators . . staging
(C) conformists . . praising
(D) traditionalists . . recognizing
(E) purists . . reinterpreting

8. A ------- person, he found the training almost unbearably monotonous, but he resolved to check his ------- and perform the basic tasks required.

(A) bitter . . submissiveness
(B) reclusive . . reserve
(C) dynamic . . restlessness
(D) mercurial . . constancy
(E) vivacious . . ambition

9. Well-publicized disagreements in the scientific community have so ------- many laypersons that they now ------- new warnings about the health effects of popular foods.

(A) inundated . . regulate
(B) exasperated . . discount
(C) bedazzled . . ridicule
(D) vindicated . . exaggerate
(E) disqualified . . minimize

10. Always ready to ------- achievement, Miller was as eager to praise a new production as the more mean-spirited critics were to ------- it.

(A) reward . . review
(B) impede . . ignore
(C) recognize . . deride
(D) expose . . study
(E) embrace . . promote

11. Eduardo Galeano's novel consists of discrete vignettes, so the reader must supply the invisible ------- binding such apparently ------- parts.

(A) emotions . . impersonal
(B) interpretations . . somber
(C) descriptions . . related
(D) connections . . independent
(E) categories . . cohesive

12. Unlike the politician, who must spend his or her energy in public show or endless meetings, the artist needs ------- for significant efforts.

(A) approval (B) prudence (C) motivation
(D) solitude   (E) perseverance

13. The fact that MTV, the cable channel devoted primarily to music, provided extensive coverage of the 1992 presidential race demonstrates how ------- politics and popular music culture have become.

(A) obscured   (B) contradictory
(C) interrelated   (D) enclosed
(E) permeated

14. Rod monochromasy, a type of color blindness that renders a person's vision strongest when light is weakest, is so rarely ------- that it is often-------.

(A) encountered . . misdiagnosed
(B) remedied . . contaminated
(C) reported . . publicized
(D) discerned . . transmuted
(E) calibrated . . unappreciated

GO ON TO THE NEXT PAGE

15. The ------- of Queen Elizabeth I impressed her contemporaries: she seemed to know what dignitaries and foreign leaders were thinking.

(A) symbiosis
(B) malevolence
(C) punctiliousness
(D) consternation
(E) perspicacity

16. Renowned for maintaining her ------- even in the most chaotic situations, Prances was utterly -------.

(A) dignity . . incorrigible
(B) composure . . imperturbable
(C) prosperity . . blunt
(D) equanimity . . clairvoyant
(E) control . . insignificant

17. Unable to attend the reunion, Marlene could enjoy it only in a ------- fashion, through the photographs taken there.

(A) gratuitous   (B) vigorous   (C) vicarious
(D) lethargic   (E) sullen

18. Many of today's physicians and patients are ------- high technology, captivated by computer designed thugs and laser surgery.

(A) nervous about
(B) defensive about
(C) tolerant of
(D) enamored of
(E) overwhelmed by

19. Joe Louis was ------- fighter: he inspired fear in many of his opponents.

(A) a serene
(B) an impetuous
(C) an insipid
(D) a malleable
(E) a redoubtable

20. In this production the king is portrayed as an initially ------- leader utterly transformed by his overwhelming thirst for power into a ------- tyrant.

(A) benevolent . . vicious
(B) heartless . . devious
(C) devoted . . reluctant
(D) prominent . . secluded
(E) notorious . . masterful

21. No one was hurt in the -------, but the fire marshals are busy searching for evidence of arson.

(A) inundation   (B) conflagration
(C) provocation   (D) confrontation
(E) substitution

22. Many experts agree that global warming is a crisis born of one ------- reality: modern societies ------- and indeed are sustained by combustible fossil fuels.

(A) indisputable. expunge
(B) trivial . . foster
(C) irrefutable . . require
(D) discreditable . . invoke
(E) ineffable . . devastate

GO ON TO THE NEXT PAGE

23. As ------- as she is -------, Lourdes Lopez has combined hard work with natural talent to succeed as a ballerina.

(A) diligent . . gifted
(B) conciliatory . . effusive
(C) stringent . . demanding
(D) accomplished . . dilatory
(E) restrained . . conditioned

24. When an already ------- machine is modified to correct existing problems, there is always a chance that the modifications will ------- more problems than they solve.

(A) perfected . . promote
(B) imposing . . curtail
(C) complex . . create
(D) intricate . . eliminate
(E) flawed . . alleviate

25. Although some political analysts do predict legislative events with ------- degree of accuracy, most analysts are ------- only 50 percent of the time, a figure that could be produced by guessing alone.

(A) a studied . . logical
(B) a slight . . unfavorable
(C) an exacting . . unknown
(D) an impressive . . correct
(E) an incalculable . . right

26. This new study of Sojourner Truth focuses primarily on her -------, on her speeches rather than her actions.

(A) reform   (B) militancy (C) strategy
   (D) principle   (E) rhetoric

27. She was a woman of contrasts: periods of ------- alternated with periods of frenetic activity.

(A) animation (B) torpor (C) invincibility
   (D) profundity   (E) ebullience

28. Though difficult, it is ------- to study shearwaters in their land-based breeding colonies; studying these birds at sea, however, poses an almost ------- problem.

(A) enterprising . . inventive
(B) helpful . . salutary
(C) necessary . . facile
(D) feasible . . insuperable
(E) possible . . implausible

29. Compared with the excitement of London, the ------- that prevails in this sleepy English village is quite remarkable.

(A) ingenuity
(B) impermanence
(C) ambivalence
(D) tranquility
(E) aestheticism

30. At that time theories concerning the type of life that might exist on other planets were still ------- because they rested on crude and ------- information about planetary atmospheres.

(A) inaccurate . . substantial
(B) nebulous . . specific
(C) authoritative . . factual
(D) speculative . . incomplete
(E) misleading . . definitive

GO ON TO THE NEXT PAGE

31. To ------- Mexico's rich cultural legacy in the United States, scholars from both countries collaborated to ------- the impressive exhibit of Mexican artifacts.

(A) celebrate . . circumvent
(B) validate . . mediate
(C) commemorate . . launch
(D) hoard . . differentiate
(E) disperse . . disrupt

32. The author's habit of indulging in obvious generalizations ------- his credibility as an expert on the details of job management.

(A) relates   (B) enhances   (C) dictates
(D) undermines   (E) cancels

33. Lately there has been a ------- of interest in Patti's writing, and it has become difficult to buy her books even in specialized secondhand bookstores.

(A) retention
(B) concealment
(C) moderation
(D) suppression
(E) resurgence

34. Contrary to what may be expected, most people are not generally ------- being asked for help but tend to welcome the chance to assist others.

(A) exasperated by
(B) condemned for
(C) agreeable to
(D) experienced in
(E) naïve about

35. They sought to oust their party chair because her proposal seemed ------- it contradicted their fundamental economic policies.

(A) garrulous   (B) remedial (C) formulaic
(D) heretical   (E) cursory

36. Those Renaissance scholars who reproduced almost verbatim the accounts written a century earlier were essentially -------, not genuine authorities on the events they recorded.

(A) historians   (B) translators
(C) researchers (D) participants
(E) transcribers

37. Shy and timid by nature, Martin became even more ------- when in the presence of his supervisor.

(A) boisterous   (B) retiring   (C) oblivious
(D) perturbed   (E) gallant

38. Because Alexander the Great was an omnipotent ruler, his death was a -------, marking the end of the old order and the beginning of chaos.

(A) tribute   (B) watershed   (C) verdict
(D) reparation   (E) connotation

SAT Sentence Completion Exercise #04
38 Questions

DIRECTIONS

Each sentence below has one or two blanks, each blank indicating that something has been omitted. Beneath the sentence are five words or sets of words labeled A through E. Choose the word or set of words that, when inserted in the sentence, best fits the meaning of the sentence as a whole.

EXAMPLE:

Though the first moon landing took place half a century ago, its legacy is far from -------; today's astronauts, scientists and engineers continue to be inspired by its -------.

(A) over .. brevity
(B) flawless .. aftermath
(C) forgotten .. achievements
(D) accurate .. clarity
(E) secure .. obscurity

Ⓐ Ⓑ Ⓒ Ⓓ Ⓔ

1. The number of African American inventors from the 1600s to the late 1800s will never be -------, since their work was often ------- by others.

(A) seen .. reintegrated
(B) determined .. expropriated
(C) withheld .. trivialized
(D) disclosed .. uncensored
(E) archived .. marketed

2. House-wares and book-bindings by designer Josef Hoffmann exemplify a range of styles, from simple and austere to ------- and opulent.

(A) basic (B) efficient (C) severe
(D) florid (E) straightforward

3. Although Christa Wolf was one of East Germany's most famous authors, her works were often ------- and, therefore, often unavailable.

(A) suppressed (B) revised (C) imitated
(D) tolerated (E) analyzed

4. A few of the people on the island may live -------, but most have no hope of ------- even the basic amenities of life.

(A) poorly .. enjoying
(B) pretentiously .. yielding
(C) responsibly .. acquiring
(D) lavishly .. attaining
(E) simply .. missing

5. The new pluralism in art ------- a great variety of styles and points of view while denying ------- to any single approach.

(A) ignores .. originality
(B) distorts .. probability
(C) espouses .. embellishment
(D) undermines .. secrecy
(E) accommodates .. dominance

6. Interest in the origin of life is -------; all cultures and societies have narratives about creation.

(A) distant (B) mythical (C) universal
(D) debatable (E) superficial

GO ON TO THE NEXT PAGE

7. Although the personality that emerges from May Sarton's autobiography seems unmistakably -------, the journals for which she became famous described her ------- life in a sparsely populated area.

(A) complex . . intricate
(B) celebrated . . humorous
(C) affable . . solitary
(D) stoic . . isolated
(E) scholarly . . intellectual

8. Negotiators predicted an early end to the strike, but the reporters were ------- because both sides refused to compromise.

(A) cordial
(B) dubious
(C) benevolent
(D) biased
(E) prophetic

9. He was always ------- in performing his tasks, waiting until the last moment to finish them.

(A) dilatory
(B) incompetent
(C) extroverted
(D) surreptitious
(E) obtrusive

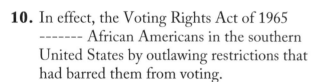

10. In effect, the Voting Rights Act of 1965 ------- African Americans in the southern United States by outlawing restrictions that had barred them from voting.

(A) inspired　(B) promulgated
　(C) enfranchised　(D) preserved
　(E) proliferated

11. The author portrays research psychologists not as disruptive ------- in the field of psychotherapy, but as effective ------- working ultimately toward the same ends as the psychotherapists.

(A) proponents . . opponents
(B) antagonists . . pundits
(C) interlocutors . . surrogates
(D) meddlers . . usurpers
(E) intruders . . collaborators

12. Despite their ------- backgrounds, those who fought for women's right to vote successfully overcame their differences in a ------- effort.

(A) incompatible . . divisive
(B) disparate . . united
(C) distinguished . . futile
(D) eccentric . . prosaic
(E) comparable . . joint

13. The usually ------- Mr. Henderson shocked his associates by reacting violently to the insignificant and moderate comments of his critic.

(A) demanding
(B) inarticulate
(C) aggressive
(D) persuasive
(E) composed

14. Disappointingly, the researchers' failure was a direct result of their -------, we had not expected that their focus would be so indistinct.

(A) egoism　(B) irreverence (C) relevance
　(D) vagueness　(E) hindsight

GO ON TO THE NEXT PAGE

15. Although her restaurant already has a large and devoted following, Magda tries to expand her ------- by offering special promotions.

(A) clientele
(B) investments
(C) coverage
(D) staffing
(E) liability

16. By showing such a large shaded area, this map of wildlife distribution encourages the ------- that certain species living in isolated spots are actually -------.

(A) misconception . . widespread
(B) impression . . remote
(C) illusion . . extant
(D) notion . . carnivorous
(E) sense . . feral

17. The candidate recognized that his attempt to build a broad base of support had been -------, but he was still ------- by the magnitude of his defeat.

(A) obstinate. elated
(B) insightful . . impenitent
(C) persuasive . . exultant
(D) thwarted . . discomfited
(E) successful. satisfied

18. Although it is not -------, Clara Rodriguez' book on Puerto Rican life is especially useful because the supply of books on the subject is so -------.

(A) intense . . vast
(B) obsolete . . outdated
(C) ostentatious . . varied
(D) comprehensive . . meager
(E) contemporary . . plentiful

19. Wave direction, apparently the primary ------- used by young turtles to navigate in water, is later ------- by their orientation to magnetic fields.

(A) mechanism . . confused
(B) vestige . . propagated
(C) restraint . . complemented
(D) agent . . propelled
(E) cue . . supplanted

20. The Uzbeks are a people of Central Asia who are chiefly -------, deriving their livelihood from growing grains and cotton.

(A) nomads   (B) industrialists (C) pillagers
      (D) technologists   (E) agriculturalists

21. The ------- of animated films on college campuses is evident from the ------- books analyzing cartoon classics that have been sold in college bookstores.

(A) availability . . limited
(B) predominance . . incidental
(C) suppression . . overdue
(D) reduction . . scholarly
(E) popularity . . numerous

22. Once a ------- issue, the idea that complex organic molecules may be present in interstellar space no longer sparks debate.

(A) laudatory (B) rare (C) controversial
      (D) plausible   (E) defunct

GO ON TO THE NEXT PAGE

23. Although his methods of composition have had a ------- and ------- influence on jazz, Thelonious Monk is unique among great jazz artists in not having attracted a legion of slavish imitators.

(A) superb . . untimely
(B) profound . . lasting
(C) pervasive . . unaccounted
(D) dubious . . universal
(E) severe . . unfavorable

24. Because scholarship in that field is still in its nascent stage, many researchers have argued that to develop ------- model would be -------, but to demonstrate progress toward a model is essential at this time.

(A) a tentative . . decisive
(B) a definitive . . premature
(C) a superfluous . . inadvisable
(D) an impressive . . vital
(E) an irrelevant . . necessary

25. The psychic claimed to know what the signs -------, but no one trusted her prophecy.

(A) disfigured
(B) deterred
(C) repudiated
(D) portended
(E) circumvented

26. From classic fiction to the latest journalism, the theme of the typical plague story is one of -------: whenever a writer describes an epidemic as a plague, an extremely fatalistic view is implied.

(A) eccentricity
(B) tedium
(C) inevitability
(D) mystery
(E) excitement

27. Unlike her brother Henry, who extolled the merits of the English, Alice James lost no opportunity to ------- them.

(A) tolerate
(B) restrict
(C) abide
(D) disparage
(E) glorify

28. During the 1960s, attorneys who ------- court orders that declared various kinds of racial segregation unconstitutional often did so at the risk of retaliation from civil rights -------.

(A) filed . . victims
(B) questioned . . skeptics
(C) defied . . opponents
(D) obtained . . foes
(E) demanded . . leaders

29. Sports can be ------- because they demonstrate the value of teamwork, fair play, and discipline.

(A) entertaining   (B) enervating
(C) individualistic   (D) educational
(E) disruptive

30. In a survey, many parents who wish to ------- virtues such as family togetherness reported that they prefer television shows about the daily lives of closely knit families to those ------- violent conflicts and adventures.

(A) discredit . . portraying
(B) identify . . criticizing
(C) promote . . depicting
(D) foster . . rejecting
(E) dispute . . satirizing

GO ON TO THE NEXT PAGE

31. Despite the critics' ------- of the actress's performance in her most recent film, their acclaim seems to have done little to further her career.

(A) perusal
(B) parody
(C) commendation
(D) extenuation
(E) ignorance

32. The ------- waters of the shallow lake made the fish clearly visible to Dr. Muraoka and his survey team.

(A) turbulent
(B) treacherous
(C) serpentine
(D) pellucid
(E) putrid

33. Dagmar did not enjoy the dessert; there was so much sugar in it that it was -------.

(A) unpalatable (B) subtle (C) caustic
(D) convoluted   (E) invigorating

34. The constriction of small blood vessels can be ------- when it leads to ------- of the blood flow; however, a reduced blood flow is sometimes actually beneficial.

(A) advantageous . . an interruption
(B) deleterious . . a stoppage
(C) healthful . . a resumption
(D) innocuous . . a coagulation
(E) injurious . . a progression

35. A study of Berthe Morisot's painting technique reveals that her apparent ------- and ------- execution were never as casual as they seemed but actually resulted from years of practice and concentration.

(A) craft . . studied
(B) improvisation . . diligent
(C) spontaneity . . rapid
(D) deception . . flawless
(E) accomplishment . . laborious

36. Jones believes that since extrasensory experiences are by their very nature subjective, they are not ------- and cannot, therefore, be ------- scientifically.

(A) intrepid . . perceived
(B) transitory . . validated
(C) extrinsic . . accepted
(D) uncanny . . increased
(E) observable . . substantiated

37. For the parade, the tailor designed an elaborate outfit too ------- for even the most foolish dandy.

(A) rustic (B) subdued   (C) demure
(D) foppish (E) trite

38. Once an occasional liar, Jessica has become ------- one in that she lies habitually.

(A) a perfidious (B) a rancorous
(C) a selective   (D) an arcane
(E) an inveterate

STOP

this is the end of the exercise

SC5 SC5
SC5 SC5

SAT Sentence Completion Exercise #05
35 Questions

DIRECTIONS

Each sentence below has one or two blanks, each blank indicating that something has been omitted. Beneath the sentence are five words or sets of words labeled A through E. Choose the word or set of words that, when inserted in the sentence, best fits the meaning of the sentence as a whole.

EXAMPLE:

Though the first moon landing took place half a century ago, its legacy is far from -------; today's astronauts, scientists and engineers continue to be inspired by its -------.

(A) over . . brevity
(B) flawless . . aftermath
(C) forgotten . . achievements
(D) accurate . . clarity
(E) secure . . obscurity

(A) (B) (C) (D) (E)

---

1. Many cultural historians believe that language has a ------- purpose: it serves not only as a means of communication but also as a means of defining culture.

(A) foreign   (B) literary   (C) false
   (D) dual   (E) direct

2. In 1859 Black pioneer Clara Brown turned the unpromising conditions that had ------- many other settlers of the mining camp into a source of ------- by starting her own business.

(A) discouraged . . reconciliation
(B) defeated . . prosperity
(C) elevated . . happiness
(D) aided . . opportunity
(E) delayed . . unity

3. While the island country's dramatists typically use ------- settings and myths, their themes are not ------- their country alone; indeed, many plays are appreciated worldwide for their insightful treatment of common human issues.

(A) ancient . . condescending to
(B) modest . . concerned with
(C) native . . limited to
(D) ordinary . . lobbying for
(E) cosmopolitan . . indebted to

4. Far from ------- the old social inequities, the law ------- new ones by virtue of the loopholes it left for the wealthy.

(A) eradicating . . created
(B) jeopardizing . . corrected
(C) placating . . eliminated
(D) duplicating . . avoided
(E) corroborating . . anticipated

5. The use of gospel music in the modem production of the ancient Greek tragedy is effective, in spite of seeming ------- to critics interested only in historical accuracy.

(A) felicitous   (B) inevitable
(C) anachronistic   (D) timeless
(E) exemplary

6. It has been suggested that the detailed listings of animals, plants, and minerals by their usefulness to humans indicate the ------- of the ancient Mesopotamians,

(A) irrationality
(B) humanity
(C) temerity
(D) serendipity
(E) anthropocentrism

GO ON TO THE NEXT PAGE

7. Buildings designed exclusively for strength and stability, structures for which only ------- considerations have been taken into account, are properly works of engineering, not true architecture.

(A) utilitarian (B) grandiose (C) imaginative
    (D) aesthetic   (E) external

8. Many healing practices that doctors once derided as ------- have now been sanctioned by the medical community.

(A) benign (B) diagnostic (C) inefficacious
    (D) discretionary   (E) therapeutic

9. Sometimes forgetting that rationality is only one part of a person's experience, Andrew takes an excessively ------- approach to life.

(A) cerebral (B) obdurate (C) sensitive
    (D) pretentious   (E) enervated

10. For centuries, the coastline of Uruguay was regarded by European mariners as a ------- place, one seemingly devoid of inhabitants.

(A) conceivable
(B) desolate
(C) fallacious
(D) prepossessing
(E) discourteous

11. Chocolate connects us to the past, for despite modern ------- in food-processing technology, the steps necessary for transforming cocoa beans into chocolate have been ------- for nearly two centuries.

(A) developments . . varied
(B) setbacks . . constant
(C) failures . . inconsistent
(D) progress . . unstable
(E) advances . . unchanged

12. The landscape was truly -------, so arid that even the hardiest plants could not survive.

(A) lurid   (B) parched   (C) drubbed
    (D) verdant   (E) variegated

13. Born -------, children will follow their natural inclination to explore their surroundings with a ------- that belies the random appearance of their play.

(A) innocent . . deviousness
(B) serious . . merriment
(C) curious . . purposefulness
(D) eager . . moderation
(E) aware . . casualness

14. Although English philosopher Anne Conway was ------- by her seventeenth-century contemporaries, she has through oversight been nearly ------- in recent times.

(A) revered . . forgotten
(B) censured . . venerated
(C) abandoned . . ignored
(D) imitated . . emulated
(E) pardoned . . absolved

GO ON TO THE NEXT PAGE

15. While the ------- explorers faced risks courageously, they were not -------, choosing instead to avoid needless dangers.

    (A) flagrant . . punctual
    (B) intrepid . . foolhardy
    (C) genial . . clandestine
    (D) resolute . . amicable
    (E) culpable . . irresponsible

16. Maxine Hong Kingston presents universal themes in the context of Chinese American culture; this has helped her achieve a literary ------- that is -------, yet speaks to the full range of human experience.

    (A) success . . indistinct
    (B) voice . . unique
    (C) convention . . encompassing
    (D) style . . comprehensive
    (E) prominence . . general

17. The grief and sadness of parting and the sorrows that seem eternal are ------- by time, but they leave their scars.

    (A) revived (B) magnified (C) nurtured
        (D) mitigated   (E) concocted

18. The traditional process of producing an oil painting requires so many steps that it seems ------- to artists who prefer to work quickly.

    (A) provocative (B) consummate
        (C) interminable (D) facile (E) prolific

19. Photography as an art form often seeks the ------- in its subjects, those qualities that cannot be expressed in words.

    (A) ineffable (B) mundane (C) onerous
        (D) incisive (E) auspicious

20. The unification of Upper and Lower Egypt around 3000 B.C. acted as a catalyst, ------- a flowering of Egyptian culture.

    (A) triggering
    (B) describing
    (C) suspending
    (D) polarizing
    (E) symbolizing

21. If his works had been regarded merely as those of a fool, he might have met with only -------, not with violent enmity and strict censorship.

    (A) brutality (B) loathing   (C) rebellion
        (D) ridicule   (E) execution

22. Recent evidence that a special brain cell is critical to memory is so ------- that scientists are ------- their theories of how the brain stores information to include the role of this cell.

    (A) pervasive . . reproducing
    (B) perplexing . . formulating
    (C) obscure . . confirming
    (D) extreme . . restoring
    (E) compelling . . revising

23. The ------- act was ------- even to the perpetrator, who regretted his deed to the end of his life.

    (A) vulgar . . unaffected
    (B) heinous . . appalling
    (C) vengeful . . acceptable
    (D) timorous . . intrepid
    (E) forgettable . . offensive

GO ON TO THE NEXT PAGE

24. The observation that nurses treating patients with pellagra did not ------- the disease led epidemiologists to question the theory that pellagra is -------.

(A) risk . . deadly
(B) fear . . curable
(C) acknowledge . . common
(D) contract . . contagious
(E) battle . . preventable

25. The general view of gorillas as menacing, ferocious King Kongs was not successfully ------- until Dian Foisse's field studies in the 1960s showed gorillas to be peaceable, rather fainthearted creatures, unlikely to ------- humans.

(A) counteracted . . please
(B) enhanced . . murder
(C) verified . . attack
(D) dispelled . . captivate
(E) challenged . . threaten

26. The quotation attributing to the mayor the view that funds for police should be cut was -------: it completely ------- the mayor's position that more police should be hired.

(A) inflammatory . . justified
(B) abbreviated . . curtailed
(C) meticulous . . misstated
(D) egregious . . underscored
(E) spurious . . misrepresented

27. A ------- is concerned not with whether a political program is liberal or conservative but with whether it will work,

(A) radical
(B) utopian
(C) pragmatist
(D) partisan
(E) reactionary

28. Thomas Jefferson's decision not to ------- lotteries was sanctioned by classical wisdom, which held that, far from being a ------- game, lots were a way of divining the future and of involving the gods in everyday affairs.

(A) expand . . sacred
(B) publicize . . vile
(C) condemn . . debased
(D) legalize . . standardized
(E) restrict . . useful

29. The visitor was of an ------- age: white-haired, but baby-faced, he might have been twenty-five or fifty.

(A) assiduous   (B) unalterable
(C) indecorous   (D) indeterminate
(E) extenuating

30. Unfortunately, for North American Indians the arrival of European settlers often meant ------- their lands, their ways of life, and even their very existence.

(A) a renewal of
(B) a respect for
(C) an assault on
(D) a retention of
(E) an idea of

31. Different species of mosquito conduct the essential activities of eating, growing, and reproducing in so many ways that no rule of mosquito behavior is without some -------.

(A) result (B) objectivity   (C) exception
(D) clarity   (E) enforcement

GO ON TO THE NEXT PAGE

32. Even more interesting than the completed masterpiece can be the ------- work of the artist: the first-draft manuscript, the initial pencil sketches, the symphony rehearsal.

(A) rough   (B) intense   (C) varied
(D) thoughtless   (E) atypical

33. Oceanographic research has shown that ridges on the ocean floor are not ------- features, but part of a 4,000-mile-long mountain range.

(A) conditional
(B) unchanging
(C) observable
(D) definable
(E) isolated

34. Although Jack and Mary Lynch are often ------- to strangers, they show only ------- to a pack of nearly extinct buffalo wolves, working seven days a week to help save the endangered species.

(A) gracious . . disdain
(B) rude . . exasperation
(C) gruff . . kindness
(D) agreeable . . gentleness
(E) condescending . . hostility

35. We need not be ------- about our performance thus far, but neither should we be -------: there is ample room for improvement.

(A) haughty . . generous
(B) lazy . . industrious
(C) apologetic . . smug
(D) opulent . . showy
(E) sympathetic . . crude

STOP

this is the end of the exercise

SAT Sentence Completion Exercise #06

37 Questions

DIRECTIONS

Each sentence below has one or two blanks, each blank indicating that something has been omitted. Beneath the sentence are five words or sets of words labeled A through E. Choose the word or set of words that, when inserted in the sentence, best fits the meaning of the sentence as a whole.

EXAMPLE:

Though the first moon landing took place half a century ago, its legacy is far from -------; today's astronauts, scientists and engineers continue to be inspired by its -------.

(A) over . . brevity
(B) flawless . . aftermath
(C) forgotten . . achievements
(D) accurate . . clarity
(E) secure . . obscurity

Ⓐ Ⓑ Ⓒ Ⓓ Ⓔ

1. The art collection of the children's museum is quite -------, ranging from furniture to sculpture to finger painting.

   (A) imaginary   (B) repetitive   (C) elusive
   (D) eclectic   (E) circumscribed

2. By subsidizing small farms, the new government is hoping to ------- the flow of people into the cities and ------- farming.

   (A) reverse . . incorporate
   (B) arrest . . encourage
   (C) boost . . initiate
   (D) enhance . . regulate
   (E) diminish . . prohibit

3. Despite Atlanta's large Black community, African American theater companies in that city are anything but ------- in fact, in 1993 there was only one, Jomandi productions.

   Adj loyg min t

   (A) legion   (B) advantageous   (C) bourgeois
   (D) nondescript   (E) wily

4. The female subject of this painting by Henri Matisse seems -------, as if Matisse sought to portray an unconquerable female spirit.

   (A) ephemeral   (B) indomitable   (C) opulent
   (D) lithe   (E) morose

5. Ironically, the same executives who brought bankruptcy to the coal fields were ------- by their contemporaries, who ------- the notion that these people were industrial heroes.

   (A) celebrated . . cherished
   (B) respected . . doubted
   (C) ignored . . belied
   (D) condemned . . rejected
   (E) antagonized . . enjoyed

6. Hoping to ------- the dispute, negotiators proposed a compromise that they felt would be ------- to both labor and management.

   (A) enforce . . useful
   (B) end . . divisive
   (C) overcome . . unattractive
   (D) extend . . satisfactory
   (E) resolve . . acceptable

GO ON TO THE NEXT PAGE ➡

7. Geneticist Olivia M. Pereira-Smith has published her findings on "immortal" cells, that is, cells that reproduce by dividing -------.

(A) indefinitely
(B) occasionally
(C) conclusively
(D) periodically
(E) precisely

8. The unusually large herb *Gunnera* is difficult to study because it is found only in ------- areas.

(A) fertile
(B) hospitable
(C) inaccessible
(D) mundane
(E) extensive

9. To ------- about craft clubs is not only ------- but foolish, for the focus of the clubs varies greatly from one town to another.

(A) brag . . necessary
(B) generalize . . difficult
(C) complain . . important
(D) rhapsodize . . fair
(E) learn . . unproductive

10. Even though some people feel historians have an exclusive right to act as the interpreters of bygone eras, most historians insist their profession has no ------- interpreting the past.

(A) interest in
(B) responsibility in
(C) consensus for
(D) monopoly on
(E) misgivings about

11. It is difficult to tell whether the attention new rock bands are receiving from audiences is that associated with ------- or that which indicates a durable -------.

(A) novelty . . popularity
(B) originality . . understanding
(C) success . . sensation
(D) longevity . . image
(E) creativity . . production

12. Fenster schemed and plotted for weeks and these ------- were rewarded when Griswold was fired and Fenster was promoted.

(A) circumlocutions
(B) affiliations
(C) shenanigans
(D) machinations
(E) renunciations

13. Each male mockingbird views his territory as ------- no other male of the same species is tolerated within its boundaries.

(A) circuitous (B) inviolable (C) dissipated
     (D) unparalleled   (E) mandated

14. Whether Mitsuko Uchida is performing music or merely discussing it, the pianist's animated demeanor ------- her passion for her vocation.

(A) misrepresents   (B) exaggerates
     (C) satisfies (D) reflects (E) disguises

15. One of the factors that ------- the understanding of the nature of cells was the limited resolution of early microscopes.

(A) aided (B) discredited   (C) increased
     (D) contradicted   (E) restricted

GO ON TO THE NEXT PAGE

16. The congresswoman is very powerful: she has more ------- than any other member of the committee.

(A) integrity (B) influence (C) restraint
(D) discrimination   (E) pretense

17. Anyone who possesses perceptiveness, insight, and unflagging vitality has invaluable -------, but the rare individual who also possesses the ability to ------- these qualities through art has genius.

(A) prospects . . delegate
(B) gifts . . express
(C) traits . . forbid
(D) flaws . . impute
(E) visions . . bequeath

18. To summarize an article is to separate that which is ------- from the ------- material that surrounds it.

(A) notable . . primary
(B) undesirable . . encompassing
(C) fundamental . . vital
(D) essential . . supporting
(E) explanatory . . characteristic

19. Sometimes fiction is marred by departures from the main narrative, but Toni Morrison's *The Bluest Eye* is instead ------- by its -------, which add levels of meaning to the principal story.

(A) enhanced . . digressions
(B) harmed . . excursions
(C) adorned . . melodramas
(D) strengthened . . criticisms
(E) unaffected . . euphemisms

20. According to the report, the investment firm had ------- several customers, swindling them out of thousands of dollars.

(A) harassed (B) sullied (C) bilked
(D) investigated   (E) incriminated

21. Because this novel is not so narrowly concerned with ------- political issues, it seems as ------- today as it did two hundred years ago.

(A) momentary . . derivative
(B) evanescent . . nostalgic
(C) transient . . fresh
(D) sagacious . . wise
(E) dated . . quaint

22. Contemptuous of official myths about great men and women that had been taught to them in school, many postwar writers, with the skepticism expected of -------, advanced the idea that there was no such thing as greatness.

(A) idealists (B) fan boys   (C) dissemblers
(D) nitpickers   (E) debunkers

23. Residents of the secluded island fear that ------- commercial development will ------- their quiet way of life.

(A) widespread . . reinforce
(B) waning . . harm
(C) diminishing . . reform
(D) encroaching . . disturb
(E) further . . aid

GO ON TO THE NEXT PAGE

24. Nicknamed the "contact lens," the device installed on the Hubble telescope successfully ------- its flawed vision, the result of a faulty mirror.

(A) corrected (B) displayed (C) generated
    (D) scrutinized (E) accentuated

25. Though it is often exclusively ------- Brazil, the Amazon jungle actually ------- parts of eight other South American countries.

(A) protected by . . threatens
(B) located in . . bypasses
(C) limited to . . touches
(D) surrounded by . . borders
(E) associated with . . covers

26. As an architect who rehabilitates older buildings, Roberta Washington objected to a city policy that resulted in the mass ------- of clearly ------- structures.

(A) demolition . . inconsequential
(B) renovation . . derelict
(C) razing . . salvageable
(D) protection . . venerable
(E) scouring . . grimy

27. Sandia Gilbert and Susan Gubar's recent book presents a ------- of detail, providing far more information than one can easily digest.

(A) modicum (B) discrepancy (C) surfeit
    (D) deficit   (E) juxtaposition

28. On the verge of financial collapse, the museum was granted a -------, getting a much-needed ------- of cash in the form of a loan.

(A) reprieve . . infusion
(B) deferment . . inducement
(C) rebate . . advance
(D) hearing . . security
(E) procurement . . account

29. More ------- than her predecessor, Superintendent Reynolds would, many predicted, have a far less ------- term of office.

(A) phlegmatic . . apathetic
(B) conciliatory . . confrontational
(C) empathetic . . compassionate
(D) vigilant . . reputable
(E) penurious . . frugal

30. Rodolfo Gonzales was once described as ------- in body and mind because of the flexibility and grace apparent in both his boxing and his writing of poetry and plays.

(A) unyielding
(B) emphatic
(C) tremulous
(D) lithe
(E) fickle

31. Galloping technological progress has made consumers -------: advances undreamed of a generation ago are so common that they seem humdrum.

(A) flabbergasted
(B) miffed
(C) jaded
(D) wary
(E) embittered

32. They use language not to explain but to
------; each statement is like a reflection in a
warped minor.
(A) preserve (B) distort (C) enlighten
(D) negate   (E) destroy

33. Many writers associated with the Harlem
Renaissance were not originally from Harlem;
drawn by the artistic community it provided,
they ------- the place as home.

(A) neglected   (B) adopted   (C) avoided
(D) criticized   (E) encountered

34. Francis learned that by ------- his anger and
resentment, and so avoiding -------, he could
overcome opponents more successfully than
could those who openly defied their
adversaries.

(A) expressing . . hostility
(B) suppressing . . conflict
(C) stifling . . temperance
(D) disguising . . deceit
(E) rousing . . wrath

35. Colonial South Carolina was characterized by
cultural -------: Europeans, Africans, and
Native Americans each absorbed some
customs of the other groups.

(A) tension   (B) conservatism (C) integrity
(D) convergence   (E) eradication

36. Ellen Swallow Richards, a -------
environmental preservation in the United
States, campaigned during the nineteenth
century to ------- responsible practices in the
discipline that has come to be known as
ecology.

(A) foil for . . expose
(B) pioneer of . . implement
(C) resource on . . squelch
(D) imitator of . . promote
(E) critic of . . exploit

37. Sleep actually occurs -------, though one may
receive clues signaling its ------- for several
minutes before one falls asleep.

(A) gradually . . abruptness
(B) erratically . . solace
(C) temporarily . . length
(D) inevitably . . approach
(E) instantaneously . . onset

STOP

this is the end of the exercise

SAT Sentence Completion Exercise #07
37 Questions

DIRECTIONS
Each sentence below has one or two blanks, each blank indicating that something has been omitted. Beneath the sentence are five words or sets of words labeled A through E. Choose the word or set of words that, when inserted in the sentence, best fits the meaning of the sentence as a whole.

EXAMPLE:
Though the first moon landing took place half a century ago, its legacy is far from -------; today's astronauts, scientists and engineers continue to be inspired by its -------.

(A) over . . brevity
(B) flawless . . aftermath
(C) forgotten . . achievements
(D) accurate . . clarity
(E) secure . . obscurity

Ⓐ Ⓑ Ⓒ Ⓓ Ⓔ

1. Laila performed her tasks at the office with -------, completing all her projects in record time,

(A) alacrity
(B) conformity
(C) deliberation
(D) recrimination
(E) exasperation

2. Anna Freud's impact on psychoanalysis was -------, coming not from one brilliant discovery but from a lifetime of first-rate work.

(A) tangential   (B) premature
(C) exorbitant   (D) indiscernible
(E) cumulative

3. The treasurer was intimidated by the ------- demeanor of the auditors who neither spoke nor smiled when they arrived.

(A) amiable   (B) ethical   (C) glacial
(D) taunting   (E) nondescript

4. Critics say that the autobiographical work Brothers and Keepers by John Edgar Wideman is surprising in that it celebrates and yet ------- his own role in the life of his brother.

(A) censures   (B) exacerbates   (C) explores
(D) duplicates   (E) delineates

5. The prosecutor termed the defendants' actions ------- because there was no justification for their intentional disregard for the law.

(A) indefensible
(B) surreptitious
(C) indefatigable
(D) comprehensive
(E) corrective

6. Acid rain is damaging lakes in ------- way, causing the virtually unnoticed ------- of these aquatic ecosystems.

(A) a manifest . . eradication
(B) a nefarious . . polarization
(C) an insidious . . destruction
(D) a methodical . . amalgamation
(E) an obvious . . stagnation

GO ON TO THE NEXT PAGE

7. Although he can ------- isolated facts, he is no scholar: he is able to ------- information but cannot make sense of it.

(A) regurgitate . . synthesize
(B) memorize . . recite
(C) falsify . . denounce
(D) misinterpret . . acquire
(E) recall . . disregard

8. The use of tools among chimpanzees is learned behavior: young chimpanzees become ------- by ------- others.

(A) socialized . . overcoming
(B) dominant . . obeying
(C) vocal . . mimicking
(D) adept . . imitating
(E) agile . . following

9. The speech was a ------- of random and contradictory information that could not be integrated into -------, consistent whole.

(A) collage . . a rambling
(B) development . . an ambiguous
(C) hodgepodge . . a coherent
(D) morass . . an amorphous
(E) harangue . . an unintelligible

10. The new concert hall proved to be a -------: it was costly, acoustically unsatisfactory, and far too small.

(A) colossus   (B) milestone   (C) debacle
     (D) consecration   (E) fabrication

11. A hypocrite may ------- reprehensible acts but escape discovery by affecting ------- .

(A) abhor . . profundity
(B) condone . . enthusiasm
(C) commit . . innocence
(D) perform . . immorality
(E) condemn . . repentance

12. The review was -------, recounting the play's felicities and its flaws without unduly emphasizing one or the other.

(A) equitable
(B) immoderate
(C) cumulative
(D) unproductive
(E) adulatory

13. Rosita Peru, who rose to become the highest-ranking female in the television industry, was ------- recruited: Spanish language program producers courted her persistently.

(A) indiscriminately
(B) enigmatically
(C) vicariously
(D) rancorously
(E) assiduously

14. Mammals of temperate zones often give birth in the spring, thereby -------, their offspring to ------- the season's abundant food.

(A) subjecting . . subsist on
(B) encouraging . . compete for
(C) tempting . . abstain from
(D) forcing . . forage for
(E) enabling . . benefit from

GO ON TO THE NEXT PAGE

15. While the dome of the nineteenth-century city hall once ------- the city's skyline, a much taller new office building now ------- the old landmark.

(A) overshadowed . . enhances
(B) dominated . . dwarfs
(C) punctuated . . resembles
(D) cluttered . . destroys
(E) beautified . . uplifts

16. Ancient cloth makers probably could not twist flax fibers until they had dipped the fibers into water to make them -------.

(A) solvent　(B) supple　(C) nonporous
(D) immutable　(E) invisible

17. In an effort to ------- people's physical discomforts, modern medicine sometimes wrongly treats the body's defense mechanisms as ------- and in need of corrective intervention.

(A) cure . . complex
(B) prescribe . . symptomatic
(C) diagnose . . suppressive
(D) relieve . . defective
(E) analyze . . medicinal

18. *Crazy Love*, by Elias Miguel Munoz, is a(n) ------- novel: it takes the form of a series of letters.

(A) grotesque (B) epistolary (C)inauspicious
(D) inconspicuous　(E)　illusory

19. The meal had ------- effect on the famished travelers: their energy was restored almost instantly.

(A) a tonic
(B) a cloying
(C) an indefinite
(D) a debilitating
(E) an intemperate

20. While cynics may ------- the goal of international disarmament as utopian, others believe that laughing contemptuously at idealism leads n where.

(A) exalt　(B) confirm　(C) renew
(D) deride　(E) defend

21. Although his memoirs contained scathing criticisms of his opponents, the politician ------- vindictiveness as his motive.

(A) disavowed
(B) claimed
(C) disparaged
(D) substantiated
(E) evaluated

22. Even in her most casual conversation, one detects the impulse to -------, to impart knowledge systematically to her listener.

(A) mystify　(B) instruct　(C) insinuate
(D) embellish　(E) meditate

GO ON TO THE NEXT PAGE

23. Ms. Turner was a(n) ------- opponent, one who never swerved from her purpose and would never compromise or yield.

(A) inexorable
(B) ambivalent
(C) eloquent
(D) impassive
(E) obstreperous

24. She thought her ------- were amusing, but the others thought such tricks were irritating.

(A) anecdotes (B) researches (C) demands
(D) pranks   (E) debts

25. Though its wings look extremely -------, the butterfly is ------- enough to fly as high as 7,000 feet.

(A) vivid . . powerful
(B) iridescent . . skillful
(C) slender . . thick
(D) beautiful . . heavy
(E) fragile . . sturdy

26. Several medieval manuscripts that were improperly -------, and thus lost within the library itself since their acquisition, have been located and are finally ------- patrons.

(A) praised . . scrutinized by
(B) displayed . . comprehensible to
(C) labeled . . accessible to
(D) administered . . overlooked by
(E) cataloged . . unobtainable by

27. Using gestures and facial expressions rather than words, the performers eloquently communicated through the art of the -------.

(A) mediator (B) ensemble (C) elocutionist
(D) pantomime   (E) troubadour

28. The ability to treat stress-related illness is limited because many conditions can ------- stress, but none of them has been singled out as the ------- cause of stress.

(A) alleviate . . original
(B) relieve . . sole
(C) induce . . predominant
(D) inhibit . . actual
(E) produce . . partial

29. Company President Carmen Sanchez intends the ------- with which she works to be an example to her employees; as a result, they find that they are expected to apply themselves to their jobs most -------.

(A) sagacity . . unscrupulously
(B) leniency . . decorously
(C) nonchalance . . tenaciously
(D) acrimony . . cheerfully
(E) ardor . . assiduously

30. George was so eager to ------- his preconceptions that he grasped at any fact that seemed to ------- the undeniable gaps in his theory.

(A) reinforce . . strengthen
(B) preserve . . bridge
(C) convey . . widen
(D) overcome . . plug
(E) disregard . . destroy

GO ON TO THE NEXT PAGE

31. That Virginia Woolf's criticism of prose is more astute than her criticism of poetry is most likely due to her ability, as a novelist and essayist, to approach prose as one of its -------.

(A) novices (B) neighbors (C) interpreters
(D) practitioners   (E) detractors

32. Since the opposing factions could reach no ------- the budget proposal, they decided to ------- it and to debate the hazardous waste bill instead.

(A) consensus on . . table
(B) opinion about . . enact
(C) decision about . . berate
(D) agreement on . . proclaim
(E) compromise on . . endorse

33. The workers were bored by the mindless routine of their jobs; their performance, therefore, was mechanical, no more than -------.

(A) querulous (B) perfunctory (C) diffuse
(D) irresolute   (E) transient

34. In the style of some ancient Chinese poets, Asian American poet Li-Young Lee speaks ------- but -------: he meditates on abstract issues while using everyday language in his writing.

(A) clearly . . simply
(B) pompously . . nonchalantly
(C) philosophically . . colloquially
(D) diffidently . . cunningly
(E) sternly . . profoundly

35. They were not ------- misfortune, having endured more than their share of -------.

(A) cognizant of . . calamity
(B) superstitious about . . prosperity
(C) jealous of . . success
(D) oblivious to . . happiness
(E) unacquainted with . . adversity

36. Pat made the descent with unusual caution, placing each foot first -------, then firmly.

(A) heavily
(B) clumsily
(C) tentatively
(D) confidently
(E) languidly

37. Because the geometry course ------- the principles governing solid structures, it was especially popular with students specializing in -------.

(A) emphasized . . architecture
(B) deleted . . geology
(C) reversed . . literature
(D) revealed . . history
(E) attacked, ,economics

STOP

this is the end of the exercise

SAT Sentence Completion Exercise #08

37 Questions

DIRECTIONS

Each sentence below has one or two blanks, each blank indicating that something has been omitted. Beneath the sentence are five words or sets of words labeled A through E. Choose the word or set of words that, when inserted in the sentence, best fits the meaning of the sentence as a whole.

EXAMPLE:

Though the first moon landing took place half a century ago, its legacy is far from -------; today's astronauts, scientists and engineers continue to be inspired by its -------.

(A) over . . brevity
(B) flawless . . aftermath
(C) forgotten . . achievements
(D) accurate . . clarity
(E) secure . . obscurity

Ⓐ Ⓑ Ⓒ Ⓓ Ⓔ

1. As their enemy grew weaker, the confidence of the allies increased and the ------- predictions they had made at the beginning of the war began to seem justified

(A) imperceptive   (B) belated
   (C) everlasting (D) optimistic
   (E) useless

2. Typically, an environmental problem worsens little by little until finally its effects can no longer be -------; organizations then emerge to raise public consciousness and to press vociferously for ------- action.

(A) preserved . . immediate
(B) disregarded . . gradual
(C) ignored . . remedial
(D) observed . . governmental
(E) distorted . . scientific

3. It is perilously easy to decry so ------- a historical figure without trying to understand the motives for his reprehensible actions.

(A) exemplary   (B) astute   (C) efficacious
   (D) prosaic   (E) villainous

4. Because that testimony had been the ------- the prosecutor's case, when it was ruled inadmissible the case collapsed.

(A) scapegoat for
(B) linchpin of
(C) bane of
(D) conundrum of
(E) buffer against

5. Samantha's distinguishing trait is her ------: she gives liberally to those less fortunate than herself.

(A) amicability
(B) inexorableness
(C) frivolity
(D) munificence
(E) venerability

6. Lacking self-assurance, he was too ------- to ------- controversial topics with people he did not know well.

(A) impassioned . . analyze
(B) timid . . discuss
(C) cautious . . suppress
(D) knowledgeable . . disregard
(E) perceptive . . defend

GO ON TO THE NEXT PAGE

7. After winning the lottery, John bought sports cars, built a mansion, and wore designer suits, but, by thus ------- his -------, he alienated his friends.

(A) enduring . . hardship
(B) flaunting . . prosperity
(C) undermining . . image
(D) calculating . . successes
(E) moderating . . consumption

8. Ballads often praise popular figures who have performed feats that many perceive as -------, such as defending the poor or resisting ------- authority.

(A) modest . . acceptable
(B) inescapable . . legitimate
(C) insufficient . . overpowering
(D) admirable . . unjust
(E) unbelievable . . tolerable

9. As ------- as the disintegration of the Roman Empire must have seemed, that disaster nevertheless presented some ------- aspects.

(A) momentous . . formidable
(B) decisive . . unavoidable
(C) unexpected . . ambiguous
(D) advantageous . . beneficial
(E) catastrophic . . constructive

10. Predictably, detail-oriented workers are ------- keeping track of the myriad particulars of a situation.

(A) remiss in
(B) adept at
(C) humorous about
(D) hesitant about
(E) contemptuous of

11. The beauty of Mount McKinley is usually cloaked: clouds ------- the summit nine days out of ten.

(A) release   (B) elevate   (C) entangle
(D) shroud   (E) attain

12. In the opening scene, the playwright creates such a strong impression of the ------- of the main characters that none of their subsequent, apparently honorable actions can ------- these characters in the eyes of the audience.

(A) integrity . . discredit
(B) conviction . . justify
(C) corruption . . redeem
(D) dignity . . excuse
(E) degradation . . convict

13. By allowing one printer to be used by several computers, this device ------- the need for many separate printers.

(A) accelerates
(B) predetermines
(C) substantiates
(D) precludes
(E) anticipates

14. In an attempt to malign and misrepresent their opponents, some candidates resort to -------.

(A) arbitration   (B) narcissism   (C) calumny
(D) tenacity   (E) solicitude

15. The stage director insisted that before the next performance the set be ------- to eliminate its dinginess.

(A) vandalized   (B) enlarged   (C) refurbished
(D) demolished   (E) relocated

GO ON TO THE NEXT PAGE

16. Most pioneers ------- this valley on their journey to the West because its rugged terrain and frequent landslides made it a ------- place for travelers.

(A) flanked . . fascinating
(B) avoided . . necessary
(C) encompassed . . curious
(D) enjoyed . . troublesome
(E) skirted . . hazardous

17. Most people would be amazed to discover how ------- their recollections are, even those memories of which they are most -------.

(A) unpleasant . . frightened
(B) repressed . . unaware
(C) inaccurate . . certain
(D) amorphous . . unsure
(E) trustworthy . . confident

18. Perhaps the most visible sign of the ------- nature of the Cherokee nation was the fact that the women who led each clan picked the chief.

(A) stoic   (B) matriarchal   (C) defensive
   (D) caustic   (E) didactic

19. Castillo's poetry has generated only enthusiastic response: praise from the general public and ------- from the major critics.

(A) condemnation
(B) sarcasm
(C) plaudits
(D) irony
(E) pathos

20. Many scientists have such specialized expertise that they look only at ------- aspects of nature, but ecologists are concerned with the ------- of the natural environment.

(A) complex . . purity
(B) detailed . . paradox
(C) isolated . . totality
(D) universal . . balance
(E) distant . . erosion

21. Notoriously ------- regarding issues of national security, the Prime Minister dumbfounded her opponents when she ------- a defense appropriations bill they had expected her to contest.

(A) evenhanded . . muddled
(B) compliant . . conceded on
(C) pacific . . opposed
(D) intransigent . . compromised on
(E) rancorous . . railed against

22. Leslie thoroughly ------- the text to avoid any lawsuits that might arise because of the new obscenity law.

(A) condensed   (B) delineated
   (C) exterminated   (D) expurgated
   (E) transcribed

23. The skepticism of some ancient philosophers ------- and helps to elucidate varieties of nihilism that appeared in the early nineteenth century.

(A) suppresses   (B) disseminates
   (C) undermines   (D) confounds
   (E) foreshadows

GO ON TO THE NEXT PAGE

24. The doctor ------- so frequently on disease-prevention techniques that her colleagues accused her of -------.

    (A) vacillated . . inconsistency
    (B) sermonized . . fidelity
    (C) wavered . . steadfastness
    (D) experimented . . inflexibility
    (E) relied . . negligence

25. It is a curious fact that soothsayers are, virtually each and every one, ------- souls, ------- to the status quo and resistant to change.

    (A) consistent . . opposed
    (B) innovative . . committed
    (C) conciliatory . . hostile
    (D) conservative . . dedicated
    (E) progressive . . unsympathetic

26. In the late 1980s there was a sudden ------- of interest in the work of Kahlo, and her paintings escalated in price as more and more people sought to purchase them.

    (A) tenacity (B) appreciation (C) fluctuation
        (D) blurring   (E) upsurge

27. In contrast to the luxury of Mexico's coastal resort areas, the ------- that characterizes many of its urban centers is striking.

    (A) incursion   (B) vibrancy
        (C) indecisiveness   (D) cacophony
        (E) poverty

28. A small number of workers at the company may get paid -------, but the majority feel that they are not ------- adequately for the services they render.

    (A) unfairly . . rewarded
    (B) bountifully . . slighted
    (C) regularly . . refunded
    (D) handsomely . . compensated
    (E) accordingly . . bequeathed

29. Anoxemia, a condition in which the normally highly oxygenated blood cells undergo an abnormal reduction in oxygen content, has so few ------- symptoms that the disease is often -------.

    (A) recognizable . . undiagnosed
    (B) reversible . . prolonged
    (C) remarkable . . revealed
    (D) distinguishable . . fatal
    (E) treatable . . concealed

30. Carlos Saura is not given to explicit statement; his films, which seem hazy because of their psychological -------, often leave the uninitiated puzzled and unmoved.

    (A) causality
    (B) poignancy
    (C) conditioning
    (D) allusiveness
    (E) ardor

31. They petitioned to dismiss their representative because they felt her position was -------; it seemed to promote policies that she wished to change.

    (A) paradoxical
    (B) trivial
    (C) malevolent
    (D) discursive
    (E) cursory

GO ON TO THE NEXT PAGE

32. In essence, Elizabeth Cady Stanton's work for universal ------- brought the vote to women, the final group to remain disenfranchised.

(A) temperance
(B) inculcation
(C) suffrage
(D) liberation
(E) equality

33. Always friendly and sociable, Jeannie grew even more ------- in large groups of people.

(A) forthright (B) convivial (C) verbose
(D) ecstatic (E) kinetic

34. Even though he had not read the book, Cameron was able to ------- its plot through conversations with his classmates.

(A) appropriate (B) pilfer (C) glean
(D) belie (E) condone

35. The scientist's success was a direct result of her -------; she refused to quit even when her efforts appeared futile.

(A) conceit (B) intellect (C) research
(D) resolve (E) inconsistency

36. Although he was ------- throughout much of his life, his later years were characterized by a ------- lifestyle that kept him constantly moving from place to place.

(A) stationary . . dormant
(B) sedentary . peripatetic
(C) secular . . missionary
(D) sluggish . . frenetic
(E) obstinate . . unconventional

37. Some mushrooms of the genus Amanita are known to be -------, inducing severe abdominal pain, vomiting, cold sweats, and excessive thirst when ingested.

(A) nourishing
(B) contagious
(C) subversive
(D) poisonous
(E) sustaining

STOP

this is the end of the exercise

SAT Sentence Completion Exercise #09
36 Questions

DIRECTIONS
Each sentence below has one or two blanks, each blank indicating that something has been omitted. Beneath the sentence are five words or sets of words labeled A through E. Choose the word or set of words that, when inserted in the sentence, best fits the meaning of the sentence as a whole.

EXAMPLE:
Though the first moon landing took place half a century ago, its legacy is far from -------; today's astronauts, scientists and engineers continue to be inspired by its -------.

(A) over . . brevity
(B) flawless . . aftermath
(C) forgotten . . achievements
(D) accurate . . clarity
(E) secure . . obscurity

(A) (B) (C) (D) (E)

1. Although the polar bear is already a beloved attraction, the zoo directors hope to increase its ------- by allowing visitors to participate in its feeding.

(A) popularity (B) habitat (C) awareness
(D) insulation   (E) cooperation

2. His sunny disposition helped him retain his -------, but she, naturally -------, accepted disappointment and failure as her fate.

(A) excitement . courageous
(B) melancholy . . hopeful
(C) optimism . . combative
(D) despondence . . contentious
(E) enthusiasm . . pessimistic

3. The attorney general was ------- woman, and even on those ------- occasions when she did lose her temper, she quickly regained her natural imperturbability.

(A) a trying . . rare
(B) a peaceable . . infrequent
(C) an informed . . memorable
(D) a belligerent . . challenging
(E) an inarticulate . . particular

4. Naomi realized that her offer of expert assistance had not been -------, but she was nevertheless ------- by the viciousness of the rebuff.

(A) authentic . . euphoric
(B) received . . impervious
(C) trenchant . . persuaded
(D) welcome . . unnerved
(E) illicit . . scathed

5. Even though it is by no means -------, Carol Gilligan's research into gender differences in moral development is particularly essential because work in this area ,has been so -------.

(A) riveting . . copious
(B) irrelevant . . unfocused
(C) grandiose . . ambivalent
(D) exhaustive . . sparse
(E) current . . abundant

GO ON TO THE NEXT PAGE

6. An inundation of slanderous television commercials has so ------- voters that they now regard with ------- even those candidates whose campaigns focus on issues instead of character attacks.

(A) mollified . . fortitude
(B) alienated . . disdain
(C) infuriated . . consideration
(D) depraved . . mockery
(E) corrupted. contempt

7. Bluegrass, a direct ------- of old-time string-band music of the late 1920s, is ------- by its more syncopated rhythm and its higher-pitched strident vocals.

(A) descendant . . distinguished
(B) variety . . disciplined
(C) outgrowth . . illustrated
(D) compromise . . characterized
(E) expression . . safeguarded

8. As financial rewards grow and the desire to win at all costs is raised to a fever pitch, the baser elements of an athlete's personality can all too easily be ------- .

(A) intensified (B) qualified (C) submerged
(D) reduced (E) rarefied

9. A Portuguese man-of-war moves over the sea -------, blown by the wind.

(A) covertly (B) motionlessly (C) defiantly
(D) passively (E) consistently

10. Her agent cultivated the actress's reputation for being ------- , hut in fact she was quite ------- in her private life and had many close friends.

(A) reclusive . . gregarious
(B) generous. frugal
(C) charming . . deranged
(D) truculent . . admirable
(E) eccentric . . garrulous

11. Though she earned her ------- as a muralist, the artist felt that she ------- more acclaim for her sculpture.

(A) anonymity . . escaped
(B) reputation . . deserved
(C) fame . . deferred
(D) distinction . . justified
(E) notoriety . . publicized

12. The city has ------- its program for recycling waste in an effort to reduce the amount of garbage that must be ------- or dumped in landfills.

(A) improved . . produced
(B) restricted . . amassed
(C) adapted . . rescued
(D) expanded . . burned
(E) abolished . . buried

13. The Austrian ethnologist Konrad Lorenz applied his studies of the instinctive behavior of fish in schools to the social dynamics of human ------- in groups

(A) fallibility   (B) interaction
(C) physiology   (D) corruption
(E) education

GO ON TO THE NEXT PAGE

14. The historian made blunt assertions about the private life of Shaka, the 19th-century Zulu leader, without adducing a ------- of evidence to ------- his position.

(A) plethora . . advocate
(B) whit . . foreshadow
(C) shred . . concede
(D) scintilla . . buttress
(E) hallmark . . enforce

15. Even though the eye perceives color at a phenomenal speed, a recently developed laser beam can record how the retina ------- light into color- reporting chemical messages to the brain.

(A) fabricates (B) translates (C) subsumes
(D) absorbs (E) relays

16. Today's small, portable computers contrast markedly with the earliest electronic computers, which were -------.

(A) effective (B) invented (C) useful
(D) destructive (E) enormous

17. The international news wire service ------- information -------, so that events are reported all over the world shortly after they happen.

(A) records . . accurately
(B) falsifies . . deliberately
(C) verifies . . painstakingly
(D) disseminates . . rapidly
(E) suppresses . . thoroughly

18. Lacking sacred scriptures or codified ------- , Shinto is more properly regarded as a legacy of traditional religious practices and basic values than as a formal system of belief.

(A) followers (B) boundaries (C) dogma
(D) dispositions   (E) strata

19. Cathedral windows are often -------, composed of thousands of pieces of luminous stained glass.

(A) mysterious (B) intricate   (C) sacred
(D) descriptive (E) burnished

20. Recent fossil evidence suggests that carnivorous dinosaurs were ------- swimmers, but some paleontologists still think that these dinosaurs ------- the water.

(A) swift . . entered
(B) nervous. loathed
(C) accomplished . . feared
(D) unskilled . . avoided
(E) natural . . enjoyed

21. Once he had intellectually ------- the difference between regional dialects, Fernando found himself speaking the language -------.

(A) rejected. considerately
(B) grasped . . effortlessly
(C) hasty . . locating
(D) prolific . . producing
(E) delicate . . storing

22. We will face the idea of old age with ------- as long a we believe that it invariably brings poverty, isolation, and illness.

(A) glee   (B) apprehension (C) chutzpah
(D) veneration   (E) reverence

GO ON TO THE NEXT PAGE

23. Though a hummingbird weighs less than one ounce, all species of hummingbirds are ------- eaters maintaining very high body temperatures and ------- many times their weight in food each day.

(A) voracious . . consuming
(B) fastidious . . discarding
(C) mastered . . implicitly
(D) forgotten . . eloquently
(E) recognized . . ambiguously

24. As a playwright, Pinter is renowned for his mundane settings, his ------- yet poetic dialogue, and his aggressive, often mean-spirited characters.

(A) comprehensive (B) lyrical (C) colloquial
(D) ethereal (E) affirmative

25. The newspaper editorial argued that allowing unfair housing practices to continue without protest gives the appearance of ------- them.

(A) condoning (B) adjusting (C) mollifying
(D) pacifying (E) compelling

26. Since child development is not one ------- process for all infants, pediatricians must carefully study and monitor the ------- growth pattern of each child.

(A) aberrant . . basic
(B) cumulative . . animated
(C) genetic . . latent
(D) homogeneous . . foremost
(E) uniform . . individual

27. Despite their fierce appearance, caymans are rarely -------, and will not attack humans unless provoked.

(A) extinct   (B) timid   (C) domesticated
(D) amphibious   (E) aggressive

28. Some historians claim that the concept of courtly love is a -------that dates from the age of chivalry, while others believe it has more ------- origins.

(A) relic . . simultaneous
(B) notion . . ancient
(C) memento . . discovered
(D) period . . documented
(E) doctrine . . amorous

29. In Shakespeare's day, -------theater audiences would often throw fruits and vegetables at actors who failed to live up to their expectations.

(A) doting   (B) ravenous   (C) jingoistic
(D) boisterous   (E) stagnant

30. Although they physically resemble each other, the brothers could not be more ------- temperamentally; while the one is quiet and circumspect, the other is brash and -------.

(A) inimical . . timid
(B) passionate . . superficial
(C) dissimilar . . audacious
(D) different . . forgiving
(E) alike . . respectful

GO ON TO THE NEXT PAGE

31. The retreat of Napoleon's army from Moscow quickly turned into a rout as French soldiers, already ------- in the snow, were ------- by Russian troops.

(A) replenishing . . ravaged
(B) pursuing . . joined
(C) sinking . . camouflaged
(D) floundering . . assaulted
(E) tottering . . upbraided

32. The Morgan Library in New York provides a ------- environment in which scholars work amidst costly tapestries, paintings, stained-glass windows, and hand-crafted furniture.

(A) realistic
(B) frugal
(C) sumptuous
(D) friendly
(E) practical

33. The lecturer's frustration was only ------- by the audience's ------- to talk during her presentation.

(A) compounded . . propensity
(B) alleviated . . invitation
(C) soothed . . authorization
(D) increased . . inability
(E) supplanted . . desire

34. The proposal to build a nuclear power plant was the most ------- issue ever to come up at a council meeting; it is astonishing, therefore, that the members' vote was unanimous.

(A) popular
(B) contentious
(C) concise
(D) exorbitant
(E) inconsequential

35. The itinerary set by their travel agent included so many stops in ------- amount of time that they received only the most ------- impressions of places visited.

(A) a limited . . lasting
(B) a brief . . cursory
(C) a generous . . favorable
(D) sufficient . . fleeting
(E) an unnecessary . . preliminary

36. Many formerly ------- peoples have moved into ------- settlements as urban areas have encroached upon their land.

(A) roving . . vulnerable
(B) despondent . . stable
(C) transitory . . covert
(D) fervid . . enduring
(E) nomadic . . permanent

STOP

this is the end of the exercise

SAT Sentence Completion Exercise #10

38 Questions

DIRECTIONS

Each sentence below has one or two blanks, each blank indicating that something has been omitted. Beneath the sentence are five words or sets of words labeled A through E. Choose the word or set of words that, when inserted in the sentence, best fits the meaning of the sentence as a whole.

EXAMPLE:

Though the first moon landing took place half a century ago, its legacy is far from -------; today's astronauts, scientists and engineers continue to be inspired by its -------.

(A) over . . brevity
(B) flawless . . aftermath
(C) forgotten . . achievements
(D) accurate . . clarity
(E) secure . . obscurity

Ⓐ Ⓑ Ⓒ Ⓓ Ⓔ

1. The ------- effect of the sleeping tablets was so that slap-still felt groggy the next day.

(A) toxic . . erratic
(B) soporific . . pronounced
(C) salubrious . . dependable
(D) pharmaceutical . . peculiar
(E) stimulating . . unreliable

2. Ozone in the upper layers of Earth's atmosphere is beneficial, ------- animal and plant life from dangerous ultraviolet radiation.

(A) reflecting   (B) withdrawing
    (C) displacing   (D) thwarting
    (E) protecting

3. While George Balanchine's choreography stayed within a classical context, he challenged convention by recombining ballet idioms in ------- ways.

(A) unexpected (B) familiar   (C) redundant
    (D) naïve   (E) awkward

4. All of today's navel oranges are ------- of a single mutant tree that began bearing seedless fruit 200 years ago.

(A) progenitors
(B) combinations
(C) descendants
(D) conglomerations
(E) spores

5. Because he consumed ------- quantities of food and drink at feasts given in his honor, King Henry VIII was considered a ------- by his subjects.

(A) enormous . . glutton
(B) prodigious . . peer
(C) minute . . luminary
(D) unhealthy . . fraud
(E) unknown . . dolt

6. The prime minister ordered the cabinet to stay on as ------- administration until a new government could be formed.

(A) an interim (B) political (C) an invalid
    (D) a premature   (E) a civilian

GO ON TO THE NEXT PAGE

7. For many years Davis had difficulty in accepting those who were in positions of authority; in fact, when he was in high school, his teachers described him as a ------- student.

(A) compliant (B) slothful (C) conscientious
(D) model   (E) recalcitrant

8. Although the actress had lived in a large city all her life, she was such a ------- performer that she became the virtual ------- of the humble farm girl she portrayed in the play.

(A) versatile . . opposite
(B) melodramatic . . understudy
(C) natural . . nemesis
(D) consummate . . incarnation
(E) drab . . caricature

9. The chairman ------- the decision of the board members, describing it as a ------- of every worthy ideal that the organization had hitherto upheld.

(A) defended . . denial
(B) lamented . . negation
(C) criticized . . fulfillment
(D) endorsed . . renunciation
(E) applauded . . repudiation

10. Even though the programmers are ------- about their new software, they are wary of publicly ------- its capabilities until further testing.

(A) anxious . . commending
(B) apprehensive . . substantiating
(C) confident . . disclosing
(D) positive . . decrying
(E) cynical . . celebrating

11. Mary Ellen Pleasant, as a ------- support of Black emancipation before the Civil War, spurned politicians who advocated quiet dissent.

(A) cavalier (B) vociferous (C) sanguine
(D) premature (E) noncommittal

12. The doctor does not believe in conservative approaches to teaching medicine: she uses the latest techniques, including -------ones.

(A) outmoded
(B) figurative
(C) experimental
(D) cursory
(E) permanent

13. Cookery ------- the ------- of science, for the observations of prehistoric cooks laid the foundations of early chemistry.

(A) ignored . . precision
(B) advanced . . development
(C) retarded . . supremacy
(D) aided . . decline
(E) betrayed . . methodology

14. The United States congress has the power to -------, that is, to charge an elected federal official for a major crime.

(A) veto   (B) convict   (C) demote
(D) impeach   (E) exonerate

15. "Bedlam," a popular name for the first English insane asylum, has come to signify any scene of ------- and confusion.

(A) collaboration (B) treachery (C) secrecy
(D) turmoil (E) placidity

GO ON TO THE NEXT PAGE

16. Although we as laypeople expect scientific accounts of the world to be ------- our commonsense understanding of reality, the paradoxes of modern physics seem to ------- our personal expectations.

(A) parallel to . . confirm
(B) consistent with . . undermine
(C) aligned against . . resist
(D) congruent with . . buttress
(E) implied in . . augment

17. The play closed after only a week because critics gave the performance ------- reviews.

(A) innocuous   (B) caustic   (C) rave
(D) gaudy   (E) contrite

18. The essay was both ------- and -------; although concise, it was profoundly moving.

(A) meandering . . denigrating
(B) compact . . enervating
(C) fictional - . . touching
(D) argumentative . . rationalistic
(E) terse . . poignant

19. The consequence of the conspirators' ------- was severe punishment of all those involved in the unsuccessful revolt.

(A) machinations   (B) ruminations
(C) reservations   (D) forebodings
(E) consolations

20. Officials charged that the bakery had engaged in ------- practices by misleading consumers about the nutritional value of certain products.

(A) legitimate (B) exacting (C) intelligible
(D) inordinate   (E) deceptive

21. As a young physics instructor, Richard Feynman discovered that he had the gift of sharing his ------- his subject and making that excitement -------.

(A) passion for . . contagious
(B) knowledge of . . inaudible
(C) contempt for . . praiseworthy
(D) propensity for . . futile
(E) commitment to . . impersonal

22. Even after hungrily devouring their entire lunch, the children were still ------- and clamored for more.

(A) scrupulous   (B) innocuous
(C) remorseful   (D) ravenous
(E) compliant

23. Some entertainers, their egos inflated by celebrity, see themselves as ------- figures to whom ordinary moral ------- do not necessarily apply.

(A) penitent . . rules
(B) privileged . . constraints
(C) pedagogical . . enticements
(D) redundant . . conventions
(E) gifted . . benefits

24. A story's theme is sometimes -------, that is, stated directly by the author, but more often it is -------.

(A) obvious . . indisputable
(B) capricious . . dramatic
(C) convoluted . . simple
(D) enigmatic . . veiled
(E) explicit . . implied

GO ON TO THE NEXT PAGE

25. The biologists who breed California condors jokingly refer to the outdoor -------, the enclosures that house the birds, as "condominiums."

(A) arboretums
(B) aquariums
(C) depots
(D) aviaries
(E) kennels

26. New York is a cosmopolitan city; its numerous newspapers in many languages reflect its ------- population.

(A) polyglot
(B) insular
(C) bemused
(D) vapid
(E) homogeneous

27. If people continually suppress their impulse to complain, whether the vexation is ------- or grave, they will appear to be automatons, ------- feeling.

(A) fluid . . defined by
(B) severe . . bereft of
(C) deserving . . incapable of
(D) frivolous . . consumed by
(E) trivial . . devoid of

28. Louisa May Alcott's ------- the philosophical brilliance of her father's intellect was ------- by her impatience with his unworldliness.

(A) exasperation with. , contradicted
(B) concealment of . . supplanted
(C) respect for . . augmented
(D) rebellion against . . qualified
(E) reverence for . . tempered

29. Perhaps one reason for the lower number of female writers is that women traditionally have lacked the------- independence and the ------- necessary to permit them to concentrate their efforts on writing.

(A) literary . . talent
(B) intellectual . . ability
(C) social . . reputation
(D) emotional . . intelligence
(E) financial . . leisure

30. After carefully evaluating the painting, the art critics unanimously agreed that the work had been done by a ------- and should be -------.

(A) progeny . . refurbished
(B) charlatan . . repudiated
(C) neophyte . . qualified
(D) prodigal . . nullified
(E) fanatic . . purchased

31. The frightened mother ------- her young daughter for darting in front of the car.

(A) implored   (B) reproved   (C) extorted
      (D) abolished   (E) exhorted

32. People who drive while intoxicated put themselves and others in -------.

(A) guile   (B) discord   (C) jeopardy
      (D) distress   (E) dissonance

33. The salesperson's ------- voice was exceptionally annoying. Potential customers avoided going anywhere near her product.

(A) exorbitant (B) uproarious (C) docile
      (D) strident (E) egocentric

GO ON TO THE NEXT PAGE

34. Everyone avoided Pete at the party after his
------- comments insulted the hostess.

(A) tenacious
(B) rancid
(C) sarcastic
(D) pessimistic
(E) sagacious

35. ------- swept the crowd when the natural
------- suddenly occurred.

(A) Infirmary . . dispensation
(B) Pandemonium . . catastrophe
(C) Vehemence . . iodides
(D) Rectification . . cravenness
(E) Turbulence . . atmosphere

36. Rather than trying to -------, one should try
-------.

(A) abolish . . destroy
(B) instigate . . change
(C) demolish . . enhance
(D) hurt . . harm
(E) console . . comfort

37. Despite their beliefs in differing political
philosophies, the politicians agreed to -------
on issues when their goals were -------.

(A) digress . . ambivalent
(B) concede . . controversial
(C) dissent . . viable
(D) demur . . provocative
(E) collaborate . . compatible

38. Although the explorers often felt -------, they
managed to ------- the desert.

(A) defeated . . achieve
(B) elated . . survive
(C) exhausted . . conquer
(D) relentless . . finish
(E) withdrawn . . subject

STOP

this is the end of the exercise

SAT Sentence Completion Exercise #11

38 Questions

DIRECTIONS

Each sentence below has one or two blanks, each blank indicating that something has been omitted. Beneath the sentence are five words or sets of words labeled A through E. Choose the word or set of words that, when inserted in the sentence, best fits the meaning of the sentence as a whole.

EXAMPLE:

Though the first moon landing took place half a century ago, its legacy is far from -------; today's astronauts, scientists and engineers continue to be inspired by its -------.

(A) over . . brevity
(B) flawless . . aftermath
(C) forgotten . . achievements
(D) accurate . . clarity
(E) secure . . obscurity

Ⓐ Ⓑ © Ⓓ Ⓔ

1. Police officers often face ------- situations where they must maintain their -------.

(A) inhospitable . . agility
(B) impossible . . gallantry
(C) unequivocal . . sternness
(D) perilous . . composure
(E) extraordinary . . strength

2. After developing a(n) ------- toward animals, she refused to visit any of her friends who had pets.

(A) derision
(B) compliance
(C) heresy
(D) inclination
(E) phobia

3. In the years previous to 1960, when men were perceived as the sole breadwinners of a family, it was ------- for women to aspire to careers outside the home.

(A) inherent
(B) decorous
(C) unconventional
(D) vital
(E) uncouth

4. The ------- activities of the villain in the movie caused the audience to cheer when he was caught by the hero.

(A) intrepid
(B) nefarious
(C) cursory
(D) jocund
(E) lurid

5. American words and phrases have been added to the lexicon of French and Japanese cultures despite the displeasure of politicians and the ------- of purists.

(A) concession   (B) neutrality
(C) endorsement   (D) resolution
(E) denunciation

6. The use of a pen with indelible ink will ------- student's ability to ------- at a later time.

(A) preclude . . erase
(B) hinder . . slander
(C) nullify . . desecrate
(D) deplete . . digress
(E) enhance . . ameliorate

GO ON TO THE NEXT PAGE ⟶

7. The Civil War was the ------- of the inability of the North and South to ------- on an interpretation of the Constitution.

(A) epitome . . concur
(B) climax . . agree
(C) drama . . unite
(D) chaos . . harmonize
(E) finalization . . cooperate

8. The ------- of the companies was inevitable since neither could profit without the assets of the other. This showed ------- behavior on the part of the owners.

(A) merger . . prudent
(B) pivot . . exemplary
(C) antagonism . . beneficial
(D) hiatus . . monotonous
(E) diversity . . fundamental

9. The gold-studded costume appeared ------- when compared to the ------- of the flannel suit.

(A) chaste . . gaudiness
(B) laconic . . opulence
(C) reserved . . savoir-faire
(D) ornate . . simplicity
(E) feudal . . raucousness

10. Henry Louis Gates, Jr. believes that Frederick Douglass ------- patterned his 1845 autobiography after the ------- of former slave Olaudah Equiano, whose life story was published in 1789.

(A) patronizingly . . reminder
(B) belatedly . . antiquity
(C) anxiously . . capture
(D) expectantly . . epitaph
(E) consciously . . narrative

11. She found her work so ------- that she lost herself in it and was completely ------- the noise surrounding her.

(A) inspiring . . annoyed by
(B) complex . . involved in
(C) absorbing . . oblivious to
(D) exhausting . . taken with
(E) repetitive . . afraid of

12. In contrast to their widespread image as ------- carnivores, many species of piranha are vegetarian.

(A) nomadic (B) lugubrious (C) voracious
     (D) covetous   (E) exotic

13. The graceful curves of the old colonial-era buildings that dominated the old part of the city contrasted sharply with the modern, ------- subway stations and made the latter appear almost anachronistic.

(A) rectilinear   (B) grimy   (C) festive
     (D) gigantic   (E) efficient

14. Although both plants control soil erosion, kudzu disrupts the local ecology while vetiver has no ------- effects.

(A) foreseeable (B) adverse (C) domestic
     (D) permanent   (E) advantagcous

15. The poet A. B. Houseman lived a lonely life, and to the end of his days maintained a ------- which only a few chosen Mends could -------.

(A) silence . . spurn
(B) career . . appreciate
(C) seclusion . . observe
(D) reserve . . penetrate
(E) gregariousness . . enjoy

GO ON TO THE NEXT PAGE

16. The world of Heinrich Boll's early novels is one of impersonal malice, thinly camouflaged with patriotic and other ------- clichés, in which relief is provided only by occasional ------- of genuine human emotion.

(A) pragmatic . . absences
(B) ideological . . manifestations
(C) conceptual . . lapses
(D) ephemeral . . loss
(E) scholarly . . vestiges

17. The plan has few elements in it that will ------- the party with the electorate; in fact, it has caused widespread resentment.

(A) involve
(B) consolidate
(C) ingratiate
(D) deprecate
(E) impeach

18. Negritude, a literary movement emphasizing the importance and value of African culture and history, was founded in Paris in the 1930s by a group of ------- students from Martinique, Senegal, and other French-speaking colonies.

(A) animated
(B) laconic
(C) expatriate
(D) radical
(E) sophisticated

19. The fullest edition of the letters of H.P. Lovecraft consists of five volumes; however, only a small fraction of Lovecraft's ------- correspondence has ever been published.

(A) laconic (B) unknown (C) voluminous
    (D) verbal   (E) popular

20. In the ------- atmosphere of the basement, the stacks of old newspapers turned yellow and -------, emitting an odor that reached all the way to the first floor.

(A) underground . . outdated
(B) dank . . musty
(C) cool . . useless
(D) shadowy . . wrinkled
(E) cluttered . . faded

21. Once a ------- population center, the city gradually lost residents to the factory towns of the North.

(A) bustling   (B) manufactured   (C) rural
    (D) seedy   (E) deserted

22. In the summertime, ------- rains often ------- the hillside slopes, causing landslides and washing away people's precarious houses.

(A) torrential . . deluge
(B) gentle . . purge
(C) treacherous . . sustain
(D) liberal . . desecrate
(E) fecund . . bolster

23. Those who reject psychological theory and point to its scientific ------- must consider that it contains a substantial amount of truth, based not on -------, but on clinical observations.

(A) inadequacies . . assumptions
(B) foundations . . data
(C) basics . . speculation
(D) strengths . . experience
(E) deficiencies . . evidence

GO ON TO THE NEXT PAGE

24. Describing Linda as an exemplary pupil, the principal lauded her academic achievements and urged the other students to ------- her performance.

(A) elucidate　(B) mollify　(C) emulate
(D) castigate　(E) reflect

25. That she found the film ------- was a surprise, given her usual ------- towards dramatic stories.

(A) predictable . . spontaneity
(B) poignant . . impassivity
(C) irrelevant . . animosity
(D) anachronistic . . perspicacity
(E) affected . . originality

26. Nearly all epiphytic ferns are ------- tropical rain forests; while they do not require soil, they cannot survive without constant moisture.

(A) uprooted to
(B) steeped in
(C) inimical to
(D) decorative in
(E) endemic to

27. Despite the scientist's conviction of the correctness of his controversial hypothesis, the consistent ------- of supporting evidence forced him to publicly ------- it.

(A) surfeit . . revise
(B) availability . . accept
(C) lack . . print
(D) dearth . . recant
(E) agreement . . deny

28. The candidate answered tough questions with ------- candor, winning over many viewers who had previously supported her rival.

(A) presumptuous
(B) dismaying
(C) unintentional
(D) dogmatic
(E) disarming

29. In the Renaissance, when few women were formally educated and most were forced to marry, the rebellious Cecilia Gonzaga succeeded in ------- scholarship and ------- the marriage planned for her

(A) obtaining . . succumbing to
(B) escaping . . subverting
(C) pursuing . . avoiding
(D) ignoring . . observing
(E) disavowing . . enjoying

30. During the day, downpours were -------, starting and stopping at nearly regular intervals.

(A) unmediated　(B) spontaneous　(C) periodic
(D) incidental　(E) endemic

31. As a physicist, Veronica is a gifted -------; she loves to go beyond particular facts and speculate about general principles.

(A) dogmatist　(B) consultant　(C) prodigy
(D) materialist　(E) theorist

GO ON TO THE NEXT PAGE

32. Although hostile demonstrations and ------- marred James Meredith's 1962 enrollment at the University of Mississippi, the commencement ceremony in which he became the university's first African American graduate was surprisingly -------.

(A) discord . . tranquil
(B) pomp . . daunting
(C) banality . . conventional
(D) turmoil. . . controversial
(E) serenity . . opportune

33. The editor's comment was not intended as a criticism, but as a ------- by which she sought further clarification.

(A) query   (B) confession   (C) dismissal
   (D) condemnation   (E) credo

34. Although Clifton often appeared -------, he actually devoted ------- amount of time trying to keep up a neat appearance.

(A) orderly . . an enormous
(B) disheveled . . an inordinate
(C) annoyed . . an unfortunate
(D) distracted . . an unrealistic
(E) agitated . . a considerable

35. In 1991 salsa ------- ketchup as the best-selling condiment in the United States, outselling ketchup by $40 million in retail stores.

(A) supplanted
(B) redoubled
(C) augmented
(D) brandished
(E) evaded

36. The Earth's oceans sustain a ------- of marine creatures, abundance that makes the seas teem with life and an activity.

(A) melee
(B) profusion
(C) configuration
(D) symmetry
(E) dimension

37. The gentle flow of the speaker's words became increasingly balanced and rhythmic; such ------- oratory was quite hypnotic.

(A) cadent   (B) specious   (C) convoluted
   (D) adulatory   (E) impassioned

38. The ------- of the art world, its "apparent inviolability," was sullied in 1997 when investigators uncovered several dubious art transactions.

(A) turpitude
(B) sacrosanctity
(C) perspicuity
(D) verisimilitude
(E) duplicity

STOP

this is the end of the exercise

SAT Sentence Completion Exercise #12

37 Questions

DIRECTIONS

Each sentence below has one or two blanks, each blank indicating that something has been omitted. Beneath the sentence are five words or sets of words labeled A through E. Choose the word or set of words that, when inserted in the sentence, best fits the meaning of the sentence as a whole.

EXAMPLE:

Though the first moon landing took place half a century ago, its legacy is far from -------; today's astronauts, scientists and engineers continue to be inspired by its -------.

(A) over . . brevity
(B) flawless . . aftermath
(C) forgotten . . achievements
(D) accurate . . clarity
(E) secure . . obscurity

Ⓐ Ⓑ ● Ⓓ Ⓔ

1. Steven tried hard to give up sweets, but he found it particularly difficult to ------- chocolate.

(A) digest   (B) extōl   (C) impugn
(D) forgo   (E) relish

2. At first merely -------, his actions grew so bewildering and bizarre as to appear entirely ------- to us.

(A) dignified . . mystifying
(B) perplexing . . inexplicable
(C) eccentric . . stolid
(D) intriguing . . reasonable
(E) logical . . questionable

3. Despite the wide-ranging curiosity about her personal life, Eleanor Roosevelt enjoyed a degree of ------- that today's highly scrutinized public figures can only -------.

(A) privacy . . envy
(B) popularity . . celebrate
(C) privilege . . imitate
(D) isolation . . regret
(E) generosity . . refuse

4. Unable to decide between a career in biology and one in philosophy, Gwen ------- her two interests and became a medical ethicist.

(A) reclaimed   (B) merged   (C) defined
     (D) abandoned   (E) conveyed

5. The incompetent judge conducted the hearing in so ------- a manner that the entire proceeding was considered a -------, an insult to the standards of the judicial system.

(A) apathetic . . victory
(B) exacting . . spectacle
(C) astute . . debacle
(D) negligent . . travesty
(E) surreptitious . . triumph

6. Constance was ------- by the speech, regarding such criticisms of her company as extremely annoying.

(A) fascinated
(B) galled
(C) uplifted
(D) soothed
(E) disoriented

GO ON TO THE NEXT PAGE ➤

7. Rather than focusing on the ------- sequence of events, the historian E.M.W. Tillyard ------- a chronological approach and portrays, instead, the dominant belief patterns of an age.

(A) rational . . acknowledges
(B) temporal . . avoids
(C) universal . . embraces
(D) qualitative . . employs
(E) unseen . . forsakes

8. The fashion designer's new line of spring clothing was described in the style section of the newspaper as -------, even -------; the runway collection had dazzled the audience.

(A) unassuming . . audacious
(B) capricious . . innocuous
(C) tawdry . . precocious
(D) vivacious . . insipid
(E) resplendent . . incandescent

9. Robb Armstrong's *Jump Stan* fills a void in the cartoon industry, namely, a ------- of comic strips representing African Americans.

(A) spate
(B) revision
(C) dearth
(D) dispersal
(E) consensus

10. Prime Minister Neville Chamberlain of Great Britain adopted a ------- approach to Hitler, even accepting Germany's annexation of Austria.

(A) hasty   (B) precarious   (C) haughty
   (D) conciliatory   (E) dependent

11. Many who were ------- enough to witness Sir Michael Redgrave's performance in the role of Uncle Tanya assert that it was the ------- of his career.

(A) close . . scourge
(B) astute . . encore
(C) fortunate . . pinnacle
(D) hapless . . height
(E) lucky . . nadir

12. Until his defeat by the newcomer, the veteran boxer won most of his bouts by knockouts and had achieved a(n) ------- series of wins.

(A) inconsequential   (B) exaggerated
   (C) able-bodied   (D) unbroken
   (E) observable

13. Bird watching requires ------- patience as well as keen powers of -------, since one must sit still for hours and remain alert to the slightest sound or motion.

(A) extreme . persuasion
(B) skilled . . concentration
(C) cheerful . . reasoning
(D) silent . . trust
(E) limitless . . observation

14. Photographer Edward Weston's work was akin to alchemy, his camera lens magically transforming -------, everyday items such as vegetables into objects of ------- beauty.

(A) inexpensive . . tawdry
(B) mundane . . resplendent
(C) small . . enormous
(D) decorative . . functional
(E) artificial . . natural

GO ON TO THE NEXT PAGE

15. The spokesperson for the group said that the issues raised by the controversy have ------- that go far beyond the matter presently under discussion.

(A) expectations
(B) ramifications
(C) proponents
(D) inferences
(E) critics

16. Whenever she felt tired after work, a brisk walk along the beach amid the ------- sea air never failed to ------- her fatigue and leave her re-energized.

(A) humid . . hasten
(B) salty . . exacerbate
(C) bracing . . alleviate
(D) damp . . reprove
(E) chilly . . aggravate

17. "Old Nick" is one of several ------- people use when they want to refer indirectly to the Devil.

(A) euphemisms
(B) banalities
(C) arguments
(D) apostrophes
(E) eulogies

18. Because its bookkeepers altered some figures and completely fabricated others, the company's financial records were entirely -------.

(A) cursory
(B) disseminated
(C) singular
(D) concealed
(E) spurious

19. Though the Greek author Thucydides used psychological insight rather than documented information to ------- speeches to historical figures, he is still considered an impartial and ------- historian.

(A) dictate . . endless
(B) transmit . . illustrious
(C) disseminate . . relevant
(D) attribute . . accurate
(E) promote . . inventive

20. The British social philosopher Thomas Malthus predicted that population growth would eventually ------- world food production, resulting in massive famine and political unrest.

(A) pressure   (B) forbid   (C) resist
   (D) surpass   (E) confront

21. While ------- a belief in intellectual discussion, Dr. Brown brooked no deviation from his ideas and cut off anyone who did not -------.

(A) regretting . . agree
(B) admitting . . debate
(C) professing . . concur
(D) avowing . . question
(E) abandoning . . protest

22. Employers often find that even if wage increases can be ------- over a particular period of serious economic difficulties, dissatisfaction is built up and demands are merely -------, not canceled.

(A) abolished . . satisfied
(B) realized . . increased
(C) overturned . . redressed
(D) requested . . relinquished
(E) moderated . . postponed

GO ON TO THE NEXT PAGE

23. Peach pits, which contain small amounts of the poisonous compound cyanide, are not usually harmful, but, if consumed in sufficient quantities, can be -------.

(A) acerbic   (B) superfluous   (C) virulent
(D) unpalatable   (E) multifarious

24. Many audiences, upon seeing the talented stand-up comic -------, find it hard to believe that she works without a script.

(A) recruit   (B) placate   (C) extemporize
(D) extricate   (E) exult

25. Readers previously ------- by the complexity and ------- of Joyce's Ulysses will find Gilbert's study of the novel a helpful introduction.

(A) charmed . . obscurity
(B) rejected . . length
(C) inhibited . . intelligibility
(D) daunted . . allusiveness
(E) enlightened . . transparency

26. As a young man, Thomas Merton underwent a religious conversion, gradually changing from -------, to a devout Roman Catholic.

(A) an archetype   (B) a bibliophile
(C) a martinet   (D) an aesthete
(E) an agnostic

27. Aware that the pace of construction had slowed, but unwilling to risk ------- the wrath of their superiors, the project managers continued to ------- that the highway extension would be completed on schedule.

(A) comprehending . . prove
(B) divulging . . argue
(C) incurring . . maintain
(D) predicting . . assert
(E) detecting . . believe

28. Although durian, a Southeast Asian fruit, has a -------, sweet taste, it also has ------- smell that some find offensive.

(A) delicate . . a floral
(B) mild . . a pungent
(C) bland . . a refreshing
(D) cloying . . an ephemeral
(E) rancid . . an acrid

29. In 1965 the ideas that Lynn Margulis presented on the origins of cellular bodies were dismissed or even -------, but now they are ------- and unanimously lauded by biologists.

(A) examined . . rejected
(B) questioned . . ignored
(C) derided . . accepted
(D) celebrated . . appreciated
(E) refuted . . discredited

30. Since the student was ------- in answering the teacher's questions about the accident, the school had to find another means of reconstructing the chain of events.

(A) concise   (B) evasive   (C) lucid
(D) alert   (E) trite

GO ON TO THE NEXT PAGE

31. The revolution was ------- experience for the citizenry because it split the nation into several contending factions.

(A) a divisive
(B) a redundant
(C) a transient
(D) an enlightening
(E) an eclectic

32. During the hibernation of arctic ground squirrels, the long periods of torpor are ------- by short periods of -------.

(A) interrupted . . rest
(B) protracted . . tension
(C) caused . . stillness
(D) punctuated . . arousal
(E) paralleled . . alertness

33. Like the author's earlier fiction, in which flashes of ------- stand out against interminable stretches of -------, these stories are uneven in quality.

(A) clarity . . interest
(B) inspiration . . creativity
(C) intensity . . passion
(D) novelty . . experimentation
(E) brilliance . . mediocrity

34. The golden eagle is known for astonishing visual -------; it can spot small prey on the ground from more than one thousand feet in the air.

(A) repetition (B) magnetism (C) acuity
(D) enticement   (E) objectivity

35. Johnson grass can ruin other crops and be hard to remove, yet such ------- were unforeseen by nineteenth-century seed vendors when they ------- this grass for its prolific yields of hay.

(A) preliminaries . . deprecated
(B) applications . . extolled
(C) effects . . ignored
(D) drawbacks . . touted
(E) trivialities . . dismissed

36. Reformers often appear oppressively ------- in describing their own good deeds, but Dr. Alice Hamilton avoided such self-righteousness in her accounts of her investigations of industrial safety conditions.

(A) moralistic (B) practical (C) whimsical
(D) impartial   (E) scathing

37. In many myths an infant destined to become a hero or heroine must be kept safe by means of a -------: the child is either disguised or kept hidden until adulthood.

(A) ruse   (B) threat (C) dispute
(D) disclosure   (E) temptation

SAT Sentence Completion Exercise #13

38 Questions

DIRECTIONS

Each sentence below has one or two blanks, each blank indicating that something has been omitted. Beneath the sentence are five words or sets of words labeled A through E. Choose the word or set of words that, when inserted in the sentence, best fits the meaning of the sentence as a whole.

EXAMPLE:

Though the first moon landing took place half a century ago, its legacy is far from -------; today's astronauts, scientists and engineers continue to be inspired by its -------.

(A) over . . brevity
(B) flawless . . aftermath
(C) forgotten . . achievements
(D) accurate . . clarity
(E) secure . . obscurity

Ⓐ   Ⓑ   Ⓒ   Ⓓ   Ⓔ

---

1. Seventeenth-century playwright Aphra Behn ------- convention: she depicted independent female characters rather than the passive women who were then the norm among male writers,

(A) broached (B) flouted (C) extrapolated
   (D) encapsulated   (E) reprised

2. Although the students did not share the opinions of the lecturer, she expressed them with an unwavering ------- that compelled attention, if not -------.

(A) certitude . . accord
(B) compliance . . suspicion
(C) professionalism . . neglect
(D) obstinacy . . complicity
(E) superficiality . . conviction

3. It is the relative ------- of the owl's ear cavities, the sheer size of those spaces, that accounts for the owl's acute sense of hearing.

(A) symmetry   (B) cumbersomeness
   (C) uniformity   (D) intricacy
(E) vastness

4. A ------- writer, Shirley Jackson published works that ranged from stories about supernatural events to humorous books about child rearing.

(A) narrow-minded
(B) lackadaisical
(C) notorious
(D) multifaceted
(E) predictable

5. It was a ------- problem, one that resisted both analysis and adequate understanding.

(A) secondary
(B) manageable
(C) preliminary
(D) perplexing
(E) practical

6. Shared allusions in the letters between the two friends imply a familiarity, even -------, that sometimes verges on a ------- language.

(A) intimacy . . private
(B) (B decorum . . personal
(C) tolerance . . tepid
(D) contempt . . veiled
(E) complicity . . pompous

GO ON TO THE NEXT PAGE ➔

7. His answers to my questions were often
------, rarely more than a yes or a no, without
clear explanations.

(A) pedantic
(B) colloquial
(C) flamboyant
(D) monosyllabic
(E) encyclopedic

8. A scientific theory is ------ and hence
amenable to revision or abandonment in light
of observations that are ------ its predictions.

(A) tentative . . inconsistent with
(B) creative . . anticipated by
(C) tenuous . . derived from
(D) doctrinal . . contrary to
(E) testable . . supportive of

9. Once little more than ------ self-promotions,
corporate trade shows have become
increasingly utilitarian and cost-effective.

(A) extravagant
(B) productive
(C) serviceable
(D) indispensable
(E) accessible

10. Because the subject of the portrait was a staid
and dignified figure, the painter's choice of
------ colors created an unsettling ------.

(A) somber . . cohesion
(B) realistic . . dichotomy
(C) garish . . disparity
(D) prosaic . . harmony
(E) monochromatic . . compromise

11. Although Ms. Harvey's disposition was
generally ------, she could become enraged
when sufficiently ------.

(A) vicious . . ignored
(B) serene . . provoked
(C) energetic . . disappointed
(D) meek . . complimented
(E) perverse . . betrayed

12. Records documenting the presence of Africans
among the crews of explorers like Christopher
Columbus ------ the antiquity of the African
presence in the Americas.

(A) create   (B) illustrate   (C) compromise
    (D) overlook   (E) modify

13. Because Congress exempted the ------ of
household products from its regulation of
hazardous waste, consumers continue to
contribute to toxic pollution by improperly
------ dangerous substances.

(A) purchase . . manufacturing
(B) enlargement . . preserving
(C) distribution . . eliminating
(D) abundance . . recycling
(E) disposal . . discarding

14. Anderson's callous habit of ------ the
suggestions of his coworkers made him seem
------ to them

(A) reviling . . amenable
(B) soliciting . . accessible
(C) revisiting . . cantankerous
(D) ignoring . . approachable
(E) deriding . . abhorrent

GO ON TO THE NEXT PAGE

15. Some of the region's ranches belong to ------- landowners; they live elsewhere and visit their ranches only rarely.

(A) domestic   (B) absentee   (C) joint
(D) bucolic   (E) rural

16. Using detailed observations made by ancient astronomers in China, Korea, and Japan to ------- data collected by modern instruments, scientists can ------- precisely when a particular star exploded.

(A) contradict . . speculate
(B) replace . . disregard
(C) simulate . . investigate
(D) disseminate . . measure
(E) complement . . establish

17. Because Ruth's parents often ------- their plans as soon as they were formed, she assumed all adults were as ------- as her parents.

(A) cancelled . . indulgent
(B) developed . . vivacious
(C) solidified . . capricious
(D) changed . . mercurial
(E) altered . . obstinate

18. Although in most of Jorge Edwards' stories the references to politics are subtle, in one of his recent works his criticism of the government is -------.

(A) astute (B) discreet   (C) scathing
(D) impersonal (E) uninspiring

19. During her interview with local students, the dignitary exchanged her ------- public manner for a friendlier, less pretentious one.

(A) lofty   (B) modest   (C) gushing
(D) amicable   (E) precocious

20. Despite their attempts at -------, the ------- between Peter and Fred was barely suppressed.

(A) camaraderie . . admiration
(B) reconciliation . . forgiveness
(C) geniality . . antipathy
(D) estrangement . . hostility
(E) earnestness . . severity

21. The playwright provides us, the audience, with the ------- feeling of -------; we revel in the power to perceive connections that the characters cannot perceive.

(A) delightful . . diligence
(B) exhilarating . . omniscience
(C) despondent . . sensitivity
(D) restful . . sarcasm
(E) frenetic . . despair

22. The exterminators ------- increased the fire ant population by using a pesticide that killed a natural predator of the species.

(A) inadvertently   (B) auspiciously
(C) unsuccessfully (D) tediously
(E) ideally

23. The professor's efforts to ------- the gravitational wave experiments of his colleagues failed; the experiments could not be repeated.

(A) contradict   (B) replicate   (C) sample
(D) explain   (E) expand

GO ON TO THE NEXT PAGE

24. Gwen Guthrie's controversial compact disc was ------- by wary radio programmers until the city's listening audience ------- her work and requested its airplay.

(A) ignored . . initiated
(B) banned . . overlooked
(C) dismissed . . praised
(D) justified . . boycotted
(E) appreciated . . enjoyed

25. The attorney was expert in identifying ------- in contracts, ambiguities that could cause difficulties and therefore needed to be revised.

(A) clauses   (B) forgeries   (C) loopholes
     (D) intervals   (E) thresholds

26. The ambassador viewed his peacemaking mission to the warring border countries with -------, expecting that ------- was unlikely in the near future.

(A) enthusiasm . . mediation
(B) cynicism . . conflict
(C) trepidation . . reconciliation
(D) satisfaction . . security
(E) elation . . compromise

27. Mavis described the recently published treatise as inane, insipid, and -------, just another affirmation of the obvious.

(A) banal (B) baleful (C) inspired
     (D) successful   (E) profound

28. The sound advice given by the eleventh-century medical scholar Trotula in her writings on women's health ------- some of our assumptions about the inadequacy of medieval medicine.

(A) belies   (B) bypasses   (C) elucidates
     (D) compounds   (E) camouflages

29. Horror movies have ------- effect, purging our fears of the unknown by giving them artistic expression.

(A) an indiscernible
(B) an analogous
(C) a malleable
(D) a transient
(E) a cathartic

30. Company employees were quite pleased with their efficient new work area because it provided an ideal climate ------- increased productivity.

(A) inimical to   (B) conducive to
     (C) shadowed by   (D) stifled by
     (E) precipitated by

31. The critics reacted to the new book with enthusiasm: not one of their reviews was -------.

(A) derogatory
(B) professional
(C) episodic
(D) didactic
(E) unsolicited

GO ON TO THE NEXT PAGE

32. Marie Curie's more ------- achievements often ------- the contributions of her daughter, Irene Joliet-Curie,   even though each woman won a Nobel Prize for Chemistry.

(A) perplexing . . clarify
(B) famous . . overshadow
(C) pioneering . . duplicate
(D) neglected . . invalidate
(E) inspiring . . complement

33. Oddly, a mere stranger managed to ------- Joanna's disappointment, while even her closest friends remained oblivious.

(A) athletes
(B) lobbyists
(C) itinerants
(D) dilettantes
(E) idealists

34. Although they never referred to it ------- the two actors had a ------- agreement never to mention the film that had almost ended their careers.

(A) vaguely . . clandestine
(B) systematically . . presumptuous
(C) longingly . . haphazard
(D) obliquely . . verbose
(E) directly . . tacit

35. Crumbling masonry is ------- of the ------- that long exposure to the elements causes to architecture.

(A) refutation . . damage
(B) reflective . . uniformity
(C) indicative . . amelioration
(D) denial . . weathering
(E) evidence . . havoc

36. At bedtime the security blanket served the child as ------- with seemingly magical powers to ward off frightening phantasms.

(A) an arsenal
(B) an incentive
(C) a talisman
(D) a trademark
(E) a harbinger

37. Military victories brought tributes to the Aztec empire and, concomitantly, made it -------, for Aztecs increasingly lived off the vanquished.

(A) indecisive
(B) pragmatic
(C) parasitic
(D) beneficent
(E) hospitable

38. Unlike sedentary people, ------- often feel a sense of rootlessness instigated by the very traveling that defines them.

(A) arouse
(B) perceive
(C) warrant
(D) discredit
(E) misrepresent

STOP

this is the end of the exercise

SAT Sentence Completion Exercise #14

37 Questions

DIRECTIONS

Each sentence below has one or two blanks, each blank indicating that something has been omitted. Beneath the sentence are five words or sets of words labeled A through E. Choose the word or set of words that, when inserted in the sentence, best fits the meaning of the sentence as a whole.

EXAMPLE:

Though the first moon landing took place half a century ago, its legacy is far from -------; today's astronauts, scientists and engineers continue to be inspired by its -------.

(A) over . . brevity
(B) flawless . . aftermath
(C) forgotten . . achievements
(D) accurate . . clarity
(E) secure . . obscurity

(A) (B) ● (D) (E)

---

1. The researchers were ------- in recording stories of the town's African American community during the Depression, preserving even the smallest details.

(A) obstreperous
(B) apprehensive
(C) compensatory
(D) radicalized
(E) painstaking

2. To her great relief, Jennifer found that wearing sunglasses in bright sunlight helped to ------- her headaches.

(A) ascertain (B) dislocate (C) mitigate
    (D) extend (E) propagate

3. With scant rainfall and a history of -------, the country is one of the world's most arid.

(A) monsoons (B) farming (C) drought
    (D) manufacturing (E) conservation

4. The three designers ------- the new project, ------- their individual talents and many years of experience.

(A) boycotted . . brandishing
(B) commended . . belittling
(C) agonized over . . compensating
(D) quarreled over . . combining
(E) collaborated on . . pooling

5. Scratching, though a useful self-remedy for an occasional itch, can ------- a problem by damaging the skin if performed too -------.

(A) exacerbate . . vigorously
(B) cure . . carefully
(C) worsen . . refreshingly
(D) clarify . . abrasively
(E) exonerate . . violently

6. Climate models do not yield ------- forecasts of what the future will bring; such models serve only as a clouded crystal ball in which a range of ------- possibilities can be glimpsed.

(A) meteorological . . discarded
(B) definitive . . plausible
(C) practical . . impeccable
(D) temporal . . scientific
(E) conventional . . forgotten

GO ON TO THE NEXT PAGE

7. The cellist Yo-Yo Ma performs both classical and contemporary works; he is honored both as an active ------- of the new and as ------- interpreter of the old.

(A) excluder . . a disciplined
(B) reviler . . an unparalleled
(C) disparager . . a pathetic
(D) champion . . an inadequate
(E) proponent . . an incomparable

8. The ------- of the program charged with developing a revolutionary reactor based on nuclear fusion confidently predicted that there would soon be proof of the reactor's -------.

(A) directors . . redundancy
(B) adversaries . . profitability
(C) originators . . futility
(D) critics . . efficiency
(E) advocates . . feasibility

9. Despite his frequent shifting of allegiance, Johnson is not a flagrant -------, but he is nonetheless a striking specimen of moral -------.

(A) novice . . excellence
(B) malefactor . . earnestness
(C) idealist . . ignorance
(D) opportunist . . equivocation
(E) paragon . . immaturity

10. Through a series of -------, Professor Juárez presented a dramatic narrative that portrayed life in the ancient Mayan city.

(A) conundrums
(B) vignettes
(C) dynamics
(D) factors
(E) tangents

11. Our society increasingly ------- survey data in making important decisions, yet many people cannot tell a ------- survey from a questionable one.

(A) scoffs at . . fascinating
(B) dispenses with . . faulty
(C) depends on . . reliable
(D) responds to . . favorable
(E) adheres to . . dubious

12. Fanatically opposed to the very idea of -------, the ------- on both sides of the dispute were committed to keeping the controversy alive.

(A) compromise . . extremists
(B) despair . . pessimists
(C) conflict . . diehards
(D) agreement . . moderates
(E) aggression . . combatants

13. Ritchie Valens's songs ------- elements from rockabilly, blues, and Mexican folk music; thus Valens was known as a songwriter influenced by ------- sources.

(A) abstracted . . predictable
(B) blended . . multifarious
(C) combined . . didactic
(D) demonstrated . . urbane
(E) united . . focused

14. Protection of elephants in the wild was provided by ------- a ban on the trade of all products derived from them.

(A) vindicating
(B) epitomizing
(C) conjuring
(D) adopting
(E) renouncing

GO ON TO THE NEXT PAGE

15. Despite his intention to make financial restitution, he soon became ------- in making the promised payments.

(A) embroiled
(B) engaged
(C) uncontrollable
(D) conscientious
(E) delinquent

16. The discovery of DNA and the genetic code did not ------- any earlier scientific hypotheses; there were few, if any, conflicting theories to be moved aside.

(A) complement   (B) clarify   (C) affirm
     (D) neglect   (E) displace

17. Harsh noise characterized the theatrical production's tumultuous battle scene, which was a confused ------- of shouting actors and ------- trumpet blasts.

(A) mélange . . blaring
(B) insinuation . . clamorous
(C) explication . . raucous
(D) hodgepodge . . muted
(E) undercurrent . . sonorous

18. The company spokesperson eventually ------- the residents' fears by proving that there was no danger from the leak.

(A) evoked   (B) ignited   (C) quelled
     (D) denigrated (E) transferred

19. The ------- quality that creates and defines this great city's culture reflects its openness to a plurality of voices and values.

(A) unalloyed   (B) cosmopolitan (D) rustic
     (C) conservative   (E) circumscribed

20. The article revealed how the once ------- Mexican weed-eating beetle became an agricultural ------- that wreaked havoc on potato crops around the world.

(A) innocuous., scourge
(B) insidious . . menace
(C) domesticated . . miracle
(D) resilient . . harbinger
(E) destructive . . pest

21. The problem of conserving the ------- population of sharks is ------- by their low reproductive rate.

(A) contracting . . encompassed
(B) stable . . overridden
(C) dwindling . . compounded
(D) expanding . . enhanced
(E) burgeoning . . exacerbated

22. The beach was completely deserted; the nearby park was similarly ------- people.

(A) overwhelmed with
(B) repopulated by
(C) devoid of
(D) defeated by
(E) exploited by

23. Even though synthetic fuel is efficient and economical to produce, its use was ------- until the ------- domestic fossil-fuel supplies resulted in the need for an alternative energy source.

(A) minimal . . depletion of
(B) significant . . preference for
(C) exorbitant . . concern for
(D) unusual . . promotion of
(E) extensive . . exhaustion of

GO ON TO THE NEXT PAGE

24. Considered in roughly ------- order, Paul Marshall's works reveal a perspective that is ever -------, extending from the Barbadian community of Brooklyn in her first novel to other world communities in later works.

(A) developmental . . inward
(B) random . . accurate
(C) qualitative . . regressive
(D) episodic . . timeless
(E) chronological . . broadening

25. The care and attention demonstrated by members of the editorial staff at that newspaper are -------, whereas their counterparts at many other serious newspapers are not nearly so -------.

(A) reprehensible . . modest
(B) commendable . . remiss
(C) exceptional . . bellicose
(D) sufficient . . reactionary
(E) exemplary . . diligent

26. With only a glance at the approaching figure, Sue recognized Lee's distinctive -------: less a stroll than a strut.

(A) status   (B) mumble   (C) gait
    (D) garb   (E) lilt

27. To protect its contents from contact with contaminants in the air, the jar was closed with ------- seal.

(A) a waterproof
(B) an introverted
(C) an unreliable
(D) a loose-fitting
(E) a permeable

28. In contrast to the Chief Executive Officer, whose remarks were concise, the other speakers on the panel were -------.

(A) informative (B) verbose (C) diffident
    (D) dour   (E) sibilant

29. Some critics described the photographer's work as -------, citing his obvious ------- of the work of his renowned predecessors.

(A) distinctive . . assimilation
(B) sycophantic . . dismissal
(C) derivative . . adaptation
(D) controversial . . veneration
(E) pedantic . . ignorance

30. Toni Cade Bambara's novels are engrossing because the protagonists, in striving to achieve goals, are not simply ------- characters.

(A) passive   (B) tangible   (C) abandoned
    (D) autonomous   (E) redundant

31. Myra laughed exuberantly and embraced her friends repeatedly, so ------- was she about having been selected.

(A) ambivalent (B) quizzical (C) euphoric
    (D) jaded   (E) exacting

32. Seeking to ------- what people view and read by determining what art and literature should be available, censorship laws directly ------- free expression.

(A) govern . . liberate
(B) juxtapose . . prescribe
(C) defer . . nullify
(D) control . . prohibit
(E) balance . . promote

GO ON TO THE NEXT PAGE

33. Because little rain falls in the district during summer, municipalities are necessarily ------- to ------- water from winter storms.

(A) ready . . squander
(B) reluctant., retain
(C) free . . absorb
(D) careful . . store
(E) unwilling . . conserve

34. Excessive secrecy tends to ------- excessive curiosity and thus serves to ------- the very impulses against which it guards.

(A) inhibit . . protect
(B) disguise . . supplant
(C) satisfy . . limit
(D) compel . . deride
(E) invite . . provoke

35. The new policy has been called a quiet revolution because, though introduced without -------, it is already producing ------- changes.

(A) warning . . specious
(B) fanfare . . momentous
(C) concealment . . transient
(D) hesitation . . ostensible
(E) debate . . negligible

36. Artists who are described as ------- are the first to experiment with new forms or concepts.

(A) aesthetic
(B) partisan
(C) decorous
(D) cerebral
(E) avant-garde

37. Once his integrity had been -------, the mayoral candidate was quick both to ------- these attacks and to issue counterattacks,

(A) debunked . . buttress
(B) restored . . recommence
(C) revoked . . relinquish
(D) impugned . . repudiate
(E) vitiated . . avoid

STOP

this is the end of the exercise

SAT Sentence Completion Exercise #15
35 Questions

DIRECTIONS

Each sentence below has one or two blanks, each blank indicating that something has been omitted. Beneath the sentence are five words or sets of words labeled A through E. Choose the word or set of words that, when inserted in the sentence, best fits the meaning of the sentence as a whole.

EXAMPLE:

Though the first moon landing took place half a century ago, its legacy is far from -------; today's astronauts, scientists and engineers continue to be inspired by its -------.

(A) over . . brevity
(B) flawless . . aftermath
(C) forgotten . . achievements
(D) accurate . . clarity
(E) secure . . obscurity

Ⓐ   Ⓑ   Ⓒ   Ⓓ   Ⓔ

---

1. When two chemical compounds are combined, a ------- effect can be achieved; the resulting combination can be more potent than either of the individual compounds alone.

(A) synergistic
(B) naturalistic
(C) competitive
(D) retroactive
(E) neutralizing

2. In frigid regions a layer of permafrost under the soil surface prevents water from sinking deep into the soil, and so the water ------- the land, helping to create bog and ------- conditions.

(A) freezes . . tropical
(B) parches . . marsh
(C) inundates . . desert
(D) aerates . . jungle
(E) floods . . swamp

3. Although visitors initially may find touring the city by subway to be ------- , they are pleased to discover that subways are an inexpensive and ------- way to get around.

(A) wasteful . . generous
(B) daunting . . efficient
(C) extravagant . . prohibitive
(D) convenient . . solitary
(E) enjoyable . . easy

4. New data measuring the ------- of land beneath the oceans permit accurate generalizations about the topography of the seafloor.

(A) models contours   (C) remnants
    (D)populations   (E) pigments

5. One critic asserts that modern urban architecture causes sensory deprivation because it fails to provide visual and tactile -------.

(A) latency   (B) stimulation   (C) derision
    (D) confusion   (E) extension

GO ON TO THE NEXT PAGE

6. It would be a waste of time for any reviewer to bother ------- a book whose worthlessness is ------- to even the least discerning reader.

(A) enjoying . . doubtful
(B) mocking . . figurative
(C) assessing . . welcome
(D) condemning . . obvious
(E) ignoring . . obnoxious

7. Although the bystander's account of the car accident at first seemed ------- , the police officer was surprised, on further investigation, to find that it was -------.

(A) dubious . . erroneous
(B) incongruous . . inconsistent
(C) implausible . . correct
(D) logical . . pertinent
(E) probable . . coherent

8. The legislation facing Congress was so ------- that it threatened to shatter the governing body's fragile bipartisanship.

(A) divisive (B) transparent (C) concordant
  (D) repetitive   (E) rhetorical

9. In *All God's Children Need Traveling Shoes*, author Maya Angelou uses -------, brief descriptive sketches, to provide ------- view of Ghana that clearly details the land and its people.

(A) missives . . an illusory
(B) themes . . a thorough
(C) vignettes . . a vivid
(D) treatises . . an authentic
(E) abstracts . . an ambiguous

10. Because an older horse is more ------- than a younger one, it is safer for a novice rider.

(A) frolicsome
(B) cantankerous
(C) gargantuan
(D) tractable
(E) precipitate

11. The library's collection is a ------- of Asian American historical documents, including rare materials about race relations.

(A) summary (B) fabrication (C) consensus
  (D) trove   (E) replication

12. Dreams are ------- in and of themselves, but, when combined with other data, they can tell us much about the dreamer.

(A) uninformative
(B) startling
(C) harmless
(D) terrifying
(E) uncontrollable

13. The Muses arc ------- deities: they avenge themselves without mercy on those who weary of their charms.

(A) rueful (B) ingenuous (C) solicitous
  (D) vindictive   (E) dispassionate

GO ON TO THE NEXT PAGE

14. Without the psychiatrist's promise of confidentiality, trust is ------- and the patient's communication limited; even though confidentiality can thus be seen to be precious in therapy, moral responsibility sometimes requires a willingness to ------- it.

(A) implicit . . extend
(B) ambiguous . . apply
(C) prevented . . uphold
(D) assumed . . examine
(E) impaired . . sacrifice

15. Having fully embraced the belief that government by persuasion is preferable to government by -------, the leaders of the movement have recently ------- most of their previous statements supporting totalitarianism.

(A) intimidation . . issued
(B) participation . . moderated
(C) proclamation . . codified
(D) demonstration . . deliberated
(E) coercion . . repudiated

16. The powers and satisfactions of primeval people, though few and meager, were ------- their few and simple desires.

(A) simultaneous with
(B) commensurate with
(C) substantiated by
(D) circumscribed by
(E) ruined by

17. Some scientists argue that carbon compounds play such a central role in life on Earth because of the possibility of ------- resulting from the carbon atom's ability to form an unending series of different molecules.

(A) deviation
(B) stability
(C) reproduction
(D) variety
(E) invigoration

18. Whereas the art critic Vasari saw the painting entitled the Mona Lisa as an original and wonderful ------- feat, the reproduction of a natural object, the aesthetes saw it as ------- that required deciphering.

(A) collaborative . . an aberration
(B) historical . . a symbol
(C) technical . . a hieroglyph
(D) mechanical . . an imitation
(E) visual . . an illusion

19. As late as 1891 a speaker assured his audience that since profitable farming was the result of natural ability rather than -------, and that an education in agriculture was therefore -------.

(A) instruction . . vital
(B) effort . . difficult
(C) learning . . useless
(D) science . . intellectual
(E) luck . . senseless

GO ON TO THE NEXT PAGE

20. In spite of the ------- nature of Scotland's terrain, its main roads are surprisingly free from severe -------.

(A) rocky . . weather
(B) mountainous . . grades
(C) uncharted . . flooding
(D) unpredictable . . damage
(E) landlocked . . slipperiness

21. Walpole's art collection was huge and fascinating, and his novel *The Castle of Otranto* was never out of print; none of this mattered to the Victorians, who ------- him as, at best, -------.

(A) dismissed . . insignificant
(B) judged . . worthwhile
(C) revered . . talented
(D) reviled . . meager
(E) taunted . . dangerous

22. Since the author frequently ------- other scholars, his objection to disputes is not only irrelevant but also -------.

(A) supports . . overbearing
(B) provokes . . frightening
(C) quotes . . curious
(D) ignores . . peevish
(E) attacks . . surprising

23. Longdale and Stern discovered that mitochondria ' and chloroplasts ------- a long, identifiable sequence of DNA; such a coincidence could be ------- only by the transfer of DNA between the two systems.

(A) manufacture . . Accomplished
(B) reveal . . repeated
(C) exhibit . . determined
(D) share . . explained
(E) maintain . . contradicted

24. Until the current warming trend exceeds the range of normal climatic fluctuations, there will be, among scientists, considerable ------- the possibility that increasing levels of atmospheric CO_2 can cause long-term warming effects.

(A) interest in
(B) uncertainty about
(C) enthusiasm for
(D) worry about
(E) experimentation on

25. Without seeming unworldly, William James appeared wholly removed from the ------- of society, the conventionality of academe.

(A) ethos   (B) idealism   (C) romance
     (D) paradoxes   (E) commonplaces

26. Created to serve as perfectly as possible their workaday ------- the wooden storage boxes made in America's Shaker communities are now ------- for their beauty.

(A) environment . . accepted
(B) owners . . employed
(C) function . . valued
(D) reality . . transformed
(E) image . . seen

27. In order to ------- her theory that the reactions are ------- the scientist conducted many experiments, all of which showed that the heat of the first reaction is more than twice that of the second.

(A) support . . different
(B) comprehend . . constant
(C) evaluate . . concentrated
(D) capture . . valuable
(E) demonstrate . . problematic

GO ON TO THE NEXT PAGE

28. The sheer bulk of data from the mass media seems to overpower us and drive us to ------- accounts for an easily and readily digestible portion of news.

(A) insular
(B) investigative
(C) synoptic
(D) subjective
(E) sensational

29. William James lacked the usual ------- death; writing to his dying father, he spoke without ------- about the old man's impending death.

(A) longing for . . regret
(B) awe of . . inhibition
(C) curiosity about . . rancor
(D) apprehension of . . eloquence
(E) anticipation of . . commiseration

30. Current data suggest that, although ------- states between fear and aggression exist, fear and aggression are as distinct physiologically as they are psychologically.

(A) simultaneous
(B) serious
(C) exceptional
(D) partial
(E) transitional

31. It is ironic that a critic of such overwhelming vanity now suffers from a measure of the oblivion to which he was forever ------- others; in the end, all his ------- has only worked against him.

(A) dedicating . . self-possession
(B) leading . . self-righteousness
(C) consigning . . self-adulation
(D) relegating . . self-sacrifice
(E) condemning . . self-analysis

32. Famous among job seekers for its ------- the company, quite apart from generous salaries, bestowed on its executives annual bonuses and such ------- as low-interest home mortgages and company cars.

(A) magnanimity . . reparations
(B) inventiveness . . benefits
(C) largesse . . perquisites
(D) discernment . . prerogatives
(E) altruism . . credits

33. There are no solitary, free-living creatures; every form of life is ------- other forms.

(A) segregated from
(B) parallel to
(C) dependent on
(D) overshadowed by
(E) mimicked by

34. The sale of Alaska was not so much an American coup as a matter of ------- for an imperial Russia that was short of cash and unable to ------- its own continental coastline.

(A) negligence . . fortify
(B) custom . . maintain
(C) convenience . . stabilize
(D) expediency . . defend
(E) exigency . . reinforce

35. Despite assorted effusions to the contrary, there is no necessary link between scientific skill and humanism, and, quite possibly, there may be something of a ------- between them.

(A) generality
(B) fusion
(C) congruity
(D) dichotomy
(E) reciprocity

STOP

this is the end of the exercise

SAT Sentence Completion Exercise #16

36 Questions

DIRECTIONS

Each sentence below has one or two blanks, each blank indicating that something has been omitted. Beneath the sentence are five words or sets of words labeled A through E. Choose the word or set of words that, when inserted in the sentence, best fits the meaning of the sentence as a whole.

EXAMPLE:

Though the first moon landing took place half a century ago, its legacy is far from -------; today's astronauts, scientists and engineers continue to be inspired by its -------.

(A) over . . brevity
(B) flawless . . aftermath
(C) forgotten . . achievements
(D) accurate . . clarity
(E) secure . . obscurity

Ⓐ Ⓑ ⓒ Ⓓ Ⓔ

1. A common argument claims that in folk art, the artist's subordination of technical mastery to intense feeling ------- the direct communication of emotion to the viewer.

(A) facilitates
(B) averts
(C) neutralizes
(D) implies
(E) represses

2. While not completely nonplussed by the unusually caustic responses from members of the audience, the speaker was nonetheless visibly ------- by their lively criticism.

(A) humiliated
(B) discomfited
(C) deluded
(D) disgraced
(E) tantalized

3. In eighth-century Japan, people who ------- wasteland were rewarded with official ranks as part of an effort to overcome the shortage of ------- fields.

(A) conserved . . forested
(B) reclaimed . . arable
(C) cultivated . . domestic
(D) irrigated . . accessible
(E) located . . desirable

4. If duty is the natural ------- of one's ------- the course of future events, then people who are powerful have duty placed on them whether they like it or not.

(A) correlate . . understanding of
(B) outgrowth . . control over
(C) determinant . . involvement in
(D) adjuvant . . preoccupation with
(E) arbiter . . responsibility for

5. Because they had expected the spacecraft Voyager 2 to be able to gather data only about the planets Jupiter and Saturn, scientists were ------- the wealth of information it sent back from Neptune twelve years after leaving Earth.

(A) disappointed in
(B) concerned about
(C) confident in
(D) elated by
(E) anxious for

GO ON TO THE NEXT PAGE →

6. Wearing the latest fashions was exclusively the ------- of the wealthy until the 1850s, when mass production, aggressive entrepreneurs, and the availability of the sewing machine made them ------- the middle class.

(A) aspiration . . disagreeable to
(B) vexation . . superfluous for
(C) bane . . profitable to
(D) prerogative . . accessible to
(E) obligation . . popular with

7. Linguists have now confirmed what experienced users of ASL—American Sign Language—have always implicitly known: ASL is a grammatically ------- language in that it is capable of expressing every possible syntactic relation.

(A) limited (B) economical (C) complete
    (D) shifting (E) abstract

8. He was regarded by his followers as something of ------- not only because of his insistence on strict discipline, but also because of his ------- adherence to details.

(A) a martinet . . rigid
(B) an authority . . sporadic
(C) a tyrant . . reluctant
(D) a fraud . . conscientious
(E) an acolyte . . maniacal

9. The influence of the *Timaeus* among early philosophical thinkers was -------, if only because it was the sole dialogue ------- in Europe for almost 1,000 years.

(A) pervasive . . available
(B) inestimable . . suppressed
(C) noteworthy . . obfuscated
(D) underestimated . . studied
(E) circumscribed . . translated

10. The Gibsons were little given to -------; not one of them was afraid of -------, of being and seeming unlike their neighbors.

(A) humility . . absurdity
(B) excellence . . mediocrity
(C) anger . . confrontation
(D) conformism . . singularity
(E) ostentation . . eccentricity

11. Even after ------- against the ------- of popular sovereignty were included, major figures in the humanistic disciplines remained skeptical about the proposal to extend suffrage to the masses.

(A) recommendations . . continuation
(B) safeguards . . excesses
(C) arguments . . introduction
(D) provisions . . advantages
(E) laws . . creation

12. A recent survey shows that, while ninety-four percent of companies conducting management training programs open them to women, women are ------- only seventy-four percent of those programs.

(A) protesting against
(B) participating in
(C) displeased by
(D) allowed in
(E) refused by

13. Thomas Paine, whose political writing was often flamboyant, was in private life a surprisingly ------- man: he lived in rented rooms, ate little, and wore drab clothes.

(A) simple
(B) controversial
(C) sordid
(D) comfortable
(E) discourteous

GO ON TO THE NEXT PAGE

14. Their ------- of loyalties is first to oneself, next to kin, then to fellow tribe members, and finally to compatriots.

(A) merging
(B) hierarchy
(C) definition
(D) judgment
(E) cognizance

15. The belief that science destroys the arts appears to be supported by historical evidence that the arts have ------- only when the sciences have been -------.

(A) declined . . attacked
(B) flourished . . neglected
(C) matured . . unconcerned
(D) succeeded . . developed
(E) floundered . . constrained

16. The action and characters in a melodrama can be so immediately ------- that all observers can hiss the villain with an air of smug but enjoyable -------.

(A) spurned . . boredom
(B) forgotten . . condescension
(C) classified, . . self-righteousness
(D) plausible . . guilt
(E) gripping . . skepticism

17. In the design of medical experiments, the need for ------- assignment of treatments to patients must be ------- the difficulty of persuading patients to participate in an experiment in which their treatment is decided by chance.

(A) independent . . amended by
(B) competent . . emphasized by
(C) mechanical . . controlled by
(D) swift . . associated with
(E) random . . reconciled with

18. Though dealers insist that professional art dealers can make money in the art market, even an ------- knowledge is not enough: the art world is so fickle that stock-market prices are ------- by comparison.

(A) amateur's . . sensible
(B) expert's . . erratic
(C) investor's . . booming
(D) insider's . . predictable
(E) artist's . . irrational

19. Many artists believe that successful imitation, far from being symptomatic of a lack of ------- is the first step in learning to be creative.

(A) elegance
(B) resolution
(C) goodness
(D) originality
(E) sympathy

20. As serious as she is about the bullfight, she does not allow respect to ------- her sense of whimsy when painting it.

(A) inspire
(B) provoke
(C) suppress
(D) attack
(E) satisfy

21. No one is ------- about Stephens; he inspires either uncritical adulation or profound ------- in those who work for him.

(A) neutral . . antipathy
(B) infuriated . . aversion
(C) worried . . anxiety
(D) enthusiastic . . veneration
(E) apprehensive . . consternation

GO ON TO THE NEXT PAGE

22. Before about 1960, virtually all accounts of evolution assumed most adaptation to be a product of selection at the level of populations; recent studies of evolution, however, have found no ------- this ------- view of selection.

(A) departures from . . controversial
(B) basis for . . pervasive
(C) bias toward . . unchallenged
(D) precursors of . . innovative
(E) criticisms of . . renowned

23. The new biological psychiatry does not deny the contributing role of psychological factors in mental illnesses, but posits that these factors may act as a catalyst on existing physiological conditions and ------- such illnesses.

(A) disguise   (B) impede (C) constrain
    (D) precipitate (E) consummate

24. During periods of social and cultural stability, many art academies are so firmly controlled by ------- that all real creative work must be done by the -------.

(A) dogmatists . . disenfranchised
(B) managers . . reactionaries
(C) reformers . . dissatisfied
(D) imposters . . academicians
(E) specialists . . elite

25. The First World War began in a context of jargon and verbal delicacy and continued in a cloud of ------- as ------- as language and literature, skillfully used, could make it.

(A) circumlocution . . literal
(B) cliché . . lucid
(C) euphemism . . impenetrable
(D) particularity . . deliberate
(E) subjectivity . . enthralling

26. Because no comprehensive ------- exist regarding personal reading practices, we do not know, for example, the greatest number of books read in an individual lifetime.

(A) records
(B) instincts
(C) remedies
(D) proposals
(E) commercials

27. In our corporation there is a ------- between male and female ------- because 73 percent of the men and 34 percent of the women polled believe that our company provides equal compensation to men and women.

(A) contrast . . stereotypes
(B) difference . . perceptions
(C) variation . . salaries
(D) resemblance . . employees
(E) similarity . . aspirations

28. The wonder of De Quincey is that although opium dominated his life, it never ------- him; indeed, he turned its use to ------- when he published the story of its influence in the *London Magazine.*

(A) overcame . . altruism
(B) intimidated . . triumph
(C) distressed . . pleasure
(D) conquered . . gain
(E) released . . necessity

29. The reduction of noise has been ------- in terms of ------- its sources, but canceling noise out completely may be more desirable.

(A) justified . . diffusing
(B) accomplished . . tracking
(C) conceived . . concealing
(D) explained . . isolating
(E) approached . . eliminating

GO ON TO THE NEXT PAGE

30. While Parker is very outspoken on issues she cares about, she is not -------; she concedes the ------- of opposing arguments when they expose weaknesses inherent in her own.

(A) fickle . . validity
(B) arrogant . . restraint
(C) fanatical . . strength
(D) congenial . . incompatibility
(E) unyielding . . speciousness

31. Hampshire's assertions, far from showing that we can ------- the ancient puzzles about objectivity, reveal the issue to be even more ------- than we had thought.

(A) adapt . . pressing
(B) dismiss . . relevant
(C) rediscover . . unconventional
(D) admire . . elusive
(E) appreciate . . interesting

32. Usually the first to spot data that were inconsistent with other findings, in this particular experiment she let a number of ------- results slip by.

(A) inaccurate
(B) verifiable
(C) redundant
(D) salient
(E) anomalous

33. There is perhaps some truth in that waggish old definition of a scholar - a siren that calls attention to a fog without doing anything to ------- it.

(A) describe
(B) cause
(C) analyze
(D) dispel
(E) thicken

34. Cryogenic energy storage has the advantage of being suitable in any -------, regardless of geography or geology, factors that may ------- both underground gas storage and pumped hydroelectric storage.

(A) location . . limit
(B) climate . . deter
(C) site . . forebode
(D) proportion, typify
(E) surface . . hamper

35. The newborn human infant is not a passive figure, nor an active one, but what might be called an actively ------- one, eagerly attentive as it is to sights and sounds.

(A) adaptive
(B) selective
(C) inquisitive
(D) receptive
(E) intuitive

36. Opponents of the expansion of the market economy, although in -------, continued to constitute ------- political force throughout the century.

(A) error . . an inconsequential
(B) retreat . . a powerful
(C) disarray . . a disciplined
(D) jeopardy . . an ineffective
(E) command . . a viable

STOP

Critical Reading
16 practice exercises

SAT Critical Reading Exercise #01
23 Questions

A mysterious phenomenon is the ability of over-water migrants to travel on course. Birds, bees, and other species can keep track of time
line without any sensory cues from the outside world,
5 and such "biological clocks" clearly contribute to their "compass sense." For example, they can use the position of the Sun or stars, along with the time of day, to find north. But compass sense alone cannot explain how birds navigate the
10 ocean: after a flock traveling east is blown far south by a storm, it will assume the proper northeasterly course to compensate. Perhaps, some scientists thought, migrants determine their geographic position on Earth by celestial
15 navigation, almost as human navigators, use stars and planets, but this would demand of the animals a fantastic map sense. Researchers now know that some species have a magnetic sense, which might allow migrants to determine their
20 geographic location by detecting variations in the strength of the Earth's magnetic field.

1. The main idea of the passage is that
(A) migration over land requires a simpler explanation than migration over water does
(B) the means by which animals migrate over water arc complex and only partly understood
(C) the ability of migrant animals to keep track of time is related to their magnetic sense
(D) knowledge of geographic location is essential to migrants with little or no compass sense
(E) explanations of how animals migrate tend to replace, rather than build on, one another

2. It can be inferred from the passage that if the flock of birds were navigating by compass sense alone, they would, after the storm, fly
(A) cast
(B) north
(C) northwest
(D) south
(E) southeast

3. In maintaining that migrating animals would need "a fantastic map sense" (line 16) to determine their geographic position by celestial navigation, the author intends to express
(A) admiration for the ability of the migrants
(B) skepticism about celestial navigation as an explanation
(C) certainty that the phenomenon of migration will remain mysterious
(D) interest in a new method of accounting for over-water migration
(E) surprise that animals apparently navigate in much the same way that human beings do

4. Of the following descriptions of migrating animals, which most strongly suggests that the animals are depending on magnetic cues to orient themselves?
(A) Pigeons can properly readjust their course even when flying long distances through exceedingly dense fogs.
(B) Bison are able to reach their destination by passing through a landscape that has been partially altered by a recent fire.
(C) Elephants are able to find grounds that some members of the herd have never seen before.
(D) Swallows are able to return to a given spot at the same time every year.
(E) Monarch butterflies coming from different parts of North America are able to arrive at the same location each winter.

GO ON TO THE NEXT PAGE

Some modern anthropologists hold that biological evolution has shaped not only human morphology but also human behavior. The role
line those anthropologists ascribe to evolution is not
5 of dictating the details of human behavior but one of imposing constraints—ways of feeling, thinking, and acting that "come naturally" in archetypal situations in any culture. Our "frailties"—emotions and motives such as rage,
10 fear, greed, gluttony, joy, lust, love-may be a very mixed assortment, but they share at least one immediate quality: we are, as we say, "in the grip" of them. And thus they give us our sense of constraints.
15   Unhappily, some of those frailties—our need for ever-increasing security among them—are presently maladaptive. Yet beneath the overlay of cultural detail, they, too, are said to be biological in direction, and therefore as natural to us as are
20 our appendixes. We would need to comprehend thoroughly their adaptive origins in order to understand how badly they guide us now. And we might then begin to resist their pressure.

5. The primary purpose of the passage is to present

(A) a position on the foundations of human behavior and on what they imply

(B) a theory outlining the parallel development of human morphology and behavior

(C) a diagnostic test for separating biologically determined behavior patterns from culture-specific detail

(D) a practical method for resisting the pressures of biologically determined drives

(E) an overview of those human emotions and motives that impose constraints on behavior

6. The author implies that control to any extent over the "frailties" (line 8) that constrain our behavior is thought to presuppose

(A) that those frailties are recognized as, currently beneficial and adaptive

(B) that there is little or no overlay of cultural detail that masks their true nature

(C) that there are cultures in which those frailties do not "come naturally" and from which such control can be learned

(D) a full understanding of why those frailties evolved and of how they function now

(E) a thorough grasp of the principle that cultural detail in human behavior can differ arbitrarily from society to society

7. Which of the following most probably provides an appropriate analogy from human morphology for the "details" (line 5) versus "constraints" (line 6) distinction made in the passage in relation to human behavior?

(A) The ability of most people to see all the colors of the visible spectrum as against most people's inability to name any but the primary colors

(B) The ability of even the least fortunate people to show compassion as against people's inability to mask their feelings completely

(C) The ability of some people to dive to great depths as against most people's inability to swim long distances

(D) The psychological profile of those people who are able to delay gratification as against people's inability to control their lives completely

(E) The greater lung capacity of mountain peoples that helps them live in oxygen-poor air as against people's inability to fly without special apparatus

8. It can be inferred that in his discussion of maladaptive frailties the author assumes that

(A) evolution does not favor the emergence of adaptive characteristics over the emergence of maladaptive ones

(B) any structure or behavior not positively adaptive is regarded as transitory in evolutionary theory

(C) maladaptive characteristics, once fixed, make the emergence of other maladaptive characteristics more likely

(D) the designation of a characteristic as being maladaptive must always remain highly tentative

(E) changes in the total human environment can outpace evolutionary change

GO ON TO THE NEXT PAGE

I became a devoted reader of Marianne
Moore's poetry while attending college in the
early 1930's. A school friend and her mother,
line both better read and more sophisticated in their
5 literary tastes than I was, were the first to
mention her poetry, and soon I had read every
poem of Moore's I could find.

I had not known poetry could be like that: her
treatment of topics as diverse as glaciers and
10 marriage struck me, as it still does, as a miracle of
language and construction. Why had no one ever
written about these things in this clear and
dazzling way before?

As luck had it, when I first began searching
15 for a copy of her volume entitled Observations, I
found that the college library didn't own one.
Eventually, though, I did borrow a copy, but
from one of the librarians, Fanny Borden, not
from the library. And I received an invitation to
20 meet Marianne Moore in the process.

In retrospect, Fanny Borden seems like a most
appropriate person to have suggested I might
meet Marianne Moore. Borden was extremely
shy and reserved and spoke in such a soft voice it
25 was hard to hear her at all. The campus rumor
was that her personality had been permanently
subdued by her family history: the notorious
Lizzie Borden of Fall River was her aunt.

Contact with Fanny Borden was rare.
30 Occasionally, in search of a book, students would
be sent to her office, shadowy and cave like, with
books piled everywhere. She weighed down the
papers on her desk with smooth, round stones,
quite big stones, brought from the seashore. My
35 roommate once commented on one in particular,
and Borden responded in her almost inaudible
voice, "Do you like it? You may have it," and
handed it over.

One day I was sent to her office about a book.
40 During our talk, I finally got up my courage to
ask her why there was not a copy of Observations
by that wonderful poet Marianne Moore in the
library. She looked ever so gently taken aback
and inquired, "Do you like Marianne Moore's
45 poems?" I said I certainly did, the few had been
able to find. She then said calmly, "I've known
her since she was a girl," and followed that with
the question that was possibly to influence the
whole course of my life: "Would you like to meet
50 her?"

I was painfully—no, excruciatingly—shy and
had run away many times rather than face being
introduced to adults of much less distinction
than Marianne Moore. Yet I immediately said,
55 "Yes."

9. To the author, Marianne Moore's poetry was
   (A) reminiscent of poems by other great
       poets
   (B) subtly satirical
   (C) too scholarly for most readers
   (D) inspiring and well crafted
   (E) difficult but rewarding

10. The major purpose of the passage is to
    (A) describe the events that led to a
        milestone in the author's life
    (B) reveal the character of a college librarian
    (C) relate the significant events of the
        author's college years
    (D) analyze the impact of Marianne Moore's
        poetry on the author
    (E) show the unexpected surprises that can
        happen in an ordinary life

11. The reference to Lizzie Borden in line 26
    provides all of the following EXCEPT
    (A) one possible reason for the librarian's
        unusually quiet manner
    (B) a piece of information about the
        librarian's family history
    (C) a suggestion that the librarian might be
        deliberately hiding her true nature
    (D) an indication that the students were
        curious about the shy librarian
    (E) a fact that might be interesting to some
        readers

12. By mentioning the extent of her shyness in
    line 48, the author primarily emphasizes
    (A) her reasons for not asking Borden to
        introduce her to Marianne Moore
    (B) her awareness of her own weakness
    (C) how important meeting Marianne
        Moore was to her
    (D) how hard it was for her to talk to people,
        even Borden
    (E) how different her encounter with
        Borden was from her roommate's

GO ON TO THE NEXT PAGE

13. The author most likely remembers Fanny Borden primarily with feelings of

(A) regret

(B) curiosity

(C) amusement

(D) gratitude

(E) loyalty

14. The passage suggests that the author's interest in meeting Marianne Moore was

(A) ultimately secondary to her interest in locating a copy of Observations

(B) prompted by a desire to have the poet explain a difficult poem

(C) motivated by the idea of writing a biography of the poet

(D) a secret dream she had cherished for many years

(E) sufficiently strong to make her behave uncharacteristically

GO ON TO THE NEXT PAGE

The thought came and went in a flash: there was not a chance in a billion years that an extraterrestrial object as large as Halley's comet would hit the Earth. But that was 15 years ago, when I had little appreciation of geological time. I did not consider then the adage that anything that can happen does happen—given the time. My intuition was right- there is not a chance in a billion years for a big hit- but there have been more than 4 billion years of Earth history. Smaller collisions have happened frequently, as evidenced by many ancient impact craters. Even during the brief period of human history, there was a very real event at Tunguska.

Tunguska was a quiet hamlet in central Siberia. At 7:00 a.m. on June 30, 1908, a fireball appeared above the horizon to the southeast. More luminous than the rising Sun, the bright light streaked across the cloudless sky and exploded somewhere to the northwest. The scale of the explosion was unprecedented in recorded history. When seismographers consulted their instruments and calculated the energy that had been released, they were stunned. In today's terms the explosion had the force of a 10-megaton nuclear detonation.

The brilliant object had been seen for hundreds of kilometers around, and the explosion was heard as far away as 1,000 kilometers.' The shockwave of wind circled the globe twice, and the ejecta from the explosion glowed over Northern Europe through the next two nights. Vast amounts of fire debris arrived at California two weeks later, noticeably depressing the transparency of the atmosphere over the state.

Fortunately, the object had exploded at a height of 8.5 kilometers above the ground, and the fall region was very sparsely populated. Hunters who were first to enter the disaster area reported that the whole forest had been flattened and gave accounts of wild forest fires. Systematic investigations did not begin until two decades later. The first team of experts visited the target area in 1927. They endured hardship to penetrate the devastated forest with horse-drawn wagons to investigate the aftereffect of the blast. Their mapping showed that trees within a radius of 30 to 40 kilometers had been uprooted and blown radially outward from the center of the blast. Within the blast zone, an area of 2,000 square kilometers had been ravaged by fire.

Study of the Tunguska site resumed after the Second World War and is still continuing. Although no meteorites have ever been found, soil samples from Tunguska contain small spherical objects similar to tektites, black glassy objects commonly believed to result from the impact of a meteorite. The material of which tektites are usually composed is only slightly contaminated by extraterrestrial substances from the meteorite itself. The spherical objects found at Tunguska have been compared to small tektites, or microtektites, which are commonly a fraction of a millimeter in diameter, but the chemical composition of the Tunguska objects resembles cosmic dust. Apparently they were not ejecta thrown out of an impact crater, but were derived directly from the explosion above the Earth, and descended as extraterrestrial fallout.

What was it that exploded on that sunny morning over Siberia? Astronomers have conjured everything from black holes to balls of antimatter, but dramatic as the Tunguska event was, it does not seem to require an exotic explanation. The more likely interpretation is conventional: the object was a large meteor.

15. In line 1, the statement "The thought came and went in a flash" refers to the idea that

(A) intuition is important in scientific research

(B) the Earth is immensely old

(C) the speed of Halley's comet is difficult to calculate

(D) the Tunguska event had an extraterrestrial origin

(E) the Earth could experience a collision with a large cornet

16. The word "appreciation" (line 5) most nearly means

(A) increase in value

(B) artistic interest

(C) understanding

(D) curiosity

(E) gratitude

17. In the third paragraph, the author mentions Northern Europe and California in order to emphasize which point about the Tunguska event?

(A) Although the explosion was locally destructive, the remainder of the world escaped harm.

(B) The magnitude of the explosion was so great that its effects were observable over much of the Northern Hemisphere.

(C) Although the explosion occurred in a remote area, more densely populated areas were also devastated.

(D) No part of the Earth can consider itself secure from the possibility of such an explosion.

(E) The explosion took place in the atmosphere rather than on the ground.

18. The word "depressing" (line 32) most nearly means

(A) reducing

(B) saddening

(C) indenting

(D) constraining

(E) probing

19. Which is most similar to the design of the fallen trees indicated in the 1927 "mapping" (line 44)?

(A) The gridlike pattern of a checkerboard

(B) The spokes of a wheel

(C) The parallel lanes of a highway

(D) The spiral of a whirlpool

(E) The steps in a staircase

20. The author uses the evidence of tektite-like objects in the soil in line 53 to establish that

(A) the Tunguska tektites were uncontaminated by extraterrestrial substances

(B) Tunguska had been the site of an earlier meteorite collision

(C) it was an extraterrestrial object that exploded above Tunguska

(D) normal tektites became deformed as a result of the impact of the Tunguska meteorite

(E) the effects of the Tunguska event were widespread

21. The author's conclusion at the end of the passage would be most directly supported by additional information concerning

(A) what quantity of cosmic dust routinely enters the Earth's atmosphere

(B) how an exploding meteor could generate conventional tektites

(C) why experts did not visit the forest until nineteen years after the explosion

(D) where and when the effect of the blast first registered on a seismograph

(E) why a large meteor would explode in the Earth's atmosphere rather than strike the Earth's surface

22. The author uses the example of the Tunguska event primarily to illustrate the

(A) origin and significance of tektites

(B) devastation caused when a meteorite strikes the surface of the Earth

(C) difference between collisions involving comets and those involving meteorites

(D) potential of the Earth's being struck by large extraterrestrial objects

(E) range of scientific theories advanced to explain an uncommon event

23. In maintaining that the Tunguska event was caused by a meteor, the author has assumed all of the following EXCEPT:

(A) The explosion was so destructive that only tiny fragments of the meteor survived.

(B) The altitude of the explosion accounts for the absence of a crater on the ground.

(C) The tektites found in the soil at Tunguska were formed by the 1908 event and not by an earlier event.

(D) The meteor that exploded near Tunguska is the largest one to have come close to the Earth.

(E) The Earth can be involved in collisions with a variety of cosmic objects.

STOP

this is the end of the exercise

SAT Critical Reading Exercise #02
25 Questions

Although language is used to transmit information, the informative functions of language are fused with older and deeper
line functions so that only a small portion of our
5 everyday utterances can be described as purely informative. The ability to use language for strictly informative purposes was probably developed relatively late in the course of linguistic evolution. Long before that time, our
10 ancestral species probably made the sorts of cries animals do to express feelings of hunger, fear, loneliness, and the like. Gradually these noises seem to have become more differentiated, transforming grunts and
15 gibberings into language as we know it today.

Although we have developed language in which accurate reports may be given, we still use language as vocal equivalents of gestures such as crying in pain or baring the teeth in
20 anger. When words are used as the vocal equivalents of expressive gestures, language is functioning in presymbolic ways. These presymbolic uses of language coexist with our symbolic system, so that the talking we do in
25 everyday life is a thorough blending of symbolic and presymbolic language.

What we call social conversation is mainly presymbolic in character. When we are at a large social gathering, for example, we all have
30 to talk. It is typical of these conversations that, except among very good friends, few of the remarks made have any informative value. We talk together about nothing at all and thereby establish rapport.
35 There is a principle at work in the selection of the subject matter we deem appropriate for social conversation. Since the purpose of this kind of talk is the establishment of communion, we are careful to select subjects about which
40 agreement is immediately possible. Having agreed on the weather, we go on to further agreements—that the rate of inflation is scandalous, that New York City is an interesting place to visit but that it would be an
45 awful place to live, and so on. With each new agreement, no matter how commonplace, the fear and suspicion of the stranger wears away, and the possibility of friendship emerges. When further conversation reveals that we have friends
50 or political views or artistic values or hobbies in

common, a friend is made, and genuine communication and cooperation can begin.

An incident in my own experience illustrates these points. Early in 1942, a few weeks after
55 war was declared between Japan and the United States and at a time when rumors of Japanese spies were still widely current, I had to wait two or three hours in a small railroad station in a city in the Midwest. I became aware as time went on
60 that the other people waiting in the station were staring at me suspiciously and feeling uneasy about my presence. One couple with a small child was staring with special uneasiness and whispering to each other. I therefore took
65 occasion to remark to the husband that it was too bad that the train should be late on so cold a night. He agreed. I went on to remark that it must be especially difficult to travel with a small child in winter when train schedules were so
70 uncertain. Again the husband agreed. I then asked the child's age and remarked that the child looked very big and strong for his age. Again agreement—this time with a slight smile. The tension was relaxing.
75 After two or three more exchanges, the man asked, "I hope you don't mind my asking, but you're Japanese, aren't you? Do you think the Japanese have any chance of winning this war?"

"Well," I replied, "your guess is as good as
80 mine. I don't know any more than I read in the papers. [This was true.] But I don't see how the Japanese with their lack of coal and steel and oil and their limited industrial capacity, can ever beat a powerful industrialized nation like the
85 United States."

My remark was admittedly neither original nor well informed, Hundreds of radio commentators and editorial writers were saying exactly the same thing during those weeks, But
90 because they were, the remark sounded familiar and was on the right side, so that it was easy to agree with. The man agreed at once, with what sounded like genuine relief. How much the wall of suspicion had broken down was indicated in
95 his next question, "Say, I hope your folks aren't over there while the war is going on?"

"Yes, they are. My father and mother and two younger sisters are over there."

"Do you ever hear from them?"
100 "How can I?"

GO ON TO THE NEXT PAGE

"Do you mean you won't be able to see them or hear from them until after the war is over?" Both he and his wife looked sympathetic.
105   There was more to the conversation, but the result was that within ten minutes after it had begun they had invited me to visit them in their city. The other people in the station ceased paying any attention to me and went back to
110 staring at the ceiling.

1. The phrase "older and deeper functions" (lines 3-4) refers to the
(A) grammatical structure of language
(B) expression of emotions through sound
(C) transmission of information
(D) statement of cultural values
(E) original meanings of words

2. The word "differentiated" (line 14) is used to mean
(A) changeable   (B) fused   (C) defined   (D) functional   (E) communicative

3. The term "presymbolic language" (line 26) means
(A) grunts and cries such as are made by animals
(B) language used between friends
(C) language that lacks an elaborate grammatical structure
(D) nonverbal expressions used in communicating
(E) language that does not convey specific information

4. The primary value of presymbolic language for humans is that it
(A) is easily understood
(B) is common to all languages rather than unique to any one language
(C) permits and aids the smooth functioning of interpersonal relationships
(D) helps us understand and express emotions
(E) allows for a desirable amount of social mobility

5. It can be from lines 27-34 ("What... rapport.") that the most important function of social conversation is to
(A) dispel suspicion among strangers
(B) discover topics that are interesting to debate
(C) impress others by expressing clever opinions
(D) perfect the use of effective gestures and facial expressions
(E) involve a large number of people in a conversation

6. Which of the following best captures the meaning of the word "communion" (line 38) in the fourth paragraph?
(A) ritual   (B) initiation   (C) conversation   (D) common ground   (E) social group

7. The comment that New York City "would be an awful place to live" (lines 44-45) is offered by the author as an example of the kind of statement that
(A) might lead to genuine communication
(B) will amuse the reader
(C) exemplifies the author's distrust
(D) is generally ignored
(E) expresses a basic emotion

8. The most crucial difference between presymbolic and symbolic language lies in the
(A) diversity of topics that can be discussed in each mode
(B) origin and developmental path of each mode in linguistic evolution
(C) degree to which each mode may be accompanied by expressive gestures
(D) purposes served by each mode
(E) clarity each mode makes possible

9. The author's remark about Japan's "industrial capacity" (line 83) helped to relieve the tension because

   (A) it showed how much the author knew about Japan
   (B) the information was already familiar to the couple
   (C) it was not directly related to the war
   (D) the author indicated that American newspapers were accurate
   (E) the author did not offer the information until the couple asked for it

10. Which of the following best explains why the onlookers in the train station went back to "staring at the ceiling" (line 110)?

    (A) They sympathized with the writer because he was separated from his family.
    (B) They did not want to get into conversation with the writer.
    (C) They were embarrassed by the fact that the writer was from a country at war with the United States.
    (D) The train was late and they had become bored.
    (E) They had stopped viewing the author as a suspicious person.

11. The author uses the incident at the train station primarily to illustrate that

    (A) distrust between strangers is natural
    (B) people react positively to someone who is nice to children
    (C) giving people the opportunity to agree with you will make it easier for them to trust you
    (D) people of Japanese ancestry living in the United States during the Second World War faced prejudice
    (E) it is easy to recognize hostility in strangers

12. Which piece of information about himself would have been most risky for the author to convey at the beginning of the conversation in the train station?

    (A) He knows only what he reads in the newspapers.
    (B) He believes that Japan lacks vital natural resources.
    (C) He does not see how a powerful nation like the United States could be defeated by Japan.
    (D) He has close relatives living in Japan.
    (E) He does not expect to hear from his family in the near future.

GO ON TO THE NEXT PAGE

Passage 1

Attempts have been made by architectural writers to discredit the garden cities on the ground that they lack "urbanity." Because the
line buildings in them are generously spaced and
5 interspersed with gardens, lawns, and trees, they rarely produce the particular effect of absolute enclosure or packed picturesqueness not undeservedly admired by visitors to many ancient cities. This is true: garden cities exhibit
10 another and a more popular kind of beauty, as well as a healthier and more convenient layout.

But the garden city is, nonetheless, truly a "city." The criticism exposes the confusion and aesthetic narrow-mindedness of the critics. If
15 the word "urbanity" is used in the accepted sense of "educated tastefulness," the charge that the garden cities are without it is an affront to the well-qualified architects who have taken part in their design. If it is used in the simple
20 etymological sense of "city-ness," the users unknowingly expose their crass ignorance of the infinite diversity that the world's cities display. And if it is used (illegitimately) as a synonym for high urban density or crowdedness, it stands
25 for a quality most city dwellers regard as a thing to escape from if they can. The word "urbanity" has been so maltreated that it should now be eliminated from town planning discussions.

Tastes differ in architectural styles as they
30 do in all the arts, and the ability to judge is complicated by changes in fashion, to which critics of the arts seem more subject than people in general. Persons vary in stability of taste: for some a thing of beauty is a joy forever, for
35 others a joy till next month's issue of an architectural periodical.

The garden cities have been obedient to the prevailing architectural fashion. Luckily for the profession, average Britons, though not highly
40 sensitive to architectural design, do not mind it, so long as the things they really care about in a house or a town are attended to. They take great pleasure in grass, trees, and flowers, with which the garden cities are well endowed. The
45 outlook from their windows is more important to them than the look of their dwellings from the street. And though they would have preferred their dwellings to have some element of individuality, they accept harmonious design
50 and grouping without resentment. Thus, given due respect for their major interest, a pleasing ensemble is attainable.

Passage 2

To the visually trained person today, the architecture of the modern city is a remorseless
55 and unremitting assault on the senses. This kind of urban anarchy is an outstanding fact of modern life, an expression of brutalism as harsh and as significant as modern warfare. Our cities are neither expressions of civilization nor
65 creators of civilized individuals.

We see this rampant ugliness not only in the crumbling hearts of older American cities, but in America's most modern urban areas as well— the tangle of superhighways that seem to
70 strangle certain West Coast cities or in suburbs that project the image of a standardized, anonymous, dehumanized person. Nor have we escaped this gloomy catalog when we visit cities that have erected "good taste" into an
75 inoffensive —but equally repugnant because false—urban "style." Urban uglification is not limited to any single country: the posters in the travel agent's office promise famous monuments and picturesque antiquities, but when you look
80 through your hotel room window you see smog, unsanitary streets, and neighborhoods ruined by rapacious speculation in land and buildings.

Those who do not reject modern cities are conditioned not to see, hear, feel, smell, or sense
85 them as they are. The greatest obstacle to seemly cities has become our low expectations, a direct result of our having become habituated to the present environment and our incapacity to conceive of any better alternative. Those of us
90 who have made this adjustment are permanently disabled in the use of our senses, brutalized victims of the modern city.

We can get at what's wrong with a city like Washington D.C. by considering the question
95 once asked seriously by a European visitor, "Where can you take a walk?" He didn't mean an arduous hike, but a stroll along a city street where you can see the people, admire the buildings, inspect the goods, and learn about life
100 in the process.

Perhaps we need a simple litmus-paper test of the good city. Who lives there? Where is the center? What do you do when you get there? A successful urban design involves urbanity, the
105 quality the garden city forgot. It is found in plazas and squares, in boulevards and promenades. It can be found in Rome's railroad station. When you find it, never let it go. It is the hardest thing to create anew.

GO ON TO THE NEXT PAGE

13. In line 4, the word "generously" most nearly means

(A) charitably
(B) helpfully
(C) unselfishly
(D) widely
(E) benevolently

14. The author of Passage 1 objects to using the "simple etymological sense" (lines 19-20) of the word "urbanity" (line 26) for which reason?

(A) Different individuals value different aspects of urban life.
(B) The traditional idea of what is desirable in a city changes greatly over time.
(C) Discovering the history of a word is often difficult.
(D) Not all of the world's cities are alike.
(E) It is dangerous to disregard the opinion of experts.

15. In Passage 1, the reference to "next month's issue of an architectural periodical" (lines 35-36) serves to

(A) show that the plans for the garden cities are well thought of in professional journals
(B) indicate that what seems like a random process is actually an ordered process
(C) suggest that some people lack their own firm ideals of beauty
(D) imply that only those who are knowledgeable about a subject should offer their opinions
(E) emphasize the importance of what the experts say

16. In Passage 1, by considering the relative importance to "average Britons" (line 39) of the view from their homes, the author of Passage 1 suggests that

(A) natural light is an important element of urban design
(B) Britons are not particularly concerned about the architectural design elements that catch the attention of critics
(C) the appeal of grass, trees, and flowers has been overrated by many architectural theorists
(D) the importance of designing buildings that have a pleasing exterior form needs to be remembered
(E) Britons often object to being treated like members of a group rather than like individuals

17. In lines 44-50 ("The...resentment."), the author acknowledges which flaw in the design of the garden city?

(A) The uniformity of the dwellings
(B) The view from many of the windows
(C) The constraint imposed by the landscape
(D) The emphasis placed on plantings
(E) The outmodedness of the architecture

18. The references in Passage 2 to "posters" (line 77) and the view from the "hotel room window" (line 80) serve to

(A) give an accurate sense of the two places
(B) highlight the distinction between the ideal and the reality
(C) show what could be, as opposed to what is
(D) criticize those who would say negative things about well-loved places
(E) invoke past splendor in order to point out present flaws

19. In Passage 2, the phrase "rapacious speculation" (line 82) refers to

(A) rapid calculations
(B) endless deliberation
(C) immoral thoughts
(D) exploitative investments
(E) illegal gambling

GO ON TO THE NEXT PAGE →

20. If modem cities are so terrible, why, according to Passage 2, do people continue to live in them?

(A) Cities provide more varied employment opportunities than other places.

(B) People see cities for what they are and actually enjoy living in such places.

(C) The cultural opportunities available in cities are more varied than those in rural areas.

(D) Despite their drawbacks, cities have a quality of life that makes them desirable as places to live.

(E) As a consequence of living in cities, people have become unable to think objectively about their environment.

21. The distinction made in Passage 2 between a "walk" (line 96) and a "hike" (line 97) can best be summarized as which of the following?

(A) The first is primarily a social experience, the second primarily exercise.

(B) The first involves a greater degree of physical exercise than the second.

(C) The first is more likely to be regimented than the second.

(D) The first covers a greater distance than the second.

(E) The first is a popular activity, the second appeals only to a small group.

22. The questions in the last paragraph of Passage 2 chiefly serve to

(A) ask the reader to compare his or her experience with the author's

(B) show that it is easier to point out problems than to find solutions

(C) suggest what the author's definition of urbanity might involve

(D) answer the charges made by the author's critics

(E) outline an area in which further investigation is needed

23. In lines 101-104 ("Perhaps…forgot."), the author of Passage 2 is critical of garden cities primarily because

(A) they are too crowded

(B) they lack that quality essential to a good city

(C) their design has not been carried out rationally

(D) people cannot readily accommodate themselves to living in them

(E) they are better places for plants than for people

24. The author of Passage 1 would most likely react to the characterization of garden cities presented in the last paragraph of Passage 2 by pointing out that

(A) recent research has shown the inadequacy of this characterization

(B) the facts of urban life support this characterization

(C) this characterization is dismissed by most authorities

(D) this characterization is neither accurate nor well defined

(E) this characterization expresses poor taste

25. How would the author of Passage 1 respond to the way the author of Passage 2 uses the word "urbanity" to describe the quality found in "Rome's railroad station" (line 107-108)?

(A) The quality is not to be found in so common a structure as a railroad station.

(B) The word "urbanity" is being used to denigrate an otherwise positive quality.

(C) The word "urbanity" has been so misused as to be no longer meaningful.

(D) "Urbanity" is, in fact, one of the leading characteristics of the garden city.

(E) It is a sign of arrogance to refuse to value this quality.

STOP

this is the end of the exercise

SAT Critical Reading Exercise #03

23 Questions

A Marxist sociologist has argued that racism stems from the class struggle that is unique to the capitalist system—that racial prejudice is
line generated by capitalists as a means of
5 controlling workers. His thesis works relatively well when applied to discrimination against Blacks in the United States, but his definition of racial prejudice as "racially-based negative prejudgments against a group generally
10 accepted as a race in any given region of ethnic competition," can be interpreted as also including hostility toward such ethnic groups as the Chinese in California and the Jews in medieval Europe. However, since prejudice
15 against these latter peoples was not inspired by capitalists, he has to reason that such antagonisms were not really based on race. He disposes thusly (albeit unconvincingly) of both the intolerance faced by Jews before the rise of
20 capitalism and the early twentieth-century discrimination against Oriental people in California, which, inconveniently, was instigated by workers.

1. The passage supplies information that would answer which of the following questions?
   (A) What accounts for the prejudice against the Jews in medieval Europe?
   (B) What conditions caused the discrimination against Oriental people in California in the early twentieth century?
   (C) Which groups are not in ethnic competition with each other in the United States?
   (D) What explanation did the Marxist sociologist give for the existence of racial prejudice?
   (E) What evidence did the Marxist sociologist provide to support his thesis?

2. The author considers the Marxist sociologist's thesis about the origins of racial prejudice to be
   (A) unoriginal
   (B) unpersuasive
   (C) offensive
   (D) obscure
   (E) speculative

3. It can be inferred from the passage that the Marxist sociologist would argue that in a non-capitalist society racial prejudice would be
   (A) pervasive
   (B) tolerated
   (C) ignored
   (D) forbidden
   (E) nonexistent

4. According to the passage, the Marxist sociologist's chain of reasoning required him to assert that prejudice toward Oriental people in California was
   (A) directed primarily against the Chinese
   (B) similar in origin to prejudice against the Jews
   (C) understood by Oriental people as ethnic competition
   (D) provoked by workers
   (E) nonracial in character

GO ON TO THE NEXT PAGE

For its nineteenth-century discoverers and explorers, Bohemia was an identifiable country with visible inhabitants, but one not marked on any map. To trace its frontiers was to cross constantly back and forth between reality and fantasy.

Explorers recognized Bohemia by certain signs: art, youth, socially defiant behavior, the vagabond life-style. To Henry Murger, the most influential mapper, Bohemia was the realm of young artists struggling to surmount the bathers poverty erected against their vocations, "all those who, driven by an unstinting sense of calling, enter into art with no other means of existence than art itself." They lived in Bohemia because they could not—or not yet—establish their citizenship anywhere else. Ambitious, dedicated, but without means and unrecognized, they had to turn life itself into an art: "Their everyday existence is a work of genius."

Yet even Murger admitted that not all Bohemians were future artists. Other reporters did not think even the majority were future artists. To that sharp-eyed social anatomist Balzac*, Bohemia was more simply the country of youth. All the most talented and promising young people lived in it, those in their twenties who had not yet made their names but who were destined eventually to lead their nation. "In fact all kinds of ability, of talent, are represented there. It is a microcosm. If the emperor of Russia bought up Bohemia for twenty million—assuming it were willing to leave the boulevard pavements—and transferred it to Odessa, in a year Odessa would be Paris." In its genius for life, Balzac's Bohemia resembled Murger's. "Bohemia has nothing and lives from what it has. Hope is its religion, faith in itself its code, charity is all it has for a budget."

Artists and the young were not alone in their ability to make more of life than objective conditions seemed to permit. Some who were called Bohemians did so in more murky and mysterious ways, in the darker corners of society. "By Bohemians," a well-known theater owner of the 1840's declared, "I understand that class of individuals whose existence is a problem, social condition a myth, fortune an enigma, who are located nowhere and who one encounters everywhere! Rich today, famished tomorrow, ready to live honestly if they can and some other way if they can't." The nature of these Bohemians was less easy to specify than either Murger's or Balzac's definitions. They might be unrecognized geniuses or swindlers. The designation "Bohemian" located them in a twilight zone between ingenuity and criminality.

These alternative images of Bohemia are ones we still recognize when we use the tam: more recent incarnations like the Beat Generation of the 1950's or the hippiedom of the 1960's contained these real or potential elements, too. Artistic, youthful, unattached, inventive, or suspect, Bohemian styles are recurring features of modern life. Have they not always existed in Western society? In a way, yes: wandering medieval poets and eighteenth-century literary hacks also exhibited features of Bohemians. But written references to Bohemia as a special, identifiable kind of We appear initially in the nineteenth century. It was in the Prance of the 1830's and 1840's that the terms "Bohemia," "La Bohème," and "Bohemian" first appeared in this sense. The new vocabulary played on the common French word for gypsy— bohémien — which erroneously identified the province of Bohemia, part of old Czechoslovakia, as the gypsies' place of origin.

From the start, Bohemianism took shape by contrast with the image with which it was commonly paired: bourgeois life. The opposition is so well established and comes so easily to mind that it may mislead us, for it implies a form of separation and an intensity of hostility often belied by experience. Bohemia has always exercised a powerful attraction on many solid bourgeois, matched by the deeply bourgeois instincts and aspirations of numerous Bohemians. This mysterious convergence sometimes leads to accusations of insincerity, even dishonesty: "Scratch a Bohemian, find a bourgeois." But the quality revealed by scraping away that false appearance of opposition is seldom hypocrisy. Like positive and negative magnetic poles, Bohemian and bourgeois were—and are—parts of a single field: they imply, require, and attract each other.

French novelist (1799-1850)

5. The passage is best described as
(A) a refutation of an ancient misconception
(B) a definition of a concept
(C) a discussion of one historical era
(D) a catalog of nineteenth-century biases
(E) an example of a class struggle

6. In the quotation at the beginning of the passage, "all those…art itself" (lines 13-15), Bohemia is presented in terms of
(A) an extended metaphor
(B) a complex argument
(C) geographic distances
(D) a logical paradox
(E) popular legend

7. Murger's Bohemians would differ most from the bourgeois in that Bohemians
(A) are motivated by strong artistic impulses
(B) are primarily political reactionaries
(C) have higher social status than the bourgeois
(D) prefer to live off inherited wealth and the generosity of friends
(E) prefer an anarchic social order to a stable one

8. Murger uses the word "unstinting" (line 14) to emphasize the Bohemians'
(A) desire for wealth
(B) power to assimilate bourgeois ideals
(C) reservations about society
(D) dedication to their goals
(E) generous nature

9. The quotation "Their… genius" (line 20-21) can best be interpreted to mean that the Bohemians
(A) are lucky to be alive
(B) are highly successful achievers
(C) are spirited and creative in spite of meager resources
(D) live at the expense of the bourgeois
(E) live chiefly by deceit, theft, and violation of accepted social codes

10. The quotations from Murger suggest that he viewed the Bohemians with
(A) reserve and suspicion
(B) benevolence yet perplexity
(C) amusement and superiority
(D) timidity and fear
(E) interest and admiration

11. In contrast to Murger's Bohemia, Balzac's Bohemia was composed of
(A) young artists struggling in poverty
(B) young bourgeois playing with a new social role
(C) the criminal as well as the genuine
(D) talented artists working together
(E) talented youths seeking to build their futures

12. The word "objective" (line 44) most nearly means
(A) unassuming
(B) fair
(C) intentional
(D) material
(E) detached

13. The quotation in lines 47-55 ("By…can't.") most probably reflects the point of view of
(A) the gypsies
(B) Murger
(C) Balzac
(D) some Bohemians
(E) some bourgeois

14. Which statement best summarizes the point made in the fifth paragraph?
(A) Bohemians have always been subjected to suspicion and scorn.
(B) The Bohemian is an inescapable feature of urban society.
(C) Bohemianism, as a way of life, is not unique to the nineteenth century.
(D) Eighteenth-century Bohemia was similar to nineteenth-century Bohemia.
(E) The province of Bohemia was home to aspiring young artists.

GO ON TO THE NEXT PAGE

15. The statement in the last paragraph ("Scratch… bourgeois") (lines 93-94) is best interpreted as conveying

(A) skepticism about the Bohemians' commitment to their life-style

(B) a desire to study the Bohemian life-style

(C) distrust of both the Bohemian and the bourgeois worlds

(D) a lack of appreciation of the arts

(E) envy of the artist's uncomplicated life

16. Which statement best summarizes the author's argument in the last paragraph?

(A) Bohemians were purposely misleading in their actions.

(B) Bohemians received considerable financial support from bourgeois customers.

(C) Bohemians and bourgeois were more similar than is often realized.

(D) Bourgeois were oblivious to the struggles of Bohemians.

(E) Bourgeois and Bohemians inherited the same cultural traditions from their ancestors.

GO ON TO THE NEXT PAGE

The question of one's identity is at the same time a simple and very complex issue. Is one to be identified by one's race, nationality,
line sex, place of birth, place of death, place of
5 longest residence, occupation, class, relationships to others, personality traits, size, age, interests, religion, astrological sign, salary, by how one perceives oneself, by how one is perceived by others? When born to
10 parents of different races or nationalities, or when born in one country, reared in another, and finally settled in a third, one cannot give a simple answer to the question of racial or national identity. When one is born female in
15 a world dominated by males of two different races, further complications ensue.

At what point does an immigrant become an American? How does one identify one's nationality if one has moved about the world
20 a great deal? Mai-Mai Sze, for example, was born in China to Chinese parents, taken to England as a young child, cared for by an Irish nanny, sent to a private high school and college in the United States, to a painting
25 school in France, and now lives in New York City. Another example is Diana Chang, whose mother was Eurasian (of Irish and Chinese ancestry) and whose father was Chinese; she was born in New York City,
30 taken to China as an infant, reared in the International Sector in Shanghai where she attended American schools, then brought back to the United States for high school and college. In the early 1970's, scholars included
35 her work in anthologies of Asian American literature but also castigated her for the lack of ethnic pride and themes.

To complicate further the question of identity, not only are parentage and
40 geographical factors significant, but external or social factors impinge as well. That recent immigrants feel a sense of alienation and strangeness in a new country is to be expected, but when American-born Chinese
45 Americans, from families many generations in the United States, are asked where they learned such good English, they too are made to feel foreign and alien. The "double consciousness" with which W. E. B. Du Bois
50 characterized the African American—"this sense of always looking at one's self through the eyes of others, of measuring one's soul by the tape of a world that looks on in amused contempt and pity"—equally characterizes
55 Chinese Americans. However, if they should go to the People's Republic of China, they would soon realize, by their unfamiliarity with conditions and customs and by the reactions of the Chinese to them, how American they are. As
60 Lindo Jong tells her daughter in Amy Tan's The Joy Luck Club, "When you go to China…you don't even need to open your mouth. They already know you are an outsider…They know just watching the way you walk, the way you carry
65 your face. They know you do not belong."

Thus, the feeling of being between worlds, totally at home nowhere, is at the core of all the writers in this study and, consequently, of the books they write.

17. The passage serves primarily to
(A) inform the reader of the conflicting senses of identity experienced by Chinese American and other multicultural writers
(B) encourage Chinese American writers to write more fully about the variety of cultural experiences they have had
(C) inform Chinese American writers about writers from other cultures who have experienced conflicts similar to theirs
(D) praise the talent and resourcefulness of contemporary Chinese American writers
(E) refute those who criticize Chinese American literature for its multicultural perspective

18. The author refers to the life of Mai-Mai Sze in the second paragraph chiefly to illustrate the
(A) difficulty of determining one's identity after many relocations
(B) beneficial effects of a multiethnic heritage
(C) influence of social rank on the perception of ethnic identity
(D) advantages of wide experiences on an author's creativity
(E) disruptive effects on a family caused by extensive travel

GO ON TO THE NEXT PAGE

19. The discussion of Diana Chang in lines 26-34 ("Another...college.") suggests that she was

(A) unfamiliar with the culture of the United States

(B) isolated from other writers

(C) concerned with developing an unusual style

(D) unwilling to identify solely with any one cultural background

(E) trying to influence a small group of specialized readers

20. Which of the following would the author consider the best example of the "external or social factors" (lines 40-41)?

(A) The ability to speak several languages

(B) The number of friends one has

(C) The political climate of the country in which one resides

(D) The number of countries one has lived in

(E) The assumptions other people make about one's identity

21. In line 41, "impinge" means

(A) enlarge

(B) contribute

(C) resolve

(D) fall apart

(E) fix firmly

22. The author's views in the third paragraph about Chinese American identity can best be summarized as which of the following?

(A) Chinese Americans are as curious about their United States heritage as they are about their Chinese heritage.

(B) Chinese Americans have made contributions to both Chinese and United States literature.

(C) Chinese Americans are perceived as foreigners in both the People's Republic of China and the United States.

(D) Chinese Americans are viewed as role models by new immigrants to the United States from the People's Republic of China.

(E) Chinese Americans find their dual heritage an advantage in their writing careers.

23. The quotation in lines 61-65 ("When... belong.") emphasizes the point that American-born Chinese Americans

(A) would have difficulty understanding the sense of separation felt by their relatives who emigrated

(B) should travel to China to learn about their heritage

(C) would feel alienated in their ancestors' homeland of China

(D) need to communicate with their relatives in China

(E) tend to idealize life in China

STOP

this is the end of the exercise

SAT Critical Reading Exercise #04
21 Questions

The world can be classified in different ways, depending on one's interests and principles of classification. The classifications (also known as
line taxonomies) in turn determine which
5 comparisons seem natural or unnatural, which literal or analogical. For example, it has been common to classify living creatures into three distinct groups—plants, animals, and humans. According to this classification, human beings
10 are not a special kind of animal, nor animals a special kind of plant. Thus any comparisons between the three groups are strictly analogical. Reasoning from inheritance in garden peas to inheritance in fruit flies, and from these two
15 species to inheritance in human beings, is sheer poetic metaphor.

Another mode of classifying living creatures is commonly attributed to Aristotle. Instead of treating plants, animals, and humans as distinct
20 groups, they are nested. All living creatures possess a vegetative soul that enables them to grow and metabolize. Of these, some also have a sensory soul that enables them to sense their environments and move. One species also has a
25 rational soul that is capable of true understanding. Thus, human beings are a special sort of animal, and animals are a special sort of plant. Given this classification, reasoning from human beings to all other species with
30 respect to the attributes of the vegetative soul is legitimate, reasoning from human beings to other animals with respect to the attributes of the sensory soul is also legitimate, but reasoning from the rational characteristics of the human
35 species to any other species is merely analogical. According to both classifications, the human species is unique. In the first, it has a kingdom all to itself; in the second, it is the peak of the taxonomy hierarchy.
40 *Homo sapiens* is unique. All species are. But this sort of uniqueness is not enough for many (probably most) people, philosophers included. For some reason, it is very important that the species to which we belong be uniquely unique.
45 It is of utmost importance that the human species be insulated from all other species with respect to how we explain certain qualities. Human beings clearly are capable of developing and learning languages. For some reason, it is
50 very important that the waggle dance performed

by bees* not count as a genuine language. I have never been able to understand why. I happen to
55 think that the waggle dance differs from human languages to such a degree that little is gained by terming them both "languages," but even if "language" is so defined that the waggle dance slips in, bees still remain bees. It is equally
60 important to some that no other species use tools. No matter how ingenious other species get in the manipulation of objects in their environment, it is absolutely essential that nothing they do count as "tool use." I, however,
65 fail to see what difference it makes whether any of these devices such as probes and anvils, etc. are really tools. All the species involved remain distinct biological species no matter what decisions are made. Similar observations hold
70 for rationality and anything a computer might do. After finding food, a bee returns to the hive and indicates, through an elaborate sequence of movements, the location of the food to other members of the hive.

1. According to the author, what is most responsible for influencing our perception of a comparison between species?
   (A) The behavior of the organisms in their natural environment
   (B) The organizational scheme imposed on the living world by researchers and philosophers
   (C) The style of language used by scientists in presenting their research
   (D) The sophistication of the communication between organisms
   (E) The magnitude of hierarchical distance between a species and Homo sapiens

GO ON TO THE NEXT PAGE

2. Which of the following is NOT possible within an Aristotelian classification scheme?

(A) Two species that both have sensory souls but one lacks a rational soul

(B) Two species that both have vegetative souls but only one has a sensory soul

(C) A species having a vegetative soul while lacking sensory and rational souls

(D) A species having vegetative and rational souls while lacking a sensory soul

(E) A species having vegetative and sensory souls while lacking a rational soul

3. Which of the following comparisons would be "legitimate" (line 31) for all living organisms according to the Aristotelian scheme described in paragraph two?

  I. Comparisons based on the vegetative soul
  II. Comparisons based on the sensory soul
  III. Comparisons based on the rational soul

(A) I only

(B) II only

(C) III only

(D) II and III only

(E) I, II, and III

4. If the author had wished to explain why "most" (line 39) people feel the way they do, the explanation would have probably focused on the

(A) reality of distinct biological species

(B) most recent advances in biological research

(C) behavioral similarities between Homo sapiens and other species

(D) role of language in the development of technology

(E) lack of objectivity in the classification of Homo sapiens

5. The author uses the words "For some reason" in line 43 to express

(A) rage   (B) disapproval   (C) despair
(D) sympathy   (E) uncertainty

6. Which best summarizes the idea of "uniquely unique" (line 44)?

(A) We are unique in the same way that all other species are unique.

(B) We are defined by attributes that we alone possess and that are qualitatively different from those of other species.

(C) We are, by virtue of our elevated rank, insulated from many of the problems of survival faced by less sophisticated species.

(D) Our awareness of our uniqueness defines us as a rational species.

(E) Our apparently unique status is an unintended by-product of classification systems.

7. In line 46, "insulated from" means

(A) warmed by

(B) covered with

(C) barred from

(D) segregated from

(E) protected from

8. In the third paragraph, the author criticizes those who believe that

(A) the similarities between *Homo sapiens* and other species are more significant than their differences

(B) the differences between Homo sapiens and other animals are those of degree, not kind

(C) *Homo sapiens* and animals belong to separate and distinct divisions of the living world

(D) *Homo sapiens* and animals have the ability to control their environment

(E) *Homo sapiens* and other organisms can be arranged in Aristotelian nested groups

GO ON TO THE NEXT PAGE

Passage 1

We came upon the Prairie at sunset. It would be difficult to say why, or how—though it was possibly from having heard and read so
line much about it—but the effect on me was
5 disappointment. Towards the setting sun, there lay stretched out before my view a vast expanse of level ground, unbroken (save by one thin line of trees, which scarcely amounted to a scratch upon the great blank) until it met the glowing
10 sky, wherein it seemed to dip, mingling with its rich colors and mellowing in its distant blue. There it lay, a tranquil sea or lake without water, if such a simile be admissible, with the day going down upon it: a few birds wheeling
15 here and there, solitude and silence reigning paramount around. But the grass was not yet high; there were bare black patches on the ground and the few wild flowers that the eye could see were poor and scanty. Great as the
20 picture was, its very flatness and extent, which left nothing to the imagination, tamed it down and cramped its interest. I felt little of that sense of freedom and exhilaration that the open landscape of a Scottish moor, or even the
25 rolling hills of our English downlands, inspires. It was lonely and wild, but oppressive in its barren monotony. I felt that in traversing the Prairies, I could never abandon myself to the scene, forgetful of all else, as I should
30 instinctively were heather moorland beneath my feet. On the Prairie I should often glance towards the distant and frequently receding line of the horizon, and wish it gained and passed. It is not a scene to be forgotten, but it is scarcely
35 one, I think (at all events, as I saw it), to remember with much pleasure or to covet the looking-on again, in after years.

Passage 2

In herding the cattle on horseback, we children came to know the open prairie round
40 about and found it very beautiful. On the uplands a short, light-green grass grew, mixed with various resinous weeds, while in the lowland grazing grounds luxuriant patches of blue joint, wild oats, and other tall forage plants
45 waved in the wind. Along the streams, cattails and tiger lilies nodded above thick mats of wide-bladed marsh grass. Almost without realizing it, I came to know the character of every weed, every flower, every living thing big
50 enough to be seen from the back of a horse.

Nothing could be more generous, more joyous, than these natural meadows in summer. The flash and ripple and glimmer of the tall sunflowers, the chirp and gurgle of red-winged
55 blackbirds swaying on the willow, the meadowlarks piping from grassy bogs, the peep of the prairie chick and the wailing call of plover on the flowery green slopes of the uplands made it all an ecstatic world to me. It was a wide
60 world with a big, big sky that alluringly hints at the more glorious unknown wilderness beyond.
Sometimes we wandered away to the meadows along the creek, gathering bouquets of pinks, sweet william, tiger lilies, and lady's
65 slippers. The sun flamed across the splendid serial waves of the grasses and the perfumes of a hundred spicy plants rose in the shimmering midday air. At such times the mere joy of living filled our hearts with word less satisfaction.
70 On a long ridge to the north and west, the soil, too wet and cold to cultivate easily, remained unplowed for several years. Scattered over these clay lands stood small wooded groves that we called "tow-heads." They stood out like
75 islands in the waving seas of grasses. Against these dark-green masses, breakers of blue joint radiantly rolled. To the east ran the river; plum trees and crabapples bloomed along its banks. In June immense crops of wild strawberries
80 appeared in the natural meadows. Their delicious odor rose to us as we rode our way, tempting us to dismount.
On the bare upland ridges lay huge antlers, bleached and bare, in countless numbers, telling
85 of the herds of elk and bison that had once fed in these vast savannas. On sunny April days the mother fox lay out with her young on southward-sloping swells. Often we met a prairie wolf, finding in it the spirit of the
90 wilderness. To us it seemed that just over the next long swell toward the sunset the shaggy brown bison still fed in myriads, and in our hearts was a longing to ride away into the "sunset regions" of our pioneer songs.
95

9. In creating an impression of the prairie for the reader, the author of Passage 1 makes use of

(A) reference to geological processes
(B) description of its inhabitants
(C) evocation of different but equally attractive areas
(D) comparison with other landscapes
(E) contrast to imaginary places

GO ON TO THE NEXT PAGE

10. In Passage 1, the author includes the detail of "a few birds" (line 14) primarily to emphasize the
(A) loneliness of the scene
(B) strangeness of the wildlife
(C) lateness of the evening
(D) dominance of the sky
(E) infertility of the land

11. The word "tamed" (line 19) most nearly means
(A) composed (B) trained (C) subdued (D) captured (E) befriended

12. In Passage 1, "abandon myself" (lines 26) most nearly means
(A) dismiss as worthless
(B) isolate from all others
(C) overlook unintentionally
(D) retreat completely
(E) become absorbed in

13. The author of Passage 1 qualifies his judgment of the prairie by
(A) pointing out his own subjectivity
(B) commenting on his lack of imagination
(C) mentioning his physical fatigue
(D) apologizing for his prejudices against nature
(E) indicating his psychological agitation

14. In Passage 2, "mere" (line 65) most nearly means
(A) tiny (B) trivial (C) simple (D) direct (E) questionable

15. In Passage 2, the author's references to things beyond his direct experience (second paragraph and last paragraph) indicate the
(A) unexpected dangers of life on the unsettled prairie
(B) psychological interweaving of imagination and the natural scene
(C) exaggerated sense of mystery that is natural to children
(D) predominant influence of sight in experiencing a place
(E) permanence of the loss of the old life of the prairie

16. In Passage 2, "masses" (line 73) metaphorically compares the tow-heads to
(A) ships on a stormy ocean
(B) birds on a pond
(C) reefs submerged by rising waters
(D) islands amidst the surf
(E) islands engulfed by a river

17. One aspect of Passage 2 that might make it difficult to appreciate is the author's apparent assumption that readers will
(A) have seen nineteenth-century paintings or photographs of the prairie
(B) connect accounts of specific prairie towns with their own experiences
(C) be able to visualize the plants and the animals that are named
(D) recognize particular pioneer songs
(E) understand the children's associations with the flowers that they gathered

18. The contrast between the two descriptions of the prairie is essentially one between
(A) misfortune and prosperity
(B) homesickness and anticipation
(C) resignation and joy
(D) bleakness and richness
(E) exhaustion and energy

19. Both authors liken the prairie to
(A) a desert (B) an island (C) an animal (D) a wilderness (E) a body of water

20. Both authors indicate that the experience of a beautiful landscape involves
(A) artistic production
(B) detached observation of appearances
(C) emotional turmoil
(D) stimulation of the imagination
(E) fanciful reconstruction of bygone times

STOP

this is the end of the exercise

SAT Critical Reading Exercise #05

19 Question

Skushno is a Russian word that is difficult to translate. It means more than dreary boredom: a spiritual void that sucks you in like a vague but
line intensely urgent longing. When I was thirteen, at
5 a phase that educators used to call the awkward age, my parents were at their wits' end. We lived in the Bukovina, today an almost astronomically remote province in southeastern Europe. The story I am telling seems as distant—not only in
10 space but also in time—as if I'd merely dreamed it. Yet it begins as a very ordinary story.
  I had been expelled by a *consilium abeundi*— an advisory board with authority to expel unworthy students—from the schools of the then
15 Kingdom of Rumania, whose subjects we had become upon the collapse of the Austro-Hungarian Empire after the first great war. An attempt to harmonize the imbalances in my character by means of strict discipline at a
20 boarding school in Styria (my people still regarded Austria as our cultural homeland) nearly led to the same ignominious end, and only my pseudo-voluntary departure from the institution in the nick of time prevented my final
25 ostracism from the privileged ranks of those for whom the path to higher education was open. Again in the jargon of those assigned the responsible task of raising children to become "useful members of society," I was a "virtually
30 hopeless case." My parents, blind to how the contradictions within me had grown out of the highly charged difference between their own natures, agreed with the schoolmasters; the mix of neurotic sensitivity and a tendency to violence,
35 alert perception and inability to learn, tender need for support and lack of adjustability, would only develop into something criminal.
  One of the trivial aphorisms my generation owes to Wilhelm Busch's Pious Helene is the
40 homily "Once your reputation's done, you can live a life of fun." But this optimistic notion results more from wishful thinking than from practical experience. In my case, had anyone asked me about my state of mind, I would have
45 sighed and answered, "Skushno!" Even though rebellious thoughts occasionally surged within me, I dragged myself, or rather I let myself be dragged, listlessly through my bleak existence in the snail's pace of days. Nor was I ever free of a
50 sense of guilt, for my feeling guilty was not

entirely foisted upon me by others; there were deep reasons I could not explain to myself; had I been able to do so, my life would have been much easier.

1. It can be inferred that the author's parents were
(A) frustrated by the author's inability to do well in school
(B) oblivious to the author's poor academic performance
(C) wealthy, making them insensitive to the needs of the poor
(D) schoolmasters who believed in the strict disciplining of youth
(E) living in Russia while their son lived in Bukovina

2. In the second paragraph, the author demonstrates that
(A) the author was an unstable and dangerous person
(B) the schools that the author attended were too difficult
(C) the tactics being used to make. the author a more stable person were failing
(D) the author was not accepted well by his classmates
(E) (B) the author's academic career was nearing an end

3. The word "ignominious" (line 22) means
(A) dangerous
(B) pitiless
(C) unappreciated
(D) disgraceful
(E) honorable

4. The word "ostracism" (line 25) most nearly means
(A) praise (B) abuse (C) appreciation (D) departure (E) banishment

GO ON TO THE NEXT PAGE

5. The passage as a whole suggests that the author felt

(A) happy because he was separated from his parents

(B) upset because he was unable to maintain good friends

(C) melancholy and unsettled in his environment

(D) suicidal and desperate because of his living in Russia

(E) hopeful because he'd soon be out of school

6. The passage indicates that the author regarded the aphorism mentioned in the last paragraph with

(A) relief because it showed him that he would eventually feel better

(B) disdain because the author found it unrealistic

(C) contempt because he saw it working for others

(D) bemusement because of his immunity from it

(E) sorrow because his faith in it nearly killed him

Members of the Jury… If you want to convict these twenty men, then do it. I ask no consideration on behalf of any one of them. They
line are no better than any other twenty men or
5 women; they are no 5 better than the millions down through the ages who have been prosecuted and convicted in cases like this. And if it is necessary for my clients to show that America is like all the rest, if it is necessary that
10 my clients shall go to prison to show it, then let them go. They can afford it if you members of the jury can; make no mistake about that…

The State says my clients "dare to criticize the Constitution." Yet this police officer (who the
15 State says is a fine, right-living person) twice violated the federal Constitution while a prosecuting attorney was standing by. They entered Mr. Owen's home without a search warrant. They overhauled his papers. They found
20 a flag, a red one, which he had the same right to have in his house that you have to keep a green one, or a yellow one, or any other color, and the officer impudently rolled it up and put another flag on the wall, nailed it there. By what right
25 was that done? What about this kind of patriotism that violates the Constitution? Has it come to pass in this country that officers of the law can trample on constitutional rights and then excuse it in a court of justice?
30 Most of what has been presented to this jury to stir up feeling in your souls has not the slightest bearing on proving conspiracy in this case. Take Mr. Lloyd's speech in Milwaukee. It had nothing to do with conspiracy.
35 Whether that speech was a joke or was serious, I will not attempt to discuss. But I will say that if it was serious it was as mild as a summer's shower compared with many of the statements of those who are responsible for
40 working conditions in this country. We have heard from people in high places that those individuals who express sympathy with labor should be stood up against a wall and shot. We have heard people of position declare that
45 individuals who criticize the actions of those who are getting rich should be put in a cement ship with leaden sails and sent out to sea. Every violent appeal that could be conceived by the brain has been used by the powerful and the
50 strong. I repeat, Mr. Lloyd's speech was gentle in comparison…

My clients are condemned because they say in their platform that, while they vote, they believe the ballot is secondary to education and
55 organization. Counsel suggests that those who

get something they did not vote for are sinners, but I suspect you the jury know full well that my clients are right. Most of you have an eight-hour day. Did you get it by any vote you ever cast?
60 No. It came about because workers laid down their tools and said we will no longer work until we get an eight-hour day. That is how they got the twelve-hour day, the ten-hour day, and the eight-hour day—not by voting but by laying
65 down their tools. Then when it was over and the victory won…then the politicians, in order to get the labor vote, passed legislation creating an eight-hour day. That is how things changed; victory preceded law…
70 You have been told that if you acquit these defendants you will be despised because you will endorse everything they believe. But I am not to defend my clients' opinions. I am here to defend their right to express their opinions. I ask you
75 then to decide this case upon the facts as you have heard them, in light of the law as you understand it, in light of the history of our country, whose institutions you and I are bound to protect.

7. Clarence Darrow's statement that "They can afford it if you members of the jury can" (lines 11-12) is most probably meant to imply that

(A) the defendants will not be harmed if convicted

(B) if the jurors convict the defendants, they will be harshly criticized

(C) the defendants do not care whether they are convicted

(D) everyone involved in the trial will be affected financially by whatever the jury decides

(E) if the defendants are found guilty, everyone's rights will be threatened

GO ON TO THE NEXT PAGE

8. Lines 17-19 ("They…warrant.") suggest that the case against Owen would have been dismissed if the judge had interpreted the Constitution in which of the following ways?

(A) Defendants must have their rights read to them when they are arrested.

(B) Giving false testimony in court is a crime.

(C) Evidence gained by illegal means is not admissible in court.

(D) No one can be tried twice for one crime.

(E) Defendants cannot be forced to give incriminating evidence against themselves.

9. The defense in lines 26-31 ("What…justice?") relies mainly on persuading the jury that

(A) the prosecution is using a double standard

(B) the evidence used by the prosecution is unreliable

(C) the defendants' views are similar to those of the jury

(D) labor unions are guaranteed the right to hold a strike

(E) a federal court is a more appropriate place to try the defendants than is a state court

10. The third and fourth paragraphs indicate that the prosecution attempted to characterize Mr. Lloyd's speech as

(A) bitter sarcasm

(B) deceptive propaganda

(C) valid criticism

(D) a frightening threat

(E) a bad joke

11. What does Clarence Darrow accuse "people in high places" (line 42) of doing?

(A) Trying to kill Communist Party members

(B) Advocating violence against labor sympathizers

(C) Lying to the jury

(D) Encouraging the use of harsh punishment against criminals

(E) Making foolish and insulting suggestions

12. The word "counsel" in line 55 refers to

(A) expert psychologists

(B) the prosecution

(C) an assembly

(D) a recommendation

(E) an expert

13. Lines 70-72 ("You…believe.") imply that the prosecution had told the jury that finding for the innocence of the defendants would be similar to

(A) denying the validity of the Constitution

(B) permitting workers to go on strike

(C) promoting passive resistance

(D) limiting freedom of expression

(E) promoting communism

14. In line 78, the word "bound" most nearly means

(A) intellectually committed

(B) personally determined

(C) morally compelled

(D) violently coerced

(E) inevitably destined

15. Darrow's defense hinges on the ability of the jurors to

(A) understand complicated legal terms and procedures

(B) sympathize with union organizers

(C) comprehend the beliefs of the Communist Labor party

(D) separate the defendants' rights from their views

(E) act in the interest of the national economy

GO ON TO THE NEXT PAGE

The transfer of heat and water vapor from the ocean to the air above it depends on disequilibrium at the interface of the water and
line the air. Within about a millimeter of the water,
5 air temperature is close to that of the surface water, and the air is nearly saturated with water vapor. But the differences, however small, are crucial, and the disequilibrium is maintained by air near the surface mixing with air higher up,
10 which is typically appreciably cooler and lower in water vapor content. The air is mixed by means of turbulence that depends on the wind for its energy. As wind speed increases, so does turbulence, and thus the rate of heat and
15 moisture transfer. Detailed understanding of this phenomenon awaits further study. An interacting and complicating phenomenon is wind-to-water transfer of momentum that occurs when waves are formed. When the wind
20 makes waves, it transfers important amounts of energy-energy that is therefore not available to provide turbulence.

16. The primary purpose of the passage is to
(A) resolve a controversy
(B) describe a phenomenon
(C) outline a theory
(D) confirm research findings
(E) classify various observations

17. According to the passage, wind over the ocean generally does which of the following?
I. Causes relatively cool, dry air to come into proximity with the ocean surface.
II. Maintains a steady rate of heat and moisture transfer between the ocean and the air.
III. Causes frequent changes in the temperature of the water at the ocean's surface.

(A) I only
(B) II only
(C) I and II only
(D) II and III only
(E) I, II, and III

18. It can be inferred from the passage that the author regards current knowledge about heat and moisture transfer from the ocean to air as
(A) revolutionary
(B) incons6quential
(C) outdated
(D) derivative
(E) incomplete

19. The passage suggests that if on a certain day the wind were to decrease until there was no wind at all, which of the following would occur?
(A) The air closest to the ocean surface would become saturated with water vapor.
(B) The air closest to the ocean surface would be warmer than the water.
(C) The amount of moisture in the air closest to the ocean surface would decrease.
(D) The rate of heat and moisture transfer would increase.
(E) The air closest to the ocean would be at the same temperature as air higher up.

GO ON TO THE NEXT PAGE

Waverly laughed. "I mean, really, June." And then she started in a deep television-announcer voice: "*Three* benefits, *three* needs, *three* reasons
line to buy…Satisfaction *guaranteed*…"
5   She said this in such a funny way that everybody thought it was a good joke and laughed. To make matters worse, my mother said to Waverly: "True, one can't teach style. June is not sophisticated like you. She must have been
10 born this way."

     I was surprised at myself, how humiliated I felt. I had been outsmarted by Waverly once again, and now betrayed by my own mother.

     Five months ago, some time after the dinner,
15 my mother gave me my "life's importance," a jade pendant on a gold chain. The pendant was not a piece of jewelry I would have chosen for myself. It was almost the size of my little finger, a mottled green and white color, intricately carved.
20 To me, the whole effect looked wrong: too large, too green, too garishly ornate. I stuffed the necklace in my lacquer box and forgot about it.

     But these days, I think about my life's importance. I wonder what it means, because my
25 mother died three months ago, six days before my thirty-sixth birthday. And she's the only person I could have asked to tell me about life's importance, to help me understand my grief.

     I now wear that pendant every day. I think the
30 carvings mean something, because shapes and details, which I never seem to notice until after they're pointed out to me, always mean something to Chinese people. I know I could ask Auntie Lindo, Auntie An-mei, or other Chinese
35 friends, but I also know they would tell me a meaning that is different from what my mother intended. What if they tell me this curving line branching into three oval shapes is a pomegranate and that my mother was wishing
40 me fertility and posterity? What if my mother really meant the carvings were a branch of pears to give me purity and honesty?

     And because I think about this all the time, I always notice other people wearing these same
45 jade pendants—not the flat rectangular medallions or the round white ones with holes in the middle but ones like mine, a two-inch oblong of bright apple green. It's as though we were all sworn to the same secret covenant, so secret we
50 don't even know what we belong to. Last weekend, for example, I saw a bartender wearing one. As I fingered mine, I asked him, "Where'd you get yours?"

     "My mother gave it to me," he said.

that only one Chinese person can ask another; in a crowd of Caucasians, two Chinese people are already like family.

     "She gave it to me after I got divorced. I
60 guess my mother's telling me I'm still worth something."

     And I knew by the wonder in his voice that he had no idea what the pendant really meant.

20. In lines 1-4, Waverly characterizes June as
(A) unsophisticated and heavy-handed
(B) somber and convoluted
(C) clear and concise
(D) humorous and effective
(E) clever and lively

21. The statement "I was surprised at myself" (line 11) suggests that June
(A) had been unaware of the extent of her emotional vulnerability
(B) was exasperated that she allowed Waverly to embarrass her in public
(C) was amazed that she could dislike anyone so much
(D) had not realized that her mother admired her friend Waverly
(E) felt guilty about how much she resented her own mother

22. For June, a significant aspect of what happened at the dinner party is that
(A) her mother had taken great pains to make Waverly feel welcome
(B) she argued openly with Waverly and lost
(C) her mother had sided against her in front of family and friends
(D) Waverly had angered June's mother
(E) Waverly had lied to June's mother

23. The description of June's encounter with the bartender primarily serves to suggest that
(A) she is not the only one who ponders the meaning of a jade pendant
(B) a jade pendant symbolizes life and death
(C) June finally understood her jade pendant
(D) strangers are easier to talk to than family
(E) the bartender is Jade's long-lost brother

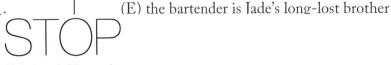

STOP

this is the end of the exercise

SAT Critical Reading Exercise #06

25 Questions

The domestic cat is a contradiction, No other animal has developed such an intimate relationship with humanity, while at the same
line time demanding and getting such independent
5 movement and action.

The cat manages to remain a tame animal because of the sequence of its upbringing. By living both with other cats (its mother and littermates) and with humans (the family that
10 has adopted it) during its infancy and kittenhood, it becomes attached to and considers that it belongs to both species. It is like a child that grows up in a foreign country and as a consequence becomes bilingual. The young cat
15 becomes bimental. It may be a cat physically but mentally it is both feline and human. Once it is fully adult, however, most of its responses are feline ones, and it has only one major reaction to its human owners. It treats them as
20 pseudoparents. The reason is that they took over from the real mother at a sensitive stage of the kitten's development and went on giving it milk, solid food, and comfort as it grew up.

This is rather different from the kind of bond
25 that develops between human and dog. The dog sees its human owners as pseudoparents, as does the cat. On that score the process of attachment is similar. But the dog has an additional link. Canine society is group-organized; feline society
30 is not. Dogs live in packs with tightly controlled status relationships among the individuals. There are top dogs, middle dogs, and bottom dogs and under natural circumstances they move around together, keeping tabs on one another the whole
35 time. So the adult pet dog sees its human family both as pseudoparents and as the dominant members of the pack, hence its renowned reputation for obedience and its celebrated capacity for loyalty. Cats do have a complex
40 social organization, but they never hunt in packs. In the wild, most of their day is spent in solitary stalking. Going for a walk with a human, therefore, has no appeal for them. And as for "coming to heel" and learning to "sit" and "stay,"
45 they are simply not interested. Such maneuvers have no meaning for them.

So the moment a cat manages to persuade a human being to open a door (that most hated of human inventions), it is off and away without a
50 backward glance. As it crosses the threshold, the cat becomes transformed. The kitten-of-human brain is switched off and the wildcat brain is on.

The dog, in such a situation, may look back to see if its human packmate is following to join
55 in the exploring, but not the cat. The cat's mind has floated off into another, totally feline world, where strange bipedal* primates have no place.

Because of this difference between domestic cats and domestic dogs, cat-lovers tend to be
60 rather different from dog-lovers. As a rule, cat-lovers have a stronger personality bias toward working alone, independent of the larger group. Artists like cats: soldiers like dogs. The much-lauded "group loyalty" phenomenon is alien to
65 both cats and cat-lovers. If you are a company person, a member of the gang, or a person picked for the squad, the chances are that at home there is no cat curled up in front of the fire. The ambitious Yuppie, the aspiring
70 politician, the professional athlete, these are not typical cat-owners. It is hard to picture football players with cats in their laps -much easier to envisage them taking their dogs for walks.

Those who have studied cat-owners and
75 dog-owners as two distinct groups report that there is also a gender bias. The majority of cat-lovers are female. This bias is not surprising in view of the division of labor evident in the development of human societies. Prehistoric
80 males became specialized as group-hunters, while the females concentrated on food-gathering and childbearing. This difference contributed to a human male "pack mentality" that is far less marked in females. Wolves, the
85 wild ancestors of domestic dogs, also became pack-hunters, so the modern dog has much more in common with the human male than with the human female.

The argument will always go on -feline self-
90 sufficiency and individualism versus canine camaraderie and good-fellowship. But it is important to stress that in making a valid point I have caricatured the two positions. In reality there are many people who enjoy equally the
95 company of both cats and dogs. And all of us, or nearly all of us, have both feline and canine elements in our personalities. We have moods when we want to be alone and thoughtful, and other times when we wish to be in the center of
100 a crowded, noisy room.

GO ON TO THE NEXT PAGE

1. The primary purpose of the passage is to
   (A) show the enmity that exists between cats and dogs
   (B) advocate dogs as making better pets than cats
   (C) distinguish the different characteristics of dogs and cats
   (D) show the inferiority of dogs because of their dependent nature
   (E) emphasize the role that human society plays in the personalities of domestic pets

2. According to the passage, the domestic cat can be described as
   (A) a biped because it possesses the characteristics of animals with two feet
   (B) a pseudopet because it can't really be tamed and will always retain its wild habits
   (C) a contradiction because although it lives comfortably with humans, it refuses to be dominated by them
   (D) a soldier because it is militant about preserving its independence
   (E) a ruler because although it plays the part of a pet, it really dominates humans

3. In line 26, the word "pseudoparents" means
   (A) part-time parents that are only partially involved with their young
   (B) individuals who act as parents of adults
   (C) parents that neglect their young
   (D) parents that have both the characteristics of humans and their pets
   (E) adoptive parents who aren't related to their young

4. The author suggests that an important difference between dogs and cats is that, unlike dogs, cats
   (A) do not regard their owners as the leader of their social group
   (B) obey mainly because of their obedient nature
   (C) have a more creative nature
   (D) do not have complex social organizations
   (E) are not skilled hunters

5. It can be inferred from the passage that the social structure of dogs is flexible abstract hierarchical male dominated somewhat exclusive
   (A) flexible
   (B) abstract
   (C) hierarchical
   (D) male dominated
   (E) somewhat exclusive

6. Lines 39-45 ("Cats…them.") emphasize
   (A) the laziness of cats that keeps them from being pack animals
   (B) the ignorance of dogs, which makes them more obedient pets
   (C) the antipathy that cats feel for humans
   (D) a difference between cats and dogs that stresses the independent nature of cats
   (E) the stubborn and complacent disposition of dogs

7. In lines 63-64, "much-lauded" means
   (A) vehemently argued
   (B) overly discussed
   (C) unnecessarily complicated
   (D) typically controversial
   (E) commonly praised

8. The "ambitious Yuppie" (line 69) is an example of a person
   (A) who is power hungry
   (B) who craves virtue
   (C) who is a stereotypical pet-owner
   (D) who has a weak personality
   (E) who seeks group-oriented status

GO ON TO THE NEXT PAGE

9. Lines 79-82 ("Human...childbearing.") indicate that human females
(A) are more like dogs than cats
(B) developed independent roles that didn't require group behavior
(C) had to gather food because they were not strong enough to hunt
(D) are not good owners for the modern dog
(E) were negatively affected by the division of labor of human societies

10. The author uses last paragraph to
(A) show that the argument stated in the passage is ultimately futile
(B) disclaim glaring contradictions that are stated in the passage
(C) qualify the generalizations used to make the author's point
(D) ensure that the reader doesn't underestimate the crux of the passage
(E) highlight a difference between individualism and dependency

11. Lines 91-100 ("But...room.") provide
(A) an example of the argument that has been made earlier
(B) a summary of the points made earlier
(C) a reason for the statements made earlier
(D) a modification of the position taken earlier
(E) a rebuttal to opposing views referred to earlier

12. The passage as a whole does all of the following EXCEPT
(A) use a statistic
(B) make parenthetic statements
(C) use a simile
(D) restate an argument
(E) make a generalization

GO ON TO THE NEXT PAGE

Passage 1

Talk to those people who first saw films when they were silent, and they will tell you the experience was magic. The silent film had
line extraordinary powers to draw members of an
5 audience into the story, and an equally potent capacity to make their imaginations work. It required the audience to become engaged—to supply voices and sound effects. The audience was the final, creative contributor to the process
10 of making a film.

The finest films of the silent era depended on two elements that we can seldom provide today— a large and receptive audience and a well-orchestrated score. For the audience, the
15 fusion of picture and live music added up to more than the sum of the respective parts.

The one word that sums up the attitude of the silent filmmakers is enthusiasm, conveyed most strongly before formulas took shape and
20 when there was more room for experimentation. This enthusiastic uncertainty often resulted in such accidental discoveries as new camera or editing techniques. Some films experimented with players; the 1915 film Regeneration, for
25 example, by using real gangsters and streetwalkers, provided startling local color. Other films, particularly those of Thomas Ince, provided tragic endings as often as films by other companies supplied happy ones.
30 Unfortunately, the vast majority of silent films survive today in inferior prints that no longer reflect the care that the original technicians put into them. The modern versions of silent films may appear jerky and flickery, but
35 the vast picture palaces did not attract four to six thousand people a night by giving them eyestrain. A silent film depended on its visuals: as soon as you degrade those, you lose elements that go far beyond the image on the surface. The
40 acting in silents was often very subtle, very restrained, despite legends to the contrary.

Passage 2

Mime opens up a new world to the beholder,
40 but it does so insidiously, not by purposely injecting points of interest in the manner of a tour guide. Audiences are not unlike visitors to a foreign land who discover that the modes, manners, and thoughts of its inhabitants are not
45 meaningless oddities, but are sensible in context.

I remember once when an audience seemed perplexed at what I was doing. At first, I tried to gain a more immediate response by using slight exaggerations. I soon realized that these actions
50 had nothing to do with the audience's understanding of the character. What I had believed to be a failure of the audience to respond in the manner I expected was, in fact, only their concentration on what I was doing;
55 they were enjoying a gradual awakening—a slow transference of their understanding from their own time and place to one that appeared so unexpectedly before their eyes. This was evidenced by their growing response to
60 succeeding numbers.

Mime is an elusive art, as its expression is entirely dependent on the ability of the performer to imagine a character and to re-create that character for each performance. As a
65 mime, I am a physical medium, the instrument upon which the figures of my imagination play their dance of life. The individuals in my audience also have responsibilities—they must be alert collaboration. They cannot sit back,
70 mindlessly complacent, and wait to have their emotions titillated by mesmeric musical sounds or visual rhythms or acrobatic feats, or by words that tell them what to think. Mime is an art that, paradoxically, appeals both to those who
75 respond instinctively to entertainment and to those 'whose appreciation is more analytical and complex. Between these extremes lie those audiences conditioned to resist any collaboration with what is played before them; and these the
80 mime must seduce despite themselves. There is only one way to attack those reluctant minds— take them unaware! They will be delighted at an unexpected pleasure.

GO ON TO THE NEXT PAGE

13. Lines 11-16 ("The…parts".) indicate that

(A) music was the most important element of silent films

(B) silent films rely on a combination of music and image in affecting an audience

(C) the importance of music in silent film has been overestimated

(D) live music compensated for the poor quality of silent film images

(E) no film can succeed without a receptive audience

14. The "formulas" mentioned in line 19 of passage 1 most probably refer to

(A) movie theaters

(B) use of real characters

(C) standardized film techniques

(D) the fusion of disparate elements

(E) contemporary events

15. The author uses the phrase "enthusiastic uncertainty" (line 21) to suggest that the filmmakers were

(A) excited to be experimenting in an undefined area

(B) delighted at the opportunity to study new acting formulas

(C) optimistic in spite of the obstacles that faced them

(D) eager to challenge existing conventions

(E) eager to please but unsure of what the public wanted

16. The author of Passage 1 uses the phrase "but the…eyestrain" (lines 34-37) in order to

(A) indicate his disgust with the incompetence of early film technicians

(B) suggest that audiences today perceive silent films incorrectly

(C) convey his regret about the decline of the old picture palaces

(D) highlight the pitfalls of the silent movie era

(E) argue for the superiority of modern film technology over that of silent movies

17. The word "legends" in line 41 of Passage 1 most nearly means

(A) arguments

(B) symbolism

(C) propaganda

(D) movie stars

(E) misconceptions

18. Lines 39-41 ("The acting…contrary.") imply that

(A) the stars of silent movies have been criticized for overacting

(B) many silent film actors became legends in their own time

(C) silent film techniques should be studied by filmmakers today

(D) visual effects defined the silent film

(E) many silent films that exist today are of poor quality

19. The word "restrained" (line 38) most nearly means

(A) sincere   (B) dramatic   (C) understated   (D) inexpressive   (E) consistent

20. The author of Passage 2 mentions the incident in the second paragraph in order to imply that

(A) the audience's lack of response was a positive sign and reflected their captivated interest in the performance

(B) she was forced to resort to stereotypes in order to reach an audience that was otherwise unattainable

(C) exaggeration is an essential part of mime because it allows the forums used to be fully expressed

(D) her audience, though not initially appearing knowledgeable, had a good understanding of the subtlety of mime

(E) although vocalization is not necessary in mime, it is sometimes helpful for slower audiences

GO ON TO THE NEXT PAGE

21. The second paragraph of Passage 2 indicates that the author of Passage 2 and the silent filmmakers of Passage 1 were similar because

(A) neither used many props

(B) both conveyed universal truths by using sophisticated technology

(C) for both trial and error was a part of the learning process

(D) both used visual effects and dialogue

(E) both had a loyal following

22. The sentence "As a...life" (lines 66-69) suggests that the author feels mimes

(A) cannot control the way audiences interpret their characters

(B) must suspend their own identities in order to successfully portray their characters

(C) have to resist outside attempts to define their acting style

(D) should focus on important events in the lives of specific characters

(E) know the limitations of performances that do not incorporate either music or speech

23. Which of the following pieces of information makes mime and silent film seem less similar?

(A) Vaudeville and theatrical presentations were also popular forms of entertainment during the silent film era

(B) Silent films presented both fictional drama and factual information.

(C) Silent film sometimes relied on captions to convey dialogue to the audience.

(D) Musicians working in movie theaters were usually employed for long periods of time

(E) Many of the characters in silent films gained wide popularity among moviegoers

24. Passages 1 and 2 are similar in that both are mainly concerned with

(A) the use of special effects

(B) differences among dramatic styles

(C) the visual aspects of performance

(D) the suspension of disbelief in audiences

(E) nostalgia for a bygone era

25. Which of the following is an element that figures in the success of the dramatic arts described in both passages?

(A) A successful combination of different dramatic styles

(B) The exaggeration of certain aspects of a character

(C) The incorporation of current events in the narrative

(D) High audience attendance

(E) The active participation of the audience

STOP

this is the end of the exercise

SAT Critical Reading Exercise #07

21 Questions

By the time the American colonists took up arms against Great Britain in order to secure their independence, the institution of Black
line slavery was deeply entrenched. But the
5 contradiction inherent in this situation was, for many, a source of constant embarrassment. "It always appeared a most iniquitous scheme to me," Abigail Adams wrote her husband in 1774, "to fight ourselves for what we are daily robbing
10 and plundering from those who have as good a right to freedom as we have."

Many Americans besides Abigail Adams were struck by the inconsistency of their stand during the War of Independence, and they were not
15 averse to making moves to emancipate the slaves. Quakers and other religious groups organized antislavery societies, while numerous individuals manumitted their slaves. In fact, within several years of the end of the War of Independence,
20 most of the Eastern states had made provisions for the gradual emancipation of slaves.

1. Which of the following best states the central idea of the passage?
(A) The War of Independence produced among many Black Americans a heightened consciousness of the inequities in American society.
(B) The War of Independence strengthened the bonds of slavery of many Black Americans while intensifying their desire to be free.
(C) The War of Independence exposed to many Americans the contradiction of slavery in a country seeking its freedom and resulted in efforts to resolve that contradiction.
(D) The War of Independence provoked strong criticisms by many Americans of the institution of slavery, but produced little substantive action against it.
(E) The War of Independence renewed the efforts of many American groups toward achieving Black emancipation.

2. The passage contains information that would support which of the following statements about the colonies before the War of Independence?
(A) They contained organized antislavery societies.
(B) They allowed individuals to own slaves.
(C) They prohibited religious groups from political action.
(D) They were inconsistent in their legal definitions of slave status.
(E) They encouraged abolitionist societies to expand their influence.

3. According to the passage, the War of Independence was embarrassing to some Americans for which of the following reasons?

I. It involved a struggle for many of the same liberties that Americans were denying to others.
II. It involved a struggle for independence from the very nation that had founded the colonies.
III. It involved a struggle based on inconsistencies in the participants' conceptions of freedom.

(A) I only
(B) II only
(C) I and II only
(D) I and III only
(E) I, II, and III

GO ON TO THE NEXT PAGE

It is April 1959, I'm standing at the railing of the Batory's upper deck, and I feel that my life is ending. I'm looking out at the crowd that has
line gathered on the shore to see the ship's departure
5 from Gdynia—a crowd that, all of a sudden, is irrevocably on the other side—and I want to break out, run back, run toward the familiar excitement, the waving hands, the exclamations. We can't be leaving all this behind —but we are.
10 I am thirteen years old, and we are emigrating. It's a notion of such crushing, definitive finality that to me it might as well mean the end of the world.

My sister, four years younger than I, is
15 clutching my hand wordlessly; she hardly understands where we are, or what is happening to us. My parents are highly agitated; they had just been put through a body search by the customs police. Still, the officials weren't clever
20 enough, or suspicious enough, to check my sister and me—lucky for us, since we are both carrying some silverware we were not allowed to take out of Poland in large pockets sewn onto our skirts especially for this purpose, and hidden under
25 capacious sweaters.

When the brass band on the shore strikes up the jaunty mazurka rhythms of the Polish anthem, I am pierced by a youthful sorrow so powerful that I suddenly stop crying and try to
30 hold still against the pain. I desperately want time to stop, to hold the ship still with the force of my will. I am suffering my first, severe attack of nostalgia, or *tesknota*—a word that adds to nostalgia the tonalities of sadness and longing. It
35 is a feeling whose shades and degrees I'm destined to know intimately, but at this hovering moment, it comes upon me like a visitation from a whole new geography of emotions, an annunciation of how much an absence can hurt.
40 Or a premonition of absence, because at this divide, I'm filled to the brim with what I'm about to lose—images of Cracow, which I loved as one loves a person, of the sunbaked villages where we had taken summer vacations, of the hours I spent
45 poring over passages of music with my piano teacher, of conversations and escapades with friends. Looking ahead, I come across an enormous, cold blankness—a darkening, and erasure, of the imagination, as if a camera eye has
50 snapped shut, or as if a heavy curtain has been pulled over the future. Of the place where we're going—Canada—"I know nothing. There are vague outlines of half a continent, a sense of vast spaces and little habitation. When my parents
55 were hiding in a branch-covered forest bunker

during the war, my father had a book with him called *Canada Fragrant with Resin* which, in his horrible confinement, spoke to him of majestic wilderness, of animals roaming without being
60 pursued, of freedom. That is partly why we are going there, rather than to Israel, where most of our Jewish friends have gone. But to me, the word "Canada" has ominous echoes of the "Sahara." No, my mind rejects the idea of being
65 taken there, I don't want to be pried out of my childhood, my pleasures, my safety, my hopes for becoming a pianist. The Batory pulls away, the foghorn emits its lowing, shofar sound, but my being is engaged in a stubborn refusal to
70 move. My parents put their hands on my shoulders consolingly; for a moment, they allow themselves to acknowledge that there's pain in this departure, much as they wanted it.

Many years later, at a stylish party in New
75 York, I met a woman who told me that she had an enchanted childhood. Her father was a highly positioned diplomat in an Asian country, and she had lived surrounded by sumptuous elegance... No wonder, she said, that when this
80 part of her life came to an end, at age thirteen, she felt she had been exiled from paradise, and had been searching for it ever since.

No wonder. But the wonder is what you can make a paradise out of. I told her that I grew up
85 in a lumpen apartment in Cracow, squeezed into three rudimentary rooms with four other people, surrounded by squabbles, dark political rumblings, memories of wartime suffering, and daily struggle for existence. And yet, when it
90 came time to leave, I, too, felt I was being pushed out of the happy, safe enclosures of Eden.

4. This passage serves mainly to

(A) provide a description of what the author loved most about her life in Poland

(B) recount the author's experience of leaving Cracow

(C) explain why the author's family chose to emigrate

(D) convey the author's resilience during times of great upheaval

(E) create a factual account of the author's family history

5. In lines 2-3, "I feel that my life is ending" most nearly reflects the author's

(A) overwhelming sense of the desperate life that she and her family have led

(B) sad realization that she is leaving a familiar place permanently

(C) unsettling premonition that she will not survive the voyage to Canada

(D) severe state of depression that may lead her to seek professional help

(E) irrational fear that she will be unexpectedly separated from her family

6. The author's description of "the crowd on the shore" (lines 3-4) suggests that

(A) her family does not expect to find a warm welcome in Canada

(B) her relatives will not be able to visit her in Canada

(C) her family's friends have now turned against them

(D) she will find it difficult to communicate with her Polish friends

(E) the step she is taking is irreversible

7. The passage as a whole suggests that the author differs from her parents in that she

(A) has happier memories of Poland than her parents do

(B) is more sociable than they are

(C) feels no response to the rhythms of the Polish anthem

(D) has no desire to wave to the crowd on the shore

(E) is not old enough to comprehend what she is leaving behind

8. For the author, the experience of leaving Cracow can best be described as

(A) enlightening

(B) exhilarating

(C) annoying

(D) wrenching

(E) ennobling

9. In lines 19-25, the author's description of the customs police suggests that the author views her encounter with them as

(A) alarming

(B) violent

(C) auspicious

(D) unnecessary

(E) unmemorable

10. In the third paragraph, the author indicates that "nostalgia" (line 33) differs from "tesknota" (line 33) in that

(A) tesknota cannot be explained in English

(B) tesknota denotes a gloomy, bittersweet yearning

(C) tesknota is a feeling that never ends

(D) nostalgia is a more painful emotion than tesknota

(E) nostalgia connotes a greater degree of desire than tesknota

11. By describing her feelings as having "shades and degrees" (line 35), the author suggests that

(A) she is allowing herself to grieve only a little at a time

(B) she is numb to the pain of her grief

(C) she is overwhelmed by her emotions

(D) her sadness is greatest at night

(E) her emotional state is multifaceted

12. The phrase "I'm destined to know intimately" (lines 35-36) implies that the author

(A) provide a detailed description of what the author loved most about her life in Poland

(B) recount the author's experience of leaving Cracow

(C) explain why the author's family chose to emigrate

(D) convey the author's resilience during times of great upheaval

(E) create a factual account of the author's family history

GO ON TO THE NEXT PAGE

13. The author refers to the "camera eye" (line 49) and the "heavy curtain" (line 50) in order to suggest

(A) the difference between reality and art

(B) the importance of images to the human mind

(C) the difference between Poland and Canada

(D) her inability to overcome her fear of death

(E) her inability to imagine her future life

14. The description of the author as "engaged in a stubborn refusal to move" (line 69-70) suggests her

(A) determination to claim her space on the crowded deck of the ship

(B) refusal to accept the change in her life

(C) wish to strike back at her parents for taking her away from Poland

(D) resolve not to become a Canadian citizen

(E) need to stay in close proximity to her family

15. In lines 70-73 ("My…it."), the author suggests that her parents' comforting gesture indicates

(A) a recognition of feelings of distress over their departure

(B) their exhilaration and relief at the thought of personal freedom

(C) a great deal of ambivalence regarding their decision

(D) pain so great that they can feel no joy in their departure

(E) a complete loss of feeling due to the stressful events

16. The word "it" (line 70) most likely refers to

(A) the pain of departing from home

(B) the migration to Canada

(C) the desperation to go home

(D) the nostalgia for things past

(E) the desire to return to Eden

GO ON TO THE NEXT PAGE

Why do some desert plants grow tall and thin like organ pipes? Why do most trees in the tropics keep their leaves year round? Why in the Arctic
line tundra are there no trees at all? After many years
5 without convincing general answers, we now know much about what sets the fashion in plant design.

Using terminology more characteristic of a thermal engineer than of a botanist, we can think of plants as mechanisms that must balance their
10 heat budgets. A plant by day is staked out under the Sun with no way of sheltering itself. All day long it absorbs heat. If it did not lose as much heat as it gained, then eventually it would die. Plants get rid of their heat by warming the air around
15 them, by evaporating water, and by radiating heat to the atmosphere and the cold, black reaches of space. Each plant must balance its heat budget so that its temperature is tolerable for life.

Plants in the Arctic tundra lie close to the
20 ground in the thin layer of still air that clings there. A foot or two above the ground are the winds of Arctic cold. Tundra plants absorb heat~ from the Sun and tend to warm up; they probably balance most of their heat budgets by radiating
25 heat to space, but also by warming the still air that is trapped among them. As long as Arctic plants are close to the ground, they can balance their heat budgets. But if they should stretch up as a tree does, they would lift their working parts, their
30 leaves, into the streaming Arctic winds. Then it is likely that the plants could not absorb enough heat from the Sun to avoid being cooled below a critical temperature. Your heat budget does not balance if you stand tall in the Arctic.
35 Such thinking also helps explain other characteristics of plant design. A desert plant faces the opposite problem from that of an Arctic plant— the danger of overheating. It is short of water and so cannot cool itself by evaporation without dehy-
40 drating. The familiar sticklike shape of desert plants represents one of the solutions to this problem: the shape exposes the smallest possible surface to incoming solar radiation and provides the largest possible surface from which the plant
45 can radiate heat. In tropical rain forests, by way of contrast, the scorching Sun is not a problem for plants because there is sufficient water.

This working model allows us to connect the general characteristics of the forms of plants in
50 different habitats with factors such as temperature, availability of water, and presence or absence of seasonal differences. Our Earth is covered with a patchwork quilt of meteorological conditions, and the patterns of this patchwork are faithfully
55 reflected by the plants.

17. The passage primarily focuses on which of the following characteristics of plants?
(A) Their ability to grow equally well in all environments
(B) Their effects on the Earth's atmosphere
(C) Their ability to store water for dry periods
(D) Their fundamental similarity of shape
(E) Their ability to balance heat intake and output

18. Which of the following could best be substituted for the words "sets the fashion in" (line 6) without changing the intended meaning?
(A) improves the appearance of
(B) accounts for the uniformity of
(C) defines acceptable standards for
(D) determines the general characteristics of
(E) reduces the heat budgets of

19. According to the passage, which of the following is most responsible for preventing trees from growing tall in the Arctic?
(A) The hard, frozen ground
(B) The small amount of available sunshine
(C) The cold, destructive winds
(D) The large amount of snow that falls each year
(E) The absence of seasonal differences in temperature

20. The author suggests that the "sticklike shape of desert plants" (line 40) can be attributed to the
(A) inability of the plants to radiate heat to the air around them
(B) presence of irregular seasonal differences in the desert
(C) large surface area that the plants must expose to the Sun
(D) absence of winds strong enough to knock down tall, thin plants
(E) extreme heat and aridity of the habitat

GO ON TO THE NEXT PAGE

21. The "contrast" mentioned in line 46 specifically concerns the
(A) availability of moisture
(B) scorching heat of the Sun
(C) seasonal differences in temperature
(D) variety of plant species
(E) heat radiated by plants to the atmosphere

STOP

this is the end of the exercise

SAT Critical Reading Exercise #08

22 Questions

This semester I have been teaching a course entitled Women and Notions of Property. I have been focusing on the ways in which gender
line affects individuals' perspectives—gender in this
5 instance having less to do with the biology of male and female than with the language of power relations, of dominance and submission, of assertion and deference, of big and little. An example of the stories we discuss is the following,
10 used to illustrate the rhetoric of power relations, whose examination, I tell my students, is at the heart of the course.

Walking down Fifth Avenue in New York not long ago, I came up behind a couple and
15 their young son. The child, about four or five years old, had evidently been complaining about big dogs. The mother was saying, "But why are you afraid of big dogs?" "Because they're big," he responded with eminent good sense. "But what's
20 the difference between a big dog and a little dog?" the father persisted. "They're big," said the child. "But there's really no difference," said the mother, pointing to a large, slavering wolf hound with narrow eyes and the calculated gamble of a
25 gangster, and then to a beribboned Pekingese the size of a roller skate, who was flouncing along just ahead of us all, in that little fox-trotty step that keeps Pekingeses from ever being taken seriously. "See?" said the father. "If you look
30 really closely you'll see there's no difference at all. They're all just dogs."

And I thought: Talk about a static, unyielding, totally uncompromising point of reference. These people must be lawyers. Where
35 else do people learn so well the idiocies of High Objectivity? How else do people learn to capitulate so uncritically to a norm that refuses to allow for difference? How else do grown-ups sink so deeply into the authoritarianism of their
40 own world view that they can universalize their relative bigness so completely as to obliterate the viewpoint of their child's relative smallness? (To say nothing of the viewpoint of the slavering wolfhound, from whose own narrow perspective
45 I dare say the little boy must have looked exactly like a lamb chop.)

I use this story in my class because I think it illustrates a paradigm of thought by which children are taught not to see what they see; by
50 which African Americans are reassured that

there is no real inequality in the world, just their own bad dreams; and by which women are taught not to experience what they experience, in deference to men's ways of knowing. The
55 story also illustrates the possibility of a collective perspective or social positioning that would give rise to a claim for the legal interests of groups. In a historical moment when individual rights have become the basis for any remedy, too often
60 group interests are defeated by, for example, finding the one four year old who has wrestled whole packs of wolfhounds fearlessly to the ground; using that individual experience to attack the validity of there ever being any
65 generalizable fear of wolfhounds by four year olds; and then recasting the general group experience as a fragmented series of specific, isolated events rather than a pervasive social phenomenon ("You have every right to think
70 that that wolfhound has the ability to bite off your head, but that's just your point of view").

My students, most of whom signed up expecting to experience that crisp, refreshing, clear-headed sensation that "thinking like a
75 lawyer" purportedly endows, are confused by this and all the stories I tell them in my class on Women and Notions of Property. They are confused enough by the idea of property alone, overwhelmed by the thought of dogs and
80 women as academic subjects, and paralyzed by the idea that property, ownership, and rights might have a gender and that gender might be a matter of words.

1. In lines 4-8, the author describes "gender" primarily in terms of
   (A) early childhood experience
   (B) genetics and hormonal chemistry
   (C) the distribution of power in relationships
   (D) the influence of role models on personality formation
   (E) the varying social conventions in different cultures

GO ON TO THE NEXT PAGE

2. In line 19, "eminent" most nearly means
   (A) famed
   (B) exalted
   (C) protruding
   (D) influential
   (E) obvious

3. The description of the two dogs in the end of the second paragraph serves primarily to
   (A) defuse a tense situation with humor
   (B) discredit what the parents are saying
   (C) emphasize the dogs' resemblance to their owners
   (D) suggest that dogs are more sensible than humans
   (E) illustrate a legal concept regarding pet ownership

4. In line 24, "calculated" most nearly means
   (A) scheming
   (B) predetermined
   (C) deliberate
   (D) predictable
   (E) estimated

5. The author uses the term "authoritarianism" (line 39) in order to
   (A) link habits of thought with political repression
   (B) ridicule the parents in the story by using comically exaggerated terms
   (C) criticize the harsh teaching methods used in law schools
   (D) show that the attitude represented by the parents is unconstitutional
   (E) allude to parental roles in societies of the past

6. The author describes the wolf hound's viewpoint (lines 42-46) in order to
   (A) refute those who disapprove of storytelling as a teaching tool
   (B) introduce an example of desirable objectivity
   (C) suggest that it is similar to the parents' viewpoint
   (D) show that viewpoints are not always predictable
   (E) lend credence to the child's point of view

7. The "paradigm of thought" (line 48) may be described as one that disposes people toward
   (A) cooperating with one another for the common good
   (B) discussing family problems frankly and openly
   (C) resorting to violence when thwarted
   (D) discounting their own experiences
   (E) suing others over trivial matters

8. The process presented by which group interests may be "defeated" (line 60) is one in which
   (A) an exception is made to look like a general rule
   (B) a logical flaw in the group's arguments is attacked
   (C) a crucial legal term is used in a misleading way
   (D) statistical evidence is distorted to the opposition's advantage
   (E) personal arguments are used to discredit group leaders

9. The author presents the idea of wrestling "whole packs of wolfhounds" (lines 61-62) as an example of
   (A) an argument that no lawyer would find plausible
   (B) an event so unusual as to be irrelevant
   (C) something that only a child would attempt
   (D) a morally reprehensible act
   (E) an easier task than studying law

GO ON TO THE NEXT PAGE

10. In the last sentence of the fourth paragraph, the "right" (line 69) is characterized as

(A) central to the concept of democracy

(B) probably not attainable without a constitutional amendment

(C) something that is hardly worth having

(D) something that powerful groups are reluctant to give up

(E) something that most people are not aware that they have

11. The final paragraph suggests that the author probably believes that a law professor's main duty is to

(A) make a highly technical subject exciting to students

(B) jar students out of unexamined assumptions about the study of law

(C) emphasize the importance of clear legal writing

(D) encourage more students from disadvantaged groups to become lawyers

(E) train students in the practical skills they will need in the courtroom

GO ON TO THE NEXT PAGE

Passage 1—Ian Watt (1957)

That Robinson Crusoe is an embodiment of economic individualism hardly needs demonstration. All of Defoe's heroes and heroines pursue
line money, and they pursue it very methodically.
5 Crusoe's bookkeeping conscience, indeed, has established an effective priority over all of his other thoughts and emotions. The various forms of traditional group relationship—family, village, a sense of nationality—all are weakened, as are
10 the competing claims of noneconomic individual achievement and enjoyment, ranging from spiritual salvation to the pleasures of recreation. For the most part, the main characters in Defoe's works either have no family or, like Crusoe, leave
15 it at an early age never to return. Not too much importance can be attached to this fact, since adventure stories demand the absence of conventional social ties. Still, Robinson Crusoe does have a home and family, and he leaves them
20 for the classic reason of economic individualism—that it is necessary to better his condition. "Something fatal in that propension of nature" calls him to the sea and adventure, and against "settling to business" in the station to
25 which he is born—and this despite the elaborate praise that his father heaps upon that condition. Leaving home, improving the lot one was born to, is a vital feature of the individualist pattern of life.
30   Crusoe is not a mere footloose adventurer, and his travels, like his freedom from social ties, are merely somewhat extreme cases of tendencies that are normal in modern society as a whole since, by making the pursuit of gain a primary
35 motive, economic individualism has much increased the mobility of the individual. More specifically, the story of Robinson Crusoe is based on some of the many volumes recounting the exploits of those voyagers who in the
40 sixteenth and seventeenth centuries had assisted the development of capitalism. Defoe's story, then, expresses some of the most important tendencies of the life of his time, and it is this that sets his hero apart from most other travelers
45 in literature. Robinson Crusoe is not, like Ulysses, an unwilling voyager trying to get back to his family and his native land: profit is Crusoe's only vocation, and the whole world is his territory.

Passage 2—James Sutherland (1971)

To Ian Watt, Robinson Crusoe is a characteristic embodiment of economic individualism. "Profit," he assures us, "is Crusoe's only vocation," and "only money—
50 fortune in its modern sense—is a proper cause of deep feeling." Watt therefore claims that Crusoe's motive for disobeying his father and leaving home was to better his economic condition, and that the argument between
55 Crusoe and his parents in the early pages of the book is really a debate "not about filial duty or religion, but about whether going or staying is likely to be the most advantageous course materially: both sides accept the economic
60 motive as primary." We certainly cannot afford to ignore those passages in which Crusoe attributes his misfortunes to an evil influence that drove him into "projects and undertakings beyond my reach, such as are indeed often the
65 ruin of the best heads in business." But surely the emphasis is not on the economic motive as such, but on the willingness to gamble and seek for quick profits beyond what "the nature of the thing permitted." Crusoe's father wished him to
70 take up the law as a profession, and if Crusoe had done so, he would likely have become a very wealthy man indeed. Crusoe's failure to accept his father's choice for him illustrates not economic individualism so much as Crusoe's
75 lack of economic prudence, indifference to a calm and normal bourgeois life, and love of travel.
    Unless we are to say - and we have no right to say it - that Crusoe did not know himself,
80 profit hardly seems to have been his "only vocation." Instead, we are presented with a man who was driven (like so many contemporary Englishmen whom Defoe either admired or was fascinated by) by a kind of compulsion to
85 wander footloose about the world. As if to leave no doubt about his restless desire to travel, Crusoe contrasts himself with his business partner, the very pattern of the economic motive and of what a merchant ought to be, who would
90 have been quite happy "to have gone like a carrier's horse, always to the same inn, backward and forward, provided he could, as be called it, find his account in it." Crusoe, on the other band, was like a rambling boy who never wanted
95 to see again what be had already seen. "My eye," he tells us, "was never satisfied with seeing, was still more desirous of wand'ring and seeing."

GO ON TO THE NEXT PAGE

12. The first paragraph of Passage 1 primarily explores the contrast between
    (A) economics and religion
    (B) business and adventure
    (C) family responsibilities and service to one's country
    (D) Crusoe's sense of duty and his desire for pleasure
    (E) economic individualism and group-oriented behavior

13. Watt refers to "spiritual salvation" (lines 12) as an example of
    (A) something in which Crusoe seemed to show relatively little interest
    (B) the ultimate goal in life for most of Defoe's contemporaries
    (C) an important difference in priorities between Crusoe and his father
    (D) something that Defoe believed was incompatible with the pursuit of pleasure
    (E) a crucial value that Crusoe's family failed to pass on to him

14. Which statement about Crusoe is most consistent with the information in Passage 1?
    (A) He left home because his father forced him to do so.
    (B) He single-mindedly pursued financial gain.
    (C) He was driven to seek pleasure through world travel.
    (D) He had a highly developed sense of morality.
    (E) He was economically imprudent to a fault.

15. In line 88, "pattern" most nearly means
    (A) configuration
    (B) duplicate
    (C) decoration
    (D) perfection
    (E) model

16. It can be inferred that Crusoe's business partner was "like a carrier's horse" (lines 90-91) in that the partner was
    (A) satisfied with a life of routine
    (B) descended from ancestors who were both noble and strong
    (C) strong enough to bear any burden
    (D) stubborn in refusing to change
    (E) loyal to Crusoe to a degree of near servility

17. In context, the phrase "find his account in it" (lines 93) can best be interpreted to mean
    (A) be exposed to new experiences
    (B) make a reasonable profit
    (C) seek adventure around the world
    (D) become popular and well known
    (E) acquire great power and responsibility

18. Crusoe's self-assessment quoted in lines 95-97 of Passage 2 serves primarily to
    (A) reveal that Crusoe did not know himself as well as he thought he did
    (B) suggest that vision entails more than merely seeing
    (C) suggest that, though boylike, Crusoe was more like Ulysses than Watt acknowledges
    (D) provide support for Sutherland's view of Crusoe
    (E) introduce one of Crusoe's traits

19. Both passages indicate that Crusoe's father was
    (A) similar to the parents of main characters in other works by Defoe
    (B) confident that his son would succeed in whatever field he chose
    (C) in favor of more prudent behavior by his son
    (D) opposed to the business partners chosen by his son
    (E) proud of his son's ability to survive comfortably after being shipwrecked

GO ON TO THE NEXT PAGE

20. In both passages, Crusoe's attitude toward the idea of "settling to business" (line 24) like his father is described as

(A) eager anticipation

(B) conventional acceptance

(C) confused uncertainty

(D) moral suspicion

(E) innate opposition

21. The authors of the two passages would apparently agree that Crusoe was

(A) motivated only by personal financial gain

(B) profoundly unaware of his basic nature and calling in life

(C) commendable in his devotion to his family and his business partners

(D) willing to take risks while traveling

(E) responsible for whatever misfortunes befell him in life

22. The primary focus of this pair of passages is

(A) earlier commentaries on Defoe's Robinson Crusoe

(B) the exact nature of the flaws in Crusoe's character

(C) the style and structure of Robinson Crusoe

(D) Defoe's positive portrayal of greed

(E) Crusoe's motivation for leaving home and traveling abroad

STOP

this is the end of the exercise

SAT Critical Reading Exercise #09

25 Questions

Several years ago, my mother began giving me unusual birthday presents. Wrapped in conventional gift paper, they pose as innocent surprises,
line but every one of them is capable of detonating.
5 One recent birthday she must have been feeling especially…What's the word to describe someone who both stirs things up and plays a deep game? Inciter? Igniter? Evocateur? Evocatrix? "Elusive presence" isn't a bad description: always there,
10 but never completely grasped.

Anyway, one recent birthday she presented me with a whole box of these time bombs from the past. Included was the December 1945 issue of LOVE Short Stories. Turning to the table of
15 contents, I saw a story by Kathleen Godwin and another by Charlotte Ashe. Beside the name Charlotte Ashe had been penciled in "Kathleen," as if I might not remember who Charlotte Ashe was.

20 When this issue of the magazine came out, we were living on Charlotte Street, in Asheville. My mother was the most glamorous person I knew. I was not completely sure of her, the way I was sure of my grandmother, who in our household
25 performed the tasks associated with motherhood while Kathleen Godwin went out in all-weather to breadwin for us, and her alter ego Charlotte Ashe concocted the extra romance for two cents a word on the weekends. (One story per author
30 to an issue was the magazine's policy.)

She was more like a magical older sister, my mother, in those impressionable days when the soft clay of my personality was being sculpted. She came and she went (mostly went, it seemed).
35 She dashed off to her various jobs each day, returning after dark in elated exhaustion. She was long since divorced by then, but was playing her cards close to her chest. "When people ask, I say your father's in the service. It's true, he's in the
40 navy. The rest is nobody's business." Many years later, she told me they were also more likely to give jobs to wives of servicemen.

Or widows. After the war ended, she was obliged to kill him off. Once he came up from
45 Florida to visit us, and she made us say he was my uncle. I obeyed, my grandmother obeyed, he obeyed—he was very good-natured about it. I was sorry not to be able to claim him to my friends, because he was so handsome and
50 amusing. But Kathleen was running the show.

His navy letters to her were in that same birthday box of explosives that included the LOVE Short Stories and her master's thesis on masques.
55 These selected birthday offerings, I have begun to understand, are not just a way of cleaning out her closets, or even of doling out to me artifacts from our shared past; they are also an art form. They are cunning little stage sets
60 through which someone who recognizes the "pieces" can then reenter the past and watch reruns of the old masques being played out in those days. Only now, the same someone would have grown out of the emotional dependencies
65 of her childhood (one would hope!) and is therefore ready to appreciate the masques artistically, as interesting embodiments of the human drama…could enter the masques, if she likes, and play the parts of the other actors. And
70 begin to make all sorts of connections about who these people were, and who she is, and what they all had in common.

*Short dramatic entertainments in which performers are in disguise

1. The narrator most likely mentions the "gift paper" (line 3) to suggest
   (A) her poignant memories of special occasions
   (B) the anticipation she feels when receiving these gifts
   (C) the contrast between the appearance and the contents of the packages
   (D) that gift paper is often more interesting than the gifts
   (E) the carelessness with which her mother prepares the gifts

2. The series of one-word questions in the first paragraph primarily reflects
   (A) a child's confusion
   (B) a child's amusement over a game
   (C) the mother's changeable personality
   (D) an adult's resentment at being tricked
   (E) an adult's attempt to find a fitting label

GO ON TO THE NEXT PAGE

3. In lines 26-29 ("Kathleen...weekends."), the narrator emphasizes Kathleen's

(A) sentimentality

(B) gullibility

(C) unconventionality

(D) dependability

(E) generosity

4. The parenthetical comment in lines 29-30 ("(One...policy.)" is most likely included to

(A) provide insight into how fame affected the mother

(B) indicate why the mother used two names

(C) indicate that the narrator had a sudden afterthought

(D) indicate the difficulties in finding subjects to write about

(E) help the narrator refocus on how her mother became a writer

5. The reference to "soft clay" (line 33) serves to

(A) show what a lasting impression the narrator made on others

(B) suggest the versatility of Kathleen's creative talents

(C) suggest Kathleen's unpretentious nature

(D) express the unreliable nature of the narrator's memories

(E) emphasize Kathleen's influence over the narrator

6. The phrase "(one would hope!)" (line 65) expresses the narrator's

(A) need for reassurance about her own talents

(B) optimism about the wisdom of human beings

(C) surprise at her mother's thoughtfulness

(D) uncertainty about having achieved full maturity

(E) confusion over her mother's intentions

7. The primary motive behind Kathleen's gift giving is to

(A) prove that all members of the family had shared in its survival

(B) provide her daughter with a vehicle for experiencing past dramas

(C) help the narrator to understand the challenges a writer faces

(D) set the stage for her future relationship with her daughter

(E) establish a link to the plots of her old stories

8. With which of the following statements would Kathleen Godwin most likely agree?

(A) Sometimes it is necessary to be less than entirely forthright.

(B) Being too innovative jeopardizes personal growth.

(C) Obstacles prevent individuals from achieving their goals.

(D) Individuals should consult others before making career choices.

(E) Traditional social practices should be rigorously respected.

9. The narrator primarily conveys which of the following regarding her mother?

(A) Amused wonderment

(B) Reluctant gratitude

(C) Unresolved insecurity

(D) Casual acceptance

(E) Suppressed resentment

In popular misconception, science is believed to be omnipotent: what it has not yet achieved, it will ultimately achieve. It is believed to be
line infallible; to say of anything that it is scientific is
5 thought to give it the impress of truth, the certainty that brooks no shadow of doubt. Even the packets of breakfast cereals bear witness to this; advertising owes much of its power to the weight carried by a so-called scientific statement;
10 to attribute scientific qualities to some process or other is to stifle criticism. Naturally, the advertiser allows no hint of uncertainty to mar claims dubbed scientific; hence they become indisputable, eternally true, profoundly
15 significant—at least they do in the eyes of those susceptible to the wiles of advertising. The television screen and the loudspeaker are as blatant and even more clamorous. Popular journalism preaches the same gospel: science is
20 certainty; the findings of a research team must be true; mistakes are never made; progress is uninterrupted.
A result of this clamor is the unquestioning acceptance of the belief that science has proven
25 such and such statements to be true; that the findings of science correspond to reality, and are therefore inevitable, indisputable, and final— claims that no scientist would make, claims that no philosopher could admit. There has been
30 another influence that bolsters this belief. This is the view that even some scientists themselves profess to have of their subject, a view that owes its origin to the immense influence of the philosopher Ernst Mach (1838-1916), who
35 developed a conception of science as a convenient summary of experience. The purpose of science, he said, was to save time and trouble in recording observations. Science was the most economical adaptation of thought to facts and was as external
40 to the facts as is a map, a timetable, or a telephone directory. It must not go beyond experience by affirming anything that cannot be tested by experience; above all, scientists must be immediately prepared to drop a theory the
45 moment an observation turns up to conflict with it. Scientists must have absolute respect for observations; they must hold scientific theories in judicial detachment. Scientists must be passionless observers, unbiased by emotion,
50 intellectually cold.
The facts are otherwise. The history of science shows us, again and again, great discoveries made by passionate adherence to ideas forged in the white heat of imagination. It
55 shows us slow construction, brick by patient

brick, of a scientific edifice, often in complete disregard of apparently conflicting evidence. And it shows us bold imaginative leaps made in the dark, in unjustified anticipation of success,
60 only later to find astonishing confirmation.

10. In line 6, the phrase "certainty…doubt" refers to which property popularly ascribed to science?
(A) Provable tenets
(B) Healthy exchange of ideas
(C) Widely held beliefs
(D) Absolute authority
(E) Unswerving dedication

11. The example of the "breakfast cereal" (lines 7) is used to support the view that
(A) responsible manufacturers ensure the quality of their products through scientific research
(B) children increasingly have become the targets of advertising
(C) scientific claims are used to enhance the appeal of certain products
(D) more scientific research is needed in the area of nutrition
(E) the effects of advertising have so far been minimal

12. The word "clamor" (line 23) is used to
(A) characterize the promulgation by the media of a certain image of science
(B) emphasize the author's view that scientific findings can seem confusing
(C) indicate the excitement in the scientific immunity over a dramatic breakthrough
(D) exaggerate the differences of opinion between advertising and journalism
(E) represent the debate that exists about the role of science in everyday matters

GO ON TO THE NEXT PAGE

13. Lines 51-54 ("The…imagination.") indicates that scientific discoveries

(A) do not always depend on ploddingly rational, organized thinking

(B) rarely hold up when they are arrived at frivolously

(C) usually reflect the personality of the scientists who made them

(D) are approached so illogically that scientists work best alone

(E) are made in such states of emotion that researchers overlook important data

14. Which example most accurately illustrates what is being described in "And it shows . . . success" (lines 58-59)?

(A) The excavation of the ruins of an ancient city to search for clay writing tablets

(B) A voyage across an ocean in search of a hypothesized new continent

(C) The microscopic inspection of muscle tissue in order to discover its anatomy

(D) The accidental discovery of a new galaxy while scanning the sky for comets

(E) An experiment in which one group of people is given a thug and another group a placebo

GO ON TO THE NEXT PAGE

Upwards of a billion stars in our galaxy have burnt up their internal energy sources, and so can no longer produce the heat a star needs to oppose *line* the inward force of gravity. These stars, of more 5 than a few solar masses, evolve, in general, much more rapidly than does a star like the Sun. Moreover, it is just these more massive stars whose collapse does not halt at intermediate stages (that is, as white dwarfs or neutron stars). 10 Instead, the collapse continues until a singularity (an infinitely dense concentration of matter) is reached.

It would be wonderful to observe a singularity and obtain direct evidence of the undoubtedly 15 bizarre phenomena that occur near one. Unfortunately in most cases a distant observer cannot see the singularity; outgoing light rays are dragged back by gravity so forcefully that even if they could start out within a few kilometers of 20 the singularity, they would end up in the singularity itself.

15. The author's primary purpose in the passage is to
(A) describe the formation and nature of singularities
(B) explain why large numbers of stars become singularities
(C) compare the characteristics of singularities with those of stars
(D) explain what happens during the stages of a singularity's formation
(E) imply that singularities could be more easily studied if observers could get closer to them

16. The passage suggests which of the following about the Sun?

I. The Sun could evolve to a stage of collapse that is less dense than a singularity

II. In the Sun, the inward force of gravity balanced by the generation of heat.

III. The Sun emits more observable light than does a white dwarf or a neutron star.

(A) I only
(B) III only
(C) I and II only
(D) II and III only
(E) I, II, and III

17. Which of the following sentences would most probably follow the last sentence of the passage?
(A) Thus, a physicist interested in studying phenomena near singularities would necessarily hope to find a singularity with a measurable gravitational field.
(B) Accordingly, physicists to date have been unable to observe directly any singularity.
(C) It is specifically this startling phenomenon that has allowed us to codify the scant information currently available about singularities.'
(D) Moreover, the existence of this extra-ordinary phenomenon is implied in the extensive reports of several physicists.
(E) Although unanticipated, phenomena such as these are consistent with the structure of a singularity.

GO ON TO THE NEXT PAGE

Passage 1 (Corcyra)

Athenians, in this situation, it is right and proper that certain points should be made clear. We have come to ask for help, but we cannot
line claim that this help is due us because of any great
5 services we have done to you in the past or on the basis of any existing alliance. We must therefore convince you first that by giving us this help you will be acting in your own interests, or certainly not against your own interests; and then we must
10 show that our gratitude can be depended on. If on you find our arguments unconvincing, we must not be surprised if our mission fails.

What has happened is that our policy in the past appears to have been against our own
15 present interests and at the same time makes it look inconsistent of us to be asking help from you. We used to think that our neutrality was a wise thing, since it prevented us from being dragged into danger by others' policies; now we
20 see it as a lack of foresight and as a source of weakness. We recognize that if we have nothing but our own national resources, it is impossible for us to survive. It should not be held against us that now we have faced the facts and are
25 reversing our old policy of keeping ourselves to ourselves. There is nothing sinister in our action; we merely recognize that we made a mistake.

If you grant our request, you will find that in many ways it was a good thing that we made it at
30 this particular time. First of all, you will not be helping aggressors, but people who are the victims of aggression. Secondly, we are now in extreme peril, and if you welcome our alliance at this moment you will win our undying gratitude.
35 And then, we are, after you, the greatest naval power in Greece. You would have paid a lot of money and still have been very grateful to have us on your side, is it not, then, an extraordinary stroke of good luck for you (and one that will
40 cause pain among your enemies) to have us coming over voluntarily into your camp, giving ourselves up to you without involving you in any dangers or any expense? It is a situation where we, whom you are helping, will be grateful to
45 you, the world in general will admire you for your generosity, and yourselves will be stronger than you were before. There is scarcely a case in history where all these advantages have been available at the same time, nor has it often
50 happened before that a power looking for an alliance can say to those whose help it asks that it can give as much honor and as much security as it will receive.

Passage 2 (Corinth)

"Wisdom" and "moderation" are the words
55 used by the Corcyraeans in describing their old policy of avoiding alliances. In fact the motives were entirely evil, and there was nothing good about them at all. They wanted no allies because their actions were wrong, and they were
60 ashamed of calling others to witness their own misdoings. The geographical situation of Corcyra gives its inhabitants a independence. The ships of other states are forced to put in to their harbors much more often than Corcyraean
65 ships visit the harbors of other states. So, in cases where a Corcyraean has been guilty of injuring some other national, the Corcyraeans are themselves their own judges, and there is no question of having the case tried by independent
70 judges appointed by treaty. So this neutrality of theirs, which sounds so innocent, was in fact a disguise adopted not to preserve them from having to share in the wrong-doings of others, but in order to give them a perfectly free hand
75 to do wrong themselves, making away with other people's property by force when they are strong enough, cheating them whenever they can manage to do so, and so enjoying their gains without any vestige of shame. Yet if they really
80 were the honorable people they pretend to be, this very independence of theirs would have given them the best possible opportunity for showing their good qualities in the relations of common justice.
85 The right course, surely, is either for you to preserve a strict neutrality or else to join us against them. At least you have treaty obligations toward Corinth, whereas you have never even had a peace treaty with Corcyra.

18. Which of the following best describes the two appeals to the Athenians?

(A) Passage 1 cites historical reasons, while Passage 2 refers to economic ones.

(B) Passage 1 focuses on the Athenians' obligations to neighboring states, while Passage 2 focuses on the dangers to the Athenians if they remain neutral.

(C) Passage 1 stresses the advantages of the alliance to Athens, while Passage 2 stresses Corcyra's untrustworthiness.

(D) Both Passage 1 and Passage 2 appeal to the Athenians' sense of pride.

(E) Both Passage 1 and Passage 2 emphasize a desperate need for assistance.

GO ON TO THE NEXT PAGE

19. The word "mission" (line 12) most nearly means
 (A) religious enterprise
 (B) vocation
 (C) conversion
 (D) diplomatic effort
 (E) group sent to a foreign country

20. The argumentative strategy used by the Corcyraeans in the first paragraph of Passage 1 can best be described as
 (A) ridiculing the opposing claims of the Corinthians
 (B) professing to be frank about Corcyra's own past behavior
 (C) appealing to the Athenians' sympathy for a city with shared cultural ties
 (D) attempting to frighten the Athenians with the consequences of not allying
 (E) attempting to make the Athenians feel guilty

21. The word "sinister" (line 26) means
 (A) ill-omened
 (B) ill-intentioned
 (C) unfavorable
 (D) gruesome
 (E) deadly

22. The word "camp" (line 41) means
 (A) a recreational facility
 (B) a military base
 (C) a temporary dwelling
 (D) a newly built settlement
 (E) a group with common interests

23. The Corinthians argue that the Corcyraeans are able to steal from others because
 (A) their political neutrality enables them to avoid legal sanctions
 (B) their alliance with the Athenians shields them from other states
 (C) their navy is strong enough to intimidate other states
 (D) (ID) there is no system of justice to regulate relations among the states
 (E) there are no trade agreements among neighboring states

24. The Corinthians' recommendations to the Athenians in Passage 2 include all of the following EXCEPT to
 (A) do what is right and proper
 (B) remain neutral
 (C) unite with the Corinthians against the Corcyraeans
 (D) punish a state that has behaved badly
 (E) promote isolationism

25. The sentence "The geographical…other states"(line 61-65) indirectly establishes that Corcyra
 (A) contained major shipping ports
 (B) was located close to its enemies
 (C) often experienced harsh weather
 (D) was very prone to violence
 (E) supplied most of Athens' ships

26. In comparison to the tone of Passage 1, the tone of Passage 2 is more
 (A) detached
 (B) condemnatory
 (C) humble
 (D) descending
 (E) sympathetic

27. Which event, had it occurred, would have been most likely to persuade the Athenians to take sides?
 (A) The Corcyraeans initiated an attack on the Corinthians.
 (B) The Corcyraeans provided proof of a planned Corinthian attack on the Athenians.
 (C) The Corcyraeafls more fully explained their earlier wish to remain unallied.
 (D) The Corinthians solicited the aid of their other allies.
 (E) The Corinthians demonstrated their skill in argumentation more effectively.

GO ON TO THE NEXT PAGE

28. Both passages discuss the
  (A) Corcyraeans' neutrality
  (B) Corcyraeans' desire to dominate the water-
       ways
  (C) Corinthians' alliance with the Athenians
  (D) Athenians' sense of fairness
  (E) Athenians' naval power

29. Which pairing best describes what the
  Corcyraeans and the Corinthians,
  respectively, believe will motivate the
  Athenians to act?
  (A) Greed versus desire for solidarity
  (B) Honor versus desire for vengeance
  (C) Self-interest versus sense of duty
  (D) Survival versus desire for domination
  (E) Power versus fear of regional threat

STOP

SAT Critical Reading Exercise #10
25 Questions

Louis Armstrong happened to be a genius. That particular word has probably been misused more regularly by writers on jazz than by those
line on any of the other arts, with the exception, of
5 course, of film. Virtually every jazz musician able to hold an instrument properly has at one time or another been described as a genius; patently, the description is usually unwarranted.

But if the term means anything at all, it
10 describes Armstrong. I take the word to mean somebody whose accomplishments are beyond analysis. An artist makes relationships; a great artist makes new and surprising ones, showing us how apparently disparate shapes can be fitted
15 together. With ordinary artists, we can discover in their background and character where they drew their material from; with geniuses, we often are unable to determine how they arrived at their startling conclusions. Armstrong's
20 melodic gift was simply astonishing, and there is no explaining where it came from or how it worked its magic. Consider this: Armstrong did not begin to play the cornet until he was fourteen, a relatively late age for a musician to
25 start. Within months, despite the fact that he could not read music, he was leader of his school band. Four years later he was cornetist with the leading jazz band in New Orleans. In another four years, when he was not yet twenty-three, he
30 was acknowledged by his peers to be the best jazz musician alive. By the time he was twenty-eight, he had made a series of records that not only changed the course of jazz history, and therefore the history of Western music as well,
35 but also remains one of the greatest achievements in jazz.

What makes Armstrong's playing so remark-able? First, there is his mastery of his instrument. His tone is warm and full, like
40 honey, in all registers. The way he begins a musical phrase is one of the strongest and cleanest of any jazz trumpeter. Where many jazz brass players employ a smooth and continuous style replete with slurs and half tonguings,
45 Armstrong always introduced a note with a razor-sharp front edge. His vibrato is broad, but slower than the slightly nervous vibrato of Joe Oliver and other New Orleans players. Although his command of the high register would not be
50 considered remarkable today, he was far ahead of

his peers in this respect; in fact, Armstrong brought high-register playing into jazz. In sum, there is no other sound in jazz like Armstrong's. It is immediately identifiable—rich and
55 welcoming. (It should also be noted that Armstrong habitually hits held notes just fractionally flat, and pulls up to true pitch, a procedure, we remember, that Milton Metfessel's phonophotography machine showed
60 to be customary with Black folksingers.)

But ultimately it is his melodic conception that dazzles us. Melody is one of those things in music that is difficult to talk about. Harmony has its theory, which is based on reasoned
65 assumptions; rhythm can be approached almost mathematically; and form has analogues in architecture, drama, and geometry. Yet why is it that a particular fragment of melody moves us? Jazz musicians have often spoken of a player's
70 "telling his story"; drummer Jo Jones claimed that he could hear actual words and indeed whole sentences in Lester Young's saxophone playing. Too, critics of classical music have spoken of the conversational element in melody.
75 It is difficult to know how much to make of this, but in the best music we do catch the feeling that the composer or improvising musician is talking to us, telling us a story, or making an important point about something we
80 can almost, but not quite, put into words. This effect is no doubt created in part by the resemblances that exist between music and speech. A story or lecture is coherent. It proceeds from here to there in logical fashion,
85 and if it is to move us it will contain certain common dramatic devices—that is, it will elaborate on an initial statement; it will contain climaxes, asides and detours, tensions and resolutions; and it will round off with a final
90 statement. The best music behaves in the same way, and it may be these formal similarities that give music the effect of speech.

This conversational element is abundantly present in Armstrong's music. He had a greater
95 sense of form than any other player in the history of jazz. His solos are not made of sequences of melodic fragments related only in mood; they consist of parts contributing to a whole. They have unity—a beginning, middle,
100 and end. Not all the time; Armstrong, like any

player, had his weak moments, and there were times when he was simply showing off. But at his best, that dramatic form is always present.

1. The author implies that, like writers on jazz, film critics
   (A) confer undeserved praise on artists
   (B) place too much emphasis on an artist's background
   (C) are usually more impressed by reputation than by quality
   (D) have too little experience of the art they analyze
   (E) have a tendency to be intolerant of minor flaws

2. In lines "I take...beyond analysis" (lines 10-12), the author is doing which of the following?
   (A) Providing a concrete example
   (B) Defining an important term
   (C) Proving an assertion
   (D) Seeking support from other authorities
   (E) Stating a fact

3. In lines "An artist...conclusions" (lines 12-19), the author differentiates between
   (A) a musician who is trained and one who is not
   (B) Armstrong and other great artists
   (C) what promotes and what holds back true creativity
   (D) an ordinary artist and a genius
   (E) social background and personal character

4. The accomplishments listed in the second paragraph reinforce which of the following ideas?
   (A) Help from his peers served to promote Armstrong's career.
   (B) Armstrong's hard work and perseverance ultimately earned him great rewards.
   (C) Armstrong was only one of the great innovators who changed the course of jazz.
   (D) Armstrong's enormous talent fueled his meteoric rise.
   (E) Armstrong built on a foundation laid by earlier musicians.

5. According to the passage, which of the following is an innovation of Armstrong's?
   (A) A smooth style of playing
   (B) A lack of vibrato
   (C) Playing jazz in the high register
   (D) Playing notes forcefully
   (E) A warm-sounding tone

6. In line 44, "replete with" means
   (A) complicated by
   (B) marred by
   (C) replaced by
   (D) in addition to
   (E) containing many

7. In lines 37-55, the author emphasizes that Armstrong's style of playing was
   (A) rhythmic and precise
   (B) spare yet memorable
   (C) emotionally draining
   (D) highly traditional
   (E) unmistakably characteristic

8. The sentence in parentheses (lines 55-60) serves primarily to
   (A) describe one aspect of Armstrong's playing that the speaker regrets
   (B) link Armstrong's playing to another musical form
   (C) satirize the use of scientific machinery for making aesthetic judgments
   (D) offer a reason for Armstrong's early success
   (E) provide an example of the result of Armstrong's lack of musical training

9. The author states that listeners are most moved by Armstrong's
   (A) harmonic complexity
   (B) melodic sensibility
   (C) rhythmic precision
   (D) well-honed technique
   (E) startling inventiveness

GO ON TO THE NEXT PAGE

10. In the fourth paragraph, the idea of telling a story is used

(A) support for the view that jazz is more emotional than is classical music

(B) an alternative to more scientific theories of harmony

(C) an analogy to explain melodic form

(D) an example of a technique used mainly by Lester Young

(E) an example of a technique that prevents excess emotional expression

11. One element that the author particularly values in the construction of a melody is

(A) logical coherence

(B) elaborate ornamentation

(C) compelling rhythm

(D) implied harmonies

(E) true pitch

12. The sentence "Not all … off" (line 100-102) is unique in the passage in that it

(A) makes no use of concrete detail

(B) is not focused on Armstrong's playing

(C) is not concerned with a theoretical aspect

(D) presents a criticism of Armstrong

(E) offers a personal assessment of Armstrong

13. In the final paragraph, the author emphasizes which of the following characteristics of Armstrong's music?

(A) Its emotional impact

(B) Its purity of tone

(C) Its innovativeness

(D) Its structure

(E) Its origins

GO ON TO THE NEXT PAGE

The education of John Quincy Adams (1767-1848) was the most superb of any of the United States Presidents, and consequently absolutely
line crippling. He was too brilliant, he knew too
5 many languages, books, nations, and political and philosophical systems (having spent many years abroad as United States minister to several European nations) to be able to preside with any grace or tolerance over the dingy republic of his
10 day.

James Monroe, who was President from 1817 to 1825, had appointed Adams as his secretary of state, at that time the country's second most important office and the surest way to the presi-
15 dency. Although Adams was generally admired—certainly he was our best secretary of state—he was not much liked. He was often bored by the politicians he had to deal with. And he himself liked neither political party: "Between
20 both, I see the impossibility of pursuing the dictates of my own conscience."

During this period General Andrew Jackson, who had become a national hero at the Battle of New Orleans in 1815, was on the rampage in
25 Spanish Florida. Jackson had interpreted the government's orders to punish some Seminole tribes as a license for invasion of foreign territory, conquest, and military executions. These capers appealed hugely to the electorate and, in the
30 presidential election of 1824, Jackson received 99 electoral college votes; Adams received 84, William H. Crawford, 41; Speaker of the House Henry Clay, 37. Since no candidate had the required majority, the election went to the House
35 of Representatives for decision. Unable to win himself, Clay gave his support to Adams, who became President in February 1825. Adams then appointed Clay as secretary of state.

Jackson and his allies were rightly indignant
40 at losing an election in which Jackson had, after all received the most votes; they regarded the alliance between Adams and Clay as corrupt.

Adams' administration proved to be a disaster. He was hopeless when it came to the
45 greasy art of survival in United States politics. He had great plans to foster education, science, commerce, and civil service reform; but his projects were too rigorous and too unpolitical to be accepted. For instance, the United States had
50 not one astronomical station, while in Europe there were 130 "lighthouses of the sky." This happy phrase of Adams was received with perfect derision by the mob. It was plain that Adams was not suited to lead a democracy. He was too
55 intelligent, too unyielding, too tactless. Needless

to say, Jackson swamped him in the 1828 election. The Jackson slogan was prophetic of the era: "Jackson who can fight, and Adams who can write."
60 But Adams saw things more clearly than did most of the mob-pleasing politicians. In 1837, after President Jackson's brutal treatment of the Creeks and Cherokees, Adams wrote: "We have done more harm to the Indians since
65 our Revolution than had been done to them by the French and English… These are crying sins for which we are answerable before a higher Jurisdiction."

14. The author most likely believes that Adams would have been a more popular President if he had

(A) deferred to Clay's judgment
(B) been more openly loyal to his party
(C) been better informed about the living conditions of ordinary Americans
(D) implemented projects to aid Native Americans
(E) sacrificed his integrity to political expediency

15. The author uses "capers" (line 27) to refer to
(A) unsuccessful escapades
(B) immoral military acts
(C) government orders
(D) legislative compromises
(E) voter reactions

16. It can be inferred from the passage that Adams agreed to appoint Clay to the post of secretary of state in order to
(A) avoid having to appoint Jackson to the post
(B) satisfy the indignant electorate
(C) repay Clay for helping him obtain the necessary House votes
(D) win back the favor of his party after a divisive campaign
(E) counteract his reputation for inaction by making a decisive move

GO ON TO THE NEXT PAGE

17. Which of the following best expresses the author's opinion of the voters during the time of the Adams presidency?

(A) They were easily misled by high-sounding speeches.

(B) They were easily fooled by corrupt politicians.

(C) They were shrewd in judgment despite a lack of sophistication.

(D) They were enthusiastic about new technologies and innovative ideas.

(E) They were easily impressed by military success.

18. The word "perfect" (line 52) means

(A) excellent

(B) complete

(C) blameless

(D) mature

(E) pristine

GO ON TO THE NEXT PAGE

Since 1953, many experimental attempts to synthesize the chemical constituents of life under "Primitive Faith conditions" have been performed, but none of these experiments has produced anything approaching the complexity of the simplest organism. They have demonstrated, however, that a variety of the complex molecules currently making up living organisms could have been present in the early ocean and atmosphere, with only one limitation: such molecules are synthesized far less readily when oxygen-containing compounds dominate the atmosphere, Therefore some scientists postulate that the Earth's earliest atmosphere, unlike that of today, was dominated by hydrogen, methane, and ammonia.

From these studies, scientists have concluded that the surface of the primitive Earth was covered with oceans containing the molecules fundamental to life. Although, at present, scientists cannot explain how these relatively small molecules combined to produce larger, more complex molecules, some scientists have precipitously ventured hypotheses that attempt to explain the development, from these larger molecules, of the earliest self-duplicating organisms.

19. According to the passage, which of the following can be inferred about the process by which the chemical constituents of life were synthesized under primitive Earth conditions?

(A) The synthesis is unlikely to occur under current atmospheric conditions.

(B) The synthesis is common in modem laboratories.

(C) The synthesis occurs more readily in the atmosphere than in the ocean.

(D) The synthesis easily produces the most complex organic molecules.

(E) The synthesis is accelerated by the presence of oxygen-containing compounds.

20. The primary purpose of the passage is to

(A) point out that theories about how life developed on Earth have changed little since 1953

(B) warn of increasing levels of hydrogen, methane, and ammonia in the Earth's atmosphere

(C) describe the development since 1953 of some scientists' understanding of how life began on Earth

(D) demonstrate that the synthesis of life in the laboratory is too difficult for modem technology

(E) describe how primitive atmospheric conditions produced the complex molecules of living organisms

21. It can be inferred from the passage that "some scientists" assume which of the following concerning "larger, more complex molecules" (lines 22-23)?

(A) The earliest atmosphere was formed primarily of these molecules.

(B) Chemical processes involving these molecules proceeded much more slowly under primitive Earth conditions.

(C) The presence of these molecules would necessarily precede the existence of simple organisms.

(D) Experimental techniques will never be sufficiently sophisticated to produce in the laboratory simple organisms from these chemical constituents.

(E) Explanations could easily be developed to explain how simple molecules combined to form these more complex ones.

22. The author's reaction to the attempts that have been made to explain the development of the first self-duplicating organisms can best be described as one of

(A) enthusiasm
(B) expectation
(C) dismay
(D) skepticism
(E) antipathy

STOP

this is the end of the exercise

SAT Writing Exercise #11
25 Questions

Widely condemned as a false or pseudo sport, televised professional wrestling constantly challenges the ideal of free and open competition. In a sport without statistics, the win-loss percentage of a wrestling star is not relevant knowledge. In wrestling, it's how one plays the game that truly counts: a hero in defeat is still heroic; a villain triumphant is still to be despised. And in this privileging of character at the expense of authenticity, professional wrestling lampoons naïve ideals associated with the winner-take-all justice of the competition ethic. Professional wrestling champions a much richer brand of justice—a justice derived from character, not conquest.

People don't bet on the outcome of professional wrestling matches, obviously, because wrestling requires the suspension of disbelief of a moviegoer, not a gambler. However, in the United States, the wrestling fan is typically ridiculed as a gullible and stupid creature, while the gambler is frequently honored as dating and clever. Assuming that some wrestling fans actually believe matches are authentic (and there is reason to believe most do not), one wonders who is the more deceived: the wrestling fan who believes in the spectacle of good versus evil, or the gambler who trusts the arbitrary amoral order of legitimate spectator sports.

A subversive sport form, professional wrestling completely calls into question assumptions about rules and rule enforcement attached to the ideal of competition. In professional wrestling, the rules are obviously and painfully arbitrary and unevenly enforced; they generally work in favor of the villain and against the hero. The referee, though usually sincere and well intentioned, is frequently distracted and often blind to villainous violations the partisan crowd can easily spot. Typically, the hero respects the rules until it becomes obvious to all that obedience will ultimately result in defeat; then, in a wonderful eruption of chaos, the hero takes the law into his own hands—and, sometimes, justice emerges from the fray. In professional wrestling, justice isn't handed down from above. Instead, justice results from individual action and an eventual disregard of arbitrary rules impeding vindication. In wrestling as in life, law and order do not equal justice and equality.

Although now located on television's fringes, professional wrestling was a prime-time spectacle during the 1950's. In those early years of broadcast

television, a wrestler named Gorgeous George became a pivotal figure in television's world of sports. George's performance emphasized character more than athletic excellence. His success did not go unnoticed by performers in more legitimate sports. indeed, George provided inspiration to one of the greatest sports stars of modern times— professional heavyweight-boxing champion Muhammad Au.

According to Ali, a performance by Gorgeous George was an epiphanic experience for him—one that illuminated the subtle dynamics of hype:

Gorgeous George came into the television studio. He made his entrance combing his long blond hair like a movie idol. "Look at my velvet skin," he purred. "Look at my pretty hair. if that bum messes up my hair tomorrow night, I'll annihilate him! I want all of you out there to come to the Sports Palace early because I'm gonna mop the floor with this bum. If he beats me, I'll cut off my golden hair and throw the hair out in the audience and go bald." The next night instead of resting for my fight, I was at the Sports Palace along with a standing-room-only crowd, wanting to see what would happen to George. I saw how this strategy had worked.

By observing George, All arrived at a key element of television stardom: personality, character, and flamboyance are as interesting to audiences and as crucial to media stardom as competitive superiority.

GO ON TO THE NEXT PAGE

1. The author uses the quotation at the beginning of the passage to emphasize which of the following?
   (A) Religious insights are an important means of arriving at the truth.
   (B) Skill and ability are not always rewarded.
   (C) Time is on the side of those who wait patiently for change.
   (D) Trickery and guile are important to achieving success.
   (E) The values represented by so-called heroes need to be examined carefully.

2. In line 13, the word "champions" most nearly means
   (A) triumphs (B) overpowers (C) rescues
   (D) engages (E) espouses

3. The author considers professional wrestling a "subversive sport" (line 31) because
   (A) it is extremely popular, even though many critics question its validity
   (B) it seems to question the underlying assumptions of most sports
   (C) it offers an escape from the dreary world of day-to-day living
   (D) the villain occasionally prospers, even though the fans are cheering for the hero
   (E) the athletic skills of professional wrestlers are actually much greater than most people realize

4. The hero's initial respect for the rules and subsequent disregard of them most nearly suggests that
   (A) the rules have no emotional, psychological, or practical relevance
   (B) by breaking the rules all contestants can make certain that justice will be done
   (C) the rules apply only to the villain, whereas the hero is free to disregard them
   (D) rules should be enforced so the spectator can enjoy an orderly match
   (E) obeying the rules does not guarantee that justice will be done

5. In lines 46-52 of the passage, the comparison between professional wrestling and life states that
   (A) wrestling is often more realistic than life
   (B) wrestling is amusing, while life is serious
   (C) life is not always fair
   (D) the so-called rules prevent the individual from acting
   (E) the so-called rules aid only the powerful

6. According to the author, professional wrestling most nearly resembles
   (A) boxing   (B) football   (C) war
   (D) theater   (E) gambling

7. In line 85-86, "this strategy" refers to
   (A) the techniques Gorgeous George used to defeat his opponent
   (B) the way in which Gorgeous George used his television appearance to thaw a crowd to his match
   (C) Gorgeous George's personal invitation to Muhammad AU to attend the match at the Sports Palace
   (D) Gorgeous George's frank admission that he might lose at the Sports Palace
   (E) Gorgeous George's delight in portraying himself as a monstrous villain

8. The author uses the example of Gorgeous George primarily to
   (A) add humor to the piece
   (B) mock old-style wrestling matches
   (C) contrast his career with that of Ali
   (D) emphasize the significance of showmanship
   (E) suggest that the hero and villain are sometimes difficult to distinguish

9. What did Muhammad Ali learn from Gorgeous George?
   (A) how to dominate one's opponents
   (B) the importance of rest between matches
   (C) Outrageous behavior attracts the attention of fans and the media.
   (D) Personal vanity can tarnish one's image.
   (E) Only demonstrations of athletic ability can rouse an audience.

GO ON TO THE NEXT PAGE

Passage 1

The curriculum in our all-girls' high school was inherited from Great Britain, and consequently it was utterly untouched by
line progressive notions in education. We read
5 British poetry, novels, and short stories. We might have been in the English countryside for all the attention we paid to Australian literature. It did not count. We, for our part, dutifully learned Shakespeare's imagery drawn from the
10 English landscape. We memorized Keats's "Ode to Autumn" or Shelley's "To a Skylark" without ever having seen the progression of seasons and the natural world they referred to. This gave us the impression that great poetry and fiction were
15 written by and about people and places far distant from Australia. As for landscape, we learned by implication that ours was ugly, because it deviated totally from the landscape of Britain.
20   Much about our way of life symbolized the colonial mentality. Its signs were visible in the maps on our classroom walls, extended depictions of the globe with much of Africa, all of the Indian subcontinent, parts of Southeast
25 Asia, and half of North America colored the bright red of the British Empire. Our uniforms, copies of those of English schools, indicated that we were only partially at home in our environment. We wore tunics, blouses, flannel
30 blazers, cotton stockings, hats, and gloves. No one paused to think that gloves and blazers had a function in damp English springs that they lacked entirely in our blazing summers.
    This kind of education can have interesting
35 effects, even years later, on a student's perception of reality. At college, when I read Engels' The Origin of the Family, Private Property and the State, I treated its discussion of women's roles in modern society as though it were about some
40 distant and different species rather than my own sex. I had unthinkingly taken on the identity of the male writer and intellect present in everything that I read and did not take in emotionally that the subordination Engels wrote about applied to me.

Passage 2
45

As a child, I didn't know that African American people wrote books. I did not read for pleasure. When I was sixteen I got a job shelving books for the public library. One day when went
50 to put a book away, I saw James Baldwin's face staring up at me. "Who in the world is this?" I wondered. I remember feeling embarrassed and did not read Baldwin's[1] book because I was too afraid. I couldn't imagine that he'd have
55 anything better or different to say than Henry Thoreau, Ernest Hemingway, William Faulkner, and a horde of other mostly White male writers that I had been introduced to in Literature 101 in high school. Not only had
60 there not been any African American authors included in any of those textbooks, but I'd never been given a clue that if we did have anything important to say, somebody would actually publish it. Needless to say, I was not just naïve,
65 but had not yet acquired an ounce of Black pride.
    And then things changed.
    It wasn't until after Malcolm X had been assassinated that I found out who he was. I
70 know I should be embarrassed, but I'm not. I read his autobiography and it literally changed my life. First and foremost, I realized that it was ridiculous to be ashamed of being Black, that we had a history and much to be proud of. I began
75 to appreciate our strength as a people. I started thinking about my role in the world and not just on my street. I started thinking —thinking about things I'd never thought about before— and the thinking turned into questions. But I
80 had more questions than answers.
    So I went to college. When I looked through the catalog and saw a class called Afro-American Literature, I signed up and couldn't wait for the first day of class. Did we really have
85 enough writers to warrant an entire class? I couldn't believe the rush I felt once I discovered Langston Hughes, Zora Neale Hurston, Ralph Ellison, Jean Toomer, Richard Wright, and Ann Petry. I'm surprised that I didn't need
90 glasses by the end of the semester. My world opened up. I accumulated and gained a totally new insight about, and perception of, our lives as Black people, as if I had been an outsider and was finally let in. To discover that our lives held
95 as much significance and importance as those of our White counterparts was more than gratifying, it was exhilarating. Not only had we lived diverse, interesting, provocative, and relentless lives, but during, though, and as a result of all
100 these painful experiences, some folks had taken the time to write it down.

[1] James Baldwin (1924-1987) was a prominent African
    American writer,

[2] Malcom X (1925-1965) was a prominent Black Muslim leader.

GO ON TO THE NEXT PAGE

10. In Passage 1, what is the author's main point about the attention given to the English landscape in her high school?

(A) It concentrated too much on a literary rather than a scientific approach.

(B) It implied that the students' own environment was less inspiring.

(C) Like the rest of the course content, it failed to interest the students.

(D) It developed in the students a permanent appreciation for English ideas of beauty.

(E) It encouraged students to appreciate English literature through English landscape paintings.

11. In Passage 1, the "colonial mentality" (line 21) is characterized as

(A) a necessary evil

(B) an inescapable presence

(C) a source of enlightenment

(D) a means to social advantage

(E) a welcome unifier of diverse peoples

12. The phrase "interesting effects" (line 34-35) most directly refers to

(A) psychological depression

(B) social snobbery

(C) a lack of self-knowledge

(D) a distrust of new ideas

(E) an opposition to injustice

13. The author of Passage 2 recounts her discovery at age sixteen of James Baldwin's book primarily to

(A) convey her pleasure in encountering a new African American author

(B) reveal her annoyance at the library's shortage of good books

(C) indicate her lack of familiarity with African American literature

(D) demonstrate that she was not interested in African American writers

(E) suggest that she was not prepared to read adult literature

14. In Passage 2, the author's initial reaction to Baldwin's picture (lines 45-47) indicates that

(A) people read with more attention when interested in the subject matter

(B) young people are more sophisticated than many adults think

(C) confronting new information can shake a person's sense of security

(D) adolescents are often rebellious against their elders' ideas

(E) adolescents generally exhibit little fear of the unknown

15. The author of Passage 2 refers to Thoreau, Hemingway, and Faulkner (lines 54-55) in making the point that

(A) she was interested in going to college

(B) she enjoyed literature more than other subjects

(C) the American literary tradition was not inferior to other literary traditions

(D) she thought everything of significance had already been said by White authors

(E) it was difficult for African American authors to get published

16. In the sentence beginning "I know I should…" (lines 69), the author indicates that she might once have been criticized for her

(A) lack of awareness of contemporary political issues

(B) failure to read novels by African American authors

(C) dismissal of authors studied in high school

(D) inability to take pleasure in reading

(E) preoccupation with ideas rather than experiences

17. Both passages recount educational experiences that are characterized by
(A) a discovery of the joys of reading
(B) a rebellion against obsolete ideas
(C) the study of complex but neglected literatures
(D) teachers who had no regard for students' physical comfort
(E) curricula that contained significant omissions

GO ON TO THE NEXT PAGE

18. A significant difference between the two passages is that Passage 1

(A) describes the effects of an upbringing, while Passage 2 describes the effects as well as a significant change

(B) focuses on an individual transformation, while Passage 2 focuses on relationships between groups of people

(C) emphasizes the strengths of a classical education, while Passage 2 criticizes its shortcomings

(D) examines curricular inadequacies, while Passage 2 traces their causes through history

(E) discusses a problem in high school education, while Passage 2 discusses a problem at the college level

19. Both passages make the point that a good education is one that

(A) provides students with both political and literary works to read

(B) stresses real-world experience over reading

(C) incorporates a diversity of viewpoints

(D) allows a student to discover reading material independently

(E) makes use of natural imagery

GO ON TO THE NEXT PAGE

In *Raisin in the* Sun, Lorraine Hansberry does not reject integration or the economic and moral promise of the American dream; rather, she
line remains loyal to this dream while looking,
5 realistically, at its incomplete realization. Once we recognize this dual vision, we can accept the play's ironic nuances as deliberate social commentaries by Hansberry rather than as the "unintentional" irony that Bigsby attributes to *the* work. Indeed, a
10 curiously persistent refusal to credit Hansberry with a capacity for intentional irony has led some critics to interpret the play's thematic conflicts as mere confusion, contradiction, or eclecticism. Isaacs, for example, cannot easily reconcile
15 Hansberry's intense concern for her race with her ideal of human reconciliation. But the play's complex view of Black self-esteem and human solidarity as compatible is no more "contradictory" than Du Bois' famous, well-considered ideal of
20 ethnic self-awareness coexisting with human unity, or Fanon's emphasis on an ideal internationalism' that also accommodates national identities and roles.

20. The author's primary purpose in this passage is t
(A) explain some critics' refusal to consider *Raisin in the Sun* a deliberately ironic play
(B) suggest that ironic nuances ally *Raisin in the Sun* with Du Bois' and Fanon's writings
(C) analyze the fundamental dramatic conflicts in Raisin in the Sun
(D) justify the inclusion of contradictory elements in *Raisin in the Sun*
(E) affirm the thematic coherence underlying *Raisin in the Sun*

21. It can be inferred from the passage that the author believes which of the following about Hansberry's use of irony in *Raisin* in *the Sun?*
(A) It derives from Hansberry's eclectic approach to dramatic structure.
(B) It is justified by Hansberry's loyalty to a favorable depiction of American life.
(C) It is influenced by the themes of works by Du Bois and Fanon.
(D) It is more consistent with Hansberry's concern for Black Americans than with her ideal of human reconciliation.
(E) It reflects Hansberry's reservations about the extent to which the American dream has been realized.

22. In which of the following does the author of the passage reinforce his criticism of responses such as Isaacs' to *Raisin in the Sun?*
(A) The statement that Hansberry is "loyal" to the American dream
(B) The description of Hansberry's concern for Black Americans as "intense"
(C) The assertion that Hansberry is concerned with "human solidarity"
(D) The description of Du Bois' ideal as "well-considered"
(E) The description of Fanon's internationalism as "ideal"

23. The author of the passage would probably consider which of the following judgments to be most similar to the reasoning of critics?
(A) The world is certainly flat; therefore, the person proposing to sail around it is unquestionably foolhardy.
(B) Radioactivity cannot be directly perceived; therefore, a scientist could not possibly control it in a laboratory.
(C) The painter of this picture could not intend it to be funny; therefore, its humor must result from a lack of skill.
(D) Traditional social mores are beneficial to culture; therefore, anyone who deviates from them acts destructively.
(E) Filmmakers who produce documentaries deal exclusively with facts; therefore, a filmmaker who reinterprets particular events is misleading us.

STOP
this is the end of the exercise

SAT Writing Exercise #12

25 Questions

It may be that as many as 38,000 Greenland right whales were killed in the Davis Strait fishery during the early part of the nineteenth century, largely by the British fleet. A sound estimate of the size of that population today is 200. What happened in the heyday of Arctic whaling represents in microcosm the large-scale advance of nonindigenous cultures into the Arctic. It is a disquieting reminder that the modern Arctic industries—oil, gas, and mineral extraction— might be embarked on a course as disastrously short-lived as that of the whaling industry. Our natural histories of this region 150 years later are still cursory and unintegrated. This time around, however, the element at greatest risk is not the whale but the coherent vision of the indigenous people. Only indigenous groups such as the Inuit, the Yupik, the Inupiat, and others can provide a sustained narrative of human relationships with the Arctic landscape independent of the desire to control or possess. Most non-indigenous views lack historical depth and are still largely innocent of what is obscure and subtle there.

Conceptions of the Arctic vary markedly. Its future disposition is not viewed in the same way by a Montreal attorney working on the settlement of Inuit land claims, by a Swedish naval architect designing an ice-breaking tanker, by an *inuk* pulling on his fishnets at the mouth of the Hayes River, by a biologist watching a caribou herd encounter the trans-Alaska pipeline, or by a tourist bound for a caviar-and-champagne luncheon at the North Pole. Such a variety of human views and interests in one particular part of the planet is not new; what is new, and troubling for people who, like me, live in the Temperate Zone, is a difference in the land itself, which changes the very nature of these considerations. In the Temperate Zone we are accustomed to dealing with landscapes that can easily accommodate opposing views, the long growing seasons, mild temperatures, great variety of creatures, and moderate rainfall make up for much human abuse. Arctic ecosystems are different—they are far more vulnerable ecologically to attempts to "accommodate both sides." Of concern in the North, then, is the impatience with which reconciliation and compromise are now sought.

As Temperate Zone people, we have long been ill-disposed toward deserts and expanses of tundra and ice. They have been wastelands for us; historically we have not cared at all what happened in them or to them. I am inclined to think, however, that their value will one day prove to be inestimable to us. Because the regimes of light and time in the Arctic are so different from what we are used to, this landscape is able to expose in startling ways the complacency of our thoughts about land in general. The unfamiliar rhythms of the Arctic, the fundamental strangeness of a land in which the sun does not set on a summer evening, point up the narrow impetuosity of the schedules of industrialized nations. The periodically frozen Arctic Ocean is at present an insurmountable impediment to timely shipping. This land, for some, is irritatingly and uncharacteristically uncooperative. To devise a plan for increased human activity in the Arctic requires a more particularized under-standing of the land itself—not a more refined mathematical knowledge but a deeper under-standing of its essence, as if it were, itself, another civilization with which we had to reach an accord.

Once in winter I was far out on the sea ice north of Melville Island in the high Arctic observing a crew drilling- for oil. I saw a seal surface at some hourless moment of the day in a moon pool, the open water directly underneath the drilling platform. The seal and I regarded each other in absolute stillness, I in my parka, arrested in the middle of an errand, the seal in the motionless water, its dark brown eyes glistening in its gray, catlike head. Curiosity held it. What held me was: how far out on the edge of the world I am-A movement of my head shifted the hood of my parka slightly, and the seal was gone in an explosion of water. Its eyes had been enormous. I walked to the edge of the moon pool and stared into the dark ocean. To contemplate what people are doing out here and ignore the universe of the seal, to consider human quest and plight and not know the land, I thought, seemed fatal—not perhaps for tomorrow, or next year, but at some point in the future of our relationship with the Arctic.

GO ON TO THE NEXT PAGE

1. In lines 1-4 the author refers to events in the Davis Strait fishery in order to provide

   (A) details about the daily operations of the British whaling fleet
   (B) an example of the ability of some species to survive human predation
   (C) a reason why whales should not be hunted or killed
   (D) an illustration of shortsighted human activity in the Arctic
   (E) estimates of Arctic whale populations whose accuracy should be challenged

2. The author discusses the nineteenth-century Arctic whaling industry in order to

   (A) correct a misconception
   (B) provide a warning
   (C) reconcile two points of view
   (D) introduce an appealing model from history
   (E) furnish a contrast to twentieth-century Arctic industries

3. The author suggests that "modern Arctic industries" (line 10) seem likely to

   (A) employ large numbers of indigenous Arctic peoples
   (B) be less successful economically than was the whaling industry
   (C) do harm regardless of their intentions
   (D) insist that unique features of the Arctic be recorded and studied
   (E) cause international conflicts

4. The reference to "Our natural histories" of the Arctic (line 13) suggests that

   (A) current versions are superior to those of the preceding century
   (B) collaborations between indigenous people and nonindigenous people have resulted in comprehensive studies of the region
   (C) modern Arctic industries are not likely to repeat mistakes made in earlier times
   (D) sustained narratives of indigenous Arctic dwellers have successfully substituted for more format studies
   (E) the region has not yet been investigated enough to allow nonindigenous people to understand it

5. In line 24, "innocent of" most nearly means

   (A) not harmful to
   (B) not guilty of
   (C) uncorrupted by
   (D) optimistic about
   (E) oblivious to

6. Why is the Arctic unable to "accommodate opposing views" (line 42-43) as easily as does the Temperate Zone?

   (A) Indigenous people and nonindigenous people have competing land claims in the Arctic.
   (B) There are fewer people and more desertlike expanses of land in the Arctic.
   (C) Industrialized nations have widely differing ideas of how to develop the Arctic.
   (D) Arctic ecosystems are more fragile than those of the Temperate Zone.
   (E) The Arctic has been subjected to more human abuse than the Temperate Zone has.

7. Which of the following would the author most likely believe about the process of "reconciliation and compromise" (line 50) in the Arctic?

   (A) It will probably be too expensive to be practical.
   (B) It is undesirable if pursued according to Temperate Zone customs.
   (C) It has been the direct cause of past environmental problems.
   (D) It will be effective only if implemented immediately.
   (E) It provides an opportunity to avoid mistakes made in the Temperate Zone.

8. The author states that Temperate Zone people view the uses made of "expanses of tundra and ice" (line 53) with

   (A) complete indifference
   (B) uncertainty and confusion
   (C) aesthetic appreciation
   (D) a sense of personal entitlement
   (E) an eye toward the future

GO ON TO THE NEXT PAGE

9. The author mentions that "the sun does not set on a summer evening" (lines 64-65) in order to

(A) provide a contrast with bitterly cold Arctic nights

(B) allude to an important symbol in indigenous Arctic cultures

(C) illustrate differences between the Arctic and other geographic regions

(D) explain why Temperate Zone people become complacent when visiting the Arctic

(E) suggest why the Arctic Ocean remains frozen during the winter

10. The author mentions "another sort of civilization" (lines 75- 76) in order to suggest the

(A) way in which technology has changed indigenous Arctic cultures

(B) way in which the land should be treated by people

(C) way outsiders are perceived by indigenous people

(D) extent to which the Arctic transforms visitors

(E) extent of the conflict between industry and science

11. The encounter with the seat in the fourth paragraph makes the author keenly aware of the

(A) helplessness of sea creatures

(B) human appetite for destruction

(C) scenic beauty of the Arctic sea ice

(D) mysterious unfamiliarity of the Arctic environment

(E) financial value of natural resources in the Arctic

12. The description of what occurred on the oil-drilling platform in the last paragraph serves chiefly to provide

(A) an example of the role of modern industry in the Arctic

(B) an illustration of an undesirable confrontation in the Arctic

(C) a personal and concrete example of the author's argument

(D) a solution to the problems discussed previously by the author

(E) rebuttal to the views summarized previously by the author

13. In lines 93-94, the phrase "universe of the seal" refers to the

(A) natural world of the Arctic

(B) area north of Melville Island

(C) tradictory nature of aquatic mammals

(D) moon pool beneath the Arctic drilling platform

(E) interrelated ecosystems of the Earth as a whole

GO ON TO THE NEXT PAGE

     In fourth grade I embarked upon a grandiose reading program. "Give me the names of important books," I would say to startled

line teachers. They soon found out that I had in mind

5 "adult books." I ignored their suggestion of anything I suspected was written for children. And whatever I read, I read for extra credit. Each time I finished a book, I reported the achievement to a teacher and basked in the praise

10 my effort earned, Despite my best efforts, however, there seemed to be more and more books I needed to read. At the library I would literally tremble as I came upon whole shelves of books I hadn't read. So I read and I read and I

15 read. Librarians who initially frowned when I checked out the maximum ten books at a time started saving books they thought I might like. Teachers would say to the rest of the class, "I only wish that the rest of you took reading as

20 seriously as Richard obviously does."

     But at home I would hear my mother, who was not an educated woman, wondering, "What do you see in your books?" (Was reading a hobby like her knitting? Was so much reading even

25 healthy for a boy? Was it a sign of "brains"? Or was it just a convenient excuse for not helping around the house on Saturday mornings?) Always, "What do you see?"

     What did I see in my books? I had the idea

30 that they were crucial for my academic success, though I couldn't have said exactly how or why. In the sixth grade I simply concluded that what gave a book its value was some major idea or theme it contained. If that core essence could be

35 mined and memorized, I would become learned like my teachers. I decided to record in a notebook the themes of the books that I read. After reading Robinson Crusoe, I wrote that its theme was "the value of learning to live by

40 oneself." When I completed *Wuthering Heights*, I noted the danger of "letting emotions get out of control." Rereading these brief moralistic appraisals usually left me disheartened. I couldn't believe that they were really the source of

45 reading's value. But for many more years, they constituted the only means I had as, of describing to myself the educational value of books.

     In spite of my earnestness, I found reading a

50 pleasurable activity, I came to enjoy the lonely good company of books. Early on weekday mornings, I'd read in my bed. I'd feel a mysterious comfort then, reading in the dawn quiet. On weekends I'd go to the public library to

55 read, surrounded by old men and women. Or, if the weather was fine, I would take my books to the park and read in the shade of a tree.

     I also had favorite writers. But often those writers I enjoyed most I was least able to value.

60 When I read William Saroyan's The Human Comedy, I was immediately pleased by the narrator's warmth and the charm of his story. But as quickly I became suspicious. A book so enjoyable to read couldn't be very "important."

65 Another summer I determined to read all the novels of Dickens. Reading his fat novels, I loved the feeling I got—after the first hundred pages—of being at home in a fictional world where I knew the names of the characters and

70 cared about what was going to happen to them. And it bothered me that I was forced away at the conclusion, when the fiction closed tight, like a fortune-teller's fist—the futures of all the major characters neatly resolved. I never knew

75 how to take such feelings seriously, however. Nor did I suspect that these experiences could be part of a novel's meaning. Still, there were pleasures to sustain me after I'd finished my books. Carrying a volume back to the library, I

80 would be pleased by its weight. I'd run my fingers along the edges of the pages and marvel at the breadth of my achievement. Around my room, growing stacks of paperback books reinforced my assurance.

85   I entered high school having read hundreds of books. My habit of reading made me a confident speaker and writer of English and in various ways, books brought me academic success as I hoped they would. But I was not a

90 good reader. Merely bookish, I lacked a point of view when I read. Rather, I read to acquire a point of view. I vacuumed books for epigrams, scraps of information, ideas, themes—anything to fill the hollow within me and make me feel

95 educated. When one of my teachers suggested to his drowsy tenth-grade English class that a person could not have a "complicated idea" until that person had read at least two thousand books. I heard the remark without detecting

100 either its irony or its very complicated truth.

GO ON TO THE NEXT PAGE

14. The author uses the phrase "embarked upon" (line 1) to emphasize which of the following?

(A) The transient nature of the fictional world

(B) His commitment to an exploration of the world of books

(C) His realization that literature can change one's outlook

(D) The fear he feels about leaving the familiar world of his parents

(E) His sense of isolation from his classmates

15. The author initially believed "important books" (lines 2-3) to be books that

(A) did not contain any references to children

(B) had been praised by critics

(C) were recommended by his mother

(D) were directed toward a mature audience

(E) were written by renowned authors

16. The author would "literally tremble" (lines 12-13) at the library because he

(A) did not know which books were important

(B) was intimidated by the librarians

(C) felt a personal connection to all the authors represented there

(D) was worried that he would never be able to read all the books

(E) was excited by the idea of being allowed to borrow books

17. The author's purpose in mentioning that some of the librarians "frowned" (line 15) is likely to

(A) indicate that his reading project was met with some skepticism at first

(B) imply that they thought children should not check out books written for adults

(C) suggest that what he was doing was wrong

(D) explain why he was so frightened at the library

(E) characterize librarians who favor intellectual children

18. The mother's attitude toward the boy's interest in reading (lines 21-28) can be best described as

(A) exasperation

(B) indignation

(C) perplexity

(D) sympathy

(E) admiration

19. In line 35, "mined" most nearly means

(A) followed   (B) dugout   (C) entrenched

(D) tunneled   (E) blown up

20. The author states that he was "disheartened" (line 43) because

(A) he was unable to find books that were of lasting value

(B) the tragic themes of the books he was reading were depressing to him

(C) his ability to write descriptions was lagging behind his reading ability

(D) his teachers were not giving him as much encouragement as he needed

(E) his desire for meaning was not being met by the themes that he wrote down

21. The fourth paragraph describes the author as

(A) comfortable only in the company of fellow scholars

(B) dissatisfied with the rate at which his reading progressed

(C) happy with his books despite his isolation from others

(D) lonely because he often had no other children around him

(E) determined to get outside and enjoy nature

GO ON TO THE NEXT PAGE

22. The author uses the phrase "the fiction closed tight" (line 72) in order to

(A) demonstrate that the endings of the novels were not believable

(B) blur the distinction between fictional works and real life

(C) indicate how impenetrable some of the novels were

(D) criticize the artificiality of Dickens' characters

(E) show his unhappiness at having to part with a fictional world

23. In line 78 "sustain" most nearly means

(A) defend

(B) support

(C) endure

(D) prolong

(E) ratify

24. The author uses the phrase "the breadth of my achievement" (lines 82) primarily in order to suggest that

(A) he was confusing quantity with quality

(B) the books he had read varied widely in difficulty

(C) he should have been prouder of himself than he was

(D) he believes every child should read as much as possible

(E) no one else knew how much he was reading

25. The author implies that "a good reader" (lines 90) is one who

(A) engages in a structured reading program

(B) reads constantly and widely

(C) reads with a critical perspective

(D) makes lists of books to be read

(E) can summarize a book's theme simply and concisely

STOP

this is the end of the exercise

SAT Writing Exercise #13
25 Questions

The new school of political history that
emerged in the 1960's and 1970's sought to go
beyond the traditional focus of political
line historians on leaders and government
5 institutions by examining directly the political
practices of ordinary citizens. Like the old
approach, however, this new approach excluded
women. The very techniques these historians
used to uncover mass political behavior in the
10 nineteenth-century United States -quantitative
analyses of election returns, for example-were
useless in analyzing the political activities of
women, who were denied the vote until 1920.
       By redefining "political activity," historian
15 Paula Baker has developed a political history
that includes women. She concludes that
among ordinary citizens, political activism by
women in the nineteenth century prefigured
trends in twentieth-century politics. Defining
20 "politics" as "any action taken to affect the
course of behavior of government or of the
community," Baker concludes that, while
voting and holding office were restricted to
men, women in the nineteenth century
25 organized themselves into societies committed
to social issues such as temperance and poverty,
In other words, Baker contends, women
activists were early practitioners of nonpartisan,
issue-oriented politics and thus were more
30 interested in enlisting lawmakers, regardless of
their party affiliation, on behalf of certain
issues than in ensuring that one party or
another won an election. In the twentieth
century, more men drew closer to women's
35 ideas about politics and took up modes of
issue-oriented politics that Baker sees women
as having pioneered.

1. The primary purpose of the passage is to
   (A) enumerate reasons why both traditional
       scholarly methods and newer scholarly
       methods have limitations
   (B) identify a shortcoming in a scholarly
       approach and describe an alternative
       approach
   (C) provide empirical data to support a
       long-held scholarly assumption
   (D) compare two scholarly publications on the
       basis of their authors' backgrounds
   (E) attempt to provide a partial answer to a
       longstanding scholarly dilemma

2. The passage suggests which of the following
   concerning the techniques used by the new
   political historians described in the first
   paragraph of the passage?
   (A) They involved the extensive use of the
       biographies of political party leaders and
       political theoretician.
   (B) They were conceived by political historians
       who were reacting against the political
       climates of the 1960's and 1970's.
   (C) They were of more use in analyzing the
       positions of United States political parties
       in the nineteenth century than in analyzing
       the positions of those in the twentieth
       century.
   (D) They were of more use in analyzing the
       political behavior of nineteenth-century
       voters than in analyzing the political
       activities of those who could not vote
       during that period.
   (E) They were devised as a means of tracing
       the influence of nineteenth-century
       political trends on twentieth-century
       political trends.

GO ON TO THE NEXT PAGE

3. It can be inferred that the author of the passage quotes Baker directly in the second paragraph primarily in order to

(A) clarify a position before providing an alternative to that position

(B) differentiate between a novel definition and traditional definitions

(C) provide an example of a point agreed on by different generations of scholars

(D) provide an example of the prose style of an important historian

(E) amplify a definition given in the first paragraph

4. According to the passage, Paula Baker and the new political historians of the 1960's and 1970's shared which of the following'?

(A) A commitment to interest-group politics

(B) A disregard for political theory and ideology

(C) An interest in the ways in which nineteenth-century politics prefigured contemporary politics

(D) A reliance on such quantitative techniques as the analysis of election returns

(E) An emphasis on the political involvement of ordinary citizens

5. Which of the following best describes the structure of the first paragraph of the passage?

(A) Two scholarly approaches are compared, and a shortcoming common to both is identified,

(B) Two rival schools of thought are contrasted, and a third is alluded to,

(C) An outmoded scholarly approach is described, and a corrective approach is called for.

(D) An argument is outlined, and counterarguments are mentioned.

(E) A historical era is described in terms of its political trends.

6. The information in the passage suggests that a pre-1960's political historian would have been most likely to undertake which of the following studies?

(A) An analysis of voting trends among women voters of the 1920's

(B) A study of male voters' gradual ideological shift from party politics to issue-oriented politics

(C) A biography of an influential nineteenth-century minister of foreign affairs

(D) An analysis of narratives written by previously unrecognized women activists

(E) A study of voting trends among naturalized immigrant laborers in a nineteenth-century logging camp

GO ON TO THE NEXT PAGE

As I tried to understand my dual roles of writer and mother, I realized that most, if not all, human lives are full of fantasy—passive
line daydreaming that need not be acted on. But to
5 write poetry or fiction, or even to think well, is not to fantasize, or even to put fantasies on paper. For a poem to coalesce, for a character or an action to take shape, there has to be an imaginative transformation of reality that is in
10 no way passive. And a certain freedom of to, the mind is needed—freedom to press on, to enter the currents of your thought like a glider pilot, knowing that your motion can be sustained, that the buoyancy of your attention
15 will not be suddenly snatched away. Moreover, if the imagination is to transcend and transform experience, it has to question, to challenge, to conceive of alternatives, perhaps to the very life you are living at that moment.
20 You have to be free to play around with the notion that day might be night, love might be hate; nothing can be too sacred for the imagination to turn into its opposite or to call experimentally by another name. For writing is
25 renaming. Now, to be maternally with small children all day in the old way, to be with a man in the old way of marriage, requires a holding back, a putting aside of that imaginative activity, and demands instead a
30 kind of conservatism. I want to make it clear that I am not saying that in order to write well, or think well, it is necessary to become unavailable to others, or to become a devouring ego. This has been the myth of the masculine
35 artist and thinker, and I do not accept it. But to be a female human being trying to fulfill traditional female functions in a traditional way is in direct conflict with the subversive function of the imagination. The word "traditional" is
40 important here. There must be ways, and we will be finding out more and more about them, in which the energy of creation and the energy of relation can be united. But in those years I always felt the conflict as a failure of love in
45 myself. I had thought I was choosing a full life: the life available to most men, in which sexuality, work, and parenthood could coexist. But I felt, at twenty-nine, guilt toward the people closest to me, and guilty toward my own
50 being. I wanted, then, more than anything, the one thing of which there was never enough:
time to think, time to write.

7. The passage is primarily concerned with the
   (A) different ways a writer uses imagination
   (B) variety of roles a woman has during her lifetime
   (C) contrasting theories of writing that are held today
   (D) tendency for authors to confuse the real and the imaginary
   (E) tension between traditional female roles and a writer's needs

8. The author's statement that "writing is renaming" (line 24-25) suggests a conviction that writing involves
   (A) gaining a large vocabulary of traditional definitions
   (B) safeguarding language from change through misuse
   (C) realizing that definitions are more important than perceptions
   (D) transforming ideas in an active and creative manner
   (E) overcoming the desire to use contradictory examples

9. The author's attitude toward those who believe a writer must become a "devouring ego" (lines 33-34) in order to write well is one of
   (A) reluctant agreement
   (B) confused ambivalence
   (C) casual indifference
   (D) emphatic disapproval
   (E) personal abhorrence

10. The author suggests that, in the future, women writers who are caring for small children will have the opportunity to
   (A) join two tasks into a single effort that requires little attention
   (B) integrate two pursuits in a way that enhances both experiences
   (C) identify two roles as a means of choosing one role over the other
   (D) articulate two impulses that have become indistinguishable
   (E) obtain the formal training necessary to accomplish two goals

GO ON TO THE NEXT PAGE

11. According to the passage, which of the following is a necessary prerequisite to writing well?

(A) Opportunities for the imagination to function actively

(B) Freedom to read widely among great writers of the past

(C) Shaping thoughts through disciplined study

(D) Complete withdrawal into the self

(E) Desire for literary continuity

GO ON TO THE NEXT PAGE

You have seen them in movies: scientists who are infallible and coldly objective—little more than animated computers in white lab coats. They take measurements and record results as if the collection of data were the sole object of their lives. The assumption: If one gathers enough facts about something, the relationships between those facts will spontaneously reveal themselves.

Nonsense!

The myth of the infallible scientist evaporates when one thinks of the number of great ideas in science whose originators were correct in general but wrong in detail. The English physicist John Dalton (1766-1844) gets credit for modern atomic theory, but his mathematical formulas for calculating atomic weights were incorrect. The Polish astronomer Copernicus, who corrected Ptolemy's ancient concept of an Earth-centered universe, nevertheless was mistaken in the particulars of the planets' orbits.

Luck, too, has played a determining role in scientific discovery. The French chemist Pasteur demonstrated that life does not arise spontaneously from air. But it may have been luck that he happened to use an easy-to-kill yeast and not the hay bacillus that another, long-forgotten, investigator had chosen for the same experiment. We now know that hay bacillus is heat-resistant and grows even after the boiling that killed Pasteur's yeast. If Pasteur had used the hay bacillus, his "proof" would not have materialized.

Gregor Mendel, the founder of modern genetics, epitomizes the humanness of the scientist. Plant hybridization intrigued and puzzled Mendel, an Augustinian monk with some training in mathematics and the natural sciences. He had read in the professional literature that crosses between certain species regularly yielded many hybrids with identical traits; but when hybrids were crossed, all kinds of strange new combinations of traits cropped up. The principle of inheritance, if there was one, was elusive.

Mendel had the basic idea that there might be simple mathematical relationships among plants in different generations. To pursue this hypothesis, he decided to establish experimental plots in the monastery garden at Brunn, raise a number of varieties of peas, interbreed them, count and classify the offspring of each generation, and see whether any reliable mathematical ratios could be deduced.

After many years of meticulously growing, harvesting, and counting pea plants, Mendel thought he had something worth talking about. So, in 1865, he appeared before the Brunn Society for the Study of Natural Science, reported on his research, and postulated what have since come to be called the Mendelian laws. Society members listened politely but, insofar as anybody knows, asked few questions and engaged in little discussion. It may even be that, as he proceeded, a certain suspicion emerged out of the embarrassed silence. After all, Mendel lacked a degree and had published no research. Now, if Pasteur had advanced this idea…

Mendel's assertion that separate and distinct "elements" of inheritance must exist, despite the fact that he couldn't produce any, was close to asking the society to accept something on faith. There was no evidence for Mendel's hypothesis other than his computations; and his wildly unconventional application of algebra to botany made it difficult for his listeners to understand that those computations were the evidence.

Mendel undoubtedly died without knowing that his findings on peas had indeed illuminated a well-nigh universal pattern. Luck had been with him in his choice of which particular traits to study. We now know that groups of genes do not always act independently. Often they are linked, their effect being to transmit a "package" of traits. Knowing nothing about genes, let alone the phenomenon of linkage, Mendel was spared failure because the traits that he chose to follow were each controlled separately. The probability of making such a happy choice in random picks is only about 1 in 163!

*Some scientists believe that Mendel actually did have some idea of linkage and did choose traits purposefully.

GO ON TO THE NEXT PAGE

12. The word "Nonsense!" (line 10) conveys the extent to which the authors

(A) object to the tendency of scientists to rely on existing data

(B) reject the way in which scientists are portrayed in the media

(C) are amused at the accidental nature of some scientific findings

(D) oppose the glorification of certain scientists at the expense of others

(E) realize the necessity of objectivity in research

13. The authors cite the example of Copernicus (line 19) to substantiate which of the following claims?

(A) The achievements of scientists are not always recognized.

(B) Scientific progress depends on a variety of factors.

(C) Scientists often suffer from professional jealousy and competition.

(D) Noted scientists are not always wholly accurate in their theories.

(E) A scientist may stumble on an important truth accidentally.

14. The term "humanness" (line 36) as it is applied to Mendel refers to

(A) the tendency to rely excessively on emotion

(B) an interest in improving the human condition through scientific research

(C) an attitude of forgiveness toward those who underrated him

(D) a combination of intellect, intuition, and good fortune

(E) a talent for persevering in the face of opposition

15. In the passage, Pasteur's use of a certain yeast is comparable to

(A) a previous investigator's use of the hay bacillus

(B) Dalton's discovery of atomic weights

(C) Mendel's choice of traits to study

(D) Copernicus' study of the universe

(E) Mendel's use of mathematical ratios

16. In lines 67-69, the authors imply that in comparison to Mendel, Pasteur

(A) was a more proficient researcher

(B) based his theories on more extensive investigations

(C) possessed a more impressive professional reputation

(D) was more meticulous in his observations

(E) devoted more energy to promoting his scientific ideas

17. The "universal pattern" (line 81) refers to

(A) the initial skepticism with which new ideas are received

(B) a tendency of botanists to resist purely theoretical proof

(C) the way peas tend to exhibit the quality of linked traits

(D) the way traits usually reappear in succeeding generations

(E) a similarity between Mendel's experiments and those of succeeding geneticists

18. The word "happy" (line 90) most nearly means

(A) joyful

(B) fortunate

(C) willing

(D) dazed

(E) pleasing

GO ON TO THE NEXT PAGE

19. The passage suggests that Mendel's contemporaries assumed that valid biological theories
    (A) are often proposed by inexperienced researchers
    (B) cannot be based on mathematical proof alone
    (C) must be supported by years of careful research
    (D) often represent a departure from established practice
    (E) must be circulated to a wide audience

20. The passage suggests that Mendel's experiments succeeded because
    (A) Mendel was able to convince his colleagues to support his research
    (B) Mendel discovered flaws in his research design and corrected them
    (C) Mendel had a thorough understanding of the concept of linlçed traits
    (D) the scientific community finally understood the connection between mathematical computations and heredity
    (E) the traits in peas happen to reappear in a distinct and predictable way

21. As described in the passage, the experiences of Mendel are most like those of
    (A) Albert Einstein, who fled Nazi Germany to become the most famous physicist of this century
    (B) Pierre Curie, whose career as a chemist was cut short by a tragic accident
    (C) Barbara McClintock, whose theories about inherited traits in corn were not understood or accepted until long after she had advanced them
    (D) Leonardo da Vinci, whose numerous attempts to make a successful flying machine resulted in failure
    (E) James Watson and Francis Crick, who competed with other teams of scientists in the race to unravel the genetic code

GO ON TO THE NEXT PAGE

During the 1960's and 1970's, the primary economic development strategy of local governments in the United States was to attract
line manufacturer industries. Unfortunately, this
5 strategy was usually implemented at another community's expense: many manufacturing facilities were lured away from their moorings elsewhere through tax incentives and slick promotional efforts, Through the transfer of
10 jobs and related revenues that resulted from this practice, one town's triumph could become another town's tragedy.

In the 1980's the strategy shifted from this zero-sum game to one called "high-technology
15 development," in which local governments competed to attract newly formed high-technology manufacturing firms. Although this approach was preferable to victimizing other geographical areas by taking their jobs, it also
20 had its shortcomings: high-tech manufacturing firms employ only a specially trained fraction of the manufacturing workforce, and there simply are not enough high-tech firms to satisfy all geographic areas.
25 Recently, local governments have increasingly come to recognize the advantages of yet a third strategy: the promotion of homegrown small businesses. Small indigenous businesses are created by a nearly ubiquitous
30 resource, local entrepreneurs. With roots in their communities, these individuals are less likely to be enticed away by incentives offered by another community. Indigenous industry and talent are kept at home, creating an
35 environment that both provides jobs and fosters further entrepreneurship.

22. The primary purpose of the passage is to
(A) advocate more effective strategies for encouraging the development of high-technology enterprises in the United States
(B) contrast the incentives for economic development offered by local governments with those offered by the private sector
(C) acknowledge and counter adverse criticism of programs being used to stimulate local economic development
(D) define and explore promotional efforts used by local governments to attract new industry
(E) review and evaluate strategies and programs that have been used to stimulate economic development

23. The passage suggests which of the following about the majority of United State, manufacturing industries before the high-technology development era of the 1980's?
(A) They lost many of their most innovative personnel to small entrepreneurial enterprise.
(B) They experienced a major decline in profits during the 1960's and 1970's.
(C) They could provide real economic benefits to the areas in which they were located.
(D) They employed workers who had no specialized skills.
(E) They actively interfered with local entrepreneurial ventures.

24. The tone of the passage suggests that the author is most optimistic about the, economic development potential of which of the following groups?
(A) Local governments
(B) High-technology promoters
(C) Local entrepreneurs
(D) Manufacturing-industry managers
(E) Economic development strategists

25. The passage does NOT state which of the following about local entrepreneurs?
(A) They are found nearly everywhere.
(B) They encourage further entrepreneurship.
(C) They attract out-of-town investors.
(D) They employ local workers.
(E) They are established in their communities.

26. The author of the passage mentions which of the following, as an advantage of high-technology development?
(A) It encourages the modernization of existing manufacturing facilities.
(B) It promotes healthy competition between rival industries.
(C) It encourages the growth of related industries.
(D) It takes full advantage of the existing workforce.
(E) It does not advantage one local workforce at the expense of another

STOP

SAT Verbal Exercise #14
23 Questions

Passage 1

Since the lineage of investigative journalism
is most directly traceable to the Progressive era
of the early 1900s, it is not surprising that the
President of the United States at the time was
5 among the first to articulate its political
dimensions. Theodore Roosevelt called
investigative reporters "muckrakers," after a
character from John Bunyan's Pilgrim's
Progress who humbly cleaned "the filth off the
10 floor." Despite the misgivings implied by the
comparison, Roosevelt saw the muckrakers as
"often indispensable to the well-being of
society":
There are in the body politic, economic and
15 social, many and grave evils, and there is
urgent necessity for the sternest war upon
them. There should be relentless exposure of
and attack upon every evil man, whether
politician or businessman.
20 Roosevelt recognized the value-laden
character of investigative journalism. He
perceived correctly that investigative reporters
are committed to unearthing wrongdoing. For
these journalists, disclosures of morally
25 outrageous conduct maximize the opportunity
for the forces of "good" to recognize and do
battle with the forces of "evil."
So, the current folklore surrounding
investigative reporting closely resembles the
30 American ideal of popular democracy. Vigilant
journalists bring wrongdoing to public
attention. An informed citizenry responds by
demanding reforms from their elected
representatives. Policymakers respond in turn
35 by taking corrective action. Partly a product of
its muckraking roots, this idealized perspective
is also an outgrowth of the commonly
perceived effects of exposés published in the
early 1970s. The most celebrated of these
40 exposés were the news stories that linked top
White House officials to Watergate crimes.*
These stories were widely held responsible for
the public's loss of confidence in the Nixon
administration, ultimately forcing the
45 President's resignation.
Investigative journalists intend to provoke
outrage in their reports of malfeasance. Their
work is validated when citizens respond by
demanding change from their leaders. By
50 bringing problems to public attention, the
"journalists of outrage" attempt to alter societal
agendas.

*The burglarizing of the Democratic party headquarters at the Watergate
complex and other crimes committed during the 1972 presidential
elections

Passage 2

What ails newspapers in the United States is
the fact that their gigantic commercial
55 development compels them to appeal to larger
and larger masses of undifferentiated people and
that the truth is the commodity that the masses
of undifferentiated people cannot be induced to
buy. The dominant citizen of democratic society,
60 despite a superficial appearance of intelligence, is
really quite incapable of anything resembling
reasoning.
So, the problem before a modern newspaper,
hard pressed by the need of carrying on a
65 thoroughly whole-some business, is that of
enlisting the interest of these masses of people,
and by interest, of course, I do not mean their
mere listless attention, but their active emotional
cooperation. Unless a newspaper can manage to
70 arouse these people's feelings it might just as well
not have at them at all, for their feelings are the
essential part of them, and it is out of their
feelings that they dredge up their obscure
loyalties and aversions. Well, and how are their
75 feelings to be stirred up? At bottom, the business
is quite simple. First scare them—and then
reassure them. First get people into a panic with a
bugaboo—and then go to the rescue, gallantly
and uproariously, with a stuffed club to lay it.
80 First fake 'em—and then fake 'em again.
The two passages below are followed by
questions based on their content and on the
relationship between the two passages. Answer
the questions on the basis of what is stated or
85 implied in the passages and in any introductory
material that may be provided.
Insofar as our public gazettes have any serious
business at all, it is the business of snouting out
and exhibiting new and startling horrors,
90 atrocities, impending calamities, tyrannies,

GO ON TO THE NEXT PAGE

villainies, enormities, mortal perils, jeopardies,
outrages, catastrophes—first snouting out and
exhibiting them, and then magnificently
circumventing and disposing of them. The
95 first part is easy. It is almost unheard of for
the mob to disbelieve in a new bugaboo. As
soon as the hideous form is unveiled it begins
to quake and cry out: the reservoir of its
primary fears is always ready to run over. And
100 the second part is not much more difficult.
The one thing demanded of the remedy is
that it be simple, more or less familiar, easy to
comprehend, that it make no draft upon the
higher cerebral centers—that it avoid leading
105 the shy and delicate intelligence of the mob
into strange and hence painful fields of
speculation. All healthy journalism in
America—healthy in the sense that it
flourishes spontaneously and needs no outside
110 aid—is based firmly upon just such an
invention and scotching of bugaboos. And so
is all politics. Whatever stands above that
fundamental imposture is an artificiality.
Intelligent and honest journalism and
115 politics—these things, in a democratic society,
have no legitimate place. They are, when they
are encountered, exotic curiosities, pale and
clammy orchids, half-fabulous beasts in cages.

1. Passage 1 suggests that Roosevelt's choice of
name for investigative reporters reflects his
belief that
(A) they were irresponsible about checking the
accuracy of their reporting
(B) their writing style was unrefined and
colloquial
(C) they were motivated by greed and desire
for fame
(D) they were unsung and underpaid
(E) they did unpleasant but necessary work

2. The terms "folklore" (line 28) and "idealized
perspective" (line 36) suggest that the author
of Passage 1 would agree that
(A) democracy and journalism are incompatible.
(B) investigative journalism depends on
creating a false villain.
(C) many people have a romanticized conception of the role of journalists.
(D) readers are easily swayed by appeals to
their patriotism.
(E) people seldom believe what they read in
newspapers.

3. The author of Passage 1 refers to the report on
the "Watergate crimes" (line 41) as an example
of
(A) a story covered better by television than by
print media
(B) editorial pandering to an ignorant public
(C) journalism that had a tangible effect on
politics
(D) a flagrant abuse of the right of free press
(E) the subversion of legitimate political power

4. In lines 46-52 of Passage 1, the author is
(A) showing how investigative reporting has
broken with its past tradition
(B) acknowledging that reporters are not
merely trying to impart information
(C) disparaging those who believe that meaningful reform is possible
(D) expressing sympathy for victims of over-
zealous reportage
(E) citing an exception to the generalization
mentioned by Roosevelt

5. The brand of journalism discussed in Passage
1 is based on the assumption that
(A) public awareness of injustice is necessary
for change to occur
(B) newspapers are read chiefly for information that will help people to get ahead
(C) most people take for granted that politicians are corrupt
(D) most people are suspicious of whistle-
blowers
(E) most people's beliefs are inconsistent with
their actions

GO ON TO THE NEXT PAGE

6. In line 59, "dominant" most nearly means
(A) compelling (B) influential (C) headstrong (D) typical (E) superior

7. The tactics described in lines 76-80 ("First…again.")
(A) main difference between reporters' and editors' attitudes toward the public
(B) immense difficulty involved in solving society's problems
(C) physical danger that occasionally awaits reporters
(D) extent to which journalism relies on manipulation
(E) reason why newspapers are so seldom profitable

8. In line 118, the author of Passage 2 mentions "orchids" and "beasts" in order to
(A) give an example of sensationalism in newspaper reporting
(B) suggest something so unusual as to be bizarre
(C) indicate a preference for fiction over news
(D) chide newspapers for dealing with excessively morbid subjects
(E) cite exceptions that disprove the previous sentence

9. Both passages indicate that a fundamental ingredient in the success of a newspaper is
(A) financial assistance from the government
(B) a thirst for truth
(C) commercial development
(D) reporters of great integrity
(E) an engaged readership

10. The author of Passage 2 would most likely respond to the journalists' view in Passage 1 of the battle between the forces of "good" (line 26) and "evil" (line 27) by
(A) praising the journalists' idealism
(B) mocking the journalists' naïveté
(C) admiring the journalists' wit
(D) arguing that good and evil are not easily defined
(E) offering exceptions to the general rule

11. Unlike Passage 2, Passage 1 assumes that newspapers generally
(A) cater to a thoughtful, responsible citizenry
(B) rely on an obedient and docile public for assent
(C) are compromised by the advertising that supports them
(D) are read by only an elite minority of subscribers
(E) require close supervision by government censors

12. Both authors' discussions assume that the public
(A) ignores the press more often than not
(B) will react when prompted by the press
(C) is indifferent to corruption
(D) has a higher degree of literacy than is found in most other countries
(E) is well-informed and astute in its political choices

13. The two authors would most likely agree with which statement?
(A) Newspapers are a powerful means of getting the public's attention.
(B) Journalism is an important force for good.
(C) Competition between newspapers tends to improve the coverage of news.
(D) Most investigative journalism is actually driven by the profit motive.
(E) A knowledge of history is more important to a journalist than is a talent for writing.

GO ON TO THE NEXT PAGE

In an attempt to improve the overall performance of clerical workers, many companies have introduced computerized
line performance monitoring and control systems
5 (CPMCS) that record and report a worker's computer driven activities. However, at least one study has shown that such monitoring may not be having the desired effect. In the study, researchers asked monitored clerical workers and
10 their supervisors how assessments of productivity affected supervisors' ratings of workers' performance. In contrast to unmonitored workers doing the same work, who without exception identified the most important
15 element in their jobs as customer service, the monitored workers and their supervisors all responded that productivity was be critical factor in assigning ratings. This finding suggested that there should have been a strong correlation
20 between a monitored worker's productivity and the overall rating the worker received. However, measures of the relationship between overall rating and individual elements of performance clearly supported the conclusion that supervisors
25 gave considerable weight to criteria such as attendance, accuracy, and indications of customer satisfaction.

It is possible that productivity may be a "hygiene factor"; that is, if it is too low, it will
30 hurt the overall rating. But the evidence suggests that beyond the point at which productivity becomes "good enough," higher productivity per se is unlikely to improve a rating.

14. According to the passage, before the final results of the study were known, which of the following seemed likely?

(A) That workers with the highest productivity would also be the most accurate

(B) That workers who initially achieved high productivity ratings would continue to do so consistently

(C) That the highest performance ratings would be achieved by workers with the highest productivity

(D) That the most productive workers would be those whose supervisors claimed to value productivity

(E) That supervisors who claimed to value productivity would place equal value on customer satisfaction

15. It can be inferred that the author of the passage discusses "unmonitored workers" (line 13) primarily in order to

(A) compare the ratings of these workers with the ratings of monitored workers

(B) provide an example of a case in which monitoring might be effective

(C) provide evidence of an inappropriate use of CPMCS

(D) emphasize the effect that CPMCS may have on workers' perceptions of their jobs

(E) illustrate the effect that CPMCS may have on workers' ratings

16. Which of the following, if true, would most clearly have supported the conclusion?

(A) Ratings of productivity correlated highly with ratings of both accuracy and attendance.

(B) Electronic monitoring greatly increased productivity.

(C) Most supervisors based overall ratings of performance on measures of productivity alone.

(D) Overall ratings of performance correlated more highly with measures of productivity than the researchers expected.

(E) Overall ratings of performance correlated more highly with measures of accuracy than with measures of productivity.

17. According to the passage, a "hygiene factor" (line 29) is an aspect of a worker's performance that

(A) has no effect on the rating of a worker's performance

(B) is so basic to performance that it is assumed to be adequate for all workers

(C) is given less importance than it deserves in rating a worker's performance

(D) is not likely to affect a worker's rating unless it is judged to be inadequate

(E) is important primarily because of the effect it has on a worker's rating

GO ON TO THE NEXT PAGE

My mother was only twenty years old, I was not quite three, and my brother was a toddler when we arrived at El Building, as the place had been christened by its residents.

I remember the way the heater pipes banged and rattled, startling all of us out of sleep until we got so used to the sound that we automatically either shut it out or raised our voices above the racket.

The hiss from the valve punctuated my sleep, which has always been fitful, like a nonhuman presence in the room—the dragon sleeping at the entrance of my childhood. But the pipes were a connection with all the other lives being lived around us. Having come from a house made for a single family back in Puerto Rico—my mother's extended-family home—it was curious to me to know that strangers lived under our floor and above our heads, and that the heater pipe went through everyone's apartment. (My first punishment in El Building came as a result of playing tunes on the pipes in my room to see if there would be an answer.) My mother was as new to this concept of beehive life as I was, but had been given strict orders by my father to keep the doors locked, the noise down, ourselves to ourselves.

It became my father's obsession to get out of the barrio[1], and thus we were never permitted to form bonds with the place or with the people who lived there. Yet the building was also a comfort to my mother, who never got over yearning for her *isla* (Puerto Rico). She felt surrounded by her language: the walls were thin, and voices speaking and arguing in Spanish could be heard all day. Salsa music blasted out of radios turned on early in the morning and left on for company.

Though Father preferred that we do our grocery shopping at the supermarket when he came home on weekend leaves, my mother insisted that she could only cook with products whose labels she could read, and so, during the week, I accompanied her and my little brother to La Bodega—a hole-in-the-wall grocery store across the street from El Building. There we squeezed down three narrow aisles jammed with various products. We would linger at La Bodega, for it was there that my mother breathed best, taking in the familiar aromas of foods she knew from Mama's kitchen, and it was also there that she got to speak to the other women of El Building without violating outright Father's dictates about fraternizing with our neighbors.

But he did his best to make our "assimilation" painless. I can still see him carrying a Christmas tree up several flights of stairs to our apartment, leaving a trail of aromatic pine. We were the only ones in El Building that I knew of who got presents both on Christmas Day and on *Dia de Reyes*,[2] the day when the Three Kings brought gifts to Hispanic children.

Our greatest luxury in El Building was having our own television set. My brother quickly became an avid watcher of Captain Kangaroo. I loved all the family series, and by the time I started first grade in school, I could have drawn a map of Middle America as exemplified by the lives of characters in "Father Knows Best," "Leave It to Beaver," and "My Three Sons." Compared to our neighbors in El Building, we were rich. My father's navy check provided us with financial security and a standard of living that the factory workers envied. The only thing his money could not buy us was a place to live away from the barrio — his greatest wish and Mother's greatest fear.

[1] A neighborhood where most of the residents are Spanish-speaking

[2] "Day of Kings," January 6, a holiday that celebrates the visit of the Three Kings to the infant Jesus

18. The details about the family members in lines 1-4 introduce which element of the overall portrait?

(A) Their cautious curiosity

(B) Their lack of experience

(C) Their capacity to bear hardship

(D) Their suspicion of authority

(E) Their desire to lean

19. The author's reference to a beehive in the second paragraph contributes to her depiction of the apartment by

(A) describing trivial but vivid details unnoticed by the adults

(B) evoking unexpected surprises, in daily life

(C) revealing unconscious fears about the large

(D) emphasizing the liveliness inside the building

(E) demonstrating the fantasies of the family

GO ON TO THE NEXT PAGE

20. The author's observations about the walls in the third paragraph help illustrate her claim that
(A) life in the barrio was confusing to her mother
(B) the environment evoked memories of her mother's cultural heritage
(C) El Building was similar to other buildings in the neighborhood
(D) the lack of privacy distressed her parents
(E) the apartment lacked adequate heat in the winter

21. The discussion of grocery shopping in the fourth paragraph highlights the
(A) parents' differing attitudes toward their neighborhood
(B) parents' ambition to achieve financial success
(C) tensions between the more traditional mother and her "Americanized" daughter
(D) children's sense of isolation from potential playmates
(E) family's carefully nurtured loyalty to Puerto Rican culture

22. By stating that "he did his best" (line 57), the author acknowledges that the father
(A) understood that adjusting to new surroundings would pose a challenge to his family
(B) felt that the best way for the family to adjust to new surroundings was to continue living as they had in Puerto Rico
(C) insisted that the family adopt new traditions right away because an abrupt change is less painful than a gradual one
(D) wanted his family to get along with its neighbors
(E) wanted his children's religious and moral education to be pleasant and enjoyable

23. Lines 58-64 ("I...children.") most directly suggests that
(A) Christmas trees were a part of the holiday traditions of most people in the building
(B) the author was alarmed at her father's weariness after carrying the heavy tree up many flights of stairs
(C) the family observed the holiday traditions of both the continental United States and Puerto Rico
(D) the author was impressed that her father purchased the tree, because the family did not have much money
(E) Puerto Rican families traditionally exchanged gifts on two winter holidays

24. When the author states "I could have drawn a map" (lines 49-70), she implies that as a child
(A) she preferred to watch educational programming
(B) she judged United States society by the high quality of television programs
(C) she believed that television depicted typical family life in the United States
(D) she watched television programs that reflected the reality of her own childhood
(E) she paid more attention to television than did most children her age

25. Lines 74-76 ("My...envied.") presents the family's prosperity as ultimately
(A) disastrous in its consequences
(B) limited in its benefits
(C) discouraging in its cultural demands
(D) disturbing in its exclusion of relatives
(E) bewildering in its suddenness

26. Which best characterizes the overall impression of the father conveyed in the passage?
(A) He was the single most dominant influence in the children's daily life.
(B) He feared losing touch with the traditions of his native land.
(C) He represented the best aspects of both cultures for his daughter.
(D) He wanted his family to adopt a new life and culture.
(E) He wanted the children to respect only

STOP
this is the end of the exercise

SAT Verbal Exercise #15

23 Questions

During the latter part of the nineteenth century, the proportion of women in the United States working for wages rose steadily,
line and most of these women entered paid
5 employment out of economic necessity. Daughters, wives, unmarried women, and widows had always worked — in the home or on the farm; they now worked also in the factory or shop. "Work" was always the content
10 of most women's lives, but this fact was at odds with the prevailing myth of "true womanhood," according to which the domestic role was a part of woman's nature—her way of being, rather than a way of life that could be chosen or
15 rejected. Women's paid work outside the home, though it was undertaken to support their families, made a mockery of the domestic ideal of wife and mother. The social status of the employed woman would remain low so
20 long as the image of the woman at home gracing her hearth, unsullied by the affairs of the world, remained the ideal.
Nevertheless, in the late nineteenth century increasing numbers of women sought
25 employment outside the home at some time in their lives. Young unmarried women were predominant in the female work force, which suggests that with marriage and motherhood most women reverted to the traditional role of
30 economic dependence—unless their husbands were unable to earn a living wage. Widows and married women whose husbands were disabled or absent constituted the second major group of working women. Only among Black
35 Americans, and among immigrants whose children worked in industry with them, were there substantial numbers of mothers who held jobs when their husbands were also employed.
All women who sought work outside the
40 home suffered repercussions from the idea that women's earning function was secondary, that women ought to be supported by someone rather than support themselves. Women were rarely paid at the same rate as men. In factories
45 at the end of the century, women workers earned on the average only about half as much as men did, yet need drove women to accept these low-paying jobs. Women workers often were accused of undercutting wages and unsettling the labor market. Young women

50 living with their parents were assumed to be earning "pin money" and thus not to be dependent on their salaries. Women workers were treated as casual laborers who had no urge for advancement and no future in an organization
55 because home and family comprised their natural interests. Women employed outside the home were seen as an anomaly by nineteenth-century standards, which rigidly prescribed separate spheres of activity for men and women, but of
60 course they were not an anomaly at all.

1. The author's view of the treatment of nineteenth century working women is best described as
   (A) shock and amazement
   (B) amused contempt
   (C) disapproval
   (D) anger
   (E) disbelief

2. The two things that are "at odds" (line 10) can best be described as the
   (A) kinds of jobs women could actually get and the work they aspired to do
   (B) harsh conditions in working women's homes and the gracious homes that women were supposed to create
   (C) actual living standards of working women and the image of the successful career woman
   (D) reasons why most women entered the work force and the high ambitions some had to improve the world
   (E) reality of women's working lives and the idealization of women's domestic role

3. In line 31, the word "living" means
   (A) active
   (B) vivid
   (C) animated
   (D) genuine
   (E) sufficient

GO ON TO THE NEXT PAGE

4. Which statement can be inferred from the discussion of nineteenth-century Black Americans and immigrants in the second paragraph?

(A) Members of these two groups constituted a majority of the industrial work force.

(B) Men in these two groups were frequently not paid enough to support their families.

(C) Men in these two groups were more likely than White, nonimmigrant men to be responsible for child care.

(D) Women in these two groups were subjected to more gender stereotyping than White, nonimmigrant women were.

(E) Women in these two groups were more likely than White, nonimmigrant women to be economically dependent on men.

5. Which question about nineteenth-century women is NOT answered in the passage?

(A) Why was it generally believed in the nineteenth century that the domestic role was natural to women?

(B) Why did even the women who were supporting families work in jobs that paid poorly?

(C) How were women workers often viewed by employers and men in the workplace?

(D) What economic consequences did women face because they were considered secondary wage earners?

(E) Why were single women more likely to work than married women

GO ON TO THE NEXT PAGE

Passage 1

For more than five years I maintained myself thus solely by the labor of my hands, and I found that, by working about six weeks in a year,
line I could meet all the expenses of living. The
5 whole of my (5 winters, as well as most of my summers, I had free and clear for study.

As I preferred some things to others, and especially valued my freedom, as I could live roughly and yet succeed well, I did not wish to
10 spend my time in earning rich carpets or fine furniture, or a house in the Grecian or the Gothic style. If there are any to whom it is no interruption to acquire these things, and who know how to use them when acquired, I
15 relinquish to them the pursuit. Some are "industrious," and appear to love labor for its own sake, or perhaps because it keeps them out of worse mischief; to such I have at present nothing to say. For myself I found that the
20 occupation of a day laborer* was the most independent of any, especially as it required only thirty or forty days in a year to support one.

In short, I am convinced both by faith and experience, that to maintain one's self on this
25 earth is not a hardship but a pastime, so long as we live simply and wisely. It is not necessary that a man earn his living by the sweat of his brow, unless he sweats easier than I do.

One young man of my acquaintance, who
30 has inherited some acres, told me that he thought he should live as I did, if he had the means. I would not have any one adopt my mode of living on any account, for I desire that there may be as many different persons in the
35 world as possible. I would have each young man be very careful to find out and pursue his own way, and not his father's or his mother's or his neighbor's instead. The youth may build or plant or sail, only let him not be hindered from doing
40 that which he tells me he would like to do.

Passage 2

Now, the one thing that is entirely fatal to leading the simple life is the desire to stimulate the curiosity of others in the matter. Thoreau, who is by many regarded as the apostle of the
45 simple life, is the most conspicuous example of this. Thoreau was a man of extremely simple tastes, it is true. He ate pulse, whatever that may be, and drank water; he was deeply interested in the contemplation of nature, and he loved to
50 disembarrass himself of all the apparatus of life.

It was really that he hated trouble more than anything in the world; he found that by working six weeks in the year, he could earn enough to enable him to live in a hut in a wood for the rest of
55 the year; he did his household work himself, and his little stock of money sufficed to buy his food and clothes, and to meet his small expenses. But Thoreau was indolent rather than simple, and what spoiled his simplicity was that he was forever
60 hoping that he would be observed and admired; he was forever peeping out of the corner of his eye, to see if inquisitive strangers were hovering about to observe the hermit at his contemplation.

And then, too, it was easier for Thoreau to
65 make money than it would be for a more ordinary youth. When Thoreau wrote his famous maxim, "To maintain oneself on this earth is not a hardship but a pastime," he did not add that he was himself a man of remarkable mechanical gifts,
70 he made, when he was disposed, admirable pencils, he was an excellent land surveyor and an author as well. Moreover, he was a celibate by nature. He would no doubt have found if he had had a wife and children, and no aptitude for
75 skilled labor that he would have had to work as hard as anyone else.

He thought and talked too much about simplicity; and the fact is that simplicity, like humility, cannot exist side by side with self-consciousness.
80 You cannot become simple by doing elaborately, and making a parade of doing, the things that the truly simple person would do without thinking about them.

6. The "pursuit" (line 15) has as its object
(A) intellectual freedom
(B) financial independence
(C) aesthetic superiority
(D) social accolades
(E) luxurious possessions

7. In line 26, "simply" most nearly means
(A) guilelessly   (B) ordinarily (C) foolishly
(D) clearly   (E) modestly

8. In line 51, "trouble" most likely refers to
(A) unnecessary exertion
(B) civil unrest
(C) financial hardship
(D) emotional distress
(E) personal conflict

GO ON TO THE NEXT PAGE

9. The depiction of Thoreau in lines 57-63 ("But Thoreau…contemplation") creates the impression of a man who
(A) plays a complex, mysterious role
(B) lies about his deepest beliefs
(C) follows a demanding ideal
(D) enjoys the company of others
(E) strikes a self-conscious pose

10. Which statement, if true, would most effectively challenge the view of Thoreau presented in lines 73-76 ("He would…anyone else")?
(A) Thoreau anonymously supported relatives in financial distress.
(B) Thoreau isolated himself because he craved notoriety.
(C) Thoreau earned a small income by writing about life in the woods.
(D) Thoreau lived sparingly in anticipation of owning a more comfortable house.
(E) Thoreau found lasting peace of mind in the contemplation of nature.

11. Overall, the author of Passage 2 characterizes Thoreau as an
(A) unreliable adviser with a limited view of social realities
(B) devious guide with questionable intentions
(C) immoral philosopher who rejects standards
(D) immature youth with insufficient knowledge of the world
(E) unscrupulous popularizer who deliberately deceives others

12. The author of Passage 2 would consider which advice most important for a young person seeking the simple life?
(A) You cannot achieve it by a deliberate attempt.
(B) You should have great respect for nature.
(C) You must have a sincere dedication to your task.
(D) You will not succeed unless you are already wealthy.
(E) You must first become a recluse.

13. Which statement is a logical extension of the argument made by the author of Passage 2?
(A) No individual leading the simple life can be as convincing as Thoreau was.
(B) No one who is living a truly simple life can write a book about simple living.
(C) The conditions of our century make it impossible to lead the simple life.
(D) Living a simple lifestyle is unnatural.
(E) None of the advocates of the simple life has been a pragmatic person.

14. Both passages assert that the simple life is
(A) not suitable for all people
(B) not acceptable in conventional societies
(C) not easy to find for one's self
(D) essential to one's peace of mind
(E) crucial for creative people

15. Which statement about self-awareness in the simple life most accurately represents the ideas expressed in the two passages?
(A) Passage 1 says it must be taught; Passage 2 believes it must be avoided.
(B) Passage 1 urges all readers to cultivate it; Passage 2 believes it is appropriate only for some.
(C) Passage 1 assumes it is important; Passage 2. considers it self-defeating.
(D) Passage 1 praises examples of it; Passage 2 mandates it.
(E) Passage 1 celebrates it; Passage 2 ignores it.

16. Which point made in Passage 1 does the author of Passage 2 fail to address?
(A) Living the simple life matters less than finding the right way of life for one's self.
(B) The simple life is an appropriate choice for a person with simple tastes.
(C) Earning one's living is not a difficult or tiresome task.
(D) An individual who lives simply can exist for months without earning money.
(E) Pursuing the simple life necessarily involves rejecting many options.

GO ON TO THE NEXT PAGE

Schools expect textbooks to be a valuable source of information for students. My research suggests, however, that textbooks that address the place of Native Americans within the history of the United States distort history to suit a particular cultural value system, In some textbooks, for example, settlers are pictured as more humane, complex, skillful, and wise than Native Americans. In essence, textbooks stereotype and deprecate the numerous Native American cultures while reinforcing the attitude that the
European conquest of the New World denotes the superiority of European cultures. Although textbooks evaluate Native American architecture, political systems, and home making, I contend that they do it from an ethnocentric, European perspective without recognizing that other perspectives are possible.

One argument against my contention asserts that, by nature, textbooks are culturally biased and that I am simply underestimating children's ability to see through these biases. Some researchers even claim that by the time students are in high school, they know they cannot take textbooks literally. Yet substantial evidence exists to the contrary. Two researchers, for example, have conducted studies that suggest that children's attitudes about particular cultures are strongly influenced by the textbooks used in schools. Given this, an ongoing, careful review of how school textbooks depict Native Americans is certainly warranted.

17. Which of the following would most logically be the topic of the paragraph immediately following the passage?

(A) Specific ways to evaluate the biases of United States history textbooks

(B) The centrality of the teacher's role in United States history courses

(C) Nontraditional methods of teaching United States history

(D) The contributions of European immigrants to the development of the United States

(E) Ways in which parents influence children's political attitudes

18. The primary purpose of the passage is to

(A) describe in detail one research study regarding the impact of history textbooks on children's attitudes and beliefs about certain cultures

(B) describe revisions that should be made to United States history textbooks

(C) discuss the difficulty of presenting an accurate history of the United States

(D) argue that textbooks used in schools stereotype Native Americans and influence children's attitudes

(E) summarize ways in which some textbooks give distorted pictures of the political systems developed by various Native American groups

19. The author mentions two researchers' studies most likely in order to

(A) suggest that children's political attitudes are formed primarily through textbooks

(B) counter the claim that children are able to see through stereotypes in textbooks

(C) suggest that younger children tend to interpret the messages in textbooks more literally than do older children

(D) demonstrate that textbooks carry political messages meant to influence their readers

(E) prove that textbooks are not biased in terms of their political presentations

20. The author's attitude toward the content of the history textbooks discussed in the passage is best described as one of

(A) indifference

(B) hesitance

(C) neutrality

(D) amusement

(E) disapproval

GO ON TO THE NEXT PAGE

21. It can be inferred from the passage that the "researchers" mentioned in line 24 would be most likely to agree with which of the following statements?

(A) Students form attitudes about cultures other than their own primarily inside the school environment.

(B) For the most part, seniors in high school know that textbooks can be biased.

(C) Textbooks play a crucial role in shaping the attitudes and beliefs of students.

(D) Elementary school students are as likely to recognize biases in textbooks as are high school students.

(E) Students are less likely to give credence to history textbooks than to mathematics textbooks.

22. The author implies that which of the following will occur if textbooks are not carefully reviewed?

(A) Children will remain ignorant of the European settlers' conquest of the New World.

(B) Children will lose their ability to recognize biases in textbooks.

(C) Children will form negative stereotypes of Native Americans.

(D) Children will develop an understanding of ethnocentrism.

(E) Children will stop taking textbooks seriously.

STOP

this is the end of the exercise

SAT Verbal Exercise #16

23 Questions

The archaeological evidence seems clear on the question of our original environment. For most of two million years, hominids lived on
line the savannas of Africa—vast, park-like lands
5 dotted by groves and scattered trees. They appear to have avoided the equatorial rain forests on one side and the deserts on the other. There was nothing inevitable about this choice. The two extreme habitats have no
10 special qualities that deny them to primates. Most monkeys and apes flourish in the rain forest, and two species of baboons are specialized for life in the relatively barren grasslands and semideserts of Africa. The
15 prehistoric species of Homo can be viewed both as the ancestors of modern human beings and as one more product among many in the development of primates. In the latter role they belong to the minority of species that hit upon
20 an intermediate topography, the tropical savanna. Most students of early human evolution agree that the bipedal locomotion and free-swinging arms fitted these ancestral forms very well to the open land, where they
25 were able to exploit an abundance of fruits, tubers, and game.

The body is predisposed to life on the savanna. But is the mind? The scientist Gordon Orians has suggested that this is
30 indeed the case. He points out that people today work hard to create a savanna-like environment in such improbable sites as formal gardens, cemeteries, and suburban shopping malls. They hunger for open spaces but not for
35 a barren landscape, for some amount of order in the surrounding vegetation but less than geometric perfection. According to his formulation, the ancestral environment contained three key features.
40 First, the savanna by itself, with nothing more added, offered an abundance of animal and plant food to which the omnivorous hominids were well adapted, as well as the clear view needed to detect animals and rival bands
45 at long distances. Second, some topographic relief was desirable. Cliffs, hillocks, and ridges were the vantage points from which to make a still more distant surveillance, while their overhangs and caves served as natural shelters at night. During longer marches, the scattered

50 clumps of trees provided auxiliary retreats, often sheltering bodies of drinking water. Finally, lakes and rivers offered fish, mollusks, and new kinds of edible plants. Because few natural enemies of humans can cross deep water, the shorelines
55 became natural perimeters of defense.

People tend to put these three elements together: it seems that whenever people are given a free choice, they move to open, tree-studded land on prominences overlooking water. This
60 worldwide tendency is no longer dictated by the hard necessities of hunter-gatherer life. It has become largely aesthetic. Those who exercise the greatest degree of free choice, the rich and powerful, congregate on high land and above
65 lakes and rivers and along an ocean bluffs On such sites they build palaces, villas, temples, and corporate retreats. Psychologists have noticed that people entering unfamiliar places tend to move toward towers and other large objects
70 breaking the skyline. Given leisure time, they stroll along shores and riverbanks.

I will grant at once the strangeness of the comparison and the possibility that the convergence is merely a coincidence. But
75 entertain for a while longer the idea that landscape architects and gardeners, and we who enjoy their creations without special instruction or persuasion, are responding to a deep genetic memory of humanity's optimal environment.
80 That statistically, given a completely free choice, people gravitate toward a savanna-like environment, The theory accommodates a great many seemingly disconnected facts from other parts of the world.
85 Not long ago I joined a group of Brazilian scientists on a tour of the upland savanna around the capital city of Brasilia. We went straight to one of the highest elevations as if following an unspoken command. We looked out across the
90 rippled terrain of high grass, parkland, and forest enclaves and watched birds circling in the sky. We scanned the cumulus clouds that tower like high mountains above the plains during the wet season. We traced gallery forests, groves of trees
95 that wind along the banks of the widely spaced streambeds. It was, all agreed, very beautiful.

The practical-minded will argue that certain environments are just "nice" and there's an end to it. So why dilate on the obvious? The answer is

GO ON TO THE NEXT PAGE >

100 that the obvious is usually profoundly
significant. Some environments are indeed
pleasant for the same general reason that sugar
is sweet and team sports exhilarating. Each
response has its peculiar meaning rooted in the
105 distant genetic past. To understand why we
have one particular set of ingrained preferences
and not another, out of the vast number of
possible preferences, remains a central question
in the study of human nature.

1. In lines 8-9 ("There…choice."), the author
does which of the following?

(A) Shows that reasons for habitat choices are
best understood in terms of evolution.

(B) Suggests that early hominids were
equipped to survive in other habitats.

(C) Claims that the views of those who seek
religious explanations are without merit.

(D) Underlines the fact that the archaeological
evidence about the early hominids is clear.

(E) Emphasizes the decisive ways in which
apes and baboons differ from early
hominids.

2. The author mentions the "extreme habitats"
(line 9) to

(A) show that all habitats have certain advantages

(B) show that climates that are suitable for one
species are not suitable for another species

(C) make the case that primates can live in a
variety of environments

(D) point out the difference between baboons
and other primates

(E) question the validity of archaeological
evidence

3. According to the passage, "Gordon Orians"
(line 29) has suggested that people have the
tendency to

(A) congregate on high land to feel secure

(B) conceal themselves behind large objects as
a means of protection

(C) seek subconsciously to re-create their
ancestral environment

(D) hunger for spaces that resemble shopping
malls

(E) enjoy leisure time in unfamiliar places

4. The author mentions "Cliffs, hillocks, and
ridges" (line 46) to give examples of
topographic features that

(A) became early sites of religious ceremonies

(B) provided a wide variety of food sources for
early hominids

(C) are characteristic of the extreme habitats
avoided by early hominids

(D) are in contrast with shopping malls and
formal gardens

(E) enabled early hominids to see approaching
prey and enemies

5. By mentioning "corporate retreats" (line 66),
the author

(A) rebukes corporate executives for their
arrogance

(B) implies that power has always tended to
corrupt

(C) makes the case that the corporate elite are
not sensitive to the environment

(D) suggests that the rich and powerful
include corporate executives

(E) argues against the human instinct to seek
protection against enemies

6. The author likens the action of the group on
the outskirts of Brasilia to a response to "an
unspoken command" (line 89) in order to

(A) show how people in groups lose their
individuality

(B) illustrate that even scientists respect
intuition

(C) indicate the distance between modern
humans and early hominids

(D) underline the importance of language in
human development

(E) suggest that the power of inherited preferences is still strong

GO ON TO THE NEXT PAGE

7. The author describes the trip to Brazil in order to

(A) illustrate a major difference between Africa and Brazil

(B) give an example of an environment that would have been hostile to hominids

(C) illustrate the author's appreciation of beauty

(D) support an argument with an example from personal experience

(E) show the importance of coincidence to the argument that has been developed

8. The author suggests which of the following about the "practical-minded" (line 97)?

(A) They fail to appreciate the profound beauty of the savanna.

(B) They value economic considerations over philosophical considerations.

(C) They are in agreement with many theorists.

(D) They fail to appreciate the beauty of the natural world.

(E) They are unwilling to ask probing questions about human nature.

9. In the last paragraph, the author assumes that our responses to such things as sugar and team sports

(A) are influenced by the genetic history of our species

(B) are largely a reflection of local culture

(C) are shared with other primates

(D) are different for different individuals

(E) are influenced by the geography in which human beings developed

10. Which statement, if true, would most directly weaken the author's argument regarding people's feelings about environments?

(A) Mountainous regions generally are more sparsely populated than plains are.

(B) Many national parks have characteristics of the savannas.

(C) Most urban planners agree that it is important, even though expensive, to set aside land for parks.

(D) Few people feel comfortable standing on cliffs, hillocks, and ridges.

(E) Successful landscape architects are those who create settings that are reminiscent of savannas.

GO ON TO THE NEXT PAGE

Once, in a cross-cultural training manual I came across a riddle. In Japan, a young man and woman meet and fall in love. They decide
line they would like to marry. The young man goes
5 to his mother and describes the situation, "I will visit the girl's family," says the mother. "I will seek their approval." After some time, a meeting between mothers is arranged. The boy's mother goes to the girl's ancestral house.
10 The girl's mother has prepared tea. The women talk about the fine spring weather: will this be a good year for cherry blossoms? The girl's mother serves a plate of fruit. Bananas are sliced and displayed in an exquisite design.
15 Marriage never is mentioned. After the tea, the boy's mother goes home. "I am so sorry," she tells her son. "The other family has declined the match."

In the training manual, the following
20 question was posed. How did the boy's mother know the marriage was unacceptable? That is easy, I thought when I read it. To a Japanese, the answer is obvious. Bananas do not go well with tea.
25 All of my life, I have been fluent in communicating through discordant fruit. The Japanese raise their daughters differently than their sons. "Gombatte!" they exhort their sons. "Have courage, be like the carp, swim
30 upstream!" "Kiotsukete," they caution their daughters. "Be careful, be modest, keep safe."

My mother was raised in a world such as this, in a house of tradition and myth. And although she has traveled across continents,
35 oceans, and time, although she considers herself a modern woman—a believer in the sunlight of science—it is a world that surrounds her still. Feudal Japan floats around my mother. Like an unwanted pool of
40 ectoplasm, it quivers with supernatural might. It followed her into our American home and governed my girlhood life.

And so, I was shaped. In that feudal code, all females were silent and yielding. Even their
45 possessions were accorded more rights than they. For, if mistreated, belongings were granted an annual holiday when they could spring into life and complain.

And so, I was haunted. If I left my clothes
50 on the floor, or my bicycle in the rain; if I yanked on the comb with roughness; if it splintered and lost its teeth (and I did these things often and deliberately, trying to challenge their spell); then my misdeeds
55 pursued me in dreams.

While other children were learning that in America you get what you ask for, I was being henpecked by inanimate objects. While other children were learning to speak their minds, I was
60 locked in a losing struggle for dominance with my clothing, my toys, and my tools.

The objects meant me no harm; they meant to humble and educate me. "Ownership," they told me "means obligation, caretaking, reciprocity."
65 And although I was a resistant student, in time I was trained. Well maintained, my possessions live long, useful, and mercifully quiet lives of service.

11. The "plate of fruit" (line 13) serves as
(A) a sign that the young woman's mother is a generous host
(B) an example of the family's goodwill
(C) a symbol of affection
(D) a means of communication
(E) an opportunity to display good taste

12. In line 17, "declined" most nearly means
(A) grown less well
(B) refused to approve
(C) sloped sharply away
(D) fallen out of love
(E) been unable to understand

13. Which of the following expresses the meaning of "fluent in communicating through discordant fruit" (line 25-26)?
(A) She has an aversion to certain foods.
(B) She is able to speak her mind clearly.
(C) She is able to adapt to the values of cultures other than her own.
(D) She understands various indirect forms of expression.
(E) She is sensitive to the feelings of others.

14. The distinction between "Gambatte" (line 28) and "Kiotsukete" (line 30) is the distinction between
(A) tradition and innovation
(B) passion and feeling
(C) age and youth
(D) intuition and wisdom
(E) perseverance and prudence

GO ON TO THE NEXT PAGE

15. The "carp" in line 29 is mentioned as
- (A) a symbol of food that the narrator likes
- (B) the behavior expected of boys
- (C) a traditional view of nature
- (D) the link between humans and nature
- (E) certain kinds of foolish behavior

16. The author felt different from other children because
- (A) they seldom faced the hardships that she had to face every day
- (B) she did not know how to take care of things as well as they did
- (C) her mother was always criticizing her
- (D) she felt guilty about rejecting the traditions of her parents
- (E) she was discouraged from asserting herself

GO ON TO THE NEXT PAGE

Many zoos in the United States have undergone radical changes in philosophy and design. All possible care is taken to reduce the
line stress of living in captivity. Cages and grounds
5 are landscaped to make this; gorillas feel immersed in vegetation, as they would be in a Congo jungle. Zebras gaze across vistas arranged to appear (to zoo visitors, at least) nearly as broad as an African plain.
10   Yet, strolling past animals in zoo after zoo, I have noticed the signs of hobbled energy that has found no release—large cats pacing in a repetitive pattern, primates rocking for hours in one corner of a cage. These truncated
15 movements are known as cage stereotypes, and usually these movements bring about no obvious physical or emotional effects in the captive animal. Many animal specialists believe they are more troubling to the people who watch than to
20 the animals themselves. Such restlessness is an unpleasant reminder that—despite the careful interior decorating and clever optical illusions— zoo animals are prisoners, being kept in elaborate cells.
25   The rationale for breeding endangered animals in zoos is nevertheless compelling. Once a species falls below a certain number, it is beset by inbreeding* and other processes that nudge it closer and closer to extinction. If the animal also
30 faces the whole-scale destruction of its habitat, its one hope for survival lies in being transplanted to some haven of safety, usually a cage. In serving as trusts for rare fauna, zoos have committed millions of dollars to caring for
35 animals. Many zoo managers have given great consideration to the psychological health of the animals in their care. Yet the more I learned about animals bred in enclosures, the more I wondered how their sensibilities differed from
40 those of animals raised to roam free.
      In the wild, animals exist in a world of which we have little understanding. They may communicate with their kind through "languages" that are indecipherable by humans.
45 A few studies suggest that some species perceive landscapes much differently than people do; for example, they may be keenly attuned to movement on the faces of mountains or across the broad span of grassy plains. Also, their social
50 structures may be complex and integral to their well-being. Some scientists believe they may even develop cultural traditions that are key to the survival of populations.
      But when an animal is confined, it lives
55 within a vacuum. If it is accustomed to covering

long distances in its searches for food, it grows lazy or bored. It can make no decisions for itself; its intelligence and wild skills atrophy from lack of use. It becomes, in a sense, one of society's
60 charges, completely dependent on humans for nourishment and care.
      How might an animal species be changed— subtly, imperceptibly—by spending several generations in a pen? I posed that question to the
65 curator of birds at the San Diego Wild Animal Park, which is a breeding center for the endangered California condor. "I always have to chuckle when someone asks me that," the curator replied. "Evolution has shaped the behavior of
70 the condor for hundreds of years. If you think I can change it in a couple of generations, you're giving me a lot of credit."
      Recently the condor was reintroduced into the California desert—only a moment after its
75 capture, in evolutionary terms. Perhaps the curator was right; perhaps the wild nature of the birds would emerge unscathed, although I was not convinced. But what of species that will spend decades or centuries in confinement before they are released?

* Inbreeding, which refers to the mating of offspring of the same parents, often amplifies any genetic weaknesses a species may have.

17. The primary purpose of the passage is to
  (A) highlight the improvements in the conditions of American zoos
  (B) examine behavioral traits of animals living in zoos
  (C) prompt scientists to conduct more research on animal behavior
  (D) raise concerns about the confinement of wild animals in zoos
  (E) suggest alternative ways of protecting endangered species

18. On the whole, the author's attitude toward captive breeding is one of
  (A) sympathy
  (B) puzzlement
  (C) indifference
  (D) ambivalence
  (E) disgust

GO ON TO THE NEXT PAGE

19. The primary function of the second paragraph is to show that
    (A) wild animals adapt to their cages by modifying their movements
    (B) improvements in zoo design have not had the intended effects
    (C) confined animals are not being harmed
    (D) zoos are designed with the reactions of spectators in mind
    (E) people are overly sensitive to seeing animals in captivity

20. One of the major implications of the passage is that
    (A) animals bred in captivity are as likely to survive in the wild as are wild animals
    (B) zoos do a disservice to animals by trying to entertain zoo visitors
    (C) animal extinctions can mainly be attributed to human activity
    (D) present methods of protecting animal populations may be flawed
    (E) public concerns about the extinction of species have been exploited by the media

21. In the fourth paragraph, the author's most important point is that animals in the wild
    (A) perceive landscapes differently than do animals in captivity
    (B) have modes of communicating that are very similar to those of humans
    (C) are likely to live longer than animals kept in zoos
    (D) depend on the care and support of others of their species
    (E) may have highly developed sensibilities about which scientists know little

22. In line 60, "charges" most nearly means
    (A) costs
    (B) responsibilities
    (C) demand
    (D) accusations
    (E) attacks

23. Which of the following best describes the relationship between the fourth paragraph and the fifth paragraph?
    (A) The fourth paragraph presents a question that is answered in the fifth paragraph.
    (B) The fourth paragraph contains an assertion that is evaluated in the fifth paragraph.
    (C) The fifth paragraph describes a contrast to the situation presented in the fourth paragraph.
    (D) The fifth paragraph discusses the second part of the process described in the fourth paragraph.
    (E) The fifth paragraph describes the cause of the situation discussed in the fourth paragraph.

24. The curator's primary point in the sixth paragraph is that
    (A) people's ideas about the power of humans to alter animal behavior are presumptuous
    (B) scientists should strive to mimic natural selection processes more closely
    (C) animals have little trouble adapting their behavior to captive environments
    (D) animals have been surviving for years without the intervention of humans
    (E) captive breeding is essential to the survival of animals

25. The author's attitude toward the curator's statement in the sixth paragraph can best be described as
    (A) ironic (B) objective   (C) hopeless
      (D) doubtful   (E) offended

26. It can be inferred from the passage that the author believes that wild animals
    (A) should be removed from their natural habitats only in dire circumstances
    (B) suffer few long-term consequences from changes in their habitat
    (C) are pawns in a political battle over the protection of wildlife habitats
    (D) provide an inadequate source of data for the experimental designs of captive breeding habitats
    (E) fulfill the expectations of zoo visitors who hope to see animals behave as they would have before they were captured

GO ON TO THE NEXT PAGE

219

Writing & Grammar
16 practice exercises

SAT Writing Exercise #01
50 Questions

DIRECTIONS

Thes following sentences test your ability to detect errors in grammar and usage. Each sentence contains either one error or no errors at all and no sentence contains more than one error. Choose the underlined word or phrase in each sentence that when changed best corrects the grammatical or usage error. Only underlined words may be changed. If the sentence is correct as written, select choice E. In making your choices keep in mind the standards requirements of standard written English.

EXAMPLE:

Super Mario Bros' Mario first <u>appeared</u> in Donkey
                                    A
Kong as Jumpman and <u>was</u> later <u>renamed</u> to Mario
                      B   C
<u>in honor to</u> Nintendo of America's landlord Mario
D
Segali. <u>No Error</u>
         E

Ⓐ Ⓑ Ⓒ ⬤ Ⓔ

1. It was upsetting to Tim to find his classmates

   <u>responding</u> so <u>sarcastic</u> to his presentation,
   A   B
   <u>on which</u> he <u>had worked</u> diligently and seri-
   C   D
   ously for days. <u>No error.</u>
                    E

2. In big cities <u>like</u> Detroit and Houston, there
                  A
   <u>isn't</u> hardly a day that goes by <u>when</u> there are
   B   C
   <u>no</u> homicides, according to the report of the
   D
   commissioner. <u>No error.</u>
                  E

3. <u>At seven</u>, when Martha went to the circus and
   A
   saw the clown act, she <u>knew</u> immediately that
                           B
   when she grew up she would like to be <u>one</u>,
                                          C
   <u>too</u>. <u>No error.</u>
   D   E

4. Dame Sophie runs what has been called a tea

   room, but it is really a mecca <u>in which</u> to
                                   A
   pause <u>from</u> a day of running around the city
          B
   or shopping, <u>to buy</u> a sandwich and a cup of
                 C
   tea, and to have <u>their</u> palms read. <u>No error.</u>
                     D   E

5. <u>After all</u>, Elizabeth is the strongest candidate
   A
   for the job, <u>since</u> her looks, experience, and
                 B
   natural intelligence <u>attracts</u> voters <u>toward</u>
                         C   D
   her. <u>No error.</u>
         E

GO ON TO THE NEXT PAGE →

6. History <u>tells</u> us that the Cossacks were
        A

nationalistic and ruthless people, <u>usually men</u>
                                  B

<u>having</u> little or no concern <u>of</u> their wives.
  C   D

<u>No error.</u>
  E

7. I fully agree with Bertram's idea that each

person is in <u>themselves</u> a complex puzzle
           A

and that all of us need to set <u>aside</u> time in our
                        B

hectic lives <u>for</u> trying <u>to</u> solve the puzzle.
         C   D

<u>No error.</u>
  E

8. Because the rescuers <u>had been</u> beset with doubt
                   A

<u>that</u> anyone could have survived the mudslide,
 B

it was all the <u>more nicer</u> for them <u>to have found</u>
          C   D

the old man and the child unharmed. <u>No error.</u>
                              E

9. Although the passage fails to state opinions <u>of</u>
                                 A

the speaker <u>in</u> which I can agree, I am thankful
          B

that Mr. Foley <u>has given</u> me an opportunity
           C

<u>to think</u> about the issues in a fresh and
  D

illuminating manner. <u>No error.</u>
              E

10. The smoke alarm, coincidentally,

<u>had been repaired</u> only the day before <u>it</u> sound
     A   B

at 3:00 o'clock in the morning and <u>awakened</u>
                             C

<u>up</u> the whole family. <u>No error.</u>
  D   E

11. <u>Although</u> a teenager may think that <u>their</u>
     A   B

parents are overprotective, parents feel <u>that</u>, by
                              C

shielding their offspring from harm, they are

merely showing how much they love <u>their</u>
                           D

child. <u>No error.</u>
      E

12. The orchestra played <u>so loudly</u>, and there was
                    A B

such a din in the ballroom throughout the

wedding reception, that <u>it</u> was <u>hardly possible</u>
                    C   D

to hold a conversation without shouting.

<u>No error.</u>
  E

13. According to the conservative view espoused <u>by</u>
                                A

Harrington, a woman is assigned a role in life,

<u>is to be</u> treated with respect, <u>and</u> is constantly
 B   C

to be reminded that <u>they are</u> appreciated and
                 D

loved. <u>No error.</u>
      E

GO ON TO THE NEXT PAGE

14. As a meek and humble clerk, Melvin never

asked for anything, never raised his voice,

never taunted anyone <u>or</u> made a <u>scenario</u> <u>about</u>
                  A   B   C

what was happening to him <u>around</u> the
                             D

office when the boss was not present. <u>No error.</u>
                                        E

15. After his death <u>it</u> had been rumored that
                A
Akaky's ghost <u>is</u> seen spooking around the city,
               B
stripping overcoats from passers-by and

<u>creating</u> havoc and fear <u>among</u> the bureaucrats
  C   D
in the ministry of courts and justice. <u>No error.</u>
                           E

16. Watching television at eleven in the evening,

<u>they</u> <u>always</u> give a summary of the day's
A   B

important news, an editorial <u>on</u> a current issue
                         C

and the weather forecast <u>for</u> the next few days.
                      D

<u>No error.</u>
 E

17. If you expect to be absent from school when

the senior paper is due, you should hand <u>it</u> in
                             A

early or, <u>if necessary one</u> should arrange for an
          B   C

extension <u>with</u> an advisor or teacher. <u>No error.</u>
         D   E

18. <u>Considering</u> the frailty of <u>his</u> health, the old
   A   B
man should not have descended the subway

stairs as <u>rapid</u> as he <u>did</u>. <u>No error.</u>
       C   D   E

19. If Tom Cruise <u>was</u> alive <u>during</u> the heyday of
              A   B
Hollywood's glamorous and debonair leading

actors, he probably would have been

<u>thought to be</u> too naive and boyish <u>to become</u>
    C   D
a big star. <u>No error.</u>
         E

20. <u>Agreeing</u> with Mr. Hearn's assessment of two
   A
Hemingway novels, A Farewell to Arms <u>is</u> by
                                 B
far the <u>better</u>, not only because of its structure
       C
<u>but also because</u> of the fascinating story it tells.
        D
<u>No error.</u>
  E

GO ON TO THE NEXT PAGE

21. Many people are taught <u>when very young</u> that
                              A
no matter what they are feeling they should

always wear a smile<u>, and</u> that is why one
                      B
person's sadness can look exactly <u>like</u>
                                    C
someone <u>else's</u> happiness. <u>No error.</u>
          D   E

22. The settlement of the healthcare issue <u>between</u>
                                             A
the union and the management came just at the

moment <u>when</u> all parties were <u>on the verge</u> of
         B   C
throwing their hands up and <u>quitting</u>. <u>No error.</u>
                              D   E

23. Because he was more than five years older

than <u>me</u> and a hundred years smarter, I never
      A
felt comfortable in his presence, not, <u>at least,</u>
                                         B
until the evening <u>when</u> he told me <u>that</u> he
                    C   D
loved me. <u>No error.</u>
            E

24. Though the peasants did not raise <u>any</u> political
                                        A
demands, they suffered <u>from</u> severe economic
                         B
oppression and were willing to appropriate

<u>by direct action</u> the land that they believed was
  C
<u>theirs</u> by right. <u>No error.</u>
  D   E

25. Don's heroism was demonstrated when <u>he</u> was
                                          A
being hunted because, <u>as an officer,</u> he was
                        B
expected to be <u>on</u> the front lines, not strolling
                 C
<u>around the streets</u> of Milan with a woman at
  D
his side. <u>No error.</u>
            E

26. <u>While</u> they were crossing the lake in a small
     A
dinghy, Catherine was scared, but <u>after</u> they
                                     B
arrived on the opposite shore she said <u>that</u> she
                                          C
<u>was not frightened</u> at all during the trip.
  D
<u>No error.</u>
  E

GO ON TO THE NEXT PAGE

DIRECTIONS

Thes following sentences test your ability to express ideas in writing effectively and efficiently. Each sentence is either partially or completely underlined. The first of the five choices given will repeat the original wording and the other four choices will contain alternative wording. Choose the change that best improves the senetence or choose A if the original is superior to any of the other choices given.

In making your choice keep in mind the standards of proper written English. Among other things, pay close attention to grammar, word choice, punctuation, precision, and correct usage of tenses. Avoid awkward and ambiguous construction.

EXAMPLE:

I want your love, and I want your revenge; you and me can write a bad romance.

(A) you and me can write
(B) you and me could write
(C) you and me writing
(D) you and I can write
(E) me and you can write

27. Neither visiting the school nor spending time with the students and teachers has prevented Mr. Ranalli to criticize the manner in which education is conducted in the local district.

   (A) has prevented Mr. Ranalli to criticize
   (B) have prevented Mr. Ranalli criticizing
   (C) have kept Mr. Ranalli from expressing opinions about
   (D) has kept Mr. Ranalli expressing opinions of
   (E) has prevented Mr. Ranalli from criticizing

28. Funds that are earned as tips and personal sale of goods and services is one of the most difficult sources of income for the IRS to monitor.

   (A) Funds that arc earned as tips and personal sales of goods and services is
   (B) How money that gets earned as tips and personal sales of goods and services is
   (C) Earning tips and funds from personal sales of goods and services are
   (D) Money earned from tips and from personal sales of goods and services is
   (E) The funds raised by tipping and by selling goods and services is

29. October 15th will mark the second anniversary of us coming to live in Allentown and it's flown by.

   (A) of us coming to live in Allentown and it's flown by.
   (B) of our coming to live in Allentown, and the time has flown by.
   (C) of our arriving to live in Allentown and it has flown by.
   (D) of living in Allentown, and its flown by.
   (E) of us coming to live in Allentown, and the time has flown by.

GO ON TO THE NEXT PAGE

30. The editorial, demanding the reversal of the Supreme Court's decision, brutally attacking the liberal justices exemplifying flammatory journalism at its worst.

   (A) The editorial, demanding the reversal of the Supreme Court's decision, brutally attacking the liberal justices, exemplifying flammatory journalism at its worst.
   (B) The editorial, an example of flammatory journalism at its worst, demands the reversal of the Supreme Court's decision and brutally attacks the liberal justices.
   (C) The editorial demands the reversal of the Supreme Court's decision, brutally attacking the liberal justices and an example of flammatory journalism at its worst.
   (D) An example of an editorial demanding the reversal of the Supreme Court's decision, and brutally attacking the liberal justices, is flammatory journalism at its worst.
   (E) An example of flammatory journalism at its worst demands the reversal of the Supreme Court's decision, brutally attacking the liberal justices.

31. The far right Libertarian Party, usually by fairly simple electronic hookups, has tried to preach their ideology on the closed-circuit TV systems of small, often rural, colleges.

   (A) Party, usually by fairly simple electronic hookups, has tried to preach their
   (B) Party uses fairly simple electronic hookups to preach its
   (C) Party, using fairly simple electronic hookups, preaches their
   (D) Party, preaching via fairly simple electronic hookups has sent out its
   (E) Party, usually by fairly simple electronic hookups, it has tried to preach its

32. Applications and interest in Mrs. Clinton's college, Wellesley, has risen because she often mentions her undergraduate days in public statements.

   (A) Applications and interest in Mrs. Clinton's college, Wellesley,- has risen
   (B) Applications to and interest in Mrs. Clinton's college, Wellesley, have raised
   (C) A rise in applications and an increased interest in Wellesley are attributed to Mrs. Clinton
   (D) Mrs. Clinton is responsible for raising applications and increasing interest in Wellesley
   (E) Mrs. Clinton is blamed for the increasing popularity of Wellesley

33. Obviously, today a great deal more violence occurs in the United States than fifty years ago, when guns were not so pervasive as they are now.

   (A) than fifty years ago
   (B) there was fifty years ago
   (C) than occurred fifty years ago
   (D) there occurred fifty years ago
   (E) then did occur there fifty years ago

34. Religious fundamentalism has become a major factor in modem Iranian society, now almost every woman follows its dress code.

   (A) society, now almost every woman
   (B) society; this being evident in how almost every Iranian woman now
   (C) society; so now that almost every woman
   (D) society; in fact, almost every woman
   (E) society, making now almost every woman

GO ON TO THE NEXT PAGE

35. Janet felt elated to find the book she had been looking for walking by the window of the used book shop of High Street.

    (A) Janet felt elated to find the book she had been looking for walking by the window of the used book shop of High Street.

    (B) Feeling elated, Janet found the book she had been looking for walking outside the window of the used book shop of High Street.

    (C) Walking by the used book shop on High Street, the book Janet had been looking for appeared in the window, much to her delight.

    (D) Janet, feeling elated over finding the book she had been looking for while walking outside the window of the used book shop of High Street.

    (E) Walking by the used book shop on High Street, Janet was elated to find the window the book for which she had been looking.

36. Dale Zheutlin, a popular contemporary ceramic artist, with sculptures mounted in homes and office buildings across tl1e country, but her studio is in New Rochelle, New York.

    (A) artist, with sculptures mounted in homes and office buildings across the country, but her studio is in New Rochelle, New York.

    (B) artist, has mounted sculptures in homes and office buildings across the country, and her studio is in New Rochelle, New York.

    (C) artist with a studio in New Rochelle, New York, has mounted her sculptures in homes and office buildings across the country.

    (D) artist, has a studio in New Rochelle, New York, meanwhile her sculptures are mounted in homes and office buildings across the country.

    (E) artist, whose sculptures are mounted in homes and office buildings across the country; New Rochelle, New York, is the location of her studio.

GO ON TO THE NEXT PAGE

37. <u>When Beethoven's music was first introduced to the public, they had found it</u> difficult to understand and unpleasant to listen to.

   (A) When Beethoven's music was first introduced to the public, they found it
   (B) When it was first introduced to the public, they found Beethoven's music
   (C) When the music of Beethoven was introduced, the public found it
   (D) To be introduced to Beethoven's music, the public found it
   (E) The public, being first introduced to Beethoven's music, found it

38. <u>Novels which were not customarily written</u> at the time, began to be received more favorably in Russia because of Pushkin's efforts to tell extended stories in prose.

   (A) Novels that were not customarily written
   (B) Novels which had not been written by custom
   (C) Novels, not customarily written
   (D) Novels, which having not been customarily written
   (E) Novels, which were not written according to custom

39. As a student at Yale, <u>Julie Ledbetter grew to love history with a passion that ultimately led</u> to an appointment as Ohio State Historian, a position she held for nearly two decades.

   (A) Julie Ledbetter grew to love history with a passion that ultimately led
   (B) where Julie Ledbetter grew to love history with a passion, ultimately leading
   (C) where she grew to love history passionately, as a result leading ultimately
   (D) Julie Ledbetter's love for history grew with a passion and it ultimately led her
   (E) where Julie Ledbetter grew to passionately love history, ultimately leading her

40. A biotechnology company in New Jersey got a patent for <u>xenografting, a technique for developing animals</u> to supply organs like hearts, livers, or kidneys for human transplant recipients.

   (A) xenografting, a technique for developing animals
   (B) xenografting, which is a technique for the development of animals
   (C) xenografting, which is when scientists use a technique for developing animals
   (D) xenografting. in which animals are developed using a technique
   (E) xenografting, a technique for animals to be developing

GO ON TO THE NEXT PAGE

41. Since dolphins are social animals, it is possible for Atlantic dolphins to speak the same basic "language" as Pacific dolphins <u>although not being able</u> to communicate exact nuances and subtleties of meaning.

   (A) although not being able
   (B) but not having the ability
   (C) even as their ability is lacking
   (D) although they are not able
   (E) even though being unable

42. Two-thirds of the schools in New York City, <u>a mecca for the arts, have no art or music teachers, they have been cut</u> from the program because of fiscal belt-tightening.

   (A) a mecca for the arts, have no art or music teachers, they have been cut
   (B) an artistic mecca that has no art or music teachers have been cut
   (C) a mecca for the arts; they have no art or music teachers, who have been cut
   (D) a mecca for the arts, have no art or music teachers; they have been cut
   (E) a mecca for the arts, have cut art or music teachers out

43. <u>There is plenty of Thoreau's practical advice about life which every reader can benefit from in his *Walden*.</u>

   (A) There is plenty of Thoreau's practical advice about life which every reader can benefit from in his *Walden*.
   (B) In Thoreau's *Walden*, he gives the reader plenty of practical and beneficial advice about life.
   (C) Reading Thoreau's *Walden*, plenty of practical advice is offered to the benefit of readers.
   (D) In *Walden*, Thoreau offers readers plenty of practical and beneficial advice about life.
   (E) Plenty of beneficial and practical advice about life is offered to readers by Thoreau's *Walden*.

44. Another dimension of Pugachev's personality, which was indeed crafty, <u>was if he found himself in trouble, he would drag someone down with him</u> to share the blame and endure the punishment.

   (A) was if he found himself in trouble, he would drag someone down with him
   (B) was his need to drag someone down with him, when he found himself in trouble,
   (C) was that when he found himself in trouble, he will drag someone down with him
   (D) was when he got nailed, be will always drag someone down with him
   (E) came about when he was in trouble; he would drag someone down with him

GO ON TO THE NEXT PAGE

DIRECTIONS

The following passage is an early draft of an essay. Some parts of the passage need to be rewritten.

Read the passage and select the best answers for the questions that follow. Some questions are about particular sentences or parts of sentences and ask you to improve sentence structure or word choice. Other questions ask you to consider organization and development. In choosing answers, follow the requirements of standard written English.

Questions 45-50 refer to the following passage.

(1) Much of Russia lies under a cover of snow and ice for most of the year. (2) Permafrost covers the tundra. (3) Ports in northern Russia are not navigable for most of the year simply because they are frozen in. (4) In the south, the Black Sea gives Russia access to warm water ports. (5) The reason that the Black Sea is important is because it gives them the ability to export timber, furs, coal, oil, and other raw materials that are traded for food and manufactured goods. (6) The Black Sea Hill will continue to help their economic growth.

(7) The English Channel has served as a barrier between Great Britain and the rest of Europe. (8) It has prevented attacks on Great Britain for hundreds of years. (9) Except for the Norman invasion over 900 years ago. (10) This allowed the nation to develop economically and remain politically stable. (11) The isolation of Great Britain allowed the industrial revolution to begin in England.

(12) Much of Egypt is covered by desert. (13) The desert is irrigated by the Nile River. (14) It is longer than any river in the world. (15) The land along the river has historically been the site of farms and other settlements. (16) For centuries, the river has deposited rich particles of soil for growing crops along its banks. (17) Since building the Aswan High Dam in 1968, the fanners downstream from the dam have been using artificial fertilizer. (18) The banks of the Nile and the river's delta are among the most productive

farming areas in the world. (19) Therefore, Egypt depends on the Nile.
(20) Russia, Great Britain, and Egypt are only three countries that have been shaped and developed by bodies of water.

45. Which is the best revision of the underlined segment of sentence 5 below?

The reason that the Black Sea is important is because it gives them the ability to export timber, furs, coal, oil, and other raw materials that are traded for food and manufactured goods.

(A) that it enables Russia to export
(B) its ability to allow exports of
(C) the ability of Russia to export
(D) because of exporting opportunities of
(E) for Russian exports of

46. In the context of the second paragraph, which is the best revision of sentences 8 and 9?

(A) The English Channel has prevented Great Britain's being attacked for hundreds of years; except for the Norman invasion in 1066.
(B) It has prevented attacks, except for the Norman invasion in 1066, on Great Britain for hundreds of years.
(C) Except for not preventing the Norman invasion over 900 years ago, the English Channel has prevented attacks on Great Britain for hundreds of years.
(D) It has prevented attacking Great Britain for 900 years, except the Normans.
(E) For hundreds of years it has prevented attacks on Great Britain, except for the Norman invasion in 1066.

GO ON TO THE NEXT PAGE ➡

47. Which is the best way to combine sentences 12, 13, and 14?

(A) The Nile, the longest river in the world, irrigates the desert that covers much of Egypt.
(B) Egypt, which is covered by desert, is irrigated by the Nile, which is longer than any river in the world.
(C) The desert, which covers much of Egypt, is irrigated by the Nile, which is longer than any river in the world.
(D) The longest river in the world, the Nile River, irrigates the Egyptian desert, which means that the river irrigates most of the country.
(E) Much of the desert covering much of Egypt lies alongside the Nile, the longest river in the world, and much of it is irrigated by it.

48. To improve the coherence of paragraph 3, which of the following sentences would be the best to delete?

(A) Sentence 15
(B) Sentence 16
(C) Sentence 17
(D) Sentence 18
(E) Sentence 19

49. Which of the following sentences is most in need of further support and development?

(A) Sentence 1
(B) Sentence 2
(C) Sentence 5
(D) Sentence 11
(E) Sentence 14

50. Considering the essay as a whole, which one of the following least accurately describes the function of paragraph 4?

(A) It summarizes the essay's main idea.
(B) It serves to unify the essay.
(C) It proves the validity of the essay's main idea.
(D) It defines the purpose of the essay.
(E) It gives a sense of completion to the essay.

STOP

this is the end of the exercise

SAT Writing Exercise #02

50 Questions

DIRECTIONS

Thes following sentences test your ability to detect errors in grammar and usage. Each sentence contains either one error or no errors at all and no sentence contains more than one error. Choose the underlined word or phrase in each sentence that when changed best corrects the grammatical or usage error. Only underlined words may be changed. If the sentence is correct as written, select choice E. In making your choices keep in mind the standards requirements of standard written English.

EXAMPLE:

Super Mario Bros' Mario first <u>appeared</u> in Donkey
                               A
Kong as Jumpman and <u>was</u> later <u>renamed</u> to Mario
                     B   C
<u>in honor to</u> Nintendo of America's landlord Mario
   D
Segali. <u>No Error</u>
        E

Ⓐ Ⓑ Ⓒ Ⓓ Ⓔ

1. Every morning the scouts gathered at the

flagpole <u>to listen to</u> the announcements for the
         A

day being read aloud <u>from</u> a clipboard by the
                      B

head counselor and to salute the flag <u>as</u>
                                       C

it was <u>risen</u> over the camp. <u>No error</u>
       D   E

2. Victor's parents can't afford to <u>lay aside</u> funds
                                        A

for luxuries <u>such as</u> a new car or a vacation,
             B

but rather must save <u>it</u> for <u>their</u> son's college
                     C   D

education. <u>No error</u>
           E

3. <u>To sing a song good,</u> <u>you</u> must focus your
       A   B

attention not only on the music but <u>on</u> the
                                     C

words <u>as well.</u> <u>No error</u>
      D   E

4. Young children should not be urged into

activities before they are ready <u>for them,</u> <u>for</u>
                                 A   B

pushing them prematurely often proves to be a

waste of time and may cause <u>children</u> <u>to feel</u>
                            C   D

failure and frustration. <u>No error</u>
                         E

5. The opposing attorneys, Mr. Kourabas and

Mr. Martin, <u>had gone</u> to the courthouse that
            A

morning determined <u>to take full advantage</u> of
                    B

the situation <u>in order to</u> promote <u>his</u> client's
              C   D

interests. <u>No error</u>
           E

GO ON TO THE NEXT PAGE

6. Since nihilists neither valued nationalism nor

patriotism, <u>nor</u> committed <u>themselves</u> to any
        A   B

cause <u>whatever</u>, they believed I was wrong to
      C

join the army or to serve <u>your</u> country in any
                          D

way. <u>No error</u>
      E

7. The class <u>especially</u> enjoyed the talk <u>by the man</u>
               A   B

who <u>has been</u> in Russia during the I 991
     C

coup that <u>overthrew</u> the Communist regime of
          D

Mikhail Gorbachev. <u>No error</u>
               E

8. The <u>womens</u> movement was <u>thought to have</u>
       A   B

come of age <u>during</u> the 1992 elections, when
          C

four women were elected <u>to the</u> United
                 D

States Senate and a record number won seats

in the U.S. House of Representatives.

<u>No error</u>
  E

9. <u>Throughout</u> the year, the park attracts tourists
   A

and campers who come <u>for</u> hiking the
               B

wilderness, climbing the mountains,

<u>water sports</u>, and catching trout and
  C

<u>other</u> prized game fish. <u>No error</u>
  D   E

10. A large formation of geese, in addition to one

white <u>and</u> graceful swan, <u>were swimming</u>
     A   B

peacefully on the surface of the lake <u>when</u> the
                    C

report of a rifle shot sent them <u>aloft</u>. <u>No error</u>
                 D   E

11. Chekhov's eye <u>for detail</u> and use of cogent
          A

language <u>make</u> <u>his</u> short stories and plays
       B C

popular the world over, even among people

who know little about literature or <u>care little</u>
                    D

for serious theater. <u>No error</u>
          E

12. Carolyn's mother was born and raised in the

<u>mainly</u> residential area of the Bronx, where
 A

she went to <u>high school</u>, got <u>married</u>, and
        B   C

<u>gave</u> birth to Carolyn on October 20, 1979.
 D

<u>No error</u>
  E

13. Tolstoy said that happiness derives from

<u>living</u> for others <u>and that</u>, if one fails to serve
  A   B

others in some fashion, when <u>life's end</u>
                 C

approaches, <u>they</u> will die with regrets.
      D

<u>No error</u>
  E

GO ON TO THE NEXT PAGE

14. <u>On</u> her application to Rutgers, Carole wrote
    A

    that medical technician <u>had</u> <u>always</u> been
                      B   C

    <u>an idea</u> that attracted her. <u>No error</u>
      D   E

15. Work in specialized fields <u>like</u> bacteriology,
                            A

    nutrition, horticulture, public health, and

    animal husbandry <u>require</u> at least a bachelor's
                  B

    degree, and for <u>a job</u> in management and
               C

    research, a master's degree <u>or even</u> a
                          D

    doctorate. <u>No error</u>
           E

16. Chilblains is a skin condition that stings,

    itches, and burns, it affects the feet
               A

    particularly, <u>mostly</u> after <u>they</u> have been
               B   C

    exposed to the cold or <u>after</u> being cold and
                   D

    wet. <u>No error</u>
        E

17. Baker, in his memoir, <u>tells</u> stories
                  A

    <u>about the time</u> before high school when he
      B

    <u>worked as</u> a paperboy and delivered
     C

    newspapers to the huge estates and mansions

    that <u>used to</u> line the riverfront. <u>No error</u>
        D   E

18. <u>Although</u> Martin Luther King's birthday <u>is</u>
      A   B

    on January 15th, <u>it</u> is celebrated on the third
                C

    Monday of January, <u>regardless</u> of the date.
                      D

    <u>No error</u>
      E

19. In the fifteenth century the French king,

    Charles VIII, flexed his army's muscles in

    what <u>are</u> now Naples and <u>Brittany; the latter</u>
        A   B

    of the two turned out <u>to be</u> the <u>weakest</u>, and
                    C   D

    soon became a part of France. <u>No error</u>
                          E

20. The collective thoughts, reflections,

    memories, and opinions <u>expressed by</u> the
                   A

    seniors in the pages of the <u>student</u> magazine
                      B

    <u>represent</u> the diversity and uniqueness that
     C

    <u>characterizes</u> Brookdale High School.
     D
    No error
      E

21. When he walked <u>in</u> the classroom from the
              A

    corridor, all the students <u>rose as one</u> and
                      B

    applauded <u>him</u> for <u>having run</u> in the New
         C   D

    York Marathon and finishing in under three

    hours. <u>No error</u>
         E

GO ON TO THE NEXT PAGE →

22. A good motorcycle rider like Johnny is

someone <u>who</u> knows how to switch gears at
.............A

the right moment, can downshift on a whim,

<u>obeys the law</u>, and <u>controls</u> <u>their</u> bike at all
.......B.................C.........D

times. <u>No error</u>
.............E

23. When Annie <u>set out</u> to find the best car
...................A

at a price she could afford, she decided that

she'd look <u>for</u> something different <u>than</u> the
...............B......................C

typical models that her friends <u>were driving</u>.
....D

<u>No error</u>
.....E

24. It was improper for an owner to beat <u>his</u>
....A

slaves at that <u>time, however</u>, there actually
......................B

<u>were</u> laws <u>on the books</u> that specified the
...C.............D

circumstances when slavebeating was justified.

<u>No error</u>
.....E

25. The award-winning *Sound of Music*

<u>has been seen</u> by more moviegoers <u>than</u>
...........A.....................................B
<u>any musical</u> film <u>in</u> the history of the movies.
.........C..........D

<u>No error</u>
.....E

26. In all of <u>Carson McCullers'</u> stories, <u>she</u> probes
.................A..............................B

the minds and the hearts of the characters,

<u>leaving</u> no detail unnoticed, no expression or
...C

gesture <u>unobserved</u>. <u>No error</u>
.............D.............E

GO ON TO THE NEXT PAGE

GO ON TO THE NEXT PAGE

DIRECTIONS

Thes following sentences test your ability to express ideas in writing effectively and efficiently. Each sentence is either partially or completely underlined. The first of the five choices given will repeat the original wording and the other four choices will contain alternative wording. Choose the change that best improves the senetence or choose A if the original is superior to any of the other choices given.

In making your choice keep in mind the standards of proper written English. Among other things, pay close attention to grammar, word choice, punctuation, precision, and correct usage of tenses. Avoid awkard and ambiguous construction.

EXAMPLE:

I want your love, and I want your revenge; you and me can write a bad romance.

(A) you and me can write
(B) you and me could write
(C) you and me writing
(D) you and I can write
(E) me and you can write

Ⓐ Ⓑ Ⓒ Ⓓ Ⓔ

27. Like Jasper Johns, Pop artist Ed Ruscha was fascinated by words, and have consistently formed the principal subject matter of his paintings and graphics.

(A) words, and have consistently formed the principal subject matter
(B) words, and words have consistently formed the principal subject matter
(C) words which have consistently fanned the principal subject matter
(D) words, consistently they have fanned the principal subject matter
(E) words, which have consistently fanned the principal subject matter

28. The strength and appearance of denim fabric account for its appeal among campers, hikers, and other outdoor enthusiasts.

(A) account for its appeal
(B) accounts for its appeal
(C) account for their appeal
(D) explains why it is appealing
(E) are the reasons for their appeal

29. The telling of tales is one of the earliest forms of human pastime, and they increased in complexity as well as sophistication as time went on.

(A) pastime, and they increased in complexity as well as sophistication
(B) pastime, they both increased in complexity and sophistication
(C) pastime, which both increased in complexity as well as in sophistication
(D) pastime, and it increased their complexity and sophistication
(E) pastime; an activity that increased in complexity as well as sophistication

30. The dilemma of loyalty to one's country versus loyalty to one's family is exemplified in the story when Thomas must decide whether to kill his own son, Andy, who had betrayed family tradition by joining the Union army for a woman.

(A) by joining the Union army for a woman.
(B) for a woman joining the Union army.·
(C) by, for the reason of a woman, joining the union army.
(D) by for a woman joined the Union army.
(A) for a woman, for joining the Union army.

31. Although dinosaurs were the hugest animals ever to roam the earth, many modern-day whales <u>are as equal in their dimensions to</u> many prehistoric dinosaurs.

(A) are as equal in their dimensions to
(B) are as large or equal to
(C) are as large as
(D) are as equally large in their dimensions as
(E) are as equal in dimensions with

32. Cervantes, the sixteenth-century Spanish author, was so far ahead of his day that, despite the instant popularity of his Don Quixote, <u>no immediate successors had come into being during his lifetime.</u>

(A) no immediate successors had come into being during his lifetime
(B) he had no immediate successors during his lifetime
(C) the corning of a successor was not to be during his lifetime
(D) there was not a coming of a successor during his lifetime
(E) during his lifetime it had no immediate successors

33. Howard stepped briskly to the counter <u>and bought a cup of black coffee with Janet's money, which he drank quickly</u> before hurrying back downtown.

(A) and bought a cup of black coffee with Janet's money, which he drank quickly
(B) and buying a cup of black coffee with Janet's money, drank it quickly
(C) and using Janet's money and buying a cup of black coffee that he drank quickly
(D) and, with Janet's money, bought a cup of black coffee, which he drank quickly
(E) and, using the money from Janet, buys a cup of black coffee which he drinks quickly

34. Soviet Olympians were supposed to be more than <u>athletes they</u> were also meant to be symbols of the greatness of the socialist system.

(A) athletes they were
(B) athletes and were
(C) athletes; they were
(D) athletes, although they were
(E) athletes; being that they were

35. Subjecting laboratory rats to cold temperatures <u>change the ratio of brown fat cells to white fat cells</u> in the animal's body.

(A) change the ratio of brown fat cells to white fat cells
(B) produce a change in the ratio between brown fat cells and white fat cells
(C) change the ratio between brown fat cells to white fat cells
(D) produce changes in the ratios between white and brown fat cells
(E) changes the ratio of brown fat cells to white fat cells

36. Another of the common characteristics <u>of the bulimic is their dependence</u> on the good opinion of others.

(A) of the bulimic is their dependence on
(B) of the bulimic is their reliability on
(C) of bulimia is her reliance on
(D) of bulimia is their reliability on
(E) of bulimics is their dependence on

GO ON TO THE NEXT PAGE

37. My grandfather owned a watchmaker's shop in South Philadelphia, and it was burglarized at least once a month. and he loved the place.

    (A) My grandfather owned a watchmaker's shop in South Philadelphia, and it was burglarized at least once a month, and he loved the place.
    (B) My grandfather loved his watchmaker's shop in South Philadelphia, in addition to being burglarized at least once a month.
    (C) Although his watchmaker's shop in South Philadelphia was burglarized at least once a month, my grandfather loved the place.
    (D) Although my grandfather owned a watchmaker's shop in South Philadelphia which was burglarized at least once a month, but he loved the place.
    (E) shop in South Philadelphia, my grandfather loved the place even though it was burglarized at least once a month.

38. Geneticists, in a relatively short time, have uncovered vast amounts of information about human heredity despite the fact of human generations being separated by twenty or more years.

    (A) despite the fact of human generations being separated by twenty or more years
    (B) despite the fact that a human generation has been separated by twenty or more years
    (C) despite human generations are separated by twenty or more years
    (D) even though human generations are separated by twenty or more years
    (E) even though a period of twenty or more years separate human generations

39. Paying for a college education in this decade is more difficult for the average family than it was in the past.

    (A) than it was in the past
    (B) than for past families
    (C) than the past
    (D) than families in the past
    (E) than it used to be in the past

40. If you wish to truly understand Jefferson's notion of "the pursuit of happiness," a person should read his letters to his son.

    (A) a person should read his letters to his son
    (B) you should read his letters to his son
    (C) you should read the letters Jefferson wrote to his son
    (D) the letters Jefferson wrote to his son should be read
    (E) Jefferson's letters to his son should be read

41. It is the sort of an offer that no one but him would refuse.

    (A) the sort of an offer that no one but him
    (B) the sort of offer that no one but he
    (C) sort of an offer that no one but him
    (D) a type of an offer that only him
    (E) the type of offer only he

42. Kate complained to her father that she ought to be able to date any boys she wanted and become as good of friends with them as she wished.

    (A) as good of friends with them
    (B) as good a friend to them
    (C) as good as friends to them
    (D) a good friend of theirs
    (E) as good as friends with them

GO ON TO THE NEXT PAGE

43. <u>Having studied the works by the ancient physicians of Greece</u> helped to kindle a rebirth of the biological sciences during the Renaissance.

(A) Having studied the works by the ancient physicians of Greece
(B) By studying the works by the ancient physicians of Greece
(C) Knowledge of the ancient physicians of Greece.
(D) Studying and knowing the works by the ancient physicians of Greece
(E) Having known and studied the work by the ancient physicians of Greece

44. In most of the cults studied by sociologists, <u>they practice a studied deception to attract young people, for example, inviting them to share a meal and to be "friends."</u>

(A) they practice a studied deception to attract young people, for example, inviting them to share a meal and to be "friends."
(B) they practice a studied deception to attract young people; for example, they invite them to share a meal and to be "friends."
(C) a studied deception is practiced; for example, young people are invited to share a meal and to be "friends."
(D) members, to attract young people, practice a studied deception, for example, to invite them to share a meal and to be "friends."
(E) young people are attracted by being invited and being "friends," for example, or sharing a meal with members who practice a studied deception

GO ON TO THE NEXT PAGE

239

DIRECTIONS

The following passage is an early draft of an essay. Some parts of the passage need to be rewritten.

Read the passage and select the best answers for the questions that follow. Some questions are about particular sentences or parts of sentences and ask you to improve sentence structure or word choice. Other questions ask you to consider organization and development. In choosing answers, follow the requirements of standard written English.

Questions 45-50 refer to the following passage.

[1] At the beginning of the twentieth century, no one knew the technological developments that would be made by the 1990s. [2] The area of communication media is one of the significant developments in the twentieth century. [3] Also nuclear energy and great advancements in medicine and the treatment of disease. [4] One important development was the invention of communication satellites which allow images and messages to be sent wirelessly around the world. [5] One advantage is that current events can be sent worldwide in seconds; [6] News used to travel by boat and take weeks or months to get overseas. [7] When a disaster struck the World Trade Center, the world saw it immediately and condemned the terrorists' actions. [8] One weak aspect of communication satellites is that they are launched from a space shuttle, and that is an extremely costly operation. [9] They also they cost millions of dollars td build and operate. [10] Therefore, many poor countries are left out of the so called "Global Village. "[11] The invention and use of nuclear energy is another important technological development.[12] One positive feature of nuclear energy is that energy is cheaper, and can be made easy. [13] This is important in countries like France where almost all oft he electricity is nuclear. [14] A negative consequence of nuclear energy is the probability of major nuclear accidents. [15] Watch out for human error and careless workmanship. [16] They were

the cause of the meltdown in Chemobyl, which killed hundreds or maybe even thousands, and radiated half the Earth. [17] There have been many significant technological advances in medicine in the twentieth century. [18] One development was the invention of the C.4.T scan. [19] The C4T scan allows doctors to make a picture of your brain to see if there is a growth on it. [20] One positive effect of the CAT scan is that doctors can diagnose brain tumors and brain cancer at an early stage. [21] Many lives have been saved. [22] One negative effect is that CAT scans are costly, so they are not used in third world countries.

45. Considering the main idea of the whole essay, which of the following is the best revision of sentence 1?

(A) In 1900 no one could anticipate the technological developments in the 1990s.
(B) Recent technological achievements would blow the mind of people at the beginning of the twentieth century.
(C) The twentieth century has seen remarkable technological achievements, but there has also been a price to pay for progress.
(D) No one knows if the twenty-first century will produce as much technological progress as the twentieth century did.
(E) Technological progress in communications, nuclear energy, and medicine is wonderful, but in the process we are destroying ourselves and our environment.

46. Which is the best revision of the underlined segment of sentence 12 below?

One positive feature of nuclear energy is that energy is cheaper and can be made easy.

(A) energy is cheaper and can be made easily

(B) energy is made cheaper and more easily made

(C) it is cheap and easy to make

(D) it is both cheap as well as made easily

(E) it's more cheaper and easier to make

47. To improve the coherence of paragraph 2, which of the following is the best sentence to delete from the essay?

(A) Sentence 5

(B) Sentence 6

(C) Sentence 7

(D) Sentence 8

(E) Sentence 9

48. In the context of the sentences that precede and follow sentence 15, which is the best revision of sentence 15?

(A) Human error and careless workmanship are almost unavoidable.

(B) Especially human error and careless workmanship.

(C) There's hardly no foolproof way to prevent human error and careless workmanship.

(D) You must never put down your guard against human error and careless workmanship.

(E) Accidents can happen accidentally by human error and careless workmanship.

49. With regard to the entire essay, which of the following best explains the writer's intention in paragraphs 2, 3, and 4?

(A) To compare and contrast three technological achievements

(B) To provide examples of the pros and cons of technological progress

(C) To analyze the steps needed for achievement in three areas

(D) To convince the reader to be open to technological change

(E) To advocate more funds for technological research and development

50. Assume that sentences 17 and 18 were combined as follows: A significant advance in medicine has been the invention of the CAT scan. Which of the following is the best way to continue the paragraph?

(A) The CAT scan allows your doctors to make pictures of a brain to see if it has a growth on it, a cancer is growing, or tumors at an early stage.

(B) The CAT scan permits your doctors to make a picture and see if your brain has a growth on it, or whether or not you have brain tumors or brain cancer at an early stage.

(C) Taking pictures with a CAT scan, your brain is studied by doctors for growths, brain tumors, and cancer at an early stage.

(D) Doctors may make pictures of your brain to see if there is a growth, a tumor, or cancer at an early stage on it

(E) With this device a doctor may look into patient's brain to check for growths and to detect cancerous tumors at an early stage.

STOP

this is the end of the exercise

SAT Writing Exercise #03
50 Questions

DIRECTIONS

Thes following sentences test your ability to detect errors in grammar and usage. Each sentence contains either one error or no errors at all and no sentence contains more than one error. Choose the underlined word or phrase in each sentence that when changed best corrects the grammatical or usage error. Only underlined words may be changed. If the sentence is correct as written, select choice E. In making your choices keep in mind the standards requirements of standard written English.

EXAMPLE:

Super Mario Bros' Mario first <u>appeared</u> in Donkey
                                A
Kong as Jumpman and <u>was</u> later <u>renamed</u> to Mario
                     B   C
<u>in honor to</u> Nintendo of America's landlord Mario
 D
Segali. <u>No Error</u>
         E

Ⓐ   Ⓑ   Ⓒ   ⬤   Ⓔ

---

1. The speaker won applause <u>by emphasizing</u> the
                             A
point that a woman must not <u>be held back</u> by
                             B
custom and tradition and by the preference of
male politicians when <u>they</u> make the difficult
                        C
decision <u>whether</u> to run for high public office.
          D
<u>No error.</u>
 E

2. No matter how self-deluded one <u>may be,</u>
                                   A
<u>there's</u> no getting around the fact that there is
 B
no person <u>who</u> can be held responsible for one's
           C
sad fate except <u>themself.</u> <u>No error.</u>
                  D   E

3. I get along reasonably <u>good</u> with my parents,
                           A
but I know that when <u>you</u> have somebody who
                      B
loves you and honestly supports everything you
do, <u>it</u> makes you <u>all the more happy.</u> <u>No error.</u>
     C   D   E

4. From the <u>students'</u> point of view, the new rules
             A
<u>regarding</u> class attendance were <u>more</u> stricter
 B   C
than the old <u>ones.</u> <u>No error.</u>
              D   E

5. When <u>one</u> works as a census taker, you become
         A
an <u>employee</u> of the United States government,
    B
but you don't get the health and other benefits
that others <u>do</u> because you have the status of
             C
<u>only</u> a temporary employee. <u>No error.</u>
 D   E

GO ON TO THE NEXT PAGE →

6. <u>At</u> the prearranged signal from
   A
   <u>Andy, the chief editor of the newspaper,</u> all the
                          B
   members of the staff <u>raised up</u> from <u>their</u>
                          C   D
   chairs and silently filed out of the meeting
   room.
   <u>No error.</u>
   E

7. <u>To grasp</u> the enormity of the crime <u>that</u>
   A   B
   <u>has been</u> committed against nature, imagine
   C
   every square inch of the Taj Mahal or
   St. Peter's Square covered <u>with</u> spray paint and
                              D
   graffiti. <u>No error.</u>
             E

8. Don had <u>little or no</u> interest <u>in listening</u> to
            A   B
   another lecture <u>on</u> tobacco, drug, and alcohol
                    C
   <u>abuse, therefore,</u> he declined to participate in
   D
   the conference. <u>No error.</u>
                   E

9. <u>A person's behavior</u> can be <u>effected</u> by outside
   A   B
   influences, but it is a fallacy <u>to believe</u> that
                                   C
   <u>in the long run</u> there will always be someone to
   D
   blame for personal misfortune. <u>No error.</u>
                                  E

10. They <u>had had</u> the foundation of their house
         A
    sealed, but <u>that</u> proved no defense against the
                B
    water that squeezed through the windowsills
    <u>and filled</u> the basement <u>to a depth</u> of four feet.
    C   D
    <u>No error.</u>
    E

11. Once the vacation starts, I will <u>have</u> a chance
                                    A
    to prepare my art project <u>by</u> choosing the
                              B
    paintings, cutting some mats, and <u>to find</u>
                                      C
    frames of the right size for the pictures
    <u>to be hung</u> in the exhibition. <u>No error.</u>
    D   E

12. When the story <u>begins,</u> Don Benedetto, a
                   A
    young clergyman, is on his way home when he
    <u>met</u> a pair of hoodlums <u>who</u> threaten to harm
    B   C
    him physically if he allows the imminent
    marriage of Renzo and Lucia <u>to take place.</u>
                                D
    <u>No error.</u>
    E

13. It turned into an adventure of a lifetime, a
    sometimes <u>dangerous but never tedious</u> three
                        A
    week trip, <u>during which</u> we spent virtually
               B   C
    every hour <u>of it</u> together. <u>No error.</u>
               D   E

GO ON TO THE NEXT PAGE

14. <u>Prior to</u> <u>her</u> exposing the scandal, an attitude
        A   B

    of cockiness and carelessness <u>were</u> widespread
                                    C

    throughout the industry, and safety rules were

    hardly taken <u>seriously</u>. <u>No error</u>.
                    D   E

15. While visiting my family in Italy last summer,

    I saw that <u>following</u> traditional family values
                  A

    <u>have</u> become one of the distinct differences
      B

    <u>between</u> the members of the older generation
      C

    and <u>me</u>. <u>No error</u>.
         D   E

16. Because of a dog's <u>more lively</u> disposition and
                          A

    aggressiveness, animal trainers prefer dogs

    <u>over</u> cats as subjects <u>to work</u> <u>with</u>. <u>No error</u>.
      B   C   D   E

17. To be a real cowboy <u>takes</u> particular qualities of
                           A

    endurance and tolerance for discomfort <u>, and</u> I
                                              B

    believe that Dan would have failed miserably

    <u>in</u> an attempt to become like <u>them</u>. <u>No error</u>.
    C   D   E

18. The scandal reveals that elected officials,

    who are chosen to represent <u>us</u> citizens,
                                  A

    <u>when granted</u> political power, <u>feel</u> nothing but
       B   C

    disdain <u>of</u> the common people. <u>No error</u>.
            D   E

19. Bartleby was a copying clerk in the office of a

    counselor-at-law, and <u>it was</u> all he intended to
                            A

    do, <u>regardless</u> of the effort <u>by</u> his employer to
         B   C

    <u>alter</u> Bartleby's assignment. <u>No error</u>.
     D   E

20. Neither of the candidates <u>are</u> yet <u>to take</u> a
                               A   B

    position on what to do about racial strife in the
    inner city, even though the issue is <u>foremost</u> in
                                           C

    the <u>voters'</u> minds. <u>No error</u>.
         D   E

21. By the end of the month the contractors,

    <u>much</u> to the <u>owner's</u> surprise, had <u>already</u> laid
      A   B   C

    out the site, cleared the land, and <u>began</u> to dig
                                          D

    the excavation. <u>No error</u>.
                      E

GO ON TO THE NEXT PAGE

22. There isn't any justification for you becoming
                                        A
so angry with Jason and him that you
                          B
can hardly deal rationally with the problem of
 C   D
their lost passports. No error.
                       E

23. If she only had done like I told her, what
                A   B
should have been an ordinary day at school

would not have turned into a regrettable
                              C
dilemma that will remain unsolved for a long
                            D
time. No error.
      E

24. When my five-year-old brother put a frog in
     A
my grandfather's bed, he only acted
                    B   C
surprised and laughed at the little fellow's
         D
impish nature. No error.
                  E

25. Reading about the chemistry of the sun in
            A
Knox's book will provide her with information
                  B
similar to that which she would have heard if
              C
she would have attended the physics class on
    D
Tuesday. No error.
          E

26. The garage attendant yelled that he does not
                              A   B
want me to park too close to the black

Mercedes, a car I later found out
                      C
had been stolen in Riverdale. No error.
 D   E

GO ON TO THE NEXT PAGE

DIRECTIONS

Thes following sentences test your ability to express ideas in writing effectively and efficiently. Each sentence is either partially or completely underlined. The first of the five choices given will repeat the original wording and the other four choices will contain alternative wording. Choose the change that best improves the senetence or choose A if the original is superior to any of the other choices given.

In making your choice keep in mind the standards of proper written English. Among other things, pay close attention to grammar, word choice, punctuation, precision, and correct usage of tenses. Avoid awkward and ambiguous construction.

EXAMPLE:

I want your love, and I want your revenge;
<u>you and me can write</u> a bad romance.

(A) you and me can write
(B) you and me could write
(C) you and me writing
(D) you and I can write
(E) me and you can write

Ⓐ   Ⓑ   Ⓒ   ⬤   Ⓔ

27. Public transportation in the suburbs and outlying areas is generally not as convenient and reliable <u>as it is</u> in the city.

(A) as it is
(B) as they are
(C) as those
(D) as buses
(E) since it's

28. While passing the fire department building, <u>the siren began to screech loud, which scared me.</u>

(A) the siren began to screech loud, which scared me
(B) the siren began screeching loudly, which scared me
(C) the screech of the loud siren scared me
(D) I was scared by the loud screech of the siren.
(E) I heard the siren screech loudly and scare me

29. <u>The public is welcome to visit the cemetery where famous and well-known composers, artists, and writers are buried every day except Thursday.</u>

(A) The public is welcome to visit the cemetery where famous and well-known composers, artists, and writers are buried every day except Thursday.
(B) The cemetery where the public, every day except Thursday, famous composers, artists, and writers are buried, is open.
(C) Every day except Thursday the public is welcome to visit the cemetery where well-known composers, artists, and writers are buried.
(D) The public is welcome to visit the cemetery every day except Thursday where famous composers, artists, and writers are buried.
(E) The cemetery where famous and well-known composers, artists, and writers are buried welcomes the public every day except Thursday.

GO ON TO THE NEXT PAGE →

30. My grandfather was the kind of a man that worked long hours for the welfare of is family and the benefit of the community.

(A) My grandfather was the kind of a man that worked
(B) My grandfather, the kind of a man that worked
(C) My grandfather was the kind of man who works
(D) My grandfather was a man, the type of which works
(E) My grandfather was the sort of a man that would work

31. You challenging the authority of the administration has brung about a change in policy.

(A) You challenging the authority of the administration has brung
(B) Your challenging the authority of the administration has brought
(C) Your challenge of the authority of the administration has brung
(D) By your challenging the authority of the administration has brought
(E) The challenge by you to the administration's authority has brought

32. The principal intem1pted classes this morning to announce that Casey McDermott was in an accident yesterday and was needing blood donations this afternoon.
(A) was in an accident yesterday and was needing
(B) was in an accident yesterday and is needing
(C) was in an accident yesterday and needs
(D) having been in an accident yesterday and needing
(E) had been involved in an accident yesterday and he will have a need for

33. The senator cared about neither what happened to his constituency, nor how tax money was spent and keeping appointments that he thought were unimportant.

(A) nor how tax money was spent and keeping appointments
(B) nor how tax money was spent, nor the keeping of appointments
(C) nor how tax money was spent, nor the keeping for keeping appointments
(D) and how tax money was spent, nor keeping appointments
(E) nor how tax money was spent; nor did he care about keeping appointments

34. Constantly encountering resistance from surrounding material, variations in the speed of underground water flows from a fraction of an inch to a few feet per day.

(A) variations in the speed of underground water flows
(B) underground water varies in its flowing distance
(C) the speed of underground water varies
(D) underground water has flown
(E) the flow of underground water varies

35. Therefore, I tip my hat to anyone who speaks up for democratic principles, even if it's for their own personal gain.

(A) even if it's for their own personal gain
(B) even if his motive is personal gain
(C) even if the motive is to be for his own personal gain
(D) whether or not it's for their own personal gain
(E) whether the motive is for their own personal gain or not

GO ON TO THE NEXT PAGE

36. In the Pacific Northwest, <u>waste products from cutting lumber, such as wood chips and sawdust, are one of the ingredients</u> of waferboard panels used in residential construction instead of plywood.

(A) waste products from cutting lumber, such as wood chips and sawdust, are one of the ingredients
(B) waste products from cutting lumber, such as wood chips and sawdust, is one of the ingredients
(C) wood chips and sawdust, waste products from cutting lumber, makes one of the ingredients
(D) lumber-cutting waste products like wood chips and sawdust is used as an ingredient
(E) the waste from cutting lumber as wood chips and sawdust, for example, is an ingredient

37. <u>Melody is the most directly appealing element in pieces of music and are what we sing and hum and whistle.</u>

(A) Melody is the most directly appealing element in pieces of music and are what we sing and hum and whistle.
(B) Melody is the most directly appealing element in a piece of music, this explains why we sing and hum and whistle it.
(C) Melody, as the most directly appealing element in a piece of music, but it is what we sing and hum and whistle.
(D) Melody, being both the part we sing and hum and whistle, and the most directly appealing element in a piece of music.
(E) Melody, the part we sing and hum and whistle, is the most directly appealing element in a piece of music.

38. Although the novel is not lengthy, it contains several subplots <u>as well as a daring and irresistible heroine which weakens the story.</u>

(A) as well as a daring and irresistible heroine which weakens the story
(B) which weakens the story, as well as a daring and irresistible heroine
(C) which weaken the story, who's heroine is daring and irresistible
(D) which weaken the story. It also has a daring and irresistible heroine.
(E) which not only include a daring and irresistible heroine but also weaken the story

39. If anyone wishes to research the techniques of transcendental meditation, <u>which is when a person completely relaxes their mind and body, they</u> will find several relevant books on the shelf.

(A) which is when a person completely relaxes their mind and body, they
(B) which is when a person completely relaxes his mind and body, he
(C) which is when s9meone completely relax their minds and bodies, they
(D) the complete relaxation of the mind and body, he
(E) which completely relaxes your mind and body, you

40. Since some expansion of government is inevitable, governors often convince themselves that extending their powers, <u>even if not having the desire</u>, is justifiable.

(A) even if not having the desire
(B) without it being something to desire
(C) although it not being a desirable action
(D) although their desire can be contrary to it
(E) while undesirable

GO ON TO THE NEXT PAGE ➔

41. Even if nursing homes follow state regulations to the letter of the law, <u>it doesn't</u> guarantee an efficient, cordial. well-trained staff and atmosphere on hand.

(A) it doesn't guarantee an efficient, cordial, well-trained staff and atmosphere on hand
(B) it doesn't guarantee neither an efficient, well-trained staff nor a cordial atmosphere on hand
(C) they don't guarantee either the efficiency and good training of its staff nor the cordiality of its atmosphere
(D) there's no guarantees of an efficient, well-trained staff and cordial atmosphere
(E) they can't guarantee an efficient, well-trained staff and a cordial atmosphere

42. Women in a hunter-gatherer society had to spend much of their time collecting plant <u>food, while carrying her baby with her she also had to be ready to run or otherwise protect herself from</u> wild animals.

(A) food, while carrying her baby with her she also had to be ready to nm or otherwise protect herself from
(B) food, while carrying her baby with her; she also had to be ready to run or otherwise protect herself from .
(C) food, while carrying their babies with them; they also had to be ready to run or otherwise protect theirselves from
(D) food while carrying their babies with them; they also had to be ready to run or otherwise protect themselves from
(E) food; while carrying their babies with them; they also had to be ready to run or otherwise protect themselves from

43. Although young children have higher metabolic rates than adults, <u>there is hardly no data that shows human infants surviving longer in severe cold compared to adults.</u>

(A) there is hardly no data that shows human infants surviving longer in severe cold compared to adults
(B) there is hardly no data showing human infants surviving longer than adults in severe cold
(C) data hardly exists to show human infants surviving longer in severe cold compared to adults
(D) there is hardly any data that shows human infants surviving longer in severe cold in comparison to adults
(E) there are hardly any data that show human infants surviving longer than adults in severe cold

44. <u>Should a college application essay be required</u> one should probably set aside a large block time and avoid doing it at the last minute.

(A) Should a college application essay be required
(B) Should you need to write a college application essay
(C) If you need to write a college application essay
(D) In an event that one needs to write a college application essay
(E) If a college application essay is necessary for anyone to write

GO ON TO THE NEXT PAGE

DIRECTIONS

The following passage is an early draft of an essay. Some parts of the passage need to be rewritten.

Read the passage and select the best answers for the questions that follow. Some questions are about particular sentences or parts of sentences and ask you to improve sentence structure or word choice. Other questions ask you to consider organization and development. In choosing answers, follow the requirements of standard written English.

Questions 45-50 refer to the following passage.

[1] For two hundred years United States citizens have taken for granted the right to life, liberty, and the pursuit of happiness. [2] From the experiences in the former Yugoslavia to the repressive regime in the People's Republic of China, Americans should know, however, that human rights are always in danger.

[3] During the period of the conquistadores and Spanish colonial rule of Latin America, for example. [4] Latin American natives were often violated and repressed by European settlers, an example of this is the fact that the land formerly owned by the native Latin Americans was taken away from them so the people lost the right to own land. [5] Secondly, the Latin American people were forced to work this land as slaves on their own land [6] These human rights violations were overcome by the independence movements led by such freedom fighters as Bolivar and San Martin in the late 1800s.

[7] In the Soviet Union, the extremely repressive Stalinist regime after WW 1l violated the rights of the Russian peasants, known as kulaks. [8] Collectivizing their farmlands by force, their rights were violated by Stalin. [9] Therefore, their private possessions were lost. [10] Another way by which they had their human rights violated was by forcing political opponents to remain silent, to labor in camps, or to be killed.

[11] After Stalin's death in 1953, one of his successors, Nikita Khruschev, attempted to denounce the Stalinis regime. [12] However, it took another thirty years and the collapse of the Soviet Union to bring about basic human rights in Russia.

[13] About the history of human rights violations, the Serbs in the former Yugoslavia and the leaders of Communist China should know that they can't go on forever. [14] Eventually, their power will be usurped, or the people will rise up to claim their God-given human rights.

45. Taking into account the sentences which precede and follow sentence 3, which of the following is the best revision of sentence 3?

(A) As an example, the time that the Spanish were expanding their empire and searching for gold,
(B) Take, for example, during the era of the conquistadores and Spanish colonial rule in Latin America.
(C) Consider, for example, the period of the conquistadores and Spanish colonial rule in Latin America.
(D) The Spanish expanded their empire into Latin America in the 16th century.
(E) For instance, the period of Spanish colonialism in Latin America, for example.

GO ON TO THE NEXT PAGE

46. Which of the following is the best revision of sentence 4?

(A) The land of Latin American natives was confiscated by European settlers. In fact, the rights of the natives to own land was violated and repressed.

(B) European settlers in Latin America have seized the land and the natives had repressed the right to own property.

(C) The colonial rulers confiscated the natives property and denied them the right to own land.

(D) Having their rights violated, the natives of Latin America had their land taken away. Then the European settlers repress their right to own any land at all.

(E) The rights of the Latin American natives were violated and repressed. For example, they took their land and they prohibited them from owning land.

47. In the context of paragraph 3, which is the best revision of sentences 8 and 9?

(A) Forcing them to collectivize their farmlands, Stalin confiscated their private property.

(B) One of the ways by which Stalin violated their rights was by forcing people to collectivize their farmlands, thus, causing them to lose their right to hold private possessions.

(C) One way in which the kulaks had their rights violated was Stalin forcing them to collectivize their farmlands and therefore, surrender private property.

(D) Having lost the right to own private property, Stalin collectivized the kulaks' farmland.

(E) The loss of private property and the collectivization of farmland was one way by which Stalin violated their rights.

48. Which of the following is the best revision of the underlined segment of sentence 10 below?

Another way by which they had their human rights violated was by forcing political opponents to remain silent, to labor in camps, or to be killed.

(A) A second method at which political opponents had their human rights violated was

(B) Stalin also violated the human rights of political opponents

(C) Stalin also violated human rights

(D) Stalin's violation of the human rights of political opponents was

(E) Political opponents' human rights were also violated by Stalin

49. Considering the content of the entire essay, which revision of the underlined segment of sentence 13 below, provides the best transition between paragraphs 3 and 4?

About the history of human rights violations, the Serbs in the fanner Yugoslavia and the leaders of Communist China should know...

(A) In conclusion,

(B) Finally,

(C) Last but not least,

(D) Based on the history of international agreements on human rights,

(E) If the experience of Latin America and the Soviet Union means anything,

50. Based on the essay as a whole, which of the following describes the writer's intention in the last paragraph?

(A) To draw a conclusion from evidence

(B) To prepare readers for the future

(C) To instruct readers about the past

(D) To offer solutions to a problem

(E) To give an example

this is the end of the exercise

SAT Writing Exercise #04

50 Questions

!

DIRECTIONS

Thes following sentences test your ability to detect errors in grammar and usage. Each sentence contains either one error or no errors at all and no sentence contains more than one error. Choose the underlined word or phrase in each sentence that when changed best corrects the grammatical or usage error. Only underlined words may be changed. If the sentence is correct as written, select choice E. In making your choices keep in mind the standards requirements of standard written English.

EXAMPLE:

Super Mario Bros' Mario first <u>appeared</u> in Donkey
                                      A
Kong as Jumpman and <u>was</u> later <u>renamed</u> to Mario
                        B   C
<u>in honor to</u> Nintendo of America's landlord Mario
      D
Segali. <u>No Error</u>
                E

(A) (B) (C) (D) (E)

---

1. The achievements as well as the failures of the

space program, <u>has</u> been a <u>matter</u> of
                  A   B

contention for many years, as interest groups

of many <u>kinds</u> compete <u>for</u> a share of the
              C   D
federal budget. <u>No error</u>.
                      E

2. Experts in marine life say that <u>there is</u> a closer
                                          A
relationship between barracudas <u>with</u> man-
                                    B
eating sharks than <u>had been thought</u> <u>to exist</u>
                          C   D
before. <u>No error</u>.
              E

3. The policeman would not have <u>went</u> into the
                                        A
building <u>had he known</u> that he <u>was going</u> to
              B   C
be ambushed by Mugsy, Frankie, and <u>him</u>.
                                          D

<u>No error</u>.
      E

4. Because Hannah was very close to her family,

<u>it</u> was inconceivable <u>to her</u>, as she read about
A   B
the Holocaust, <u>to imagine</u> what it must <u>be</u>
                      C   D
for children to be severed forcibly from their

parents. <u>No error</u>.
              E

5. <u>As</u> Kathy opened the refrigerator, she
    A
immediately noticed that a huge chunk of

chocolate icing had been <u>bit</u> <u>off</u> the birthday
                              B   C
cake and instantly suspected that Mark <u>was</u>
                                            D
responsible. <u>No error</u>.
                    E

GO ON TO THE NEXT PAGE →

6. Edith Wharton's novel *Ethan Frome* <u>was</u>
A
made into a movie <u>that</u> failed to capture the
B
<u>mood and meaning</u> of <u>her</u> story. <u>No error.</u>
C   D   E

7. One evening when Diana arrived at the

center, Michelle told <u>her</u> that she <u>had been</u>
A   B
astonished <u>to learn</u> from the secretary in the
C
office that <u>she</u> had been fired. <u>No error.</u>
D   E

8. The book's main point is <u>that</u> a number of
A
executive jobs <u>are now thought</u> to be
B
unsuitable for women, or at least incompatible

with <u>her</u> other duties <u>as</u> mother or
C   D
homemaker. <u>No error.</u>
E

9. <u>Unfortunately</u>, the old city of Mostar was
A
severely <u>effected</u> by the war <u>that altered</u> the
B   C
political and economic landscape of the

former Yugoslavia for decades <u>to come</u>.
D
<u>No error.</u>
E

10. The reasons for the Vietnam defeat included

weak support on the home front, the

<u>unfamiliarity</u> of American soldiers <u>of</u> guerilla
A   B
warfare, and the problems of jungle fighting

<u>not knowing friend from foe</u>. <u>No error.</u>
C   D   E

11. When they walked <u>in</u> the museum they took a
A
sharp right, and went down the corridor until

they found the door to the office <u>that</u> <u>belongs</u>
B   C
to Michael and <u>him</u>. <u>No error.</u>
D   E

12. An incident that <u>further</u> embittered the
A
colonists occurred in a Boston street when

British troops <u>fired</u> on a mob of citizens,
B
<u>killing</u> five and wounding six <u>of them</u>.
C   D
<u>No error.</u>
E

13. On the Dallas Cowboys <u>they</u> have three
A
players who grew up in Altoona,

Pennsylvania, and <u>graduated</u> from <u>its</u>
B   C
<u>high school</u>, although not at the same time.
D
<u>No error.</u>
E

GO ON TO THE NEXT PAGE

14. The confrontation that took place between he
                                                    A
and his family during the dinner scene caused

Tom to run away, but <u>as</u> his final speech
                        B
<u>suggests</u>, he never was <u>able</u> to forget his
    C   D
mother and sister. <u>No error</u>.
                        E

15. How, one may ask, does one judge the

morality of <u>another's</u> behavior <u>if</u> <u>you don't</u>
              A   B   C
even know how to define or explain one's

own, <u>in spite of</u> ample opportunity to think
        D
about it. <u>No error</u>.
              E

16. The philosophy of communism <u>is thought</u> to
                                        A
<u>be born</u> in Marx's writings and to have
    B
<u>resulted in</u> one of the most widespread
    C
economic and political upheavals that the

world <u>has seen</u>. <u>No error</u>.
        D   E

17. <u>Reflecting</u> on the magnitude of the national
        A
debt, one might <u>well</u> ask <u>themselves</u>
                    B   C
how the most powerful nation on earth; the

United States, could have <u>gotten</u> itself into
                              D
such an impossible position. <u>No error</u>.
                                  E

18. If you read the <u>sports</u> section of the paper,
                        A
<u>they</u> say that the Oakland A's, <u>the team</u> that
    B   C
has won the division title <u>for four</u> of the last
                              D
five years, are likely to win again. <u>No error</u>.
                                          E

19. The assignment <u>included</u> forming <u>into</u> groups
                        A   B
of four, discussing the questions <u>about</u> the
                                      C
book, choosing a format, and <u>a presentation</u>
                                  D
in front of the class. <u>No error</u>.
                            E

20. <u>Of</u> the hundreds of actors and actresses! who
        A
have played Hamlet since Shakespeare <u>wrote</u>
                                          B
the play, not one of them, I am sure, <u>have</u>
                                          C
done as masterful <u>a job</u> as Mel Gibson.
                      D
<u>No error</u>.
    E

21. The earliest pirates in this hemisphere,

<u>who lived on</u> West Indies islands, stole cattle,
    A
smoked the meat and sold <u>it</u> to passing ships,
                            B
attacked and burned colonial settlements, and

<u>were stealing</u> gold and jewels <u>from</u> Spanish
    C   D
galleons. <u>No error</u>.
              E

GO ON TO THE NEXT PAGE

22. Necca's beauty and kindness, <u>in addition to</u>
                                      A

her bravery during the <u>two-year</u> occupation of
                        B

her town by an enemy battalion, <u>is what</u>
                                 C

appeal to <u>most readers</u> about the young girl.
           D

<u>No error.</u>
   E

23. They had busy schedules, <u>so</u> finally they met
                                  A

after work and drove together to a meeting at

<u>the school, where</u> Philip gave <u>his</u> talk on the
        B   C

use of computers <u>in</u> biomedical research.
                  D

<u>No error.</u>
   E

24. <u>Either</u> rice or oats <u>is</u> the grain used <u>as</u> the
        A   B   C

foundation of most natural breakfast cereals,

although neither wheat nor bran <u>lag</u> far
                                 D

behind in popularity. <u>No error.</u>
                          E

25. If the driver of the dump truck <u>would have</u>
                                        A

checked his brakes before descending the

steep hill, the vehicle <u>might</u> never have
                          B

swerved <u>from</u> the road, and the driver would
         C

not be lying in the hospital, <u>as</u> he is, with a
                               D

cast on his leg. <u>No error.</u>
                     E

26. The tickets <u>that</u> allowed three people free
                    A

admission to the concert were waiting at the

box office half an hour prior to the start, just

<u>like</u> Sarah <u>had said</u> they <u>would be</u>. <u>No error.</u>
  B   C   D   E

GO ON TO THE NEXT PAGE

DIRECTIONS

Thes following sentences test your ability to express ideas in writing effectively and efficiently. Each sentence is either partially or completely underlined. The first of the five choices given will repeat the original wording and the other four choices will contain alternative wording. Choose the change that best improves the senetence or choose A if the original is superior to any of the other choices given.

In making your choice keep in mind the standards of proper written English. Among other things, pay close attention to grammar, word choice, punctuation, precision, and correct usage of tenses. Avoid awkward and ambiguous construction.

EXAMPLE:

I want your love, and I want your revenge;
<u>you and me can write</u> a bad romance.

(A) you and me can write
(B) you and me could write
(C) you and me writing
(D) you and I can write
(E) me and you can write

27. <u>This article paints Mrs. Strauss as being brilliant ruthless, and likely to resign soon.</u>

    (A) This article paints Mrs. Strauss as being brilliant ruthless, and likely to resign soon.
    (B) Mrs. Strauss, painted in this article as being brilliant, ruthless, and soon resign.
    (C) In this article Mrs. Strauss is painted as brilliant, ruthless, and she is likely to resign soon.
    (D) This article, in which Mrs. Strauss is painted as being brilliant, ruthless ·and likely to resign soon.
    (E) This article paints Mrs. Strauss, who is likely to resign soon, as being brilliant and ruthless.

28. The President said <u>softly but with firmness that all citizens must contribute their fair share</u> to the reduction of the national debt.

    (A) softly but with firmness that all citizens must contribute their fair share
    (B) softly but firmly that all citizens must contribute their fair share
    (C) softly but firmly that all citizens must contribute his fair share
    (D) softly but with firmness that all citizens must contribute his fair share
    (E) softly but with firmness that all citizens must contribute a fair share

29. During February <u>the amount of students absent from school with colds were</u> very high.

    (A) the amount of students absent from school with colds were
    (B) the amounts of students absent from school with colds were
    (C) the number of students absent from school with colds was
    (D) colds that kept the amount of students absent from school were
    (E) absenteeism of students from colds was

30. <u>It said on the news that they discovered the remains of a four-thousand-year-old man in the Alps.</u>
    (A) It said on the news that they discovered the remains of a four-thousand-year-old man in the Alps.
    (B) They said on the news in the Alps that they discovered the remains of a four-thousand-year-old man
    (C) On the news it said that in the Alps they discovered the remains of a four-thousand-year old-man.
    (D) During the news it said that the remains of a four-thousand-year-old man was discovered in the Alps.
    (E) The news said that the remains of a four-thousand-year-old man were discovered in the Alps.

GO ON TO THE NEXT PAGE

31. Mr. Winters claimed that it was the job of <u>us peer counselors to be certain that everyone who is a freshman were included</u> in the survey.

(A) us peer counselors to be certain that every- one who is a freshman were included
(B) us peer counselors, to assure that everyone who is a freshman were included
(C) we peer counselors to ascertain that every- one who is a freshman were included
(D) us peer counselors to see that everyone who is a freshman was included
(E) we peer counselors to be sure that no freshmen were left out

32. <u>Addressing themselves to the improvement of the arts program, the committee spent the first two months of its tenure.</u>

(A) Addressing themselves to the improvement of the arts program, the committee spent the first two months of its tenure.
(B) Addressing itself to the improvement of . the arts program in the school, the Committee spent the first two months of its tenure.
(C) The committee spent the first two months of its tenure addressing the improvement of the arts program.
(D) During the first two months of their tenure, improving the arts program was discussed by the committee.
(E) The improvement of the arts program during the first two months of their tenure was discussed by the committee.

33. Standing on the bridge of the ship, <u>there blew the most strong winds</u> that I had seen for at least a decade at sea.

(A) there blew the most strong winds
(B) there were the strongest winds
(C) the strongest winds were blowing
(D) I experienced the most strong winds
(E) I observed the strongest winds

34. <u>The bureau not only is charged with the responsibility of administering public lands, but</u> inherited a monumental problem.

(A) The bureau not only is charged with the responsibility of administering public lands, but
(B) The bureau is not only charged with the responsibility to administer public lands, but also have
(C) The bureau is charged both with the responsibility of administering public lands, while it
(D) The bureau, both charged with the responsibility of administering public lands and
(E) The bureau, which is charged with the responsibility of administering public lands, has

35. <u>It saves the taxpayers billions of dollars since there has been</u> no moon flights since the 1970s.

(A) It saves the taxpayers billions of dollars since there has been
(B) To save taxpayers billions of dollars, there have been
(C) Saving the taxpayers billions of dollars, there has been
(D) The savings to taxpayers billions of dollars there have been ·
(E) By saving the taxpayers billions of dollars, there have been

GO ON TO THE NEXT PAGE

36. It was in Istanbul that an Englishwoman, Florence Nightingale by name, set up headquarters <u>from which to conduct one of the most heroic and most brave</u> campaigns in the history of medicine.

(A) from which to conduct one of the most heroic and most brave
(B) in which to conduct one of the most heroic and bravest
(C) where to conduct one of the bravest
(D) where she would conduct one of the bravest
(E) from which she would be conducting among the most heroic and brave

37. The story's underlying theme is <u>about seeking revenge after</u> the death of the king.

(A) about seeking revenge after
(B) about the seeking of revenge of
(C) searching a revenge for
(D) seeking vengeance over
(E) the search for revenge after

38. <u>What helps soccer give my life meaning is</u> kicking the ball over the goalkeeper's hands for a score, hearing praise from the coach, and applause from the crowd.
(A) What helps soccer give my life meaning is
(B) What makes soccer give my life meaning by
(C) Helping soccer give meaning to my life by
(D) Being that soccer gives meaning to my life by my
(E) Since soccer gives meaning to my life

39. When caffeine is added to food, as it often is to sodas and colas, <u>it has the exact same effect in</u> the human body as the caffeine found naturally in coffee and tea.

(A) it has the exact same effect in
(B) it has the same effect on
(C) its effectiveness is the same to
(D) the exact same effects take place in
(E) it effects

40. The ferryboat had been a vessel of considerable <u>beauty, full of good woods and brass for most of her career it has carried passengers</u> between Brett Island and the mainland.

(A) beauty, full of good woods and brass for most of her career it has carried passengers
(B) beauty, full of good woods and brass. For most of its career it carried passengers
(C) beauty, full of good woods and brass, for most of her career she carried passengers
(D) beauty, full of good woods and brass; for most of its career it has carried passengers
(E) beauty. Full of good woods and brass for most of its career; it carried passengers

41. At one time the city fathers had envisioned building a nuclear desalinization plant, <u>and financial woes make that an impossible dream.</u>

(A) and financial woes make that an impossible dream
(B) and that dream becomes impossible due to financial woes
(C) but that dream had been made impossible by financial woes
(D) but financial woes made that an impossible dream
(E) however, the financial woes made the dream an impossible one

GO ON TO THE NEXT PAGE

42. For instance, <u>the author, showing us the modern city of Astoria in the opening paragraphs by cleverly combining</u> the history of the Flavel family with the folklore of the Columbia River.

(A) the author, showing us the modern city of Astoria in the opening paragraphs by cleverly combining
(B) we are shown the modern city of Astoria in the opening paragraphs, and the author cleverly combines
(C) the author shows us the modern city of Astoria in the opening paragraphs by cleverly combining
(D) author, who shows us the modern city of Astoria in the opening paragraphs, and cleverly combines
(E) we are shown the modern city of Astoria in the opening paragraphs by the author, cleverly combined

43. One event in Richard's life story that moved me greatly was <u>when he was separated from his family.</u>

(A) when he was separated from his family
(B) when he and his family were separated
(C) his separation from his family
(D) the separating from his family
(E) the separation between he and his family

44. The White House Chief of Staff, in addition to the President's children and spouse, <u>are in a position to influence policy despite that they were not elected.</u>

(A) are in a position to influence policies despite that they were not elected
(B) hold a position to influence policy despite being unelected
(C) is in a position to influence policy, yet being unelected
(D) although not elected, may hold positions that influence policy
(E) although not elected, may influence policy

GO ON TO THE NEXT PAGE

DIRECTIONS

The following passage is an early draft of an essay. Some parts of the passage need to be rewritten.

Read the passage and select the best answers for the questions that follow. Some questions are about particular sentences or parts of sentences and ask you to improve sentence structure or word choice. Other questions ask you to consider organization and development. In choosing answers, follow the requirements of standard written English.

Questions 45-50 refer to the following passage.

[1] It is difficult to deny that the world of music has changed greatly in the past thirty years. [2] The style, sound, technology, and lyrics of music have been altered greatly. [3] In the last three decades, several new categories of music have come into being. [4] One reason why music has changed so greatly is that artists use music as a tool to publicize certain social messages. [5] Although many artists of the 1970s used this method as well, their issues were not as severe that banning their album was possible. [6] For example, one rap-singer, Ice-T, used his album to promote "cop-killing." [7] The idea was so offensive that many believed the album should be banned. [8] The controversy caused by Ice- T made the Arista record company refuse to continue production of the album.

[9] Another way in which music has changed is lyrics. [10] When you listen to certain heavy met- al or rap groups, one may notice foul and obscene language used. [11] Some of the references to sex are shocking. [12] In past eras, such language in recorded music was unheard of

[13] Technological changes in music have occurred. [14] With the advent of highly advanced musical devices and many digital effects, the sounds of music have been completely altered. [15] Rock and roll was invented in the early 1950s. [16] When you listen to heavy metal,

you hear more distorted guitar sounds than in music of the 60s and 70s. [17] In the era of electronic instruments, the variety of possible sounds is incredible. [18] Present day sounds could never have been achieved in previous years because the technology was not at hand. [19] New music utilizes electronically produced sounds never heard before. [20] Computers generate everything from the human voice under water to the sound of whales. [21] There are no limits to what the music of the future will sound like.

45. Which of the following is the best revision of the underlined segment of sentence 5 below?

Although many artists of the 1970s used this method as well, <u>their issues were not as severe that banning their album was possible.</u>

(A) the issues were less severe than those which caused banning their album to be possible
(B) their issues were not as severe that their albums were in danger of being banned
(C) they never raised issues that could have caused their albums to be banned
(D) the issues they raised were not serious enough that banning their album was a possibility
(E) they raised less serious issues and banning their albums was not likely

46. Taking into account the sentences which precede and follow sentence 10, which is the most effective revision of sentence 10?
    (A) Listening to certain heavy metal or rap groups, lyrics containing obscenities are often heard.
    (B) Obscene language is common in the songs of heavy metal and rap groups.
    (C) Certain heavy metal and rap groups use foul and obscene language.
    (D) Obscenities are often heard when one listens to the lyrics of certain heavy metal or rap groups.
    (E) Listening to obscene language and listening to the lyrics of certain heavy metal and rap groups.

47. In the context of the entire essay, which revision of sentence 13 provides the most effective transition between paragraphs 3 and 4?
    (A) Technological changes in music also have occurred.
    (B) Also, technology has changed musical sounds.
    (C) Noticeable changes in music's sounds have come about through technological changes.
    (D) Changes in musical technology has changed musical sound, too.
    (E) But the most noticeable change in music has been its sound.

48. In a revision of the entire essay, which of the following sentences most needs further development?
    (A) Sentence 3
    (B) Sentence 7
    (C) Sentence 8
    (D) Sentence 19
    (E) Sentence 20

49. Which of the following sentences should be deleted to improve the unity and coherence of paragraph 4?
    (A) Sentence 14
    (B) Sentence 15
    (C) Sentence 16
    (D) Sentence 17
    (E) Sentence 18

50. Taking into account the organization of the entire essay, which is the best revision of sentence 2 in the introductory paragraph?
    (A) In the past thirty years, not only the style, sound, and technology has changed, but the lyrics have, too.
    (B) Having undergone a change in the style, sound, technology, musical lyrics have altered also.
    (C) Changes in musical sound have occurred, while the technology and lyrics have tremendously altered the style of music.
    (D) Musicians have changed the purpose and the lyrics of music, and technology has changed its sound.
    (E) Along with changes in sound and technology, the lyrics of music have changed, too.

STOP

this is the end of the exercise

SAT Writing Exercise #05

50 Questions

!

DIRECTIONS

Thes following sentences test your ability to detect errors in grammar and usage. Each sentence contains either one error or no errors at all and no sentence contains more than one error. Choose the underlined word or phrase in each sentence that when changed best corrects the grammatical or usage error. Only underlined words may be changed. If the sentence is correct as written, select choice E. In making your choices keep in mind the standards requirements of standard written English.

EXAMPLE:

Super Mario Bros' Mario first <u>appeared</u> in Donkey
                                    A
Kong as Jumpman and <u>was</u> later <u>renamed</u> to Mario
                          B   C
<u>in honor to</u> Nintendo of America's landlord Mario
     D
Segali. <u>No Error</u>
              E

Ⓐ Ⓑ Ⓒ ⬤ Ⓔ

1. Beethoven's music, <u>now</u> loved throughout the
                              A
world, aroused considerable controversy when

it was first <u>played, however</u>, its power a n d
                    B
nobility <u>came</u> to be widely accepted and even
              C
praised before <u>its</u> composer died. <u>No error</u>.
                    D   E

2. As an indication of the <u>play's</u> power to hold
                                  A
<u>its</u> audience, when the final curtain
  B
descended, there <u>was</u> only one man and one
                      C
woman <u>remaining</u> in the theater. <u>No error</u>.
          D   E

3. <u>As</u> implied in the author's biography, to show
     A
<u>how</u> the tenant farmers <u>had been</u> exploited by
  B   C
the owners was the whole point of <u>him</u>
                                        D
writing the book. <u>No error</u>.
                        E

4. <u>Despite</u> exploitation by gold-seeking
     A
marauders, the tribe survived and <u>even</u>
                                        B
flourished because their pride in themselves

was <u>stronger than almost</u> any <u>other</u> people.
          C   D
<u>No error</u>.
     E

GO ON TO THE NEXT PAGE

5. Neither the chameleon, a lizard known for <u>its</u>
                                                    A
ability to change color, nor many other lizards

<u>having</u> the same attribute, <u>is</u> able to assume
B   C
more than a few green and brown shades

when the temperatures <u>fall</u> below freezing.
                            D
<u>No error.</u>
E

6. <u>Regardless</u> of her credentials, which were
       A
indeed impressive and which included three

<u>years'</u> experience as a cook, her skills in the
B
kitchen were <u>fewer</u> than a <u>beginner</u>. <u>No error.</u>
                C   D   E

7. Interest in the marching band, in the

orchestra, and <u>in learning</u> to play instruments,
                    A
<u>have</u> doubled <u>within</u> the <u>last half</u> year.
B   C   D
<u>No error.</u>
E

8. <u>Being</u> lost in the mountains of Colorado for
       A
two days as a boy, Dave <u>was careful</u> always
                              B
<u>to take</u> a detailed map with him <u>when he set</u>
C   D
out for a backpacking adventure in the

wilderness. <u>No error.</u>
            E

9. The false alarm <u>had frightened</u> everyone in
                        A
the condo, and <u>she</u> more than the other
                B
residents <u>who lived</u> there, <u>since</u> she had once
            C   D
been living in a building that was destroyed by

fire. <u>No error.</u>
       E

10. <u>It's</u> not the <u>end result</u> of the trial that may
        A   B
forever damage a defendant's <u>reputation</u>; it's
                                C
the fact that he <u>went</u> to trial in the first place
                    D
that could cause him irrevocable harm.

<u>No error.</u>
E

11. <u>Ever since</u> the beginning of the year, the
        A
shelter, <u>like</u> the cardboard shack the homeless
          B
man had been forced <u>nightly</u> to sleep in,
                        C
<u>has been</u> rather cold comfort for him.
D
<u>No error.</u>
E

12. During the war in Vietnam, American troops

<u>observed</u> <u>that</u> the local mountain tribesman
A   B
made an excellent soldier loyal, and <u>always</u>
                                        C
ready and willing to die for <u>their</u> cause.
                                D
<u>No error.</u>
E

GO ON TO THE NEXT PAGE

13. Even though the bill for an amendment
       A

appeared feasibly to the sponsoring
          B

congressman, it was voted down unanimously.
         C   D

No error
  E

14. Since Edwin conscientiously practices diving
     A

every day for hours after school, he is
        B

continually rising the difficulty of his dives.
       C   D

No error
  E

15. If everybody kept his car in good shape, he
           A

would find that its value would diminish little
         B   C

over the years, if not actually appreciate.
        D

No error
  E

16. Dieting and exercise is not the answer to all
         A   B

weight problems, but they should do the trick
            C

for most waistlines. No error
  D   E

17. My art history professor prefers admiring
         A

Michelangelo's sculpture to viewing his
         B

painting, although Michelangelo himself was
         C

more proud of the ladder. No error
      D   E

18. Randy bought a new pair of pants because his
      A   B

last pair was just delivered to the laundry the
      C   D

morning of graduation exercises. No error
             E

19. Between the three old friends present there
    A   B

had been many memorable experiences
  C

throughout the years. No error
  D   E

20. If the engineer had had competent assistants
         A

to help him finish the project, he
    B

would not have completed it so late. No error
    C   D   E

21. Less college students are choosing liberal arts
    A   B

majors because the cost of a college education
         C

is prohibitive. No error
  D   E

22. The purpose of Mark Twain's writings were
             A

not merely to entertain but also to educate,
         B

although that doesn't prevent one from
         C

enjoying his yarns. No error
    D   E

GO ON TO THE NEXT PAGE

23. The charm <u>of</u> Lofting's book <u>lies in</u> the
              A   B

    humorous reversal <u>of</u> roles-the animals guide,
                     C

    assist, and generally <u>they take</u> care of the
                        D

    helpless humans. <u>No error</u>
                  E

24. Confucianism is more a code of ethics

    <u>than like</u> a religion; it presents no deities
      A

    <u>but fosters</u> <u>instead</u> a respect for one's ancestors
      B   C

    and for an <u>orderly</u> society. <u>No error</u>
               D   E

25. The black squirrels <u>drew</u> a crowd of students,
                     A

    <u>for</u> it had <u>never been seen</u> on the campus
      B C   D

    before. <u>No error</u>
            E

26. The construction of a waterway linking the

    Atlantic and Pacific oceans <u>was first proposed</u>
                              A

    in 1524, <u>but not until</u> the Panama Canal
              B

    opened in 1914 did <u>such a project</u> become
                    C

    <u>a reality</u>. <u>No error</u>
      D   E

GO ON TO THE NEXT PAGE

DIRECTIONS

Thes following sentences test your ability to express ideas in writing effectively and efficiently. Each sentence is either partially or completely underlined. The first of the five choices given will repeat the original wording and the other four choices will contain alternative wording. Choose the change that best improves the senetence or choose A if the original is superior to any of the other choices given.

In making your choice keep in mind the standards of proper written English. Among other things, pay close attention to grammar, word choice, punctuation, precision, and correct usage of tenses. Avoid awkward and ambiguous construction.

EXAMPLE:

I want your love, and I want your revenge; you and me can write a bad romance.

(A) you and me can write
(B) you and me could write
(C) you and me writing
(D) you and I can write
(E) me and you can write

Ⓐ   Ⓑ   Ⓒ   ⬤   Ⓔ

27. For many a brilliant architect, being free to innovate is more important than being well paid.

(A) being free to innovate is more important
(B) having freedom of innovation is more important
(C) there is more importance in the freedom to innovate
(D) freedom to innovate has more importance
(E) to have the freedom to innovate is more important

28. Industrial growth that was being stifled by the country's dictatorship, but now they are developing their full economic potential.

(A) Industrial growth that was being stifled by the country's dictatorship, but now they are developing their full economic potential.
(B) The dictatorship had stifled industrial growth, but the country is now developing their full economic potential.
(C) Industrial growth was stifled by the country's dictatorship, and so now they are developing their full economic potential.
(D) Though the dictatorship had stifled industrial growth, the country is now developing its full economic potential.
(E) Now developing their full economic potential, the country's dictatorship had stifled industrial growth.

29. Although gale-fore winds often pass through the Eiffel Tower, causing it to sway no more than four inches.

(A) causing it to sway no more
(B) and yet it sways no more
(C) they do not cause it to sway more
(D) and they do not cause it to sway more
(E) yet causing it to sway no more

GO ON TO THE NEXT PAGE →

30. Tickets are available <u>at the box office they can be picked up one hour before the performance</u>.

   (A) at the box office they can be picked up one hour before the performance
   (B) at the box office; they can be picked up one hour before the performance
   (C) one hour before the performance, they can be picked up at the box office
   (D) and that can be picked up at the box office one hour before the performance
   (E) at the box office, one hour before the performance is when they can be picked up

31. By interweaving musical and choreographic material more closely, <u>the aesthetic standards of ballet were raised by Tchaikovsky to a higher level</u> than had been known before his time.

   (A) the aesthetic standards of ballet were raised by Tchaikovsky to a higher level
   (B) Tchaikovsky raised the aesthetic standards of ballet to a higher level
   (C) a higher level of aesthetic standards for ballet were reached by Tchaikovsky
   (D) ballet's aesthetic standards were raised to a higher level by Tchaikovsky
   (E) Tchaikovsky's aesthetic ballet standards rose to a higher level

32. The Pony Express was an ingenious system for carrying <u>mail; it was in existence only briefly, however,</u> before the telegraph system made it obsolete.

   (A) mail; it was in existence only briefly, however,
   (B) mail, for it was in existence only briefly, however,
   (C) mail; however ,existing only briefly
   (D) mail, having existed only briefly
   (E) mail, but was existing only briefly

33. Even the film's most heroic characters are played with straightforward realism, <u>this restraint results in a very powerful story</u>.

   (A) this restraint results in a very powerful story
   (B) with this restraint resulting in a very powerful story
   (C) and a very powerful story being the result of this restraint
   (D) and this restraint results in a very powerful story
   (E) a very powerful story results from this restraint

34. The diving suit enabled marine biologist Sylvia Earle to explore the seafloor at 1,250 feet <u>and she could ascend</u> without stopping for decompression.

   (A) and she could ascend
   (B) as well as ascending
   (C) so she could ascend
   (D) and an ascension
   (E) and to ascend

GO ON TO THE NEXT PAGE

35. Charlie Chaplin developed definite ideas about the art of comedy and as a result of <u>sentiment, satire, and social criticism were introduced</u> into his work.

    (A) sentiment, satire, and social criticism were introduced
    (B) sentiment, satire, and social criticism were introduced by him
    (C) had introduced sentiment, satire, and social criticism
    (D) introduced sentiment, satire, and social criticism
    (E) the introduction of sentiment, satire, and social criticism

36. In the past, many famous painters ground their own colors, <u>an attention to detail that is noteworthy</u>.

    (A) an attention to detail that is noteworthy
    (B) inasmuch as they showed attention to detail, it is noteworthy
    (C) this makes it noteworthy in showing their attention to detail
    (D) an idea that is noteworthy in showing their attention to detail
    (E) which is noteworthy and it shows an attention to detail

37. The majority of people in this country still do not vote <u>despite major campaigns by celebrities</u> to encourage them.

    (A) despite major campaigns by celebrities
    (B) with major campaigns by celebrities
    (C) however great the effort made by celebrities
    (D) when even celebrities are making the effort
    (E) even though major campaign by celebrities

38. After the flood of recent complaints, the school board voted against mandatory mathematics in all grades, <u>and they thereby achieved their goal</u>.

    (A) and they thereby achieved their goal
    (B) by which means they achieved their goal
    (C) thereby achieving their goal
    (D) achieving a goal they had hoped to
    (E) to which end they were able to achieve their goal

39. The two goals put out by the architectural committee <u>was to maintain a harmony with the natural settings in the area, and keeping the efficiency of the homes high</u>.

    (A) was to maintain a harmony with the natural settings in the area, and keeping the efficiency of the homes high
    (B) were maintaining a harmony with the natural settings in the area, and to keep the efficiency of the homes high
    (C) was to maintain a harmony with the natural settings in the area, and to keep the efficiency of the homes high
    (D) were to maintain a harmony with the natural settings in the area, and to keep the efficiency of the homes high
    (E) was maintaining a harmony with the natural settings in the area, and keeping the efficiency of the homes high

GO ON TO THE NEXT PAGE

40. His latest best-seller having been published, the author Stephen King became obsessed with getting some of the critical acclaim that had long eluded him.

    (A) His latest best-seller having been published
    (B) Having been the latest best-seller published
    (C) His best-seller, having been the latest published
    (D) When having had the latest best-seller published
    (E) Having published his latest best-seller

41. Anyone with a little ingenuity can make his or her own clothes, the difficulty being that the time involved is usually quite great.

    (A) clothes, the difficulty being that the time involved
    (B) clothes, unfortunately for most the time that clothes can be involved
    (C) clothes; you may find, however, that the time involved
    (D) clothes, but the time involved
    (E) clothes; the difficulty being that in sewing clothes, the time involved

42. Successful entrepreneurship is often a result not only of creativity but also of hard work.

    (A) often a result not only of creativity but also of hard work
    (B) as often a result of not only creativity but hard work as well
    (C) sometimes a result of creativity and also a factor of hard work
    (D) often a result of creativity as well as hard work
    (E) often considered as much creativity as hard work

43. Artists can offer startling representations of the world but with their responsibility to elevate humanity.

    (A) but with their responsibility
    (B) with the responsibility
    (C) having also the responsibility
    (D) but ought also
    (E) their responsibility being as well

44. Using the desperate campaign tactics of lying, snooping, and negative ads as well, Smithers was soundly defeated by her opponent.

    (A) Using the desperate campaign tactics of lying, snooping, and negative ads as well
    (B) Because of her desperate tactics of lying, snooping, and using negative ads
    (C) Using the desperate tactics of lying, snooping, and negative ads
    (D) By using the desperate tactics of lying, snooping, as well as negative ads
    (E) With the desperate tactics of lying, snooping, as well as negative ads

GO ON TO THE NEXT PAGE

DIRECTIONS

The following passage is an early draft of an essay. Some parts of the passage need to be rewritten.

Read the passage and select the best answers for the questions that follow. Some questions are about particular sentences or parts of sentences and ask you to improve sentence structure or word choice. Other questions ask you to consider organization and development. In choosing answers, follow the requirements of standard written English.

Questions 45-50 refer to the following passage.

(1) In the last fifty years, computers in many forms have become increasingly accessible. (2) For example, today the calculator is regarded as an essential tool for basic calculation by students and businesspeople. (3) The word processor, is considered indispensable by most writers, researchers, and office workers. (4) In addition, many families use computers to organize information, to balance budgets, and to provide entertainment.

(5) In spite of the growing popularity of computers, some people are genuinely afraid of these machines. (6) They fear that computers have intelligence and that they will take control over people and things. (7) Because of this fear, people lack the confidence to try the new technology.

(8) This is unfortunate. (9) Computers perform many important functions. (10) What would happen if we did not have any computers? (11) Not only would the cost of communications increase, and many processes would require more time than before to carry out. (12) Further, technological achievements such as space programs and scientific discoveries would probably be slow down. (13) Computers have become an integral and important part of daily life. (14) To those of you who are afraid, we should remember that computers are simply afraid, we should remember that computers are simply advanced adding machines and typewriters!

45. Which of the following would be the most suitable sentence to insert immediately after sentence 1?

(A) The race is on to produce the "ultimate" computer.
(B) I have found the computer somewhat difficult to learn to operate.
(C) Many people are understandably intimidated by computers.
(D) They are now so common that they have a profound effect on daily life.
(E) Modern telephones belong to the family of computers.

46. To best connect sentence 3 to the rest of the first paragraph, which is the best word or phrase to insert after "*The word processor,*" in sentence 3 (reproduced below)?

The word processor, is considered indispensable by most writers, researchers, and office workers.

(A) surely,
(B) however,
(C) another form of computer,
(D) you see,
(E) contrastingly,

47. In context, sentence 8 could be made more precise by adding which of the following words after "*This*"?

(A) technology
(B) confidence
(C) example
(D) computer
(E) situation

GO ON TO THE NEXT PAGE

48. The function of sentence 10 is to

(A) set up a hypothetical circumstance
(B) raise doubt in the reader's mind about the usefulness of computers
(C) allow the writer to take on a pose of humility
(D) contest a common assertion about computers
(E) show the writer's bewilderment about some aspect of computers

49. Which of the following is the best revision of the underlined portion of sentence 11 (reproduced below)?

Not only would the cost of communications increase, and many processes would require more time than before to carry out.

(A) but so would the many processes require more time to carry out
(B) and also many processes require more time to carry out
(C) but they would require more time to carry out the process
(D) as well as to require more time for many processes to be carried out
(E) but so would the time required to carry out many processes

50. Which of the following versions of the underlined portion of sentence 14 (reproduced below) best suits the context?

To those of you who are afraid, we should remember that computers are simply advanced adding machines an typewriters!

(A) (As it is now)
(B) You who are fearing it should remember that computers
(C) But remember, you may be afraid that computers
(D) Those who are fearful should remember that computers
(E) What we fear about computers is that we see that they

STOP

this is the end of the exercise

SAT Writing Exercise #06
50 Questions

DIRECTIONS

Thes following sentences test your ability to detect errors in grammar and usage. Each sentence contains either one error or no errors at all and no sentence contains more than one error. Choose the underlined word or phrase in each sentence that when changed best corrects the grammatical or usage error. Only underlined words may be changed. If the sentence is correct as written, select choice E. In making your choices keep in mind the standards requirements of standard written English.

EXAMPLE:

Super Mario Bros' Mario first <u>appeared</u> in Donkey
　　　　　　　　　　　　　　A
Kong as Jumpman and <u>was</u> later <u>renamed</u> to Mario
　　　　　　　　　　　B　　　　C
<u>in honor to</u> Nintendo of America's landlord Mario
D
Segali. <u>No Error</u>
　　　　　E

Ⓐ Ⓑ Ⓒ ⬤ Ⓔ

1. When Ms. Ruiz <u>arrived</u> at the holiday sale, she
　　　　　　　　A
realized <u>that</u> she <u>had left</u> her wallet at home
　　　　　B　　　　C
<u>and must</u> go back to get it. <u>No error</u>
　　D　　　　　　　　　　　E

2. If America <u>were</u> invaded by foreign forces, <u>all</u>
　　　　　　A　　　　　　　　　　　　　　B
able-bodied men <u>would</u> <u>without hardly</u> a doubt,
　　　　　　　　　C　　　　D
enlist at the nearest armed services recruitment
center. <u>No error</u>
　　　　　E

3. The pilot's carelessness, <u>as well as</u> her
　　　　　　　　　　　　　A
equipment's malfunctioning, <u>was</u>
　　　　　　　　　　　　　B
<u>responsible for</u> the <u>near-disaster</u> at Kennedy
　C　　　　　　　D
Airport. <u>No error</u>
　　　　　E

4. <u>Instead of</u> concentrating <u>on doing their</u>
　　A　　　　　　　　　B
homework <u>as</u> they should, many teenagers
　　　　　C
watch television, talk on the phone, and
<u>they listen to the radio.</u> <u>No error</u>
　　D　　　　　　　　E

5. The twins wanted to be a <u>member</u> of the team,
　　　　　　　　　　　A
<u>but</u> the captain <u>had already made</u> <u>her selections</u>.
　B　　　　　C　　　　　　D
<u>No error</u>
　E

6. <u>It's</u> a good thing that the folks in the cast live
　A
<u>close by</u>, so <u>they</u> won't have to travel <u>very far</u> to
　B　　　　C　　　　　　　　D
get home after the show. <u>No error</u>
　　　　　　　　　　　E

GO ON TO THE NEXT PAGE

7. The crowd of onlookers grew larger as the
        A   B
   veterans which were picketing the White
              C
   House began shouting. No error
          D   E

8. Of the nominees for the Nobel Prize in
   A   B
   Literature this year, few are as qualified as the
                        C   D
   English novelist Anthony Powell. No error
                                      E

9. The confrontation between domestic businesses
                        A
   and foreign competitors has reached a dead-
                            B
   end that will take an Act of Congress
              C
   to resolve. No error
       D   E

10. Psychologists have long debated the connection
                    A   B
    between violence on television plus actual
                      C   D
    crime. No error
            E

11. The continual improvements in athletic
            A
    training methods has made performances
                      B
    that would have been considered impossible
            C
    a generation ago everyday occurrences.
            D
    No error
      E

12. A good teacher should not only convey
                     A   B
    information and should also instill his students
                C
    with a love for learning. No error
          D   E

13. Most of the contestants feel that the rules that
    A   B
    pertains to the race are far too strict. No error
      C   D   E

14. The building developer had hoped to keep the
                          A
    location of the housing project a secret
              B
    to prevent neighborhood resident groups
       C
    from interfering. No error
          D   E

15. Unless scientists discover new ways to increase
       A
    food production, the earth will not be able to
                              B
    satisfy the food needs for all its inhabitants.
                        C   D
    No error
      E

16. The fact that the Senator has never broke any
        A   B
    of his campaign promises has made his third
                              C
    re-election a virtual certainty. No error
                  D   E

GO ON TO THE NEXT PAGE

17. <u>Not until</u> each one of us <u>take</u> <u>responsibility for</u>
      A   B   C

    world peace will we ever move towards <u>it</u>.
                                            D

    <u>No error</u>
       E

18. A number of scientists <u>have begun</u> speculating
                            A

    <u>whether</u> life <u>actually began</u> as crystal of clay
       B   C

    rather <u>than</u> as organic molecules. <u>No error</u>
            D   E

19. <u>Although</u> Maria has a better voice than <u>him</u>,
       A   B

    Larry <u>insists on</u> leading his class <u>during</u> the
            C   D

    national anthem. <u>No error</u>
                        E

20. <u>Revered as</u> one of the world's most versatile
       A

    geniuses, Leonardo Da Vinci excelled <u>in</u> every
                                           B

    endeavor he attempted and <u>serving</u> as
                                C

    <u>a prototype</u> for the Renaissance Man. <u>No error</u>
       D   E

21. To have read that book <u>in</u> three days, Edwin
                             A

    would have <u>to sacrifice</u> many of the enjoyable
                 B

    details <u>of</u> plot <u>and</u> character development.
             C   D

    <u>No error</u>
       E

22. <u>After checking</u> her closets and drawers
       A

    <u>thoroughly</u>, Katina <u>walked through</u> her old
       B   C

    apartment one last time before <u>moving out</u>.
                                     D

    <u>No error</u>
       E

23. After being <u>hampered with</u> red tape and
                  A

    innumerable regulations <u>for decades</u>, many
                              B

    businesses <u>welcome</u> the trend towards fewer
                 C

    legal <u>restrictions on</u> small companies. <u>No error</u>
            D   E

24. Florence is an <u>exceedingly</u> beautiful city <u>largely</u>
                     A   B

    because <u>they</u> have successfully blended
              C

    <u>the modern</u> with the ancient. <u>No error</u>
       D   E

25. <u>With the growing popularity</u> of word
       A

    processors, the handwriting <u>of many people</u>
                                  B

    <u>has become</u> barely <u>intelligent</u>. <u>No error</u>
       C   D   E

26. Only after the floodwaters had <u>rose</u> two feet
                                     A

    <u>was</u> the mayor willing <u>to order</u> the
       B   C

    <u>evacuation of</u> some homes. <u>No error</u>
       D   E

GO ON TO THE NEXT PAGE

DIRECTIONS

Thes following sentences test your ability to express ideas in writing effectively and efficiently. Each sentence is either partially or completely underlined. The first of the five choices given will repeat the original wording and the other four choices will contain alternative wording. Choose the change that best improves the senetence or choose A if the original is superior to any of the other choices given.

In making your choice keep in mind the standards of proper written English. Among other things, pay close attention to grammar, word choice, punctuation, precision, and correct usage of tenses. Avoid awkward and ambiguous construction.

EXAMPLE:

I want your love, and I want your revenge;
you and me can write a bad romance.

(A) you and me can write
(B) you and me could write
(C) you and me writing
(D) you and I can write
(E) me and you can write

Ⓐ   Ⓑ   Ⓒ   ⬤D   Ⓔ

27. Positions in the police and fire departments once were traditionally filled by men, but becoming increasingly popular among women.

(A) becoming increasingly popular among women.
(B) have become increasingly popular among women.
(C) have among women increased in popularity.
(D) become increasingly popular among women.
(E) women have increasingly found them to be popular.

28. Unless they become more responsible about investing money, many college students will soon rebel against their administrations.

(A) Unless they become more responsible
(B) Unless becoming more responsible
(C) Unless colleges become more responsible
(D) Unless it becomes more responsible
(E) Unless more responsibility is shown

29. The average person should eat more vegetables if they want to develop strong bodies and maintain their health.

(A) The average person should eat more vegetables if they want to develop strong bodies and maintain their health.
(B) The average person should eat more vegetables to develop strong bodies and maintain their health.
(C) The average person should eat more vegetables if he wants to develop a strong body and maintain his health.
(D) The average person, wishing to develop a strong body and maintain his health, should eat more vegetables.
(E) The average person should eat more vegetables in order to develop strong bodies and maintain their health.

30. Many parents and children argue often about responsibility; this would be avoided if they had more trust in them.

(A) they had more trust in them.
(B) their trust in them was more.
(C) their trust were more.
(D) their parents had more trust in them.
(E) their parents had more trust from their children.

GO ON TO THE NEXT PAGE

31. Unprepared for such a strong rebuttal, <u>the lawyer's attempt at winning the case failed.</u>

    (A) the lawyer's attempt at winning the case failed.
    (B) the lawyer's attempt failed to win the case.
    (C) the lawyer failed to win the case.
    (D) the lawyer failed in this attempt to win the case.
    (E) the lawyer attempted to win her case, but failed.

32. Goethe's poetry is <u>different from any others</u> in that it lyrically expresses profound thoughts.

    (A) different from any others
    (B) different from that of any other poet
    (C) different from any other poet
    (D) different than anyone else's
    (E) different than anyone else

33. It is true that plastic surgery can improve a person's outward appearance <u>but your personality will not change unless you make it.</u>

    (A) but your personality will not change unless you make it.
    (B) but your personality will not be changed unless you make it.
    (C) but a personality will not change unless you make it.
    (D) but a personality will not change without an effort.
    (E) but a personality will not change unless you make an effort.

34. <u>When reading</u> the reviews of his recently published romantic novel, Father O'Malley threw his manuscript into a blazing fireplace.

    (A) When reading
    (B) Having read
    (C) When he had read
    (D) When he reads
    (E) Reading

35. <u>When first implicated in it, Nixon denied any wrongdoing in the Watergate Scandal, but soon the evidence against him was overwhelming.</u>

    (A) When first implicated in it, Nixon denied any wrongdoing in the Watergate Scandal, but soon the evidence against him was overwhelming.
    (B) When Nixon was first implicated in the Watergate scandal, he denied any wrongdoing and the evidence against him was soon overwhelming.
    (C) When first implicated in the Watergate Scandal, the evidence against Nixon was soon overwhelming but he denied any wrongdoing.
    (D) When he was first implicated in the Watergate Scandal, Nixon denied any wrongdoing, but soon he was overwhelmed by the evidence against him.
    (E) Nixon first denied any wrongdoing in it, but soon the overwhelming evidence implicated him in the Watergate Scandal.

36. Michael Jackson <u>always has and probably will always be</u> one of the most exciting pop singers in the world.
    (A) always has and probably will always be
    (B) always has been and probably will always be
    (C) always has been and probably will be
    (D) has been and probably will be always
    (E) always has and probably always will

GO ON TO THE NEXT PAGE

37. To survive an airplane hijacking, <u>it demands remaining calm</u> and well-behaved.

    (A) it demands remaining calm
    (B) it demands calmness
    (C) one is demanded to remain calm
    (D) one should remain calm
    (E) demands one to remain calm

38. Vacationing in foreign countries provides one not only with relaxing experiences but also <u>cultures different from theirs are better understood.</u>

    (A) cultures different from theirs are better understood.
    (B) a better understanding of cultures different from theirs.
    (C) with a better understanding of different cultures.
    (D) cultures different from theirs are better understood.
    (E) cultures, although different, are better understood.

39. Georgia O'Keefe painted <u>landscapes and they express</u> the mystique of both the desert and the mountains of the Southwest.

    (A) landscapes and they express
    (B) landscapes, being the expressions of
    (C) landscapes, they express
    (D) landscapes that express
    (E) landscapes, and expressing in them

40. Professor Koshland argued that although many colleges have excelled at training future scientists, <u>the failure is in their not educating</u> humanities majors in the methods of scientific thought.

    (A) the failure is in their not educating
    (B) the failure they have is in their not educating
    (C) they failed not to educate
    (D) they have failed to educate
    (E) failing in their education of

41. The amount of garbage produced in the United States could be reduced by recycling trash, minimizing packaging, <u>and developing new technology</u> for incinerators and landfills.

    (A) and developing new technology
    (B) and if they develop new technology
    (C) also by developing new technology
    (D) and new technology being developed
    (E) and if there was new technology

42. <u>Having an exceptionally dry and stable atmosphere, astronomers chose Mauna Kea</u> as the prospective site of the world's largest optical telescope.

    (A) Having an exceptionally dry and stable atmosphere, astronomers chose Mauna Kea
    (B) Astronomers who chose Mauna Kea for its exceptionally dry and stable atmosphere saw it
    (C) Mauna Kea's exceptionally dry and stable atmosphere led to its choice by astronomers
    (D) Because its atmosphere is exceptionally dry and stable, astronomers chose Mauna Kea
    (E) Based on its exceptionally dry and stable atmosphere, Mauna Kea was chosen by astronomers

GO ON TO THE NEXT PAGE

43. Several of Frank Stella's <u>paintings were inspired by the shapes of waves and whales, titled</u> after chapter headings from *Moby-Dick*.

　(A) paintings were inspired by the shapes of waves and whales, titled

　(B) paintings had their inspiration from the shapes of waves and whales with titles

　(C) paintings, inspired by the shapes of waves and whales, are titled

　(D) paintings, which were inspired by the shapes of waves and whales and which are titled

　(E) paintings, being inspired by the shapes of waves and whales, titled

44. <u>The notion that a biography should be full of praise and free from criticism prevailed during most of the nineteenth century.</u>

　(A) The notion that a biography should be full of praise and free from criticism prevailed during most of the nineteenth century.

　(B) The notion that prevailed about a biography during most of the nineteenth century was that of being full of praise and free from criticism.

　(C) During most of the nineteenth century was that of being full of praise and free from criticism.

　(D) Prevalent as a notion during most of the nineteenth century was for a biography to be full of praise and free from criticism.

　(E) Prevalent during most of the nineteenth century, they thought that a biography should be full of praise and free from criticism.

GO ON TO THE NEXT PAGE

Questions 45-50 refer to the following passage.

(1) At one point in the movie "Raiders of the Lost Ark," the evil archaeologist Bellocq shows the heroic Indiana Jones a cheap watch. (2) If the watch were to be buried in the desert for a thousand years and then dug up, Bellocq says, it would be considered priceless. (3) I often think of this scene whenever I consider the record album collecting phenomenon, it being one of the more remarkable aspects of popular culture in the United States. (4) Collecting record albums gives us a chance to make a low-cost investment that just might pay dividends in the future.

(5) When my aunt collected them in the mid-sixties, nobody regarded them as investments. (6) A young fan shelled out dollar after dollar at the corner record store for no other reason than to assemble a complete collection of her favorite musical groups-in my aunt's case, the Beatles and the Supremes. (7) By committing so much of her allowance each week to the relentless pursuit of that one group not yet in her collection-the immortal Yardbirds, let us say-she was proving her loyalty to her superstars.

(8) The recording industry is a capitalist enterprise and so this hobby has become one. (9) Just as everyone has heard of the exorbitant prices being paid for the Beatles' first album in mint condition, so everyone is certain that a payoff is among each stack of old records. (10) But if that

album was buried somewhere in my aunt's closet full of dusty records, she never knew it. (11) Long before she learned it, she had thrown them out.

45. The sentence that best states the main idea of the passage is

(A) sentence 1
(B) sentence 2
(C) sentence 3
(D) sentence 4
(E) sentence 7

46. In the context of the first paragraph, which revision is most needed in sentence 3?

(A) Insert "As a matter of fact" at the beginning.
(B) Omit the word "scene".
(C) Omit the words "it being".
(D) Change the comma to a semicolon.
(E) Change "Think" to "thought" and "consider" to "considered".

47. Which of the following sentences is best inserted at the beginning of the second paragraph, before sentence 5??

(A) Not everyone, however, starts collecting records to make a profit.
(B) It is obvious that these early investments pay off.
(C) No two experiences are exactly alike when it comes to collecting records.
(D) Allow me to tell you about my aunt's attempt to achieve wealth.
(E) Many hobbies have advantages that are not readily apparent to you in the beginning.

GO ON TO THE NEXT PAGE

48. Of the following, which is the best version of sentence 8 (reproduced below)?

The recording industry is a capitalist enterprise and so this hobby has become one.

(A) (As it is now)
(B) Becoming more and more like the recording industry has been the hobby of collecting records, a capitalist enterprise.
(C) It is said that the recording industry has been transformed into a capitalist enterprise, much like this hobby.
(D) Like the recording industry itself, this hobby has become a capitalist enterprise.
(E) Finally, like the capitalist enterprise of recording, record collecting will be transformed.

49. Which of the following is the best version of the underlined portion of sentence 10 (reproduced below)?

But if that album was buried somewhere in my aunt's closet full of dusty <u>records, she never knew it.</u>

(A) records, they would never know it.
(B) records; they would never know.
(C) records, who would know that?
(D) records, my aunt will never know.
(E) records, they never knew it.

!

50. In context, which of the following is the best version of sentence 11 (reproduced below)?

Long before she learned it, she had thrown them out.

(A) (As it is now)
(B) Long before she learned that the records could be valuable, she had thrown them out.
(C) Long before she has learned about the records, she throws them out.
(D) It was long before she learned about the records that she threw them out.
(E) She throws the records out long before she hears about them.

SAT Writing Exercise #07
50 Questions

1. Before <u>the advent</u> of modern surgical
      A
techniques, <u>bleeding patients</u> with leeches
         B
<u>were considered</u> <u>therapeutically effective</u>.
    C   D
<u>No error</u>
 E

2. The <u>recent</u> establishment <u>of</u> "Crime Busters,"
    A   B
officially sanctioned neighborhood block-
watching groups, <u>have</u> dramatically improved
          C
relations <u>between</u> citizens and police. <u>No error</u>
       D   E

3. The masterpiece auctioned so <u>successfully</u>
                 A
today depicts a Biblical <u>scene in which</u> the,
             B
king is on his throne with his <u>counselors</u>
             C
standing <u>respectively</u> below. <u>No error</u>
       D   E

4. During the election campaign, the major political parties agreed that minorities must be given the opportunity <u>to advance</u>, <u>to seek</u>
            A   B
justice, and <u>to the kinds</u> of special treatment
        C
that might compensate <u>in part</u> for historical
         D
inequities. <u>No error</u>
     E

5. Most of the delegates <u>which</u> attended the
   (A)
   convention <u>felt</u> the resolution was <u>too strongly</u>
           B   C

   worded, and the majority voted <u>against</u> it.
                                       D

   <u>No error</u>
     E

6. <u>Lost in the forest</u> on a cold night, the hunters
        A

   <u>built</u> a fire <u>to keep themselves</u> warm and
     B   C

   <u>to frighten away</u> the wolves. <u>No error</u>
        D   E

7. The effort <u>to create appropriate</u> theatrical
                 A

   effects <u>often result</u> in settings that cannot be
         B

   <u>effective</u> without an imaginative <u>lighting</u> crew.
     C   D
   <u>No error</u>
     E

8. Every one of the shops in the town <u>were closed</u>
                                 A

   on Thursday <u>because</u> of the <u>ten-inch</u> rainfall
                B   C

   that <u>had fallen</u> during the day. <u>No error</u>
        D   E

9. <u>According to</u> the directions on the package,
       A

   the contents <u>are</u> intended for external use <u>only</u>
              B   C

   and <u>should not be</u> swallowed, even in small
          D

   quantities. <u>No error</u>
            E

10. <u>The late president's numerous memoirs</u> now
                 A

    <u>about to be published promises</u> to be of special
                B   C

    <u>historical</u> interest. <u>No error</u>
       D   E

11. Mr. Webster's paper is <u>highly imaginary</u> and
                        A
    <u>very creative</u>, <u>but</u> <u>lacking</u> in cogency. <u>No error</u>
      B   C   D   E

12. The point at issue <u>was whether</u> the dock
                   A

    workers, <u>which</u> were <u>an extremely vocal group</u>,
           B   C

    <u>would decide to return</u> to work. <u>No error</u>
         D   E

13. <u>Raising</u> living costs, <u>together</u> with escalating
      A   B

    taxes, <u>have</u> proved to be a burden for ·
           C

    <u>everyone</u>. <u>No error</u>
       D   E

14. A number of <u>harried</u> department store
                  A

    employees <u>were congregating</u> <u>around</u> the
            B   C

    water cooler <u>to compare and discuss</u> their
                  D

    grievances. <u>No error</u>
            E

!
!
!
!
!
!
!

GO ON TO THE NEXT PAGE

15. The deep-sea diver <u>considered himself</u> not
A
only a <u>competent</u> barnacle scraper but
B
<u>capable of</u> collecting interesting <u>specimens of</u>
C   D
seashells. <u>No error</u>
E

16. A round robin <u>is where</u> each team <u>must</u>
A   B
compete <u>against</u> every <u>other</u> team. <u>No error</u>
C   D   E

17. The voters were <u>dismayed</u> at <u>him retiring</u> from
A   B
<u>elected</u> office at such an early age, seemingly
C
<u>at the outset of</u> a brilliant career. <u>No error</u>
D   E

18. <u>Having a reasonable amount of</u> intelligence
A
and <u>steady persistence</u> <u>assure</u> one of acquitting
B   C
oneself <u>creditably</u> in any undertaking.
D
<u>No error</u>
E

19. "Elementary, my dear Watson," <u>was</u> a <u>frequent</u>
A   B
observation <u>of</u> the <u>imminent</u> Sherlock Holmes.
C   D
<u>No error</u>
E

20. <u>As</u> a college student, Delaney was hesitant
A
to <u>participate</u> <u>in any</u> rallies or demonstrations
B   C
because he hoped <u>for having</u> a political career
D
someday. <u>No error</u>
E

21. The castaways' situation was <u>beginning</u> to look
A
<u>desperate</u>: They had <u>drank</u> the last of their
B   C
water the night <u>before</u>, and there was only one
D
flare left in the emergency kit. <u>No error</u>
E

22. <u>Among</u> the many factors contributing to the
A
revival of the medieval economy <u>was</u> the
B
<u>cessation</u> of Viking raids and the <u>development</u>
C   D
of the heavy plow. <u>No error</u>
E

GO ON TO THE NEXT PAGE

23. Raoul gave Frederick very little warning before

striking a match and setting fire to his entire
   A   B

collection of documents, which had been
                          C

painstakingly compiled over the course of
      D

several decades. No error
                  E

24. Native to New Zealand, the kiwi has few
            A   B

natural predators but is currently endangered
                      C

by deforestation and human encroachment.
 D

No error
   E

25. If the current rate of progress in raising school
                                  A

standards is to be accelerated, every pupil,
            B

teacher, and parent in the neighborhood must
      C

assume their share of the responsibility.
         D

No error
   E

26. Diabetes can strike anyone, irregardless of age;
                              A

nevertheless, many people still make the
   B   C

mistake of considering it a geriatric disease.
            D

No error
   E

GO ON TO THE NEXT PAGE

DIRECTIONS

Thes following sentences test your ability to express ideas in writing effectively and efficiently. Each sentence is either partially or completely underlined. The first of the five choices given will repeat the original wording and the other four choices will contain alternative wording. Choose the change that best improves the senetence or choose A if the original is superior to any of the other choices given.

In making your choice keep in mind the standards of proper written English. Among other things, pay close attention to grammar, word choice, punctuation, precision, and correct usage of tenses. Avoid awkward and ambiguous construction.

EXAMPLE:

I want your love, and I want your revenge; <u>you and me can write</u> a bad romance.

   (A) you and me can write
   (B) you and me could write
   (C) you and me writing
   (D) you and I can write
   (E) me and you can write

              Ⓐ Ⓑ © Ⓓ Ⓔ

27. Congress was in no doubt <u>about who would take credit</u> for winning the war on inflation.

   (A) about who would take credit
   (B) about who takes credit
   (C) about whom would take credit
   (D) of who would take credit
   (E) over who would take credit

28. After depositing and burying her eggs, the female sea turtle returns to the water, <u>never to view or nurture the offspring that she is leaving behind.</u>

   (A) never to view or nurture the offspring that she is leaving behind
   (B) never to view or nurture the offspring which she had left behind
   (C) never to view nor nurture the offspring that are being left behind
   (D) never to view or nurture the offspring she has left behind
        never to view or nurture the offspring who she has left behind

29. Laval, the first bishop of Quebec, exemplified aristocratic vigor and concern <u>on account of his giving up his substantial inheritance to become an ecclesiastic</u> and to help shape Canadian politics and education.

   (A) on account of his giving up his substantial inheritance to become an ecclesiastic
   (B) since he gave up his substantial inheritance to become an ecclesiastic
   (C) since giving up his substantial inheritance to become an ecclesiastic
   (D) because of his having given up his substantial inheritance for the purpose of becoming an ecclesiastic
   (E) as a result of becoming an ecclesiastic through giving up his substantial inheritance

GO ON TO THE NEXT PAGE >

30. In the United States, an increasing number of commuters <u>that believe their families to be</u> immune from the perils of city life.

(A) that believe their families to be
(B) that believe their families are
(C) believes their families are
(D) who believe their families to be
(E) believe their families to be

31. <u>Developed by a scientific team at his university,</u> the president informed the reporters that the new process would facilitate the diagnosing of certain congenital diseases.

(A) Developed by a scientific team at his university
(B) Having been developed by a scientific team at his university
(C) Speaking of the discovery made by a scientific team at his university
(D) Describing the developments of a scientific team at his university
(E) As it had been developed by a scientific team at his university

32. In *War and Peace*, Tolstoy presented his theories on history and <u>illustrated them</u> with a slanted account of actual historical events.

(A) illustrated them
(B) also illustrating them
(C) he also was illustrating these ideas
(D) then illustrated the theories also
(E) then he went about illustrating them

33. One ecological rule of thumb states that there is opportunity for the accumulation of underground water reservoirs <u>but in regions where vegetation remains undisturbed.</u>

(A) but in regions where vegetation remains undisturbed
(B) unless vegetation being left undisturbed in some regions
(C) only where undisturbed vegetation is in regions
(D) except for vegetation remaining undisturbed in some regions
(E) only in regions where vegetation remains undisturbed

34. The ancient Chinese were convinced that air was composed of two kinds of particles, <u>one inactive and one active, the latter of which they called yin and which we today call oxygen.</u>

(A) one inactive and one active, the latter of which they called yin and which we today call oxygen
(B) an inactive and an active one called yin, now known as oxygen
(C) an inactive type and the active type they called yin we now know to be oxygen
(D) inactive and active; while they called the active type yin, today we call it oxygen
(E) contrasting the inactive type with the active ones they named yin and we call oxygen

GO ON TO THE NEXT PAGE

35. There are several rules <u>which must be followed by whomever</u> wants to be admitted to this academy.

(A) which must be followed by whomever
(B) that must be followed by whomever
(C) which must get followed by whom
(D) that must be followed by whoever
(E) which must be followed by those who

36. Developing a suitable environment for house plants <u>is in many ways like when you are managing</u> soil fertilization for city parks.

(A) is in many ways like when you are managing
(B) is in many ways similar to when you are managing
(C) in many ways is on a par with managing your
(D) is in many ways similar to the managing of
(E) is in many ways like managing

37. When he arrived at the hospital, the doctor found that <u>several emergency cases had been admitted before</u> he went on duty.

(A) several emergency cases had been admitted before
(B) there were several emergency cases admitted prior to
(C) two emergency cases were being admitted before
(D) a couple of emergency cases were admitted before
(E) several emergency cases was admitted before

38. Most students would probably get better grades if <u>writing were to be studied by them</u>.

(A) writing were to be studied by them
(B) they studied writing
(C) writing was studied by them
(D) they would have studied writing
(E) they were to have studied writing

39. Having read the works of both Henry and William James, I'm convinced that Henry is <u>the best psychologist and William the best writer</u>.

(A) the best psychologist and William the best writer
(B) a better psychologist, William is the best writer
(C) the best as a psychologist, William the best as a writer
(D) the best psychologist, William the better writer
(E) the better psychologist and William the better writer

40. The variety of Scandinavian health care services offered to residents at reduced cost <u>far exceeds low-cost health programs</u> available in the United States.

(A) far exceeds low-cost health programs
(B) far exceeds the number of low-cost health programs
(C) tends to be greater than low-cost programs
(D) far exceed the number of low-cost health programs
(E) are greater than comparable low-cost health programs

GO ON TO THE NEXT PAGE

41. Recently, scientists concerned about the growing popularity of astrologers have begun to speak out against them.

(A) Recently, scientists concerned about the growing popularity of astrologers have begun to speak out against them.

(B) Recently, scientists who are concerned about the growing popularity of astrologers have begun to speak out against such things.

(C) Recently, scientists, concerned about the growing popularity of astrologers, are beginning to speak out against them.

(D) Recently, scientists concerned with the growing popularity of astrologers have begun to speak out about it.

(E) Recently, scientists concerned about the growing popularity of astrologers have begun to speak out against what they will be doing.

42. The politician is benefiting from behavioral research, there are new techniques for them to utilize and new broadcasting methods to experiment with.

(A) research, there are new techniques for them

(B) research; he has new techniques

(C) research; there are new techniques for them

(D) research, there are new techniques for him

(E) research; they have new techniques

43. The Equal Rights Amendment to Islandia's constitution is dying a lingering political death, many dedicated groups and individuals have attempted to prevent its demise.

(A) many dedicated groups and individuals have attempted

(B) although many dedicated groups and individuals have attempted

(C) many dedicated groups and persons has attempted

(D) despite many dedications of groups and individuals to attempt

(E) however, many dedicated groups and individuals have attempted

44. If they do not go into bankruptcy, the company will probably survive its recent setbacks.

(A) If they do not go into bankruptcy

(B) Unless bankruptcy cannot be avoided

(C) If they can avoid bankruptcy

(D) If bankruptcy will be avoided

(E) Unless it goes bankrupt

GO ON TO THE NEXT PAGE

DIRECTIONS

The following passage is an early draft of an essay. Some parts of the passage need to be rewritten.

Read the passage and select the best answers for the questions that follow. Some questions are about particular sentences or parts of sentences and ask you to improve sentence structure or word choice. Other questions ask you to consider organization and development. In choosing answers, follow the requirements of standard written English.

Questions 45-50 refer to the following passage.

(1) Many young people think there is no point in studying liberal arts anymore. (2) They think this because with the kinds of jobs out there today, it's hard to see the relevance of them. (3) They say, "What's the point of reading Shakespeare if it's not going to help me get any sort of job?" (4) I thought things like this too.

(5) Not long ago, my English teacher asked me if I wanted to compete in a school-wide quiz show, and I said yes. (6) I did well on the show. (7) I was invited to join the school Trivia Team. (8) We were competing at high schools across the state. (9) It was a lot of fun and we won prize money. (10) Then came the championship game. (11) Nervous, my palms sweating, it was time for the tiebreaker question. (12) The host pulled the card from the envelope. (13) "What is the name of the wife of the jealous Moor in Shakespeare's Othello?" (14) I knew the answer. (15) I just read that play in my English class. (16) My hand hit the buzzer. (17) "Desdemona!" I shouted. (18) My teammates cheered and everyone hugged me. (19) We won!

(20) The next time I hear someone say there's no point in reading Shakespeare, I'll tell that person my story. (21) Who knows, maybe I'll appear on Jeopardy!™ some day.

45. Which of the following best replaces the word "them" in sentence 2?

(A) many people
(B) liberal arts
(C) jobs
(D) Shakespeare's plays
(E) things like this

46. Which of the following sentences, if added after sentence 4, would best link the first paragraph with the rest of the essay?

(A) It's hard to see the point of reading Shakespeare when people with Ph.D.'s are out of work.
(B) With so much television everywhere, hardly anyone reads anymore.
(C) It was becoming more and more difficult for me to complete my school assignments.
(D) However, I recently had an experience that caused me to change my mind.
(E) My parents and teachers tried to convince me otherwise, to no avail

GO ON TO THE NEXT PAGE

47. Which of the following is the best way to revise and combine sentences 6 and 7 (reproduced below)?

I did well on the show. I was invited to join the school Trivia Team.

(A) After doing well on the show, I was invited to join the school Trivia Team.

(B) (B) In order to be invited to join the school Trivia Team, I first had to do well on the show.

(C) Doing well on the show and being invited to join the school Trivia Team were the next two things that happened to me.

(D) Joining the school Trivia Team, I did well on the show.

(E) Because I was doing well on the show, I was being invited to join the school Trivia Team.

48. In context, which of the following is the best way to revise sentence 11 (reproduced below)?

Nervous, my palms sweating, it was time for the tie-breaker question.

(A) (As it is now)

(B) Nervous, my palms sweating, the tiebreaker question arrived.

(C) Nervous and sweating, my palms waited for the arrival of the tie-breaker question.

(D) Nervous, my palms sweating, I waited for the tie-breaker question.

(E) Being nervous and having sweating palms, I was waiting for the arrival of the tie-breaker question.

49. To vary the pattern of short, choppy sentences in the second paragraph, which of the following would be the best way to revise and combine sentences 14 and 15 (reproduced below)?

I knew the answer. I just read that play in my English class.

(A) I knew the answer, I just read that play in my English class.

(B) Although I just read that play in my English class, I knew the answer.

(C) Having just read that play in my English class, I knew the answer.

(D) I have known the answer to that question ever since I had been reading that play in my English class.

(E) In my English class, where I was reading that play, I knew the answer.

50. All of the following strategies are used by the writer of the passage EXCEPT

(A) refuting the assertion put forth in the first paragraph

(B) recounting a personal anecdote in order to make a point

(C) creating suspense by making references to the passage of time

(D) providing specific details

(E) including examples of jobs that require knowledge of liberal arts

!
!
!

STOP

this is the end of the exercise

SAT Writing Exercise #08
50 Questions

DIRECTIONS

Thes following sentences test your ability to detect errors in grammar and usage. Each sentence contains either one error or no errors at all and no sentence contains more than one error. Choose the underlined word or phrase in each sentence that when changed best corrects the grammatical or usage error. Only underlined words may be changed. If the sentence is correct as written, select choice E. In making your choices keep in mind the standards requirements of standard written English.

EXAMPLE:

Super Mario Bros' Mario first <u>appeared</u> in Donkey
　　　　　　　　　　　　　　　　　A
Kong as Jumpman and <u>was</u> later <u>renamed</u> to Mario
　　　　　　　　　　　B　　　　　C
<u>in honor to</u> Nintendo of America's landlord Mario
　D
Segali. <u>No Error</u>
　　　　　　E

Ⓐ Ⓑ Ⓒ ● Ⓔ

1. The more scientists learn about subatomic

   particles, <u>the more closely</u> they come
   　　　　　　　　　　A
   <u>to being able</u> to describe <u>the ways in which</u> the
   　　B　　　　　　　　　　C
   universe <u>operates</u>. <u>No error</u>
   　　　　　D　　　E

2. To have <u>reached a verdict</u> so quickly, the
   　　　　　　A　　　　　B
   members of the jury <u>would have to make up</u>
   　　　　　　　　　　　　C
   <u>their minds</u> before leaving the courtroom.
   　　D
   <u>No error</u>
   　E

3. <u>Drinking carbonated beverages</u> and eating
   　　　　　　　A
   food <u>that</u> <u>contain</u> chemical preservatives can
   　　　B　　C
   be unhealthy <u>when indulged in to excess</u>.
   　　　　　　　　　D
   <u>No error</u>
   　E

4. Albert Schweitzer <u>was</u> not only
   　　　　　　　　A
   <u>an accomplished doctor</u> but also
   　　　　　B
   <u>a talented musician</u> <u>as well</u>. <u>No error</u>
   　　　C　　　　　D　　　E

5. Harley Goodsleuth, private detective, <u>found</u>
   　　　　　　　　　　　　　　　A
   the <u>incriminating</u> evidence <u>where</u> the murderer
   　　　B　　　　　　　　C
   had left it. <u>No error</u>
   　D　　　E

GO ON TO THE NEXT PAGE

6. When the tall, cloaked figure had finished his

bleak <u>pronouncement about</u>
                    A

the <u>strange destiny</u> of the twins, <u>he vanished</u>
              B   C

<u>without hardly</u> a trace. <u>No error</u>
         D   E

7. <u>Many people feel</u> that a large defense budget
         A

<u>is necessary</u> <u>in order to</u> make the United States
         B   C

stronger <u>than any country in the world</u>.
                         D

<u>No error</u>
    E

8. <u>Drawn</u> by the large crowd <u>gathered</u> outside
         A   B

the tent, <u>the small boy</u> <u>standing</u> listening to
                    C   D

the hoarse conversation of the circus barker.

<u>No error</u>
    E

9. Not only <u>the poorest residents</u> of the city,
                         A

<u>but also</u> the wealthiest man in town <u>eat at</u>
    B   C

the <u>popular</u> cafeteria. <u>No error</u>
         D   E

10. Typhoid fever is a <u>bacterial</u> infection <u>that is</u>
                              A   B

<u>transmitted by</u> contaminated water, milk,
         C

shellfish, or <u>eating other foods</u>. <u>No error</u>
                    D   E

11. <u>Virtually</u> all of the members <u>who</u> attended the
         A   B

meeting <u>agreed to</u> the president's viewpoint on
              C

<u>the issue of budgetary restraints</u>. <u>No error</u>
         D   E

12. <u>Fewer</u> U.S. citizens are visiting
         A

Europe <u>as</u> American currency dwindles in
              B

exchange value and prices <u>raise</u> <u>in</u> several
                              C   D

European countries. <u>No error</u>
                              E

13. The first public school in North America,

Boston Latin School, <u>begun teaching</u> <u>its</u>
                              A   B

classical curriculum in 1635, one year <u>before</u>
                                             C

Harvard University <u>was founded</u>. <u>No error</u>
                         D   E

14. <u>Of all</u> the disasters that occurred during the
         A

movie's production, the death of the two stars

<u>who</u> performed their own stunts <u>were</u> surely
    B   C

<u>the worst</u>. <u>No error</u>
    D   E

GO ON TO THE NEXT PAGE

15. There is no sense <u>in continuing</u> the research,
                              A
now that the assumptions <u>on which</u> it
                                    B
<u>was based</u> <u>had been</u> disproved. <u>No error</u>
   C   (D)   E

16. The councilwoman could not understand how

the mayor <u>could declare</u> that the city
              A
<u>is thriving</u> <u>when</u> the number of firms declaring
    B   C
bankruptcy <u>increase</u> every month. <u>No error</u>
             (D)   E

17. Arthur Rubinstein was long ranked <u>among</u> the
                                         A
world's finest pianists, <u>although</u> he was some-
                            B
times known <u>as playing</u> several wrong notes
               C
<u>in a single</u> performance. <u>No error</u>
    D   E

18. The new office complex is beautiful, but <u>full</u>
                                              (A)
two hundred longtime residents <u>were forced</u>
                                    B
to move when <u>they</u> <u>tore down</u> the old
               C   D
apartment buildings. <u>No error</u>
                        E

19. Neither the singers <u>on stage</u> <u>or</u> the announcer
                           A   (B)
in the wings <u>could be heard</u> <u>over</u> the noise of
                C   D
the crowd. <u>No error</u>
              E

20. The delegates <u>among which</u> the candidates
                       (A)
circulated <u>became</u> <u>gradually less</u> receptive and
             B   C
more determined <u>to elicit</u> candid responses.
                    D
<u>No error</u>
  (E)

21. None of this injury <u>to life</u> and damage to prop-
                          A
erty <u>wouldn't have</u> happened if the amateur
       (B)
pilot <u>had only</u> heeded the weather forecasts
        C
and <u>stayed</u> on the ground. <u>No error</u>
      D   (E)

22. The doctor recommended that young athletes

with <u>a history</u> of severe asthma take <u>particular</u>
A   B   C
care <u>not to exercise</u> alone. <u>No error</u>
      (D)   E

GO ON TO THE NEXT PAGE

23. The piano, although <u>considerably less</u> capable
                                  A

of expressive nuance <u>than many other</u> musical
                          B

instruments, <u>are</u> <u>marvelously dramatic</u>.
                C   D

<u>No error</u>
     E

24. <u>Of</u> the respondents surveyed, <u>more</u> European
         A   B

travelers preferred taking the train <u>to</u> flying,
                                        C

<u>even</u> for long trips. <u>No error</u>
   D   E

25. By the time World War I <u>broke out</u>, there <u>was</u>
                                    A   B

<u>scarcely any</u> region of the world that <u>had not</u>
       C   D

been colonized by the Western powers.

<u>No error</u>
     E

26. <u>When in Rome</u>, we <u>should do</u> <u>as</u> the Romans
         A   B   C

do, but in English-speaking countries,

<u>they call</u> the Italian city Livorno "Leghorn."
     D

<u>No error</u>
     E

GO ON TO THE NEXT PAGE

DIRECTIONS

Thes following sentences test your ability to express ideas in writing effectively and efficiently. Each sentence is either partially or completely underlined. The first of the five choices given will repeat the original wording and the other four choices will contain alternative wording. Choose the change that best improves the senetence or choose A if the original is superior to any of the other choices given.

In making your choice keep in mind the standards of proper written English. Among other things, pay close attention to grammar, word choice, punctuation, precision, and correct usage of tenses. Avoid awkward and ambiguous construction.

EXAMPLE:

I want your love, and I want your revenge;
<u>you and me can write</u> a bad romance.

(A) you and me can write
(B) you and me could write
(C) you and me writing
(D) you and I can write
(E) me and you can write

Ⓐ   Ⓑ   Ⓒ   ⬤   Ⓔ

27. Mary Cassatt, an American painter strongly influenced by French <u>impressionism, she also responded</u> to Japanese paintings exhibited in Paris in the 1890s.

(A) impressionism, she also responded
(B) impressionism, also responded
(C) impressionism, also responding
(D) impressionism, nevertheless, she responded
(E) impressionism before responding

28. The choreographer Katherine Dunham <u>having trained as an anthropologist, she studied</u> dance in Jamaica, Haiti, and Senegal and developed a distinctive dance method.

(A) having trained as an anthropologist, she studied
(B) was also a trained anthropologist, having studied
(C) was also a trained anthropologist and a student of
(D) was also a trained anthropologist who studied
(E) training as an anthropologist, she studied

29. <u>Because its glazed finish resembles a seashell's surface is why porcelain china derives its name from the French word for the cowrie shell.</u>

(A) Because its glazed finish resembles a seashell's surface is why porcelain china derives its name from the French word for the cowrie shell.
(B) Its glazed finish resembling a seashell's surface, therefore, porcelain china derives its name from the French word for the cowrie shell.
(C) Resembling a seashell's surface in its glazed finish, that is why porcelain china derives its name from the French word for the cowrie shell.
(D) The French word for the cowrie shell gives its name to porcelain china because, with its glazed finish, its resemblance to a seashell's surface.
(E) Because its glazed finish resembles a seashell's surface, porcelain china derives its name from the French word for the cowrie shell.

GO ON TO THE NEXT PAGE

30. The few surviving writings of Greek philosophers before Plato <u>are not only brief and obscure, but also figurative</u> at times.

(A) are not only brief and obscure, but also figurative

(B) are not only brief and obscure, they can be figurative too

(C) not only are brief and obscure, but also figurative

(D) while not only brief and obscure, they also are figurative

(E) being not only brief and obscure, are also figurative

31. <u>In 1891, the Chace Copyright Act began protecting British authors, until then</u> American publishers could reprint British books without paying their writers.

(A) In 1891, the Chace Copyright Act began protecting British authors, until then

(B) The Chace Copyright Act began, in 1891, protecting British authors, whom, until then

(C) Although the Chace Copyright Act began to protect British authors in 1891, until which time

(D) Before 1891, when the Chace Copyright Act began protecting British authors,

(E) Finally, the Chace Copyright Act began protecting British authors in 1891, however, until then

32. Theorists of extraterrestrial intelligence depend on astronomical observations, chemical research, <u>and they draw inferences about nonhuman biology</u>.

(A) and they draw inferences about nonhuman biology

(B) while they infer biologically about non-human life

(C) and biologically infer about nonhuman life

(D) as well as drawing inferences biologically about non-human life

(E) and biological inferences about nonhuman life

33. Initiated in 1975, <u>sandhill cranes must unwittingly cooperate in the conservationists' project to raise</u> endangered whooping crane chicks.

(A) sandhill cranes must unwittingly cooperate in the conservationists' project to raise

(B) sandhill cranes' unwitting cooperation is required in the conservationists' project to raise

(C) the conservationists require that sandhill cranes unwittingly cooperate in their project of raising

(D) the conservationists require sandhill cranes to cooperate unwittingly in their project to-raise

(E) the conservationists' project requires the unwitting cooperation of sandhill cranes in raising

GO ON TO THE NEXT PAGE

34. Even after becoming blind, <u>the poet John Milton's daughters took dictation of his epic poem Paradise Lost.</u>

(A) the poet John Milton's daughters took dictation of his epic poem Paradise Lost
(B) the poet John Milton's daughters taking dictation, his epic poem Paradise Lost was written
(C) the epic poem Paradise Lost was dictated by the poet John Milton to his daughters
(D) the epic poem Paradise Lost was dictated to his daughters by the poet John Milton
(E) the poet John Milton dictated his epic poem Paradise Lost to his daughters

35. Delighted by the positive response to his address, <u>the candidate instructed his speechwriter to only concentrate on similar themes</u> for the remainder of the campaign.

(A) the candidate instructed his speechwriter to only concentrate on similar themes
(B) the candidate gave instructions to his speechwriter to concentrate on similar themes only
(C) the candidate's speechwriter was instructed to concentrate only on similar themes
(D) the candidate told the speechwriter to only concentrate on similar themes
(E) the candidate instructed his speechwriter to concentrate only on similar themes

36. Modem dance and classical ballet help strengthen concentration, tone muscles, <u>and for creating a sense of poise.</u>

(A) and for creating a sense of poise
(B) thereby creating a sense of poise
(C) and the creation of a sense of poise
(D) and create a sense of poise
(E) so that a sense of poise is created

37. Historians of literacy encounter a fundamental <u>obstacle, no one can know for certain</u> how many people could read in earlier centuries.

(A) obstacle, no one can know for certain
(B) obstacle; no one can know for certain
(C) obstacle; no one being able to know for certain
(D) obstacle; none of whom can know with certainty
(E) obstacle and no one can know for certain

38. Beethoven bridged two musical eras, in that <u>his earlier works are essentially Classical; his later ones, Romantic.</u>

(A) his earlier works are essentially Classical; his later ones, Romantic
(B) his earlier works are essentially Classical, nevertheless, his later ones are Romantic
(C) his earlier works being essentially Classical; his later are Romantic
(D) whereas essentially, his earlier works are Classical, his later ones would be Romantic
(E) despite his earlier works' being essentially Classical; his later are more Romantic

GO ON TO THE NEXT PAGE

39. In the grip of intense anxiety, <u>tears swept over the actress who</u> actually seemed to live her role.

(A) tears swept over the actress who
(B) tears provoked the actress who
(C) the actress was swept by tears as she
(D) the actress' tears fell as she
(E) the actress was crying tears who

40. <u>The journalist lived and conversed with the guerrilla rebels and he</u> was finally accept an informed interpreter of their cause.

(A) The journalist lived and conversed with the guerrilla rebels and he
(B) The journalist living and conversing with the guerrilla rebels, and he
(C) The journalist, who lived and conversed with the guerrilla rebels,
(D) The journalist's having lived and conversed with the guerrilla rebels,
(E) While living and conversing with the guerrilla rebels, the journalist

41. <u>Bearing an uncanny resemblance to the famous man</u> was no handicap for the ambitious entertainer.

(A) Bearing an uncanny resemblance to the famous man
(B) His uncanny resemblance to the famous man
(C) Resembling uncannily the famous man
(D) Having an uncanny resemblance upon the famous man
(E) It was found by him that bearing an uncanny resemblance to the famous man

42. None of the hysterical bystanders <u>was clear-sighted enough to remain calm or offer assistance</u> to the victim.

(A) was clear-sighted enough to remain calm or offer assistance
(B) were clear-sighted enough to remain calm or offer assistance
(C) were clear-sighted enough to remain calm or offering assistance
(D) was clear-sighted enough to have remained calm or offer assistance
(E) was clear-sighted enough to be remaining calm or offering assistance

43. With his plays, George Bernard Shaw tested the limits of British <u>censorship; the purpose being to</u> make audiences aware of social inequities.

(A) censorship; the purpose being to
(B) censorship and the purpose was to
(C) censorship, with the purpose to
(D) censorship; so that he could
(E) censorship to
!
!

44. The method of printing fabric called batik originated in Southeast Asia; wax is applied to patterned areas, <u>then boiled off after dyeing.</u>

(A) then boiled off after dyeing
(B) then, after dyeing, it is boiled off
(C) later it is boiled off after dyeing
(D) after which, dyers boil it off
(E) but then it is boiled off after dyeing

!
!

GO ON TO THE NEXT PAGE ➡

Questions 45-50 are based on the following essay, which is a response to an assignment to write about an economic issue facing the United States.

[1] Last year, my social studies class attended a talk given by a young woman who worked in a factory in Central America making shirts for a popular U.S. retail chain. [2] The working conditions she described were horrific. [3] She spoke of being forced to work 14-hour days and even longer on weekends. [4] The supervisors often hit her and the other women, most of whom were teenagers, to get them to work faster. [5] They gave them contaminated water to drink and were only allowed to go to the bathroom twice a day. [6] She urged us to boycott the retail chain and to inform consumers about the conditions in their factories.
!

[7] A group of us decided to meet with a representative of the chain and we would discuss our concerns and would announce our plans to boycott. [8] The representative said that low wages were necessary to keep costs down. [9] And she claimed a boycott would never work because it would be impossible to stop people from shopping at such a popular store. [10] "Nobody is going to listen to a bunch of teenagers," she said. [11] We decided to prove her wrong.

[12] First, we calculated that the workers' wages accounted for less than one percent of the price people paid for the shirts in the United States. [13] We argued that if the chain were willing to make slightly lower profits, it could afford to pay the workers more without raising prices. [14] And when we began informing people about the conditions under which the shirts they bought were made, they were horrified. [15] Many were agreeing to shop there no longer, they even wrote letters to the president of the chain in which he was urged to do something about the conditions in the factories. [16] Even local politicians got involved. [17] The winner of that year's City Council election pledged to change the conditions in the factories or shut the store down once and for all. [18] Finally, with business almost at a standstill, the store agreed to consumers' demands.

45. In context, which is the best version of the underlined portion of sentence 5 (reproduced below)?

They gave them contaminated water to drink and were only allowed to go to the bathroom twice a day.

(A) (As it is now)
(B) and were only allowing them to go
(C) and only allowed them to go
(D) and they were only given permission to go
(E) and were allowed to only go

46. In context, which of the following best replaces the word *"their"* in sentence 6?

(A) the consumers'
(B) its
(C) the workers'
(D) the supervisors'
(E) the students'

47. Which of the following versions of the underlined portion of sentence 7 (reproduced below) is best?

A group of us decided to meet with a representative of the chain <u>and we would discuss our concerns and would announce</u> our plans to boycott.

(A) (As it is now)
(B) to discuss our concerns and announce
(C) for the purpose of discussing our concerns and announcing
(D) where we would discuss our concerns and announce
(E) with whom we would be discussing our concerns and to whom we would announce

48. Which of the following would be the best replacement for the word "And" at the beginning of sentence 9?

(A) Moreover,
(B) Rather,
(C) However,
(D) Even so,
(E) Instead,

49. In context, which of the following is the best way to revise the underlined portion of sentence 15 (reproduced below)?

Many were agreeing to shop there no longer, they even wrote letters to the president of the chain in which he was urged to do something about the conditions in the factories.

(A) (As it is now)
(B) Many were agreeing to no longer shop there and even writing to the president of the chain in order that he be urged
(C) Agreeing to shop there no longer, many even wrote letters to the president of the chain urging him
(D) Many agreed to no longer shop there and also to urge the president of the chain by writing letters in which they asked him ·
(E) Shopping there no longer, many agreed to write letters to the president of the chain and also to urge him

50. Which sentence would most appropriately follow sentence 18?

(A) Despite the boycott, people were not willing to pay more for clothing.
(B) Unfortunately, people rarely do things for selfless reasons.
(C) Simply informing others is not enough; a plan of action must be devised.
(D) We should have listened to the young factory worker in the first place.
(E) We had proven the representative wrong; people had listened to "a bunch of teenagers."

SAT Writing Exercise #09

50 Questions

!

DIRECTIONS

Thes following sentences test your ability to detect errors in grammar and usage. Each sentence contains either one error or no errors at all and no sentence contains more than one error. Choose the underlined word or phrase in each sentence that when changed best corrects the grammatical or usage error. Only underlined words may be changed. If the sentence is correct as written, select choice E. In making your choices keep in mind the standards requirements of standard written English.

EXAMPLE:

Super Mario Bros' Mario first <u>appeared</u> in Donkey
　　　　　　　　　　　　　　A
Kong as Jumpman and <u>was</u> later <u>renamed</u> to Mario
　　　　　　　　　　B　　　　　C
<u>in honor to</u> Nintendo of America's landlord Mario
　　D
Segali. <u>No Error</u>
　　　　E

Ⓐ　Ⓑ　Ⓒ　Ⓓ　Ⓔ

---

1. <u>Before</u> Ms. Winchester <u>spoke to</u> the
　　A　　　　　　　　　　B
assembled crowd, she quietly called her

bodyguards' attention <u>to</u> a man who
　　　　　　　　　　C
<u>seemed to be carrying</u> a weapon. <u>No error</u>
　　　　D　　　　　　　　　　　　　E

2. The document, written by the local burghers

in 1757, <u>shows</u> <u>little</u> concern <u>in</u> law's
　　　　　　A　　　B　　　　　　C
effects on their constituents. <u>No error</u>
　　D　　　　　　　　　　　　　E

3. <u>Despite</u> the Preservation Society's efforts
　　A
<u>at saving</u> the old mill, the <u>overwhelming</u>
　　B　　　　　　　　　　　　C
majority of city council members voted

to raze it. <u>No error</u>
　D　　　　E

4. A Midwesterner <u>who</u> relocates to the urban
　　　　　　　　A
northeast <u>may find</u> his new colleagues unso-
　　　　　　B
ciable <u>if they</u> pass him in the workplace
　　　　C
<u>without hardly</u> a word. <u>No error</u>
　　D　　　　　　　　E
!

5. <u>Fewer buildings</u> with granite facades are
　　A
<u>being erected</u> as skilled stonecarvers die out
　　B
and <u>as</u> the cost of granite <u>will soar</u>. <u>No error</u>
　　C　　　　　　　　　　D　　　　E

GO ON TO THE NEXT PAGE →

6. We <u>expect</u> this election <u>to be hotly contested</u>,
  A   B

  <u>since already</u> both the incumbent and her chal-
  C

  lenger <u>have complained</u> of negative campaign-
                   D

  ing. <u>No error</u>
       E

7. However strong the desires for freedom and

  independence, there <u>are</u> <u>invariably</u> a conflict-
                        A   B

  ing urge <u>towards</u> security, <u>as well as</u> an emo-
              C   D

  tional need for stability. <u>No error</u>
                              E

8. Hiking along mountain trails <u>is</u> less expen-
                                    A

  sive but <u>considerably</u> <u>more demanding</u>
              B   C

  vacation activity than <u>to cruise</u> in the Bahamas.
                            D

  <u>No error</u>
   E

9. <u>Among</u> divergent schools of psychology, dif-
   A

  ferences of opinion <u>about</u> human motivation
                         B

  <u>have led</u> to <u>widely different</u> methods of treat-
   C   D

  ment and research. <u>No error</u>
                      E

10. Even though <u>their</u> commissions <u>are paid</u> by
                     A   B

  the musicians, the <u>typical</u> booking agent repre-
                       C

  sents the interests <u>of</u> the nightclub owners and
                        D

  Managers. <u>No error</u>
             E

11. Even students <u>who know</u> about the grant
                       A

  rarely apply for it, because <u>you</u> hate <u>to fill out</u>
                                 B   C

  <u>so many</u> forms. <u>No error</u>
   D   E

12. The Haitian religious cult of voodoo combines

  <u>elements of</u> Roman Catholic ritual <u>beside</u> reli-
   A   B

  gious and magical practices <u>that</u> <u>originated in</u>
                                C   D

  the African nation of Dahomey. <u>No error</u>
                                  E

13. Daniel Defoe wrote successful fictional

  memoirs <u>like</u> Robinson Crusoe in the early
             A

  1700s, but Samuel Richardson <u>is judged</u> by
                                 B

  some <u>to introduce</u> the modern novel twenty
         C

  years <u>later</u>. <u>No error</u>
          D   E

GO ON TO THE NEXT PAGE

14. Not the cotton gin <u>that made</u> him famous, but
A

<u>his</u> <u>concept</u> of interchangeable machine parts
B   C

<u>were</u> Eli Whitney's greatest contribution to
D

U.S. industry. <u>No error</u>
E

15. The first woman aviator <u>to cross</u> the English
A

Channel, Harriet Quimby <u>flown</u>
B

<u>by monoplane</u> from Dover, England, to
C

Hardelot, France, <u>in</u> 1912. <u>No error</u>
D   E

16. The French philosopher Jean-Paul Sartre

<u>is often assumed</u> to have initiated existential
A

philosophy, <u>but</u> the Danish philosopher
B

Kierkegaard <u>has developed</u> similar ideas
C

<u>much earlier.</u> <u>No error</u>
D   E

17. The reproductive behavior of sea horses

<u>is notable</u> <u>in respect of</u> the male, <u>who,</u>
A   B   C

<u>instead of</u> the female, carries the fertilized
D

eggs. <u>No error</u>
E

18. German-born architects Walter Gropius and

Ludwig Mies van der Rohe <u>are thought</u>
A

to have been <u>a major influence</u> on architectural
B   C

training in the United States <u>since</u> the 1930s.
D

<u>No error</u>
E

19. <u>Although</u> Charles Darwin incubated his
A

theory of evolution <u>for twenty years</u>, he wrote
B

On the Origin of Species <u>relatively rapid</u> once he
C

<u>began</u> composing. <u>No error</u>
D   E

20. An <u>eminent</u> historian <u>who</u> lectured here last
A   B

week <u>lay</u> out an array of causes <u>leading to</u> the
C   D

Civil War. <u>No error</u>
E

GO ON TO THE NEXT PAGE

21. Early <u>experience of</u> racial discrimination <u>made</u>
              A   B
an <u>indelible</u> <u>impression for</u> the late Supreme
       C   D
Court Justice Thurgood Marshall. <u>No error</u>
                                        E

22. More journalists <u>as</u> you would suspect are
                         A
<u>secretly</u> writing plays or novels, <u>which</u> they
    B   C
hope someday <u>to have published.</u> <u>No error</u>
                    D   E

23. <u>As long ago as</u> the twelfth century, French
         A
alchemists <u>have</u> perfected techniques
              B
<u>for refining</u> precious metals <u>from</u> other ores.
     C   D
<u>No error</u>
     E

24. Galileo begged Rome's indulgence for his
<u>support</u> of a Copernican system <u>in which</u> the
    A   B
earth circled the sun <u>instead of</u> <u>occupied</u> a
                           C   D
central position in the universe. <u>No error</u>
                                        E

25. <u>Squandering</u> his inheritance, the prodigal
         A
<u>felt no compunction at</u> wasting his <u>father's</u>
         B   C   D
hard-earned fortune. <u>No error</u>
                          E

26. Although the piano <u>as we know it today</u> did
                              A
not exist in Bach's time, he <u>was writing</u> many
                                  B
pieces <u>that are</u> now frequently played
           C
<u>on that instrument.</u> <u>No error</u>
         D   E

GO ON TO THE NEXT PAGE

DIRECTIONS

Thes following sentences test your ability to express ideas in writing effectively and efficiently. Each sentence is either partially or completely underlined. The first of the five choices given will repeat the original wording and the other four choices will contain alternative wording. Choose the change that best improves the senetence or choose A if the original is superior to any of the other choices given.

In making your choice keep in mind the standards of proper written English. Among other things, pay close attention to grammar, word choice, punctuation, precision, and correct usage of tenses. Avoid awkward and ambiguous construction.

EXAMPLE:

I want your love, and I want your revenge; you and me can write a bad romance.

(A) you and me can write
(B) you and me could write
(C) you and me writing
(D) you and I can write
(E) me and you can write

27. In the grip of intense anxiety, tears swept over the actress who actually seemed to live her role.

(A) tears swept over the actress who
(B) tears provoked the actress who
(C) the actress was swept by tears as she
(D) the actress' tears fell as she
(E) the actress was crying tears who

28. Delighted by the positive response to his address, the candidate instructed his speechwriter to only concentrate on similar themes for the remainder of the campaign.

(A) the candidate instructed his speechwriter to only concentrate on similar themes
(B) the candidate gave instructions to his speechwriter to concentrate on similar themes only
(C) the candidate's speechwriter was instructed to concentrate only on similar themes
(D) the candidate told the speechwriter to only concentrate on similar themes
(E) the candidate instructed his speechwriter to concentrate only on similar themes

29. None of the hysterical bystanders was clear-sighted enough to remain calm or offer assistance to the victim.

(A) was clear-sighted enough to remain calm or offer assistance
(B) were clear-sighted enough to remain calm or offer assistance
(C) were clear-sighted enough to remain calm or offering assistance
(D) was clear-sighted enough to have remained calm or offer assistance
(E) was clear-sighted enough to be remaining calm or offering assistance

GO ON TO THE NEXT PAGE

30. <u>Bearing an uncanny resemblance to the famous man</u> was no handicap for the ambitious entertainer.

   (A) Bearing an uncanny resemblance to the famous man
   (B) His uncanny resemblance to the famous man
   (C) Resembling uncannily the famous man
   (D) Having an uncanny resemblance upon the famous man
   (E) It was found by him that bearing an uncanny resemblance to the famous man

31. The Islandian government, under pressure to satisfy the needs of consumers, <u>and loosening its</u> control of the economy.

   (A) and loosening its
   (B) by loosening its
   (C) is loosening their
   (D) but loosening their
   (E) is loosening its

32. Night-shift workers lead a strange life, working while the rest of us are sleeping, <u>then sleeping</u> while the rest of us are working.

   (A) then sleeping
   (B) after which they sleep
   (C) then they sleep
   (D) until they go to sleep
   (E) but soon they are sleeping

33. The new freshman class <u>being larger than last year's.</u>

   (A) being larger than last year's
   (B) is large, more so than last year
   (C) which is larger than the one last year
   (D) is larger than last year's
   (E) by far larger than the last

34. The difference between the jobs is that <u>one is exciting; the other, boring.</u>

   (A) one is exciting; the other, boring
   (B) of one being exciting, the other is boring
   (C) one is exciting; the other being boring
   (D) one is exciting, although the other is boring
   (E) of an exciting one and one that is boring

35. <u>The lovers eventually returned to the grassy spot where they had left their sandwiches, strolling hand in hand.</u>

   (A) The lovers eventually returned to the grassy spot where they had left their sandwiches, strolling hand in hand.
   (B) Eventually, the lovers returned to the grassy spot where they had left their sandwiches, strolling hand in hand.
   (C) Strolling hand in hand, the grassy spot where they had left their sandwiches was returned to by the lovers.
   (D) The lovers, returning to the grassy spot where they had left their sandwiches, while strolling hand in hand.
   (E) Strolling hand in hand, the lovers eventually returned to the grassy spot where they had left their sandwiches.

GO ON TO THE NEXT PAGE

36. <u>Amelia Earhart, who was born in Kansas, was the first person to fly from Hawaii to California.</u>

(A) Amelia Earhart, who was born in Kansas, was the first person to fly from Hawaii to California.

(B) Amelia Earhart being the first person to fly from Hawaii to California and was born in Kansas.

(C) Being the first person to fly from Hawaii to California, Amelia Earhart was born in Kansas.

(D) Amelia Earhart was the first person to fly from Hawaii to California and was born in Kansas.

(E) Amelia Earhart was the first person to fly from Hawaii to California and she was born in Kansas.

37. To conserve calories, to promote digestion, or <u>so that they are less vulnerable to predators,</u> wild animals rest during many of their waking hours.

(A) or so that they are less vulnerable to predators

(B) or to remain less visible to predators

(C) or so that their predators cannot see them

(D) or in order that their predators find them less visible

(E) of for the purpose of remaining less visible to predators

38. Samuel Johnson's Dictionary, published in 1755, <u>was neither the first for English nor the largest,</u> but its quotations illustrating definitions made it the best for many decades.

(A) was neither the first for English nor the largest

(B) neither was it the first for English nor the largest

(C) neither was the first for English nor the largest

(D) neither was the first for English, and it was not the largest either

(E) was neither the first for English, nor was it the largest

39. There is scholarly consensus that, while Walt Whitman often referred to illegitimate children <u>of whom he claimed to be the father, he never had any outside of "dream children."</u>

(A) of whom he claimed to be the father, he never had any outside of "dream children."

(B) whom he claimed to have fathered, he had only "dream children."

(C) who he claimed fatherhood of, he was having only "dream children."

(D) of whom he said he was the father, "dream children" were his only ones.

(E) who he claimed to be the father of, he never had anything outside of "dream children."

GO ON TO THE NEXT PAGE

40. In the Middle Ages, when no one understood most astronomical phenomena, <u>the comets that seemed to portend</u> military conflicts or other social crises.

(A) the comets that seemed to portend
(B) the comets seeming to portend
(C) the comets seemed to portend
(D) the comets apparently portending
(E) and when the cornets seemed to portend

41. Unusual numbers of playwrights and artists <u>flourishing in the England of Shakespeare's time</u>, and the Italy of Michelangelo's day, when cultural conditions combined to promote creativity.

(A) flourishing in the England of Shakespeare's time
(B) by flourishing in the England of Shakespeare's time
(C) while flourishing in Shakespeare's England
(D) flourished in the England of Shakespeare's time
(E) having flourished in Shakespeare's England

42. During World War I, U.S. Army psychologists administered a forerunner of today's I.Q. tests, <u>where it had directions that</u> were given orally in acoustically poor and crowded rooms.

(A) where it had directions that
(B) whereby there were directions that
(C) whose directions
(D) and for it they had directions which
(E) and it had directions which

43. A dispute arose between Rimland and Heartland over the eastern provinces from which twenty years before a great many people <u>had emigrated.</u>

(A) had emigrated
(B) emigrated
(C) had immigrated
(D) immigrated
(E) migrated

44. Even though the senators on the committee <u>were reluctant to schedule</u> a formal inquiry, they went on record as favoring one.

(A) were reluctant to schedule
(B) were reluctant as far as scheduling
(C) were reluctant in scheduling
(D) have been reluctant at scheduling
(E) have had reluctance to schedule

GO ON TO THE NEXT PAGE

Questions 45-50 are based on the following essay.

(1) I used to be sure that I would never really win anything great whenever I entered a piano competition: that always happened to other people. (2) Maybe I'd get a plaque. (3) I wouldn't win anything that would change my life.

(4) I'm not your average teenager. (5) My friends spend their weekends playing sports. (6) I play the piano. (7) One day my music teacher told me about a piano competition with the first prize of a free trip to Europe! (8) I'm always happy to perform in public, whether it's in a competition or just for fun. (9) Anyway, I decided to apply for a spot in the competition.

(10) I pretty much forgot about the whole thing. (11) Then the notice from the music judges came to my house a few weeks later telling me when the competition would be held. (12) I was a little nervous. (13) But instead of getting scared and rejecting the whole idea, I just started practicing. (14) After about a month, the day of the recital competition came. (15) I played really well, but I assumed I'd never hear from the recital committee again. That is, until just a few days after the event, when I got a call from one of the judges. (17) She began by saying "I have some

good news for you…" (18) I had actually won something, an all expenses paid trip to Europe.

45. Which of the following is the best edit of the underlined portions of sentences 2 and 3 (reproduced below) so that the two are combined into one sentence?

    Maybe I'd get <u>a plaque. I wouldn't win</u> anything that would change my life.

    (A) a plaque, so I do win
    (B) a plaque, while there was no winning
    (C) a plaque, but I wouldn't win
    (D) a plaque, but wouldn't be winning
    (E) a plaque, and I couldn't win

46. Which sentence listed below, if placed after sentence 3, would best tie in the first paragraph with the rest of the essay?

    (A) After all, the competitions were usually too difficult for me.
    (B) However, something happened to me recently that made me reconsider my pessimistic attitude.
    (C) I never really wanted to take part in piano competitions anyway, since the pressure was too great.
    (D) Sometimes I'd take part in these recitals and win, but the prizes were never very impressive.
    (E) My parents encouraged me to try out for competitions with better prizes.

47. Which is the best way to combine sentences 5 and 6 (reproduced below) into one sentence?

My friends spend their weekends playing sports. I play the piano.

(A) Unlike my friends, who spend their weekends playing sports, I play the piano.
(B) Although my friends spend their weekends playing sports, I play the piano.
(C) My friends spend their weekends playing sports and I play the piano.
(D) When my friends spend their weekends playing sports, I play the piano.
(E) My friends are spending their weekends playing sports and I am playing the piano.

48. Which of the following versions of sentence 7 (reproduced below) is clearest?

One day my music teacher told me about a piano competition with the first prize of a free trip to Europe!

(A) My music teacher was telling me about a piano competition that had featured a free trip to Europe as its first prize!
(B) My music teacher one day told me about a piano competition having a first prize of a free trip to Europe!
(C) One day my musk teacher is telling me about a piano competition with the first prize being a free trip to Europe!
(D) One day my music; teacher told me about a piano competition that was having as its first prize a free trip to Europe!
(E) One day my music teacher told me about a piano competition featuring a free trip to Europe as its first prize!

49. Which of the following, in light of the information in the essay, is a more appropriate replacement for "Anyway," beginning sentence 9 (reproduced below)?

Anyway, I decided to apply for a spot in the competition.

(A) Finally,
(B) That's why
(C) Eventually,
(D) Despite this,
(E) Apparently,

50. Which is the best version of the underlined portions of sentences 16 and 17 (reproduced below)?

That is, until just a few days after the event, when I got a call from one of the judges. She began by saying "I have some good news for you .... "

(A) (As it is now)
(B) That is, until just a few days after the event, having been called by one of the judges, who began by saying
(C) Until, that is, just a few days after the event, being called by one of the judges. She began by saying
(D) That is, until just a few days after the event, being called from one of the judges. She began by saying
(E) That is, when I got a call from one of the judges, who began by saying

this is the end of the exercise

SAT Writing Exercise #10
50 Questions

!

DIRECTIONS

Thes following sentences test your ability to detect errors in grammar and usage. Each sentence contains either one error or no errors at all and no sentence contains more than one error. Choose the underlined word or phrase in each sentence that when changed best corrects the grammatical or usage error. Only underlined words may be changed. If the sentence is correct as written, select choice E. In making your choices keep in mind the standards requirements of standard written English.

EXAMPLE:

Super Mario Bros' Mario first <u>appeared</u> in Donkey
                                      A
Kong as Jumpman and <u>was later renamed</u> to Mario
                         B   C
<u>in honor to</u> Nintendo of America's landlord Mario
    D
Segali. <u>No Error</u>
             E

Ⓐ Ⓑ © ● Ⓔ

!

1. The chemist Sir Humphrey Davy was a friend

   <u>of the poet</u> William Wordsworth; <u>he</u>
    A   B
   <u>would visit</u> with several other guests <u>at</u> a
    C   D
   tiny cottage in the English Lake District.

   <u>No error</u>
     E

2. There are times <u>where</u> we must make
                      A
   <u>decisions</u> purely <u>on the basis of</u> the financial
    B   C
   resources at <u>our</u> disposal. <u>No error</u>
                   D   E

3. <u>Like</u> the poetry of Milton, <u>Dryden generally</u>
    A   B
   <u>adheres to</u> classical forms and
    C
   <u>traditional themes.</u> <u>No error</u>
      D   E

4. The work of Byron <u>has been underrated</u> more
                        A
   often by <u>so-called</u> modernists in the field of
             B
   literary criticism <u>than</u> any <u>other</u> Romantic
                        C   D
   poet. <u>No error</u>
           E

5. The convict escaped <u>with the aid</u> of a <u>recent</u>
                         A   B
   released prisoner, a career criminal <u>who knew</u>
                                          C
   the prison grounds <u>intimately.</u> <u>No error</u>
                         D   E

GO ON TO THE NEXT PAGE ⟶

6. Grading research papers over the years, the
  A   B
professor became expert at recognizing
                          C
submissions that have been plagiarized or
                          D
inadequately documented. No error
                                E

7. Although he had planned a more pessimistic
  A   B
ending. Thomas Hardy was persuaded by his
                          C
readers to close The Return of the Native with
          D
marriage. No error
            E

8. During the military coup, the deposed prime
minister's property was put up for sale
                          A
without him having any opportunity to object.
  B   C   D
No error
  E

9. The proposals for insurance reform of the so-
                                A
called moderate candidate for governor were
                                          B
as conservative as, or more conservative than,
                          C
his rival. No error
  D   E

10. It did not occur to the interviewer to ask
  A   B
either the job applicant nor his reference
                          C
whether the applicant had completed the
  D
project he initiated. No error
                        E

11. The Ivorian students considered it more disre-
                          A
spectful to look directly into an elder's eyes
          B   C
than to refuse to answer a teacher's question.
                  D
No error
  E

12. Having little concern for others, as well as
  A   B
a lack of curiosity about the unknown,
  C
the woman made an ineffectual teacher.
  D
No error
  E

13. There was a huge public outcry over the cruel
        A   B
methods employed at the animal pound, but
                  C
in the end, nothing came of them. No error
                          D   E

GO ON TO THE NEXT PAGE

14. A pioneering scholar <u>of</u> anthropology, Ruth
A
Benedict <u>was also</u> a spokesperson <u>against</u>
B   C
ethnic bigotry <u>which</u> recognized that cultures
D
influence ideas about gender. <u>No error</u>
E

15. <u>Not far from</u> the finest <u>remaining</u> examples of
A   B
Federal architecture <u>stands</u> a geometric struc-
C
ture <u>of</u> glass, steel, and chrome. <u>No error</u>
D   E

16. Alexander Calder <u>first</u> studied
A
<u>mechanical engineering</u>, <u>but later</u> was able
B   C
<u>for inventing</u> a new form of sculpture, the
D
mobile. <u>No error</u>
E

17. The political <u>climate of</u> a stable nation can be
A
expected <u>to change</u>, but <u>far more gradually</u>
B   C
than trends in art or music <u>do</u>. <u>No error</u>
D   E

18. A research paper <u>requires</u> footnotes or end-
A
notes and a bibliography <u>irregardless</u> <u>of which</u>
B   C
references and sources the writer <u>uses</u>.
D

<u>No error</u>
E

19. Since the government <u>was</u> bankrupt, many of
A
the soldiers <u>which</u> were sent <u>to quell</u> the riots
B   C
had <u>not been</u> paid in months. <u>No error</u>
D   E

20. Although <u>they had been</u> political rivals on
A
<u>more than one</u> occasion, John Quincy Adams
B
<u>remained</u> one of Thomas Jefferson's closest
C
friends until <u>his</u> death. <u>No error</u>
D   E

21. Even <u>those who</u> profess <u>to care</u> about "green"
A   B
issues often fail to consider <u>how</u> their daily
C
choices <u>effect</u> the environment. <u>No error</u>
D   E

22. Ants, <u>which</u> have inhabited the earth for at
A
least 100 million years, <u>are without doubt</u> the
B
<u>more successful</u> of all the social insects of the
C
Hymenoptera, an order <u>that also</u> includes
D
wasps and bees. <u>No error</u>
E

23. For my sister and <u>I</u>, the trip to Paris was the
A
<u>fulfillment of</u> a lifelong wish we <u>had scarcely</u>
B   C
<u>dared to express</u>. <u>No error</u>
D   E

GO ON TO THE NEXT PAGE

24. The volunteers, <u>upon discovering</u> that
                       A
<u>a large number</u> of the village children <u>were</u>
      B   C
infected by parasites <u>from</u> unclean drinking
                        D
water, decided to make the well-digging

project their highest priority. <u>No error</u>
                                   E

25. Although farmers complained that the

company's new product was expensive,

malodorous, and <u>dangerous to handle</u>,
                        A
<u>there was</u> few who <u>would dispute</u> its
   B   C
effectiveness <u>as</u> an insecticide. <u>No error</u>
               D   E

26. In the wake <u>of</u> recent thefts, the town's
                     A
wealthier residents <u>have installed</u> gates, alarm
                         B
systems, and even video surveillance

equipment in their neighborhoods, hoping

<u>that it will</u> prevent <u>future burglaries</u>. <u>No error</u>.
   C   D   E

GO ON TO THE NEXT PAGE

DIRECTIONS

Thes following sentences test your ability to express ideas in writing effectively and efficiently. Each sentence is either partially or completely underlined. The first of the five choices given will repeat the original wording and the other four choices will contain alternative wording. Choose the change that best improves the senetece or choose A if the original is superior to any of the other choices given.

In making your choice keep in mind the standards of proper written English. Among other things, pay close attention to grammar, word choice, punctuation, precision, and correct usage of tenses. Avoid awkward and ambiguous construction.

EXAMPLE:

I want your love, and I want your revenge; you and me can write a bad romance.

(A) you and me can write
(B) you and me could write
(C) you and me writing
(D) you and I can write
(E) me and you can write

Ⓐ   Ⓑ   Ⓒ   🄳   Ⓔ

27. Patients with Alzheimer's disease typically exhibit symptoms such as confusion, memory loss, and their language skills are impaired.

(A) and their language skills are impaired
(B) and it also impairs their language skills
(C) and impaired language skills
(D) besides their language skills being impaired
(E) in addition to their language skills being impaired

28. Upon entering the jail, the prisoners' personal belongings are surrendered to the guards.

(A) Upon entering the jail, the prisoners' personal belongings are surrendered to the guards.
(B) Upon entering the jail, the prisoners surrender their personal belongings to the guards.
(C) The prisoners' personal belongings having been surrendered to the guards upon entering the jail.
(D) Upon entering the jail, the guards are to whom the prisoners surrender their personal belongings.
(E) Upon entering the jail, the prisoners will have been surrendering their personal belongings to the guards.

29. The albatross has a broad wing span, it is graceful in the air but ungainly on dry land.

(A) The albatross has a broad wingspan, it is graceful in the air but ungainly on dry land.
(B) The albatross, with its broad wingspan, is graceful in the air but ungainly on dry land.
(C) Having a broad wingspan, the albatross is graceful in the air, however it is ungainly on dry land.
(D) The albatross, which has a broad wingspan, graceful in the air but ungainly on dry land.
(E) The albatross, although having a broad wingspan, is graceful in the air but ungainly on dry land.

GO ON TO THE NEXT PAGE

30. King John of England is remembered not so much for his administrative successes <u>but for failing in military engagements</u>.

(A) but for failing in military engagements
(B) but more for the fact that he failed in military engagements
(C) than he was for having failed militarily
(D) the reason being that he failed in military engagements
(E) as for his military failures

31. <u>During the winter months, several feet of snow cover the narrow mountain pass, which is the only route to the monastery.</u>

(A) During the winter months, several feet of snow cover the narrow mountain pass, which is the only route to the monastery.
(B) The only route to the monastery, several feet of snow cover the narrow mountain during the winter months.
(C) Several feet of snow cover the narrow mountain pass during the winter months which is the only route to the monastery.
(D) Several feet of snow cover the narrow mountain pass, which is the only route to the monastery during the winter months.
(E) During the winter months, covering the narrow mountain pass which is the only route to the monastery is snow.

32. The border crossing proved more unpleasant than the two American reporters had <u>expected, having their cameras seized</u> and their tape recorders smashed by belligerent soldiers.

(A) expected, having their cameras seized
(B) expected, their cameras being seized
(C) expected: their cameras were seized
(D) expected; when their cameras were seized
(E) expected and so their cameras had been seized

33. The Townshend Acts, a piece of British legislation enacted on June 29, 1767, <u>were intended for the raising of revenue, to tighten customs enforcement, and assert</u> imperial authority in America.

(A) were intended for the raising of revenue, to tighten customs enforcement, and assert
(B) were intended to raise revenue, tighten customs enforcement, and assert
(C) were with the intention of raising revenue, tightening customs enforcement, and assert
(D) had for their intention the raising of revenue, tightening of customs enforcement, and asserting
(E) were intended to raise revenue, also to tighten customs enforcement and assert

34. <u>Were it not for the warming effects of the Gulf Stream, England's climate would resemble that of Greenland.</u>

(A) Were it not for the warming effects of the Gulf Stream, England's climate would resemble that of Greenland.
(B) Had the Gulf Stream not such warming effects, England's climate would resemble Greenland.
(C) Without the warming effects of the Gulf Stream, England's climate were resembling Greenland's.
(D) If not for the warming effects of the Gulf Stream, therefore England's climate would have resembled that of Greenland.
(E) If the Gulf Stream would not have had its warming effects, England's climate would resemble that of Greenland.

GO ON TO THE NEXT PAGE

35. Perhaps best known for his portrayal of T. E. Lawrence in the film Lawrence of Arabia, <u>Peter O'Toole's distinguished acting career spans nearly five decades.</u>

  (A) Peter O'Toole's distinguished acting career spans nearly five decades

  (B) Peter O'Toole has a distinguished acting career spanning nearly five decades

  (C) Peter O'Toole spans nearly five decades in his distinguished acting career

  (D) Peter O'Toole's distinguished acting career will have spanned nearly five decades

  (E) nearly five decades have been spanned by Peter O'Toole's distinguished acting career

36. In their haste to complete the new stadium before the Olympic games, the contractors disregarded safety <u>codes, thereby they endangered the lives of thousands of spectators.</u>

  (A) codes, thereby they endangered the lives of thousands of spectators

  (B) codes they have endangered the lives of thousands of spectators

  (C) codes and so endangered the lives of thousands of spectators

  (D) codes; thus the lives of thousands of spectators endangered

  (E) codes, they endangered the lives of thousands of spectators as a result

37. Many researchers contend that driving while talking on a cellular phone poses essentially the same risks <u>than if you drive</u> while intoxicated.

  (A) than if you drive

  (B) than to drive

  (C) as if one drives

  (D) as driving

  (E) as it does when driving

38. Before 1988, the corporation's board of directors included one hundred and fifty-three <u>members, none of the members were women.</u>

  (A) members, none of the members were women

  (B) members; and no women

  (C) members, none of them women

  (D) members, and of the members not one of them was a woman

  (E) members; none of them being women

39. <u>The client was waiting for fifteen minutes when</u> the receptionist suddenly looked up from her work, noticed him, and informed him that his appointment had been canceled.

  (A) The client was waiting for fifteen minutes when

  (B) The client, having waited for fifteen minutes, when

  (C) Already the client was waiting for fifteen minutes when

  (D) When the client waited for fifteen minutes,

  (E) The client had been waiting for fifteen minutes when

40. <u>Because the polar ice caps are melting, therefore many</u> scientists and environmentalists fear that several small island nations will be completely covered by water in only a few decades.

  (A) Because the polar ice caps are melting, therefore many

  (B) Because the polar ice caps are melting, many

  (C) The polar ice caps are melting, therefore many

  (D) Because the polar ice caps are melting; many

  (E) The polar ice caps are melting; and many

GO ON TO THE NEXT PAGE

41. One of the great literary artists of the nineteenth century was Gustave Flaubert known for his obsession with the writer's craft.

(A) century was Gustave Flaubert known for his obsession with the writer's craft

(B) century, Gustave Flaubert's obsession with the writer's craft was well known

(C) century, Gustave Flaubert was known for his obsession with the writer's craft

(D) century, Gustave Flaubert, known for his obsession with the writer's craft

(E) century was Gustave Flaubert: known for his obsession with the writer's craft

42. When Dr. Park presented an abridged version of his paper at the conference, several tantalizing theories about the origins of life on earth were introduced, but these were not fully developed by him.

(A) several tantalizing theories about the origins of life on earth were introduced, but these were not fully developed by him

(B) he introduced several tantalizing theories about the origins of life on earth but they had not been fully developed

(C) several tantalizing theories about the origins of life were introduced by him and not fully developed

(D) several tantalizing theories about the origins of life on earth were introduced, but he did not fully develop these

(E) he introduced, but did not fully develop, several tantalizing theories about the origins of life on earth

43. A spokesman for the arms dealers boasted that the new weapon was lightweight, effective, and virtually undetectable by the security equipment most commonly used in airports.

(A) and virtually undetectable by the security equipment most commonly used in airports

(B) and the security equipment most commonly used in airports could not detect it

(C) and virtually undetectable for the security equipment most commonly used in airports

(D) and had gone virtually undetected by the security equipment most commonly used in airports

(E) and the security equipment most commonly used in airports virtually unable to detect it

44. According to older fishermen, cod and haddock were once plentiful in the North Sea, but years of over-fishing and pollution have had a negative overall impact on the fish stocks.

(A) had a negative overall impact on the fish stocks

(B) impacted the fish stocks negatively

(C) the result that the fish stocks are diminished

(D) depleted the fish stocks

(E) been depleting the fish stocks overall

GO ON TO THE NEXT PAGE

DIRECTIONS

The following passage is an early draft of an essay. Some parts of the passage need to be rewritten.

Read the passage and select the best answers for the questions that follow. Some questions are about particular sentences or parts of sentences and ask you to improve sentence structure or word choice. Other questions ask you to consider organization and development. In choosing answers, follow the requirements of standard written English.

Questions 45-50 are based on the following passage.

[1] Last summer I was fortunate enough to be able to spend a month in France. [2] It was the most exciting time of my life. [3] I stayed with a family in Montpellier, which is in the south of France. [4] It was very different from my life back in the United States. [5] Every morning we bought fresh bread from the bakery and had coffee in a bowl instead of a cup. [6] The milk came in bottles fresh from the dairy.

[7] Back home in Winnetka, Illinois, I wouldn't think anything of taking a ten-minute shower every day, or even twice a day in the summer. [8] In Montpellier, we only showered once every two days and were using far less water. [9] First you turn the water on to get wet, then turn it off and soap yourself up, then you turned it on again to rinse off, so the water is only on for about maybe two minutes. [10] And it was pretty hot there in the summer; I'd never taken showers in cold water before! [11] I couldn't imagine what it was like in the winter. [12] I also noticed that although the family had a car, they hardly ever used it. [13] The father took the bus to work in the morning and the mother rode her bicycle when doing errands. [14] Since the family wasn't poor, they were well off, I realized that gas is much more expensive in France than in the U.S. [15] I realized that as Americans, we can afford to take long showers and drive everywhere because we pay much less for energy. [16] Living in Montpellier and seeing how frugally people lived there, I get angry thinking of the resources wasted in the U.S. [17] When I came home, I was much more energy conscious. [18] I didn't drink coffee out of a bowl anymore, but I started riding my bike to school and turning the thermostat down at night.

45. Which of the following sentences, if added after sentence 6, would best link the first paragraph with the rest of the essay?

(A) These differences were superficial; however I was soon to discover other, more important ones.
(B) How I longed for my familiar existence back in the United States!
(C) I was not prepared for the culture shock I experienced.
(D) But I didn't let such minor inconveniences ruin my overseas experience.
(E) Although it took a while, eventually I got used to the new way of doing things.

46. In context, which of the following versions of sentence 8 (reproduced below) is best?

In Montpellier, we only showered once every two days and were using far less water.

(A) Showering only once every two days, Montpellier was where I used far less water.
(B) Showering only once every two days and using far less water were things we did in Montpellier.
(C) In Montpellier, we showered only once every two days and used far less water.
(D) In Montpellier, where once every two days was when we showered, a lot less water was used.
(E) In Montpellier, we were only showering once every two days and using far less water.

GO ON TO THE NEXT PAGE →

47. In context, which of the following is the best way to revise sentence 9 (reproduced below)?

First you turn the water on just to get wet, then turn it off and soap yourself up, then you turned it on again to rinse off, so the water is only on for about maybe two minutes.

(A) First I turn the water on just to get wet, then turn it off and soap myself up, then turn it on again to rinse off, so the water is only on for about maybe two minutes.

(B) First turning the water on just to get wet, then turning it off and soaping yourself off, you turned it on again to rinse off, the water being on for only about maybe two minutes.

(C) First one turns the water on just to get wet, then turns it off and soaps oneself up, then one turns it on again to rinse off, so the water is only on for about maybe two minutes.

(D) First we turned the water on just to get wet, then turned it off and soaped our-. selves up, then turned it on again to rinse off, so that the water was only on for about two minutes.

(E) First we turn the water on just to get wet, then turn it off and soap ourselves up, then turn it on again to rinse off, so the water is only on for about two minutes.

48. Which of the following best replaces the word "And" at the beginning of sentence 10?

(A) But
(B) Although
(C) Yet
(D) When
(E) Which

49. In context, which is the best version of the underlined portion of sentence 14 (reproduced below)?

Since the family wasn't poor, they were well off, I realized that gas is much more expensive in France than in the U.S.

(A) The family not being poor, they were well off,
(B) Well off, not poor, being the family,
(C) Since the family was well off, they were not poor,
(D) The family wasn't poor but well off,
(E) Since the family was well off rather than poor,

50. Sentence 16 could best be improved by

(A) including a definition of resources
(B) providing examples
(C) changing it to the past tense
(D) using the first person plural instead of the first person singular
(E) moving it to the end of the essay

STOP

this is the end of the exercise

SAT Writing Exercise #11
50 Questions

DIRECTIONS

Thes following sentences test your ability to detect errors in grammar and usage. Each sentence contains either one error or no errors at all and no sentence contains more than one error. Choose the underlined word or phrase in each sentence that when changed best corrects the grammatical or usage error. Only underlined words may be changed. If the sentence is correct as written, select choice E. In making your choices keep in mind the standards requirements of standard written English.

EXAMPLE:

Super Mario Bros' Mario first <u>appeared</u> in Donkey
                                    A
Kong as Jumpman and <u>was</u> later <u>renamed</u> to Mario
                      B   C
<u>in honor to</u> Nintendo of America's landlord Mario
    D
Segali. <u>No Error</u>
            E

Ⓐ Ⓑ © ⬤Ⓓ Ⓔ

---

1. <u>To repair</u> the damage <u>that</u> time and the
        A   B
elements <u>had wrought</u> on the ancient fresco,
              C
the restorer used a simple mixture <u>from</u>
                                      Ⓓ
plaster, pigment, and a little water. <u>No error</u>
                                          E

2. Opponents of the Act <u>argued that</u> the
                              A
legislation <u>was not only</u> vaguely formulated
              B
and unconstitutional, but also impossible
to <u>enforce</u> in an international <u>and virtually</u>
    C   D
unregulated arena. <u>No error</u>
                        Ⓔ

3. One reason that a growing number of people
<u>have no</u> family doctor <u>may be that</u> fewer and
    A   B
fewer medical students <u>are choosing to train</u> as
                          C
a general practitioner. <u>No error</u>
          D   E

4. <u>That</u> J. L. Solomon's first novel
        A
<u>was selected for</u> several major literary prizes
          B
<u>was surprising to</u> no one who had read his
          C
<u>previous</u> collections of short stories, poems,
    D
and essays. <u>No error</u>
                Ⓔ

GO ON TO THE NEXT PAGE

5. When questioned, <u>a surprising</u> number of
　　　　　　　　　　A

fifth-graders said that telling the truth-even

if it meant <u>being</u> punished-was preferable
<u>B</u>　　　　C

<u>than living</u> with a lie. <u>No error</u>
　　D　　　　　　　　　E

6. Citizens <u>protesting the</u> planned demolition of
　　　　　　　A

the historic YMCA building claim

<u>that without</u> the YMCA, many young people
　B

in the town <u>would of</u> grown up <u>with no</u> access
　　　　　　　C　　　　　　　D

to sports facilities and no place for after-

school recreation. <u>No error</u>
　　　　　　　　D

7. <u>Though</u> Patricia's resume was <u>not nearly as</u>
　　A　　　　　　　　　　　B

long and impressive as <u>the other applicant</u>,
　　　　　　　　　　C

her personal charisma was <u>so great that</u> Mr.
　　　　　　　　　　　D

Alvarez hired her on the spot. <u>No error</u>
　　　　　　　　　　　　E

8. <u>Under</u> the proposed law, which many <u>deem</u>
　　A　　　　　　　　　　　B

too harsh, any motorist <u>convicted of</u> drunk
　　　　　　　C

lose <u>their license</u> for five years. <u>No error</u>
　　D　　　　　　　　　　E

9. When <u>it became apparent</u> to Clive that not
　　　　A

one of the remaining jurors <u>were going to</u>
　　　　　　　　　　B

believe his <u>client's</u> alibi, he began to reconsider
　　　　　　　C

the District Attorney's <u>offer of</u> a plea bargain.
　　　　　　　　　　D

<u>No error</u>
　E

10. <u>If only</u> the factory owners <u>had conducted</u>
　　　A　　　　　　　　　B

regular safety inspections <u>of</u> their equipment,
　　　　　　　　　C

the horrible accident of 1969 <u>may have been</u>
　　　　　　　　　　　D

averted. <u>No error</u>
　　　　E

11. The symphony <u>had not</u> hardly begun <u>when</u> a
　　　　　　　A　　　　　　　B

group of schoolchildren, who <u>had been forced</u>
　　　　　　　　　　C

to attend, began irritating the rest of the

audience <u>by talking loudly</u> and kicking the
　　　　　D

seats. <u>No error</u>
　　　E

12. The gods of Greek mythology, who

<u>were neither</u> omniscient nor <u>particularly</u>
　A　　　　　　　　B

ethical, amused themselves <u>by taking on</u>
　　　　　　　　C

disguises and <u>meddling in</u> the affairs of
　　　　　　D

mortals. <u>No error</u>
　　　E

GO ON TO THE NEXT PAGE

13. As an indication of the play's power to hold its
                                    A   B

audience, when the final curtain descended,

there was only one man and one woman
        C

remaining in the theater. No error.
      D   E

14. As implied in the author's biography, to show
    A

how the tenant farmers had been exploited by
    B   C

the owners was the whole point of him writing
                                         D

the book. No error.
         E

15. Despite exploitation by gold-seeking
    A

marauders, the tribe survived and even
                             B

flourished because their pride in themselves

was stronger than almost any other people.
        C   D

No error.
    E

16. Neither the chameleon, a lizard known for its
                                         A

ability to change color, nor many other lizards!

having the same attribute, is able to assume
    B   C

more than a few green and brown shades when

the temperatures fall below freezing. No error.
                    D   E!

!

17. The false alarm had frightened everyone in the
                    A

condo, and she more than the other residents
             B

who lived there, since she had once been
    C   D

living in a building that was destroyed by fire.

No error
E

18. It's not the end result of the trial that may
    A   B

not a real term

forever damage a defendant's reputation; it's
                                       C

the fact that he went to trial in the first place
                  D

that could cause him irrevocable harm.

No error
E

19. Ever since the beginning of the year, the
    A

shelter, like the cardboard shack the homeless
         B

man had been forced nightly to sleep in,
                       C

has been rather cold comfort for him.
    D

No error
E

GO ON TO THE NEXT PAGE →

20. During the war in Vietnam, American troops

observed that the local mountain tribesman
  A   B
made an excellent soldier loyal, and always
                                    C
ready and willing to die for their cause.
                              D

No error
  E

21. Beethoven's music, now loved throughout the
                        A
world, aroused considerable controversy when

it was first played, however, its power and
                B
nobility came to be widely accepted and even
        C
praised before its composer died. No error
          D   E

22. Regardless of her credentials, which were
        A
indeed impressive and which included three

years' experience as a cook, her skills in the
  B
kitchen were fewer than a beginner. No error
            C   D   E

23. Interest in the marching band, in the

orchestra, and in learning to play instruments,
                  A
have doubled within the last half year.
  B   C   D
No error
  E

24. Being lost in the mountains of Colorado for
      A
two days as a boy, Dave was careful always
                        B
to take a detailed map with him when he set
  C   D
out for a backpacking adventure in the

wilderness. No error
              E

25. Of the four members of the mountain-
      A
climbing team, none were more frightened
                  B
and inexperienced than she. No error
                  C   D   E

26. Dr. Mfume's team is attempting to cure a
                        A
disease that, although harmless to human
                  B   C
beings, regularly decimates cattle herds in
        D
Africa and parts of Asia. No error
                              E

GO ON TO THE NEXT PAGE

DIRECTIONS

Thes following sentences test your ability to express ideas in writing effectively and efficiently. Each sentence is either partially or completely underlined. The first of the five choices given will repeat the original wording and the other four choices will contain alternative wording. Choose the change that best improves the senetece or choose A if the original is superior to any of the other choices given.

In making your choice keep in mind the standards of proper written English. Among other things, pay close attention to grammar, word choice, punctuation, precision, and correct usage of tenses. Avoid awkward and ambiguous construction.

EXAMPLE:

I want your love, and I want your revenge;
you and me can write a bad romance.

(A) you and me can write
(B) you and me could write
(C) you and me writing
(D) you and I can write
(E) me and you can write

ⒶⒷⒸ●Ⓔ

27. For success in school, it is important not only to be smart but also to do your homework.

(A) to be smart but also to do
(B) being smart but also to do
(C) to be smart but also doing
(D) being smart but also doing
(E) that you be smart but also that you do

28. There is scholarly consensus that, while Walt Whitman often referred to illegitimate children of whom he claimed to be the father, he never had any outside of "dream children."

(A) of whom he claimed to be the father, he never had any outside of "dream children."
(B) whom he claimed to have fathered, he had only "dream children."
(C) who he claimed fatherhood of, he was having only "dream children."
(D) of whom he said he was the father, "dream children" were his only ones.
(E) who he claimed to be the father of, he never had anything outside of "dream children."

29. In an effort to sound like an expert, the director's speech which was riddled with esoteric references and specialized terms.

(A) the director's speech which was riddled with esoteric references
(B) the director's speech was riddled with esoteric references
(C) the director delivered a speech riddled with esoteric references
(D) his speech which was riddled with esoteric references
(E) the speech of the director was riddled with esoteric references

30. His ambition was not only to study but also mastering the craft of journalism.

(A) not only to study but also mastering
(B) not only studying but to try and master
(C) not studying only, but also mastering
(D) not only to study but also to master
(E) to study, and, as well, to master

GO ON TO THE NEXT PAGE →

31. <u>The poet Oscar Wilde was known for his aphoristic wit and brilliant conversation, he</u> wrote a number of memorable literary essays including "The Critic as Artist."

(A) The poet Oscar Wilde was known for his aphoristic wit and brilliant conversation, he
(B) The poet Oscar Wilde, known for his apho~ istic wit and brilliant conversation; he
(C) Known for his aphoristic wit and brilliant conversation, the poet Oscar Wilde
(D) The poet Oscar Wilde was known for his, aphoristic wit and brilliant conversation, however he
(E) Oscar Wilde, the poet, known for his aphoristic wit and brilliant conversation, and, he

32. According to Westin's book, <u>the typical Victorian family was more interested in maintaining the appearance of propriety than in</u> securing happiness for its individual members.

(A) the typical Victorian family was more interested in maintaining the appearance of propriety than in
(B) the appearance of propriety was more interesting to the typical Victorian family than
(C) the typical Victorian family, more interested in maintaining the appearance of propriety than it was in
(D) for a Victorian family it was typical that they would be more interested in maintaining the appearance of propriety than in
(E) the typical Victorian family was more interested in the appearance of propriety than in

33. <u>Once an enclave of privileged white males, the Wodehouse Club's directors have</u> now decided to adopt a more inclusive membership policy.

(A) Once an enclave of privileged white males, the Wodehouse Club's directors have
(B) The directors of the Wodehouse Club, which was once an enclave of privileged white males, have
(C) Though once an enclave of privileged white males, the Wodehouse Club's directors
(D) Once an enclave of privileged white males, the Wodehouse Club's directors having
(E) The directors of the enclave of privileged white males, the Wodehouse Club, has

34. Wanting to reward her assistant for loyalty, <u>Sheila gave a bonus to him as large as his paycheck.</u>

(A) Sheila gave a bonus to him as large as his paycheck
(B) given to him by Sheila was a bonus as large as his paycheck
(C) he was given a bonus as large as his paycheck by Sheila
(D) Sheila gave him a bonus as large as his paycheck
(E) Sheila gave him a paycheck to him as large as his bonus

35. <u>If the construction strike has not occurred</u>, the contractor would have had no problem finishing the restaurant on time.

(A) If the construction strike has not occurred
(B) If the construction strike would not have occurred
(C) Had the construction strike not of occurred
(D) Had it not been that the construction strike had occurred
(E) Had it not been for the construction strike

GO ON TO THE NEXT PAGE

36. Supporters of the Eighteenth Amendment thought that banning alcohol would improve citizens' morals and enhance their quality of life by removing the temptation to drink; <u>national prohibition</u> ushered in thirteen years of bootlegging, speakeasies, and violent gangster crime.

(A) national prohibition
(B) in fact, national prohibition
(C) furthermore, national prohibition
(D) but national prohibition
(E) consequently; national prohibition

37. Though multimedia presentations have their place in the school curriculum, it is ridiculous to claim, as some do, <u>that children learn as much from watching a one-hour video as a book.</u>

(A) that children learn as much from watching a one-hour video as a book
(B) that children will learn as much from watching a one-hour video as they did from a book
(C) that children learn as much from watching a one-hour video as they do from reading a book
(D) that a 'one-hour video teaches more to children than book-reading
(E) that children watching a one-hour video learn as much as reading a book

38. Finland's national epic; the *Kalevala*, <u>based on an oral tradition that</u> the alto-Finnish people preserved for some 2,500 years despite the upheavals of history and the pressures of foreign domination.

(A) based on an oral tradition that
(B) being based on an oral tradition that
(C) is based on an oral tradition; this
(D) basing itself on an oral tradition which
(E) is based on an oral tradition that

39. The island of Santa Ynez was once a playground for wealthy American tourists; in recent years, however, civil unrest and a series of natural disasters <u>have made it so that it is not nearly as appealing</u> as a vacation spot.

(A) have made it so that it is riot nearly as appealing
(B) are causing it to be made less appealing
(C) greatly reducing its appeal
(D) have greatly lessened its appeal
(E) have not nearly made it as appealing

40. In retrospect, one can see the folly of trying to unite a region containing some four hundred distinct ethnic groups, <u>each with its own language, laws, and traditions.</u>

(A) each with its own language, laws, and traditions
(B) each of them has its own language, laws, and traditions
(C) each with their own language, laws, and traditions
(D) and each of them having its own language, laws, and traditions
(E) when they each have their own language, laws, and traditions

GO ON TO THE NEXT PAGE

41. In retrospect, one can see the folly of trying to unite a region containing some four hundred distinct ethnic groups, <u>each with its own language, laws, and traditions</u>.

(A) each with its own language, laws, and traditions

(B) each of them has its own language, laws, and traditions

(C) each with their own language, laws, and traditions

(D) and each of them having its own language, laws, and traditions

(E) when they each have their own language, laws, and traditions

42. Proponents of campaign finance reform point out that people who make large, donations to politicians expect to be rewarded with special favors <u>and gaining easy access</u> to the corridors of power.

(A) and gaining easy access

(B) and they gain easy access

(C) and easy access

(D) as well as gaining easy access

(E) and to be rewarded with easy access

43. <u>Had Churchill sent planes to defend Coventry</u> from the German air raid, the Nazis would have realized that their secret code had been broken by the Allies.

(A) Had Churchill sent planes to defend Coventry

(B) If Churchill would have sent planes to defend Coventry

(C) Churchill having sent planes to defend Coventry

(D) If Churchill sent planes to defend Coventry

(E) Churchill, by sending planes to Coventry to defend it

44. <u>Television shows such as M*A*S*H and *All in the Family* took</u> months or even years to build a large audience, most new series today never get that chance.

(A) Television shows such as M*A*S*H and *All in the Family* took

(B) Although television shows such as M*A*S*H and *All in the Family* took

(C) With television shows such as M*A*S*H and *All in the Family* taking

(D) Such television shows as M*A*S*H and *All in the Family* took

(E) When television shows such as M*A*S*H and *All in the Family* took

GO ON TO THE NEXT PAGE

DIRECTIONS

The following passage is an early draft of an essay. Some parts of the passage need to be rewritten.

Read the passage and select the best answers for the questions that follow. Some questions are about particular sentences or parts of sentences and ask you to improve sentence structure or word choice. Other questions ask you to consider organization and development. In choosing answers, follow the requirements of standard written English.

Questions 45-50 are based on the following essay, which is a response to an assignment to write a letter to a local newspaper protesting cuts in funding for after-school sports programs.

[1] I disagree with the editor's view that after-school sports programs should be cut in our city government's search for ways to reduce spending. [2] The editor argues that extra-curricular sports play a less important role to academic studies, distracting students from the opportunity to increase their knowledge after school is out. [3] However, I myself believe that playing sports enhances students' academic performance. [4] Why is sports so effective in this regard? [5] The main reason is that sports teaches people to excel. [6] It gives students the chance to strive for greatness. [7] It shows them that it takes courage and discipline to succeed in competition with others. [8] Top athletes such as Michael Jordan become role models for young people everywhere, inspiring them with his brilliant individual performances. [9] In addition to these personal attributes, playing in team sports show young people how to interact with each other, achieving shared goals. [10] Such principles have a direct impact on how students perform in their academic studies. [11] I know that being selected for the school lacrosse team taught me many valuable lessons about working with others. [12] Not only that,

friendships which I have made there were carried into the rest of my school life. [13] In summary, I would urge the editor to strongly reconsider his stance on extra-curricular sports. [14] There are doubtless other ways of city government saving the money they require.

45. Which of the following is the best way to revise the underlined portion of sentence 3 (reproduced below)?

However, I myself believe that playing sports enhances students' academic performance.

(A) However, I myself believe that playing sports should enhance
(B) Playing sports, however, I believe enhances
(C) However, I personally believe that playing sports enhances
(D) I believe, however, that playing sports enhances
(E) However, I myself believe that to play sports is to enhance

46. Which of the following is the best way to revise and combine sentences 6 and 7 (reproduced below)?

It gives students the chance to strive for greatness. It shows them that it takes courage and discipline to succeed in competition with others.

(A) Although it gives students the chance to strive for greatness, it also shows them that it takes courage and discipline to succeed in competition with others.
(B) While it gives students the chance to strive for greatness, also showing them that it takes courage and discipline to succeed in competition with others.
(C) It gives students the chance to strive for greatness, showing them that it takes courage and discipline to succeed in competition with others.
(D) Because it gives students the chance to strive for greatness, they are shown that it takes courage and discipline to succeed in competition with others.
(E) I gives students the chance to strive for greatness and show them that it takes courage and discipline to succeed in competition with others.

47. In the context of the second paragraph, which of the following is the best version of the underlined portion of sentence 8 (reproduced below)?

Top athletes such as Michael Jordan become role models for young people everywhere, inspiring them with his brilliant individual performances.

(A) (As it is now)
(B) inspiring him with their
(C) inspiring them with their
(D) to inspire them with his
(E) inspiring him with his

48. Which of the following is the best way to revise the underlined portion of sentence 12 (reproduced below)?

Not only that, friendships which I have made there were carried into the rest of my school life.

(A) And,
(B) Moreover,
(C) Nevertheless,
(D) Sequentially,
(E) Finally,

49. Which of the following best describes the author's approach in the passage as a whole?

(A) defending an unpopular point of view
(B) criticizing an opponent's opinion
(C) supporting an argument with evidence
(D) considering the merits of two competing proposals
(E) citing statistics to disprove a theory

50. The author could best improve sentence 14 by

(A) making an analogy to historical events
(B) taking alternative points of view into account
(C) including a personal anecdote about her participation in team sports
(D) speculating about the motivations of those advocating cuts
(E) providing examples of other areas in which spending could be reduced

STOP

this is the end of the exercise

SAT Writing Exercise #12
50 Questions

!

1. The young scholar's research proposal

<u>consisted in</u> little more than <u>a series of</u> half-
    A   B
formulated ideas, loosely <u>strung</u> together
                            C
and <u>poorly</u> documented. <u>No error</u>
    D   E

2. Many physicists believe <u>that</u> interstellar travel
                              A
will never be possible <u>due to</u> the distances
                        B
<u>involved</u> are <u>simply</u> too great. <u>No error</u>
    C   D   E

3. If one wishes <u>to succeed</u> in business,
                    A
<u>you should</u> acquire good communication
    B
skills, <u>which</u> corporate leaders agree
         C
<u>are of paramount</u> importance. <u>No error</u>
    D   E

4. Analysts were surprised <u>that neither</u> the crises
                              A
facing the nation's public schools <u>nor</u> the
                                    B
decay of urban centers <u>were</u> included in the
                        C
party's official platform. <u>No error</u>
    D   E

5. The twins were indistinguishable <u>from</u> one
                                       A
another in every respect <u>but</u> one: Mary, the
                          B
<u>youngest</u> one, had longer hair than her <u>sister</u>.
    C   D
<u>No error</u>
    E

6. Thomas Becket, <u>who</u> the pope elevated to
                     A
sainthood shortly after 1170, <u>is</u> generally
                                B
believed <u>to have been</u> murdered <u>on</u> the orders
          C   D
of King Henry II. <u>No error</u>
                   E

GO ON TO THE NEXT PAGE

7. The university's library, designed during a

period <u>when</u> architects prized function <u>over</u>
      A   B

form, is a drab, utilitarian structure that

<u>clashes</u> with the graceful, Gothic buildings on
  C

either side <u>of it</u>. <u>No error</u>
           D   E

8. Even today, there are many who <u>would</u> say
   A   B

that the old tribal practice of <u>paying</u> blood-
                               C

money to families of murder victims

<u>are more</u> just than our modern system of trial
  D

and punishment. <u>No error</u>
              E

9. <u>Though</u> some critics deride Warhol's work as
  A

worthless commercial trash, others <u>hail</u> him
                                B

<u>as the most</u> <u>innovative</u> artist of the modem
    C   D

age. <u>No error</u>
      E

10. The <u>much-publicized</u> study was <u>deemed</u>
         A   B

unscientific because it failed to takc <u>into</u>
                             C

account such variables <u>as</u> heredity and
                    D

income. <u>No error</u>
        E

11. The early Egyptian monks <u>sought</u> complete
                      A

solitude so <u>that</u> they <u>might</u> pray without
          B   C

distraction, pursue an ideal of perfection,

and <u>to attain</u> a higher level of religious
      D

experience. <u>No error</u>
         E

12. Perhaps the coach was remembered

<u>so fondly</u> because he was <u>always</u> less
  A   B

interested in winning than in <u>making sure</u>
                            C

that all the boys participated <u>with</u> the game.
                         D

<u>No error</u>
  E

13. Thirty years ago, one could say that those

<u>who</u> the president nominated to <u>serve</u> on
  A   B

the Supreme Court were <u>chosen not</u>
                       C

because of their political leanings,

<u>but because</u> of their fine legal minds and their
      D

judicial expertise. <u>No error</u>
                 E

14. In a move <u>that</u> distressed the clergy as
            A

much as <u>it</u> delighted the barons, King Arnulf
        B

<u>named</u> one of his illegitimate sons <u>as</u> heir
  C   D

and successor to the throne. <u>No error</u>
                           E

GO ON TO THE NEXT PAGE ⟶

15. Hopefully, it is not too late to reverse the
       A   B

damage that years of neglect and harsh
             C

weather have wrought on the beautiful old
             D

mansion. No error
                E

16. Though the young author's most recent play

is undeniably exciting, well written, and
       A

memorable, it would be a mistake to place
              B

his work on a par with David Mamet.
          C   D

No error
   E

17. Many teachers feel that any parent who fails
                       A   B

to discipline their own child has no right to
               C   D

complain when the child is punished for

unruly, disrespectful behavior in school.

No error
   E

18. The rebels had less guns than their enemies
                    A

and hardly any ammunition; nevertheless,
       B   C

they were able to overthrow their country's

military government with the help of a
                        D

restless and sympathetic population.

No error
   E

19. A number of immigrants find that
       A   B

loneliness, along with the challenge of

learning a new language, hinder their
       C   D

efforts to assimilate into a new culture.

No error
   E

20. The recent discovery that at least one of
                A

Jupiter's moons possesses an internal heat
                 B

source has led to speculation that
             C

there may be life elsewhere in our solar system.
       D

No error
   E

21. Though Mikhail Gorbachev's policy of
       A

glasnost ushered in freedoms that

would have been inconceivable a decade
       B

before, many Russians still felt that economic
   C

and political reform was not proceeding

quick enough. No error
   D   E

GO ON TO THE NEXT PAGE

22. When asked whether he was ready to give up
              A

his quixotic campaign against coeducation,

Buford replied that he had not scarcely begun
                    B   C   D

to fight. No error
          E

23. As soon as the employees realized that
        A   B

management would never accede with their
                                   C

demands for a shorter work week, a strike

became inevitable. No error
       D   E

24. Lacking an objective standard by which to
        A   B

judge the contestants, the sponsors of the

pageant finally resorted to drawing a name
        C   D

at random from a hat. No error
                      E

25. The aurora borealis is a dazzling phenomena
                                        A

that occurs when the earth's magnetic field
     B

interacts with the solar wind, producing
         C   D

ionized atoms and molecules. No error
                             E

26. So great was John Lennon's fame as he
        A   B

could scarcely walk out his door without
C

being accosted by fans and photographers.
D

No error
E

27. Returning to her home town after a twenty-year absence, <u>the desperate poverty Savka saw there shocked and saddened her.</u>

(A) the desperate poverty Savka saw there shocked and saddened her
(B) the desperate poverty Savka saw there was shocking and also sad to her
(C) Savka, shocked and saddened by the desperate poverty she saw there
(D) Savka was shocked and saddened by the desperate poverty she saw there
(E) was a desperate poverty that shocked and saddened Savka

28. The stereotype of the idle, wealthy snob bears little resemblance to real Ivy League students, the majority <u>of them receive</u> financial aid in the form of jobs, loans, and grants.

(A) of them receive
(B) of which receive
(C) which receive
(D) of them receiving
(E) of whom receive

29. The brochure for the writing camp promises that by the time you leave the camp, you <u>complete an entire manuscript</u>.

(A) complete an entire manuscript
(B) would complete an entire manuscript
(C) will have completed an entire manuscript
(D) have complete an entire manuscript
(E) had completed an entire manuscript

30. The viscount was having such a merry time drinking and carousing <u>and he did not notice</u> the dark stranger who stole into the banquet hall and absconded with his treasured painting.

(A) and he did not notice
(B) that he did not notice
(C) not noticing
(D) for he did not notice
(E) and failing to notice

31. Her eyes shining with tears, Aunt Helga told us over and over again how much she appreciated <u>us coming to her</u> ninetieth birthday party.

(A) us coming to her
(B) our coming to her
(C) us having come to her
(D) that we come to her
(E) us for the fact of our coming to her

GO ON TO THE NEXT PAGE

32. Having read the works of Hemingway, Fitzgerald, and Steinbeck, <u>Hemingway is definitely overrated as a writer</u>.

   (A) Hemingway is definitely overrated as a writer
   (B) Hemingway has definitely been overrated as a writer
   (C) I am convinced that Hemingway is overrated as a writer
   (D) the writing abilities of Hemingway are overrated, I am convinced
   (E) I am convinced as a writer that Hemingway is overrated

33. When the electrochemists Stanley Pons and Martin Fleischmann declared in 1989 that they had achieved <u>cold fusion; scientists around the world tried to duplicate the process, they were not successful</u>.

   (A) cold fusion; scientists around the world tried to duplicate the process, they were not successful
   (B) cold fusion then scientists around the world tried to duplicate the process only without succeeding
   (C) cold fusion, consequently scientists around the world, without success, tried to duplicate the process
   (D) cold fusion, scientists around the world tried without success to duplicate the process
   (E) cold fusion however, scientists around the world tried to duplicate the process without success

34. Freud's complex theory based on the death instinct is, for most people, one that is <u>with difficult understanding</u>.

   (A) with difficult understanding
   (B) difficult to understand
   (C) to understand difficultly
   (D) having difficult being understood
   (E) difficult for understanding

35. In the nineteenth century, trains were more than <u>machines they were</u> expressions of the greatness of the United States.

   (A) machines they were
   (B) machines and were
   (C) machines; they were
   (D) machines, although they were
   (E) machines, but were

36. In the sunlight, the cherry <u>blossoms that burst</u> out everywhere, like foam on breaking waves.
   (A) blossoms that burst
   (B) blossoms bursting
   (C) blossoms, which are bursting
   (D) blossoms burst
   (E) blossoms, which burst

37. <u>When Dorothy Richardson decided to become</u> a novelist, she knew that her writing would leave her little time for other work.

   (A) When Dorothy Richardson decided to become
   (B) After the decision was made by Dorothy Richardson to become
   (C) After the decision by Dorothy Richardson to become
   (D) When Dorothy Richardson decides to become
   (E) When Dorothy Richardson decided about becoming

GO ON TO THE NEXT PAGE

38. The difference between the twins is that <u>one is humorous; the other, serious.</u>

    (A) one is humorous; the other, serious
    (B) of one being humorous, the other is serious
    (C) one is humorous; the other being serious
    (D) one is humorous, although the other is more serious
    (E) of a humorous one and one that is serious

39. The United States did not go on the gold standard <u>until 1900, it went off it thirty-three years later.</u>

    (A) until 1900, it went off it thirty-three years later
    (B) until 1900; however, going off after thirty-three years
    (C) until 1900, although going off in thirty-three years
    (D) until 1900, it was thirty-three years later when it went off it
    (E) until 1900 and went off it thirty-three years later

40. <u>Many memos were issued by the director of the agency that</u> had an insulting tone, according to the staff members.

    (A) Many memos were issued by the director of the agency that
    (B) Many memos were issued by the director of the agency who
    (C) The issuance of many memos by the director of the agency which
    (D) The director of the agency issued many memos that
    (E) The director of the agency, who issued many memos that

41. The widespread slaughter of buffalo for their skins profoundly <u>shocked and angered Native Americans.</u>

    (A) shocked and angered Native Americans
    (B) shocked Native Americans, angering them
    (C) shocked Native Americans, and they were also angry
    (D) was a shock and caused anger among Native Americans
    (E) was shocking to Native Americans, making them angry

42. Consumers are beginning to take notice of electric cars because they are quiet, <u>cause no air pollution, and gasoline is not used.</u>

    (A) cause no air pollution, and gasoline is not used
    (B) air pollution is not caused, and gasoline is not used
    (C) cause no air pollution, and use no gasoline
    (D) causing no air pollution and using no gasoline
    (E) air pollution is not caused, and no gasoline is used

GO ON TO THE NEXT PAGE

43. Because she was a woman was why Sharon Frontiero, a lieutenant in the United States Air Force, felt that she w as being treated unfairly.

(A) Because she was a woman was why Sharon Frontiero, a lieutenant in the United States Air Force, felt that she was being treated unfairly.

(B) Sharon Frontiero, a lieutenant in the United States Air Force, felt that she was being treated unfairly because she was a woman.

(C) Because she was a woman, Sharon Frontiero felt that this was why she was being treated unfairly as a lieutenant in the United States Air Force.

(D) Sharon Frontiero, a lieutentant in the United States Air Force, feeling that she was being treated unfairly because she was a woman.

(E) A woman, Sharon Frontiero, felt t hat because she was a lieutenant in the United States Air Force, that she was being treated unfairly.

44. A major difference between people and apes is brain size, a person's brain is three times as large as the brain of an ape.

(A) size, a person's brain is

(B) size, with a person's brain being

(C) size; a person's brain is

(D) size; a person's brain, it is

(E) size, in that it is

GO ON TO THE NEXT PAGE

DIRECTIONS

The following passage is an early draft of an essay. Some parts of the passage need to be rewritten.

Read the passage and select the best answers for the questions that follow. Some questions are about particular sentences or parts of sentences and ask you to improve sentence structure or word choice. Other questions ask you to consider organization and development. In choosing answers, follow the requirements of standard written English.

Questions 45-50 are based on the following essay.

[1] There is no way I expected to enjoy summer camp this year. [2] All of my friends were being sent to fashionable camps in the Berkshires and Vermont. [3] Not only did these camps specialize in sports that I've always wanted to try [tennis, canoeing, and white water rafting are examples]. [4] Additionally everyone I knew got to go with their best friends.

[5] Was this what my parents did? [6] Instead, Dad decided to send me to this camp in New Hampshire where he'd gone as a kid. [7] Old Deer Head Falls, NH, twenty miles from the nearest signal of human habitation. [8] The camp's main and primary activity was hiking in the rocky, rainy trails of the nearby White Mountains. [9] Thanks a lot, Dad. [10] Regarded as one of the least fit students in my class, this summer had all the hallmarks of a disaster for me. [11] It took a couple of hikes, participation in a handful of camp fire sing-alongs, and bursting many a blister on my feet to change my mind. [12] The scenery in the mountains was a major factor. [13] Another was that [even though I am a self-confessed couch potato] I actually discovered the exercise to be enjoyable. [14] I made new friends, and to my surprise I liked the camp counselors a lot. [15] There were counselors from all over the world. [16] The debates at rest stops got pretty interesting. [17] After a summer above the treeline, I returned with better stories than my friends who went to "fashionable" resorts!

45. Which of the following is the best way to revise the underlined portion of sentences 3 and 4 (reproduced below) so that the two sentences are combined into one?

Not only did these camps specialize in sports that I've always wanted to <u>try (tennis, canoeing, and white water rafting are examples). Additionally everyone</u> I knew got to go with their best friends.

(A) try, examples being tennis, canoeing, and white water rafting, but all the people

(B) try, such as tennis, canoeing, and white water rafting, but all the people

(C) try: tennis, canoeing, and white water rafting for example, plus they all

(D) try, examples being tennis, canoeing, and white water rafting, furthermore all the people

(E) try, such as tennis, canoeing, and white water rafting, and everyone

46. Which of the following sentences, if inserted in place of sentence 5, would provide the best transition between the first paragraph and the rest of the essay?

(A) However, my parents chose not to send me to a "fashionable" camp.

(B) Unlike my friends, my parents chose something else altogether.

(C) Rather than being sent to a "fashionable camp," Dad chose otherwise.

(D) Unfortunately, this situation was not the case with my parents.

(E) You might have expected that my parents would have been doing the same.

GO ON TO THE NEXT PAGE

47. In the context of the second paragraph, which of the following is the best version of the underlined portion of sentence 10 (reproduced below)?

Regarded as one of the least fit students in my class, this summer had all the hallmarks of a disaster for me.

(A) (As it is now)
(B) I predicted that this summer would be a disaster for me
(C) this summer was beginning to look disastrous for me
(D) and for me, this summer had all the hallmarks of a disaster
(E) so this summer had all the hallmarks of a disaster for me

48. Which of the following versions of the underlined portion of sentence 11 (reproduced below) is clearest?

It took a couple of hikes, participation in a handful of campfire sing-alongs, and bursting many a blister on my feet to change my mind.

(A) (As it is now)
(B) a handful of camp fire sing-alongs, and bursting many blisters
(C) the participation in some camp fire sing-alongs, and the bursting of many a blister
(D) a handful of camp fire sing-alongs, and many a burst blister
(E) my participating in a handful of camp fire sing-alongs, and my bursting many a blister

49. In the context of paragraph 2, which of the following is the best way to link sentences 15 and 16 (reproduced below)?

There were counselors from all over the world. The debates at rest stops got pretty interesting.

(A) Even though there were counselors from all over the world, the debates at rest stops still got pretty interesting.
(B) With there being counselors from all over the world, the debates at rest stops got pretty interesting.
(C) Since there were counselors from all over the world, the debates at rest stops got pretty interesting.
(D) There were counselors from all over the world, the debates at rest stops got pretty interesting.
(E) Whereas there were counselors from all over the world, the debates at rest stops got pretty interesting.

50. Which of the following, if added after sentence 17, would be the most logical concluding sentence for the passage?
(A) Everyone should be open to new experiences, because they can be unexpectedly rewarding.
(B) I have never found stories about "fashionable" resorts particularly interesting, anyway.
(C) I learned that money isn't everything; there's something to be said for hard work, too.
(D) If you start out with a positive attitude, almost anything can be made enjoyable.
(E) Facing challenges alone is often more important than being with friends.

STOP

this is the end of the exercise

SAT Writing Exercise #13

50 Questions

!

1. A few scientists claim that food additives

<u>not only</u> improve the <u>quality of</u> foods but
   A   B
also <u>made</u> <u>them</u> safer. <u>No error</u>
      C   D   E

2. It is <u>rumored that</u> the names <u>of them</u>
              A   B
<u>to be promoted</u> will be announced tomorrow,
   C
but I believe the choices <u>have not been made</u>
                              D
yet. <u>No error</u>
        E

3. In 1957, the appearance of <u>the first</u> Soviet
                                      A
satellite <u>has created</u> a panic in the United
              B
States that continued <u>for</u> <u>nearly</u> a decade.
                          C   D
<u>No error</u>
   E

4. In appreciation <u>about</u> her work, the committee
                         A
presented <u>its</u> retiring director with,
              B
<u>among other</u> gifts, a <u>plaque describing</u> her
   C   D
accomplishments. <u>No error</u>
                     E

5. For <u>many people</u>, hang-gliding, an
              A
<u>increasingly</u> popular sport, seems <u>satisfying</u>
   B   C
the urge <u>to fly</u>. <u>No error</u>
            D   E

6. Despite <u>much</u> research, there <u>are</u> still certain
                 A   B
<u>elements in</u> the life cycle of the cicada that are
   C
not <u>fully understood</u>. <u>No error</u>
        D   E

7. Louise's fair skin <u>was</u> sunburned <u>so badly</u> that
                             A   B
she looked <u>as if</u> she had <u>fell into</u> a bucket of
              C   D
red paint. <u>No error</u>
              E

GO ON TO THE NEXT PAGE

8. Whenever we hear of a natural disaster,
     A

even in a distant part of the world, you feel
    B   C

sympathy for the people affected. No error
  D   E

9. Late in the war, the Germans, retreating
                         A

in haste, left many of their prisoners go free.
  B   C   D

No error
  E

10. In many states, there seems to be a belief,
      A   B

openly expressed by educators, that the
  C

methods of teaching reading should be

changed. No error
  D   E

11. Throughout the Middle Ages women
      A

work beside men, knowing that the efforts of
  B   C

men and women alike were essential to
                     D

survival. No error
         E

12. Without hardly a doubt, the novels of Thomas
       A

Pynchon are more complex than the novels of
      B   C

many other contemporary writers. No error
  D   E

13. The leading roles in the widely acclaimed
                       A

play, a modern version of an Irish folktale,
     B

were performed by Jessica and he. No error
  C   D   E

14. In the reserve section of the library, there is
                           A

two volumes of essays by James Baldwin on
     B   C

the relation of the Black artist and intellectual

to society. No error
  D   E

15. Many studies have tried to determine
                A

whether or not seeing violence on television
      B

makes children behave more violent. No error
  C   D   E

16. Between ten and twenty percent of the
          A

textbook appears to be new; the rest is a
      B   C

revision of the previous edition. No error
  D   E

17. Some people seem remarkably insensitive to
             A

physical pain, and this insensitivity
             B

does not mean that they are able to endure
  C   D

other kinds of pain. No error
         E

GO ON TO THE NEXT PAGE →

18. During the meeting, Congresswoman Barbara
　　　　＿＿＿＿＿＿＿＿＿
　　　　　　　A
Jordan stressed that educators and legislators
　　　　＿＿＿＿＿＿
　　　　　　B
must cooperate where the goal of equal
　　　　　　＿＿＿＿
　　　　　　　Ⓒ
opportunity is to be reached. No error
　　　　　＿＿　　　　　＿＿＿＿＿＿
　　　　　D　　　　　　　　　E

19. The population of American alligators,

dangerously small a few years ago, are now
＿＿＿＿＿＿　　　　　　　　　　＿＿＿＿
　　A　　　　　　　　　　　　　　Ⓑ
estimated at more than one million. No error
＿＿＿＿＿＿＿　＿＿＿＿＿　　　　　＿＿＿＿＿＿
　　C　　　　　　D　　　　　　　　　E

20. Such novels as *Heidi* and *Little Women*
＿＿＿
　A
have long been considered by young and old
＿＿＿＿＿＿＿＿＿＿＿＿＿
　　　　　B
alike to be a classic of children's literature.
　　　　　＿＿＿＿＿＿＿
　C　　　　　Ⓓ
No error
＿＿＿＿＿
　E

21. Anyone who gathers mushrooms for the
＿＿＿＿＿＿＿
　　A
purpose of eating them must distinguish
　　　　　　＿＿＿＿
　　　　　　　B
carefully between poisonous and
＿＿＿＿＿＿ ＿＿＿＿＿＿＿
　C　　　　　D
nonpoisonous species. No error
　　　　　　　　　＿＿＿＿＿
　　　　　　　　　　Ⓔ

22. In regards to the energy crisis, the President
＿＿＿＿＿＿＿＿＿
　Ⓐ
urged all homeowners to keep their
＿＿＿＿　　　　　＿＿＿＿＿＿＿
　B　　　　　　　　C　　　D
thermostats at sixty-five degrees in

winter. No error
　　　　＿＿＿＿＿
　　　　　E

23. Long ago, well before the invention of the
　　　　　　＿＿＿＿＿＿＿＿＿ ＿＿＿＿＿＿＿＿＿
　　　　　　　　　A　　　　　　　　B
printing press, poets often sung their poetry to
　　　　　　　　　　　　　＿＿＿ ＿＿＿＿
　　　　　　　　　　　　　　Ⓒ　　D
small, interested audiences. No error
　　　　　　　　　　　　　＿＿＿＿＿＿
　　　　　　　　　　　　　　　E

24. Because of extreme weather conditions,
＿＿＿＿＿＿＿＿
　　A
starvation exists in some countries where they
　　　　＿＿＿＿＿　　　　　　　　　　　＿＿＿＿
　　　　　B　　　　　　　　　　　　　　Ⓒ
must struggle every day to stay alive. No error
　　　　　　　　　　　＿＿＿＿＿＿＿＿ ＿＿＿＿＿＿
　　　　　　　　　　　　　D　　　　　　　E

25. The energy question, along with several other
　　　　　　　　　　　　　　　　＿＿＿＿＿＿＿＿＿
　　　　　　　　　　　　　　　　　　　A
issues, are going to be discussed at the next
＿＿＿＿＿＿＿＿＿＿＿＿ ＿＿＿＿＿＿＿＿＿＿ ＿＿＿＿＿
　　Ⓑ　　　　　　　　　C　　　　　　　D
meeting of the state legislature. No error
　　　　　　　　　　　　　　　　＿＿＿＿＿
　　　　　　　　　　　　　　　　　E

26. If you find that it is difficult to concentrate
＿＿＿＿＿＿＿ ＿＿＿＿＿＿＿＿
　A　　　　　　B
in noisy surroundings, one should try to find a
＿＿＿＿＿＿＿＿＿＿＿＿＿ ＿＿＿＿＿＿＿＿
　　　　　C　　　　　　　　　Ⓓ
quiet place to study. No error
　　　　　　　　　　＿＿＿＿＿＿
　　　　　　　　　　　E

GO ON TO THE NEXT PAGE

DIRECTIONS

Thes following sentences test your ability to express ideas in writing effectively and efficiently. Each sentence is either partially or completely underlined. The first of the five choices given will repeat the original wording and the other four choices will contain alternative wording. Choose the change that best improves the senetence or choose A if the original is superior to any of the other choices given.

In making your choice keep in mind the standards of proper written English. Among other things, pay close attention to grammar, word choice, punctuation, precision, and correct usage of tenses. Avoid awkward and ambiguous construction.

EXAMPLE:

I want your love, and I want your revenge; you and me can write a bad romance.

(A) you and me can write
(B) you and me could write
(C) you and me writing
(D) you and I can write
(E) me and you can write

27. Joseph Conrad was born and educated in Poland and he wrote all of his novels in English.

   (A) Joseph Conrad was born and educated in Poland and he
   (B) Joseph Conrad, being born and educated in Poland,
   (C) Although being born and educated in Poland, Joseph Conrad
   (D) Although Joseph Conrad was born and educated in Poland, he
   (E) Being from Poland, where he was born and educated, Joseph Conrad

28. The process of how European immigrant groups being absorbed into American society is complex.

   (A) of how European immigrant groups being absorbed
   (B) for European immigrants being absorbed
   (C) where European immigrant groups were absorbed
   (D) by which European immigrant groups have been absorbed
   (E) whereby the absorption of European groups has been

29. Mr. Howe's class has organized a special program for our school; the purpose being to help us increase our understanding of Japanese culture.

   (A) school; the purpose being to
   (B) school and the purpose is to
   (C) school, the purpose is to
   (D) school, being to
   (E) school to

30. Light reaching earth from the most distant stars originated billions of years ago.

   (A) reaching earth from the most distant stars
   (B) which reaching earth from the most distant stars
   (C) from the most distant stars reaching earth
   (D) that is from the most distant stars and reaches earth
   (E) reaching earth which is from stars that are most distant

31. Today's fashion designers must consider both how much a fabric costs and its wearability.

   (A) its wearability
   (B) is it going to wear well
   (C) if it has wearability
   (D) how well it wears
   (E) the fabric's ability to wear well

GO ON TO THE NEXT PAGE

32. This year's Puerto Rican Day parade <u>being more impressive than last year's</u>.

    (A) being more impressive than last year's
    (B) it was impressive, more so than last year
    (C) which was more impressive than last year's
    (D) was more impressive than last year's
    (E) by far more impressive than the last

33. <u>Josh was relieved to find his lost keys walking along the street in front of his apartment building.</u>

    (A) Josh was relieved to find his lost keys walking along the street in front of his apartment building.
    (B) Much to his relief, Josh found his lost keys walking along the street in front of his apartment building.
    (C) Walking along the street in front of his apartment building, Josh's lost keys were found by him, much to his relief.
    (D) Josh, relieved to find his lost keys, while walking along the street in front of his apartment building.
    (E) Walking along the street in front of his apartment building, Josh found his lost keys, much to his relief.

34. It was not until the sixteenth century that chairs became <u>common, before that time a chair was an authority symbol.</u>

    (A) common, before that time a chair was an authority symbol
    (B) common; before that time a chair was a symbol of authority
    (C) common; in prior times a chair was a symbol of authority, however
    (D) common because earlier chairs were considered authority symbols
    (E) common in that earlier they were authority symbols

35. Changing to the metric system means using grams rather than ounces, liters rather than quarts, and <u>to using kilometers rather than miles.</u>

    (A) to using kilometers rather than miles
    (B) to the use of kilometers rather than miles
    (C) kilometers rather than miles
    (D) replacing miles with kilometers
    (E) to kilometers rather than miles

36. <u>The two carpenters are building their own shop, which is satisfying to them.</u>

    (A) The two carpenters are building their own shop, which is satisfying to them.
    (B) Building their own shop, that is satisfying to the carpenters.
    (C) The two carpenters find that building their own shop is a satisfying experience.
    (D) The two carpenters, who are building their own shop, which is satisfying
    (E) A satisfying experience, the carpenters are building their own shop.

37. <u>When Dorothy Richardson decided to become</u> a novelist, she knew that her writing would leave her little time for other work.

    (A) When Dorothy Richardson decided to become
    (B) After the decision was made by Dorothy Richardson to become
    (C) After the decision by Dorothy Richardson to become
    (D) When Dorothy Richardson decides to become
    (E) When Dorothy Richardson decided about becoming

GO ON TO THE NEXT PAGE

38. When Robert E. Lee was well past forty, <u>he competed with his sons in high jumping</u>.

    (A) he competed with his sons in high jumping
    (B) him and his sons were competing in high jumping
    (C) he and his sons have competed in high jumping
    (D) he was in competition in high jumping with his sons
    (E) competition with his sons in high jumping took place

39. It is not easy to arrive at a single set of values in a pluralistic society, <u>where it has divergent views that challenge conventional thinking.</u>

    (A) where it has divergent views that
    (B) in which divergent views
    (C) whereby divergent views
    (D) and the reason is if the views of those diverging
    (E) because in it the views of those diverging

40. The steel industry, under pressure to give women equal job opportunities, <u>and changing its</u> all-male image.

    (A) and changing its
    (B) by changing its
    (C) is changing their
    (D) but changing their
    (E) is changing its

41. Alice Walker, one of America's best-known <u>writers, she has published</u> both poetry and prose.

    (A) writers, she has published
    (B) writers, has published
    (C) writers, and publishing
    (D) writers since publishing
    (E) writers when she published

42. <u>The patient recovered quickly and was quite ill earlier in the week.</u>

    (A) The patient recovered quickly and was quite ill earlier in the week.
    (B) The patient recovered quickly, earlier in the week he was quite ill.
    (C) The patient's recovery was quick after being quite ill earlier in the week.
    (D) The patient, who was quite ill earlier in the week, recovered quickly.
    (E) The patient, who recovered quickly, being quite ill earlier in the week.

43. Foreign correspondents are like birds of passage, resting for a few weeks, <u>then flying off again</u> to a new place.

    (A) then flying off again
    (B) after which again they fly off
    (C) then they fly off again
    (D) when once again they fly off
    (E) but soon they are flying off again

44. Hoping to add a touch of humor to his mother's birthday party, <u>Jim gave a huge box to her containing a very small gift.</u>

    (A) Jim gave a huge box to her containing a very small gift
    (B) given to her by Jim was a huge box containing a very small gift
    (C) she was given a huge box containing a very small gift by Jim
    (D) Jim gave her a huge box containing a very small gift
    (E) Jim gave a very small gift to her contained in a huge box

GO ON TO THE NEXT PAGE

their careers may cause, and work to lessen these problems wherever possible.

DIRECTIONS

The following passage is an early draft of an essay. Some parts of the passage need to be rewritten.

Read the passage and select the best answers for the questions that follow. Some questions are about particular sentences or parts of sentences and ask you to improve sentence structure or word choice. Other questions ask you to consider organization and development. In choosing answers, follow the requirements of standard written English.

Questions 45-50 are based on the following essay, which is a response to an assignment to write about a current issue facing the United States.

[1] In more and more families, both husbands and wives work, and with this there are new problems that result. [2] One reason that there are so many two-career couples is that the cost of living is very high. [3] Another is because both women and men enjoy working.

[4] An example of a two-career couple is Mark and Dawanna Long. [5] Dawanna is a university professor. [6] Mark works for a large corporation as a personnel counselor. [7] They have two children. [8] The number of two-career couples is likely to increase. [9] A married woman is still expected to continue to fulfill the traditional roles of companion, housekeeper, mother, and hostess. [10] Thus, as the Longs have experienced, conflicts arise in many ways. [11] When career opportunities clash, it is difficult for them to decide which career is more important.

[12] There are some basic things that can be done to try to solve a couple's problems. [13] Partners should discuss issues with each other openly. [14] Keep to a realistic estimate on how much can be done. [15] Each partner must set priorities, make choices, and agree to trade-offs. [16] From the beginning, men and women need to be aware of the problems that

45. Which of the following is the best way to revise the underlined portion of sentence 1 (reproduced below)?

In more and more families, both husbands and wives work, and with this there are new problems that result.

(A) a situation that is causing new problems
(B) and, this is what is causing new problems
(C) and this makes them have new problems as a result
(D) and with it are new problems
(E) they are having new problems

46. Which of the following is the best way to combine sentences 5, 6, and 7 (reproduced below])?

Dawanna is a university professor. Mark works for a large corporation as a personnel counselor. They have two children.

(A) Dawanna, a university professor, and Mark, a personnel counselor for a large corporation, have two children.
(B) As a personnel counselor for a large corporation and as a university professor, Mark and Dawanna Long have two children.
(C) Having two children are Mark and Dawanna Long, a personnel counselor for a large corporation and a university professor.
(D) She is a university professor and he is a personnel counselor for a large corporation and they have two children.
(E) They have two children-he is a personnel counselor for a large corporation and she is a university professor.

GO ON TO THE NEXT PAGE

47. In the context, which of the following best describes the purpose of the second paragraph?

   (A) To summarize contradictory evidence.
   (B) To propose a solution to a problem
   (C) To provide a specific illustration
   (D) To evaluate opinions set forth in the first paragraph
   (E) To convince the reader to alter his or her opinion.

48. In context, which of the following should be inserted at the beginning of sentence 9?

   (A) Even though
   (B) For example,
   (C) However,
   (D) As a result,
   (E) Basically

49. In context, which of the following is the best way to revise the phrase "*things that can be done*" in sentence 12?

   (A) statements that can be made
   (B) theories that can be studied
   (C) details that can be considered
   (D) guidelines that can be followed
   (E) arguments that can be won

50. In context, which of the following is the best way to revise sentence 14 (reproduced below)?

   Keep to a realistic estimate on how much can be done.

   (A) You should keep a realistic estimate of how much you can do.
   (B) Estimate realistically how much can be done.
   (C) Keep estimating realistically about how much can be done.
   (D) They should have estimated realistically how much they could do.
   (E) They should estimate realistically how much they can do.

!

STOP

this is the end of the exercise

SAT Writing Exercise #14

50 Questions

!

DIRECTIONS

Thes following sentences test your ability to detect errors in grammar and usage. Each sentence contains either one error or no errors at all and no sentence contains more than one error. Choose the underlined word or phrase in each sentence that when changed best corrects the grammatical or usage error. Only underlined words may be changed. If the sentence is correct as written, select choice E. In making your choices keep in mind the standards requirements of standard written English.

EXAMPLE:

Super Mario Bros' Mario first <u>appeared</u> in Donkey
                                  A
Kong as Jumpman and <u>was</u> later <u>renamed</u> to Mario
                       B   C
<u>in honor to</u> Nintendo of America's landlord Mario
    D
Segali. <u>No Error</u>
            E

Ⓐ Ⓑ Ⓒ ⬤D Ⓔ

1. The speaker claimed that no other modern

   <u>nation devotes</u> so small <u>a portion of</u> <u>its wealth</u>
        A   B   C
   to public assistance and health <u>as</u> the United
                                      D
   States does. <u>No error</u>
                     E

2. The thought <u>of trying to</u> persuade <u>their</u> three-
                     A   B
   year-old <u>to sit in</u> a high chair did not appeal to
                C
   either the mother <u>nor</u> the father. <u>No error</u>
                        D   E

3. The <u>bright</u> fiberglass sculptures of Luis
          A
   Jimenez <u>has received</u> critical acclaim <u>not only</u>
              B   C
   in his home state, New Mexico, but also <u>in</u>
                                              D
   New York. <u>No error</u>
                  E

4. Doctors see a <u>connection between</u> <u>increased</u>
                      A   B
   amounts of leisure time spend sunbathing <u>and</u>
                                               C
   the increased <u>number of</u> cases of skin cancer.
                      D
   <u>No error</u>
       E

5. <u>Whether or not</u> credit card companies should
       A
   prevent <u>their</u> customers <u>to acquire</u> substantial
              B   C
   debts was the issue <u>discussed at</u> the meeting.
                            D
   <u>No error</u>
       E

6. The board's final recommendations <u>included</u>
                                          A
   hiring <u>additional</u> personnel, dismissing the
              B
   <u>head of</u> research, and <u>a reorganized marketing</u>
       C   D
   division. <u>No error</u>
                  E

GO ON TO THE NEXT PAGE

7. Some people <u>prefer</u> attending movies
                    A
   <u>to television</u> because <u>they</u> dislike the <u>frequent</u>
        B   C   D
   interruptions of programs for commercials.

   <u>No error</u>
        E

8. <u>Like</u> many factory workers <u>of</u> a century ago,
   A   B
   <u>women today</u> are developing organizations to
        C
   <u>represent</u> their interests. <u>No error</u>
        D   E

9. In a prominent city newspaper, <u>they claim</u>
                                        A
   that the number <u>of</u> unregistered <u>participants in</u>
                    B   C
   this year's marathon was half <u>that of</u>
                                    D
   last year's. <u>No error</u>
                    E

10. <u>For</u> the past three years, the puppet troupe has
    A
    <u>went</u> to schools <u>throughout</u> the state to present
    B   C
    programs <u>that teach</u> children about Black
                    D
    history. <u>No error</u>
                E

11. <u>Of all</u> the written sources from which history
    A
    <u>can be</u> reconstructed, diaries <u>are undoubtedly</u>
        B   C
    the <u>more</u> entertaining. <u>No error</u>
            D   E

12. Diplomatic relations <u>between</u> Great Britain
                            A
    and Iceland improved <u>once it had agreed to</u>
                            B   C   D
    observe the fishing restrictions. <u>No error</u>
                                            E

13. <u>When Zora Neale Hurtson began to write</u>
        A   B
    short stories <u>in the late</u> 1920's, she <u>initiated</u>
                    C   D
    the second stage of the Harlem Renaissance.

    <u>No error</u>
        E

14. A stunt man often is able <u>for working</u> only
                                A
    two weeks <u>a month</u> <u>because of</u> the injuries
                B   C
    he suffers <u>on the job</u>. <u>No error</u>
                    D   E

15. If <u>there is</u> funds budgeted <u>for purchasing</u>
        A   B
    new books, your request <u>will probably</u>
                                C
    <u>be approved</u>. <u>No error</u>
        D   E

16. Many scientists <u>are convinced that</u> individuals
                        A
    who have been <u>working at</u> asbestos in
                        B
    <u>their jobs</u> are <u>likely</u> to develop health
        C   D
    problems. <u>No error</u>
                    E

GO ON TO THE NEXT PAGE

17. For the recent exhibition, the museum

acquired a rock <u>from</u> a volcano that
<u>A</u>   <u>B</u>

<u>has erupted</u> <u>more than</u> two thousand
        C   D

years ago. <u>No error</u>
                    E

18. Some researchers <u>have theorized</u> that
                                    A

<u>there may be</u> a connection between hormones
        B

<u>with</u> the body's <u>ability to</u> heal damaged
  C   D

organs. <u>No error</u>
                E

19. <u>Whether</u> relaxing with visitors or <u>lecturing to</u>
        A   B

an audience, the mayoral candidate <u>freely</u>
                                              C

offered her opinions <u>on all subjects.</u> <u>No error</u>
                            D   E

20. <u>According to</u> recent reports, more women
        A

<u>are working</u> as <u>the manager</u> of small business
        B   C

firms <u>than ever</u> before. <u>No error</u>
            D   E

21. <u>Although</u> the language of *The Canterbury*
        A

Tales <u>seems strange</u> to us, <u>it reflects</u> the
          B   C

language <u>talked</u> in Chaucer's time. <u>No error</u>
              D   E

22. <u>To a much greater extent</u> than is <u>generally</u>
                A   B

<u>realized</u>, the economy of the United
    C

States <u>relies on</u> agriculture. <u>No error</u>
            D   E

23. Gustave Flaubert is <u>thought to be</u> <u>one of</u> the
                                A   B

three or four writers <u>which</u> were influential
                            C

<u>in</u> the creation of the modern realistic novel.
  D

<u>No error</u>
    E

24. <u>Even with</u> a calculator, you must have a basic
        A

<u>understanding of</u> mathematics if <u>one expects</u>
        B   C
to

solve complex problems <u>correctly.</u> <u>No error</u>
                                D   E

25. In the last decade, some college graduates

<u>will have defaulted</u> on federal <u>loans</u> for <u>their</u>
            A   B   C

education <u>by declaring</u> bankruptcy. <u>No error</u>
                D   E

26. <u>In their</u> report to the <u>treasurer and I</u>, the
        A   B

members of the subcommittee argued

<u>in favor of</u> <u>establishing</u> a library. <u>No error</u>
    C   D   E

GO ON TO THE NEXT PAGE

DIRECTIONS

Thes following sentences test your ability to express ideas in writing effectively and efficiently. Each sentence is either partially or completely underlined. The first of the five choices given will repeat the original wording and the other four choices will contain alternative wording. Choose the change that best improves the senetence or choose A if the original is superior to any of the other choices given.

In making your choice keep in mind the standards of proper written English. Among other things, pay close attention to grammar, word choice, punctuation, precision, and correct usage of tenses. Avoid awkward and ambiguous construction.

EXAMPLE:

I want your love, and I want your revenge;
you and me can write a bad romance.

(A) you and me can write
(B) you and me could write
(C) you and me writing
(D) you and I can write
(E) me and you can write

Ⓐ Ⓑ Ⓒ Ⓓ Ⓔ

27. Although Jonathan is very much interested in Mexican culture, he does not speak Spanish and has never visited Mexico.

(A) he does not speak Spanish and has never visited Mexico
(B) it is without being able to speak Spanish or having visited in Mexico
(C) he does not speak Spanish and has never visited there
(D) he does not speak Spanish nor has he ever visited there
(E) it is without speaking Spanish now having visited there

28. Justice Thurgood Marshall, who was appointed by Lyndon Johnson, is the first Black American to serve on the Supreme Court.

(A) Justice Thurgood Marshall, who was appointed by Lyndon Johnson, is the first Black American to serve on the Supreme Court.
(B) Justice Thurgood Marshall being the first Black American to serve on the Supreme Court and was appointed by Lyndon Johnson.
(C) Being the first Black American to serve on the Supreme Court, Justice Thurgood Marshall was appointed by Lyndon Johnson.
(D) Justice Thurgood Marshall is the first Black American to serve on the Supreme Court and was appointed by Lyndon Johnson.
(E) Justice Thurgood Marshall is the first Black American to serve on the Supreme Court, and he was appointed by Lyndon Johnson.

29. The turning point in the battle of Actium clearly was Cleopatra, who was fleeing.

(A) Cleopatra, who was fleeing
(B) Cleopatra, in that she fled
(C) Cleopatra's flight
(D) when Cleopatra was fleeing
(E) that Cleopatra took flight

30. Juggling two careers is common among state legislators, the majority of them serve in states where the legislature is in session only part of the year.

(A) of them serve
(B) of them are serving
(C) which serve
(D) of whom serve
(E) serve

GO ON TO THE NEXT PAGE

31. <u>Having command of pathos, tragedy, as well as</u> <u>humor,</u> George Eliot is considered to be a great English novelist.

(A) Having command of pathos, tragedy, as well as humor,
(B) Having command of pathos, tragedy, and her humorous side,
(C) By being in command of both pathos and tragedy and also humor,
(D) With her command of pathos and tragedy and being humorous,
(E) Because of her command of pathos, tragedy, and humor,

32. Issued in Great Britain in 1840, <u>the first</u> <u>gummed postage stamp in history was known</u> <u>as</u> the "Penny Black."

(A) the first gummed postage stamp in history was known as
(B) they called the first gummed postage stamp in history
(C) history refers to the first gummed postage stamp as
(D) was the first gummed postage stamp in history
(E) the first gummed postage stamp in history being known as

33. <u>Whether the ancient Egyptians actually sailed</u> <u>or did not</u> to South America remains uncertain, but that they could have was demonstrated by Heyerdahl's Ra II expedition.

(A) Whether the ancient Egyptians actually sailed or did not
(B) Whether in actuality the ancient Egyptians sailed or did not
(C) The actuality of which the ancient Egyptians sailed
(D) That the ancient Egyptians actually did sail
(E) If the ancient Egyptians may have sailed

34. After visiting their friends in Paris, my parents told me that <u>in France they sometimes</u> do not wear bathing suits on the beach.

(A) in France they sometimes
(B) in France some people
(C) some French people
(D) in France there are some who
(E) in France, men and women

35. Today's computers <u>are becoming not only</u> <u>more varied and powerful, but also less</u> <u>expensive.</u>

(A) are becoming not only more varied and powerful but also less expensive
(B) not only are becoming more varied and powerful, they cost less
(C) become not only more varied and powerful, they become less expensive
(D) becoming more varied and powerful, but also less expensive
(E) become more varied and powerful, not only, but also less expensive

36. <u>Getting off the chairlift, Neil adjusted his boot</u> <u>buckles, polished his goggles, and skied down</u> <u>the slope.</u>

(A) Getting off the chairlift, Neil adjusted his boot buckles, polished his goggles and skied down the slope.
(B) He got off the chairlift, Neil adjusted his boot buckles, polished his goggles, and skied down the slope.
(C) After getting off the chairlift, Neil adjusted his boot buckles, polished his goggles, and then he went skiing down the slope.
(D) Neil, after getting off the chairlift, adjusted his boot buckles, polished his goggles, and was skiing down the slope.
(E) After he got off the chairlift, Neil adjusted his boot buckles, polished his goggles, and skied down the slope.

GO ON TO THE NEXT PAGE

37. Since they have been told not to do so in their school books, students often hesitate to write in their personal books; yet, circling an unknown word or underlining an important phrase is <u>critically when one wishes to truly learn something.</u>

(A) is critically when one wishes to truly learn something
(B) is critically being as one might wish to truly learn something
(C) is critical when one wishes to truly learn something
(D) is critical when you truly want to learn that something has been
(E) can only be seen as critical when one wishes to truly learn something

38. Unprepared for such a strong rebuttal, <u>the lawyer's attempt at winning the case failed.</u>

(A) the lawyer's attempt at winning the case failed.
(B) the lawyer's attempt failed to win the case.
(C) the lawyer failed to win the case.
(D) the lawyer failed in his attempt to win the case.
(E) the lawyer attempted to win her case, but failed.

39. <u>Unless they become more responsible</u> about investing money, many college students will soon rebel against their administrations.

(A) Unless they become more responsible
(B) Unless becoming more responsible
(C) Unless colleges become more responsible
(D) Unless it becomes more responsible
(E) Unless more responsibility is shown

40. <u>One of Humphrey Bogart's earlier movies, Samuel Space is a detective trying to solve the mystery of his partner's death in *The Maltese Falcon.*</u>

(A) One of Humphrey Bogart's earlier movies, Samuel Spade is a detective trying to solve the mystery of his partner's death in *The Maltese Falcon.*
(B) One of Humphrey Bogart's earlier movies, *The Maltese Falcon* is a movie in that Samuel Space, detective, tries to solve the mystery of his partner's death.
(C) One of Humphrey Bogart's earlier movies, *The Maltese Falcon* is a mystery in which Samuel Spade tries to solve his partner's death.
(D) In *The Maltese Falcon*, one of Humphrey Bogart's earlier movies, Samuel Spade is a detective trying to solve the mystery of his partner's death.
(E) In *The Maltese Falcon*, one of Humphrey Bogart's roles is that of Samuel Spade, a detective trying to solve the mystery of his partner's death, and it was also one of his earlier movies.

41. Many parents and children argue often about responsibility; this would be avoided if <u>they had more trust in them.</u>

(A) they had more trust in them
(B) their trust in them was more.
(C) their trust were more
(D) their parents had more trust in them
(E) their parents had more trust from their children

GO ON TO THE NEXT PAGE

42. While Boudin's own paintings have never been held in that high regard, he is seen as having played a critical role in the education of Impressionist painter Monet.

(A) While Boudin's own paintings have never been held in that high regard, he is seen as having played a critical role in the education of Impressionist painter Monet.

(B) While Boudin's own paintings were never regarded highly, Monet is seen as having been on of his most educated students.

(C) It is seen that Boudin's critical role in educating the Impressionist painter Monet was held in higher regard than his paintings.

(D) Since Boudin's own paintings have never been held in that high regard, he has been seen as having played a critical role in the education of Impressionist painter Monet.

(E) Since Boudin's own paintings, which were never held in that high regard, were seen as having played a critical role in the education of Impressionist painter Monet.

43. Although everyone was forewarned about the upcoming exam, yet only three students out of the entire class passed it.

(A) yet only three students out of the entire class

(B) only three students out of the entire class

(C) only three students, which was out of the entire class,

(D) yet only three students that were forewarned out of the entire class

(E) but only three students out of the entire class

44. Positions in the police and fire departments once were traditionally filled by men, but becoming increasingly popular among women.

(A) becoming increasingly popular among women.

(B) have become increasingly popular among women.

(C) have among women increased in popularity.

(D) become increasingly popular among women.
    women have increasingly found them to be popular

GO ON TO THE NEXT PAGE

DIRECTIONS

The following passage is an early draft of an essay. Some parts of the passage need to be rewritten.

Read the passage and select the best answers for the questions that follow. Some questions are about particular sentences or parts of sentences and ask you to improve sentence structure or word choice. Other questions ask you to consider organization and development. In choosing answers, follow the requirements of standard written English.

Questions 45-50 are based on the following draft of an essay.

Our town needs to make more of an effort to make its museums accessible to children. [2] Raised with frequent exposure to sculpture and paintings, it is much more likely that young people will mature into artists and patrons of the arts.

[3] It is often quite easy to accomplish a great deal simply. [4] Placed slightly lower on the walls, paintings become more visible to children. [5] But extensive programs to encourage children to appreciate art are often not a necessity. [6] Children have a natural enjoyment of art. [7] A museum is an excellent place for a child. [8] We must only understand that these young museum patrons can not help acting like them. [9] Children should not be asked to be silent, or spend long periods of time in front of any one piece. [10] If necessary, museums should set up special "children's times" during which young people may roam through the building, enjoying the artwork in their own way. [11] A wonderful learning experience! [12] Children can have a great time, and at the same time gain an appreciation of art. [13] Precautions could be taken to make sure that no damage was done.

[14] This is necessary because places like museums must be available for everyone. [15]

These changes cannot happen overnight, but if we volunteered and were helping to make these changers in our town's museums, we can realize the goal of making them accessible to people of all ages.

45. Which of the following represents the best revision of sentence 4 (reproduced below)?

Placed slightly lower on the walls, paintings become more visible to children.

(A) (As it is now)
(B) Placing them slightly lower on the walls, the paintings become more visible to the children.
(C) For example, placing paintings slightly lower on the walls makes them more visible to children.
(D) For example, when placed slightly lower on the walls, children can see the paintings better.
(E) Placed paintings that are lower on the walls are more visible to children.

46. Which of the following could best replace the word "*But*" in sentence 5 (reproduced below)?

But extensive programs to encourage children to appreciate art are often not a necessity.

(A) However,   (B) Rather,   (C) Indeed,
(D) Notwithstanding,   (E) And yet,

47. Which version of the underlined portion of sentence 8 (reproduced below)?

We must only understand that these young museum patrons cannot help acting like them.

(A) (as it is now)
(B) like it
(C) as if they were
(D) like what they are
(E) like children

GO ON TO THE NEXT PAGE

48. Which of the following is the best way to revise sentences 10 and 11 (reproduced below)?

If necessary, museums should set up special "children's times" during which young people may roam through the building, enjoying the artwork in their own way. A wonderful experience!

(A) To avoid disrupting everyone else, create "children's times" in the museum, during which children could roam throughout the building, enjoying the artwork in their own way and a wonderful learning experience.
(B) Museums should set up "children's times." This would be a wonderful learning experience. Children could roam through the museum. Children could enjoy the artwork in their own way.
(C) If necessary, museums should set up a wonderful learning experience called "children's times." During it, young people could roam throughout the building, enjoying the artwork in their own way.
(D) To enjoy artwork in their own way, children should be given the freedom to roam throughout the building. This would be a wonderful learning experience, and it could be called "children's times."
(E) To avoid disrupting other museum-goers, museums should set up special "children's times." During these times, children would be allowed to roam throughout the building and enjoy the artwork in their own way. What a wonderful learning experience!

49. Sentence 13 could be best improved if the author were to

(A) Describe possible damage
(B) Explain the precautions to be taken
(C) Give a historic precedent
(D) Extend her argument to include other institutions
(E) Explain the mission of a museum

50. In context, sentence 14 could be made more precise by changing the phrase "*This is*" to which of the following?

(A) That is
(B) These changes are
(C) The reasons for these changes is that they are
(D) It is
(E) These changes, as mentioned above, are also

!

STOP

this is the end of the exercise

SAT Writing Exercise #15
50 Questions

!

1. <u>Because</u> eighteenth-century literature is
        A
<u>filled up with</u> <u>references to</u> Greek mythology,
    B   C
it often intimidates those who <u>have not studied</u>
                                D
ancient myths. <u>No error</u>
                  E

2. <u>There is</u> a number of reasons, <u>both</u> economic
        A   B
and ecological, <u>for</u> Oregon's desire <u>to limit</u>
                 C   D
population growth. <u>No error</u>
                      E

3. A deer herd <u>can be expected</u> to double in size
                    A
every two or three years <u>until</u> its territory
          B   C
<u>becomes crowded.</u> <u>No error</u>
          D   E

4. Those interviewed said that <u>they</u> <u>excepted</u> the
                                  A   B
principle of equal employment and believed
that every effort <u>should be made</u> <u>to end</u> sex
                    C   D
discrimination. <u>No error</u>
                  E

5. <u>Even though</u> she had the impressive title <u>of</u>
        A   B
executive assistant, her salary <u>was lower</u> than
                                  C
<u>a secretary.</u> <u>No error</u>
    D   E

6. The similarities <u>between</u> the two societies
                        A
Heyerdahl <u>studied</u> tend to support his theory
            B   C
that the origins of the Polynesians were <u>in</u>
                                          D
South America. <u>No error</u>
                  E

7. To learn more about Hispanic culture, we
   A
   invited a lecturer who had spoken frequently
              B
   with regard to the life of early settlers in Santa
   C   D
   Fe. No error
   E

8. In the nineteenth century, a number of
   A
   occupations came to be viewed as
                 B
   unsuitable for women or incompatible with her
   C   D
   work in the home. No error
                     E

9. The pamphlet from the insurance company

   reported that good drivers change lanes
                       A
   cautiously, are constantly alert, and react swift
              B   C
   when danger threatens. No error
   D   E

10. Many readers of Leon Damas's poetry

    do not realize that much of his work was
    A   B
    inspired by the sounds and rhythms of African
    C   D
    music. No error
           E

11. If Carol had not warned her guests about the
                                    A
    flooded streets, they might have ran into
    B   C
    difficulty on the way to her house. No error
    D   E

12. Members of the Parti Québécois were

    threatening seceding from Canada, for they
                A   B   C
    considered their interests to be different from
                                    D
    those of English speaking Canadians. No error
                                         E

13. The idea of romantic love is often thought
                            A
    to originate in the Middle Ages and to have
    B   C
    resulted from a misinterpretation of Ovid's
    D
    writings. No error
              E

14. The good politican, like most other perceptive
                          A
    people, learns more from their opponents
            B   C
    than from supporters. No error
    D   E

15. Either the manager or the customer-relations
                      A
    representative are supposed to respond to
                    B   C
    complaints about damaged goods. No error
    D   E

16. The friendship between Alicia and Karen
        A
    developed when she agreed to help with the
             B   C   D
    preliminary design for the new municipal

    building. No error
              E

GO ON TO THE NEXT PAGE

17. Recent protests <u>against</u> nuclear power plants
                              A
<u>have</u> much <u>in common with</u> some of the social
  B   C
protests of the <u>preceding</u> two decades.
                          D
<u>No error</u>
        E

18. The supply of oak, hickory, and birch logs <u>are</u>
                                                          A
<u>sufficient to keep</u> the family warm, <u>even if</u> this
              B   C
winter is as cold as <u>the last one</u>. <u>No error</u>
                              D   E

19. Shrewd politicians <u>speculate</u> that people will
                                  A
stand in line <u>longer</u> at the polls to vote against
                    B
somebody <u>than they will</u> <u>voting</u> for somebody.
                    C   D
<u>No error</u>
        E

20. The camera crew looked <u>skeptical</u> at the
                                      A
director as <u>he described</u> his <u>plan</u> to film,
                  B   C
<u>without stopping</u> for any reason, two hours in
          D
the life of a Portuguese fisherman. <u>No error</u>
                                              E

21. Skilled weavers <u>are found</u> <u>only in</u> those few
                              A   B
communities <u>whereby</u> weaving is an important
                    C
skill <u>developed</u> from childhood. <u>No error</u>
            D   E

22. In her novels, Nella Larson <u>focused on</u> the
                                          A
problems of young Black women <u>which</u>
                                          B
<u>lived in</u> Europe and America <u>during the</u>
      C   D
1920's. <u>No error</u>
              E

23. The energy question, along with <u>several other</u>
                                              A
issues, <u>are going</u> <u>to be dicussed</u> <u>at the next</u>
            B   C   D
meeting of the state legislature. <u>No error</u>
                                          E

24. Few people <u>cannot hardly</u> <u>tell</u> the difference
                        A   B
between purple and fuchsia, <u>even when</u>
                                      C
samples of these related colors <u>are</u> placed side
                                      D
by side. <u>No error</u>
              E

25. The exhibit includes both a collection of
pictures <u>taken by</u> a celebrated photographer
              A
<u>in addition to</u> prints <u>made</u> recently
      B   C
by <u>comparatively</u> unknown artists. <u>No error</u>
        D   E

26. <u>Whenever</u> we hear of a natural disaster,
          A
<u>even in</u> a distant part of the world, <u>you</u>
      B   C
<u>feel sympathy</u> for the people affected. <u>No error</u>
        D   E

GO ON TO THE NEXT PAGE

DIRECTIONS

Thes following sentences test your ability to express ideas in writing effectively and efficiently. Each sentence is either partially or completely underlined. The first of the five choices given will repeat the original wording and the other four choices will contain alternative wording. Choose the change that best improves the senetence or choose A if the original is superior to any of the other choices given.

In making your choice keep in mind the standards of proper written English. Among other things, pay close attention to grammar, word choice, punctuation, precision, and correct usage of tenses. Avoid awkard and ambiguous construction.

EXAMPLE:

I want your love, and I want your revenge;
you and me can write a bad romance.

(A) you and me can write
(B) you and me could write
(C) you and me writing
(D) you and I can write
(E) me and you can write

27. The committee chairpersons agreed to return to their respective committees and they would discuss the proposals made by the executive board.

(A) To return to their respective committees and they would discuss
(B) Upon return to their respective committees, thereby discussing
(C) To return to her respective committees and discuss
(D) To return to their respective committees discussing
(E) To return to their respective committees and discuss

28. The clog has come back into fashion recently, yet few people know that originally it was called the sabot, made by hollowing a single piece of wood, and was worn by peasants in Europe.

(A) it was called the sabot, made by hollowing a single piece of wood, and was worn by peasants in Europe
(B) it was called the sabot, making it by hollowing a single piece of wood, and worn by peasants in Europe
(C) it was called the sabot, made by hollowing a single piece of wood, and worn by peasnts in Europe
(D) it was called the sabot, making it by hollowing a single piece of wood, and was worn by peasants in Europe
(E) it was called the sabot, and the peasants made it by hollowing a single of wood, and wore it in Europe

29. Many say that, after inventing an explosive more powerful than any then known, Alfred Nobel instituted the Nobel Peace Prizes to atone for his "accomplishment" and relieve his conscience.

(A) after inventing an explosive more powerful than any then known
(B) after inventing an explosive that was more powerful than any that were then known
(C) after he invented an explosive more powerful than he or any others had then known
(D) after he invented an explosive, it being more powerful than any then known
(E) after inventing an explosive more powerful then any then known

GO ON TO THE NEXT PAGE

30. For many a brilliant actor, <u>being free to interpret their character as they wish</u> is more important than being well paid

(A) being free to interpret their character as they wish

(B) being free to interpret his or her character as they wish

(C) being free to interpret their character as they wishes

(D) being free to interpret his or her character as he or she wishes

(E) being free to interpret his or her character as he or she wish

31. On Sunday afternoons, Omar and his family enjoy playing Monopoly with the neighbors, <u>and they always win</u>.

(A) And they always win

(B) Even though they always win

(C) Even though the neighbors always win

(D) And the neighbors, they always win

(E) It being that the neighbors always win

32. Goethe's poetry is <u>different from any others</u> in that it lyrically expresses profound thoughts.

(A) different from any others

(B) different from that of any other poet

(C) different from any other poet

(D) different than anyone else's

(E) different than anyone else

33. Although he was not a advocate of psychiatrists, <u>Sigmund Freud was respected by Albert Einstein as a social philosopher, and worked with him to promote peace</u> during the Nazi uprising.

(A) Sigmund Freud was respected by Albert Einstein as a social philosopher, and worked with him to promote peace

(B) Sigmund Freud was respected by Albert Einstein, since he was a social philosopher, and they worked to promote peace

(C) Albert Einstein respected Sigmund Freud as a social philosopher, and they together worked to promote peace

(D) Albert Einstein respected Sigmund Freud as a social philosopher who was working with him to promote peace

(E) Albert Einstein respected Sigmund Freud as a social philosopher, and worked with him to promote peace

34. After getting her driver's license, Jenny used her father's car <u>as often as possible, and her father said to put less miles on it</u> by walking to school and work.

(A) As often as possible, and her father said to put less miles on it

(B) As often as possible; eventually her father told her to put fewer miles on it

(C) As often as possible, but then eventually her father told her to be putting fewer miles on it

(D) As often as possible; eventually her father told her to put less miles on it

(E) As often as possible, and her father said to be putting less miles on it

GO ON TO THE NEXT PAGE →

35. It is true that plastic surgery can improve a person's outward appearance <u>but your personality will not change unless you make it.</u>

(A) but your personality will not change unless you make it.

(B) but your personality will not be changed unless you make it.

(C) but a personality will not change unless you make it.

(D) but a personality will not change without an effort.

(E) but a personality will not change unless you make an effort.

36. To survive an airplane hijacking, <u>it demands remaining calm</u> and well-behaved.

(A) it demands remaining calm

(B) it demands calmness

(C) one is demanded to remain calm

(D) one should remain calm

(E) demands one to remain calm

37. Vacationing in foreign countries provides one not only with relaxing experiences but also <u>cultures different from theirs are better understood.</u>

(A) cultures different from theirs are better understood.

(B) a better understanding of cultures different from theirs.

(C) with a better understanding of different cultures.

(D) cultures different from theirs are better understood.

(E) cultures, although different, are better understood.

38. <u>When reading</u> the reviews of his recently published romantic novel, Father O'Malley threw his manuscript into a blazing fireplace.

(A) When reading

(B) Having read

(C) When he had read

(D) When he reads

(E) Reading

39. <u>When first implicated in it, Nixon denied any wrongdoing in the Watergate Scandal, but soon the evidence against him was overwhelming.</u>

(A) When first implicated in it, Nixon denied any wrongdoing in the Watergate Scandal, but soon evidence against him was overwhelming.

(B) When Nixon was first implicated in the Watergate scandal, he denied any wrongdoing and the evidence against him was soon overwhelming.

(C) When first implicated in the Watergate Scandal, the evidence against Nixon was soon overwhelming but he denied any wrongdoing.

(D) When he was first implicated in the Watergate Scandal, Nixon denied any wrongdoing, but soon he was overwhelmed by the evidence against him.

(E) Nixon first denied any wrongdoing in it, but soon the overwhelming evidence implicated him in the Watergate Scandal.

GO ON TO THE NEXT PAGE

40. <u>The average person should eat more</u> <u>vegetables if they want to develop strong</u> <u>bodies and maintain their health.</u>

(A) The average person should eat more vegetables if they want to develop strong bodies and maintain their health.
(B) The average person should eat more vegetables to develop strong bodies and maintain their health.
(C) The average person should eat more vegetables if he wants to develop a strong body and maintain his health.
(D) The average person, wishing to develop a strong body and maintain his health, should eat more vegetables.
(E) The average person should eat more vegetables in order to develop strong bodies and maintain their health.

41. Georgia O'Keeffe painted <u>landscapes and they</u> <u>express</u> the mystique of both the desert and the mountains of the Southwest.

(A) landscapes and they express
(B) landscapes, being the expressions of
(C) landscapes, they express
(D) landscapes that express
(E) landscapes, and expressing in them

42. The amount of garbage produced in the United States could be reduced by recycling trash, minimizing packaging, <u>and developing new</u> <u>technology</u> for incinerators and landfills.

(A) And developing new technology
(B) and if they develop new technology
(C) also by developing new technology
(D) and new technology being developed
(E) and if there was new technology

43. Professor Koshland argued that although many colleges have excelled at training future scientists, <u>the failure is in their not educating</u> humanities majors in the methods of scientific thought.

(A) The failure is in their not educating
(B) The failure they have is in their not educating
(C) They failed not to educate
(D) They have failed to educate
(E) Failing in their education of

44. <u>Having an exceptionally dry and stable</u> <u>atmosphere, astronomers chose Mauna Kea</u> as the prospective site of the world's largest optical telescope.

(A) Having an exceptionally dry and stable atmosphere, astronomers chose Mauna Kea
(B) Astronomers who chose Mauna Kea for its exceptionally dry and stable atmosphere saw it
(C) Mauna Kea's exceptionally dry and stable atmosphere led to its choice by astronomers
(D) Because its atmosphere is exceptionally dry and stable, astronomers chose Mauna Kea
(E) Based on its exceptionally dry and stable atmosphere, Mauna Kea was chosen by astronomers

GO ON TO THE NEXT PAGE

DIRECTIONS

The following passage is an early draft of an essay. Some parts of the passage need to be rewritten.

Read the passage and select the best answers for the questions that follow. Some questions are about particular sentences or parts of sentences and ask you to improve sentence structure or word choice. Other questions ask you to consider organization and development. In choosing answers, follow the requirements of standard written English.

Questions 45-50 are based on the following passage.

At one point in the movie "Raiders of the Lost Ark," the evil archaeologist Bellocq shows the heroic Indiana Jones a cheap watch. (2) If the watch were to be buried in the desert for a thousand years and then dug up, Bellocq says, it would be considered priceless. (3) I often think of this scene whenever I consider the record album-collecting phenomenon, it being one of the more remarkable aspects of popular culture in the United States. (4) Collecting record albums gives us a chance to make a low-cost investment that just might pay dividends in the future.

(5) When my aunt collected them in the mid-sixties, nobody regarded them as investments. (6) A young fan shelled out dollar after dollar at the corner record store for no other reason than to assemble a complete collection of her favorite musical groups – in my aunt's case, the Beatles and the Supremes. (7) By committing so much of her allowance each week to the relentless pursuit of that one group not yet in her collection – the immortal Yardbirds, let us say – she was proving her loyalty to her superstars.

(8) The recording industry is a capitalist enterprise and so this hobby has become one. (9) Just as everyone has heard of the exorbitant prices being paid for the Beatles' first album in mint condition, so everyone is certain that a payoff is among each stack of old records. (10) But if that album was buried somewhere in my aunt's closet full of dusty records, she never knew it. (11) Long before she learned it, she had thrown them out.

45. The sentence that best states the main idea of the passage is

(A) Sentence 1
(B) Sentence 2
(C) Sentence 3
(D) Sentence 4
(E) Sentence 7

46. In the context of the first paragraph, which revision is most needed in sentence 3?

(A) Insert "As a matter of fact" at the beginning.
(B) Omit the word "scene".
(C) Omit the words "it being".
(D) Change the comma to a semicolon.
(E) Change "think" to "thought" and "consider" to "considered".

47. Which of the following sentences is best inserted at the beginning of the second paragraph, before sentence 5?

(A) Not everyone, however, starts collecting records to make a profit.
(B) It is obvious that these early investments pay off.
(C) No two experiences are exactly alike when it comes to collecting records.
(D) Allow me to tell you about my aunt's attempt to achieve wealth.
(E) Many hobbies have advantages that are not readily apparent to you in the beginning.

GO ON TO THE NEXT PAGE

48. Of the following, which is the best version of sentence 8 (reproduced below)?

The recording industry is a capitalist enterprise and so this hobby has become one.

(A) (As it is now)
(B) Becoming more and more like the recording industry has been the hobby of collecting records, a capitalist enterprise.
(C) It is said that the recording industry has been transformed into a capitalist enterprise, much like this hobby.
(D) Like the recording industry itself, this hobby has become a capitalist enterprise.
(E) Finally, like the capitalist enterprise of recording, record collecting will be transformed.

49. Which of the following is the best version of the underlined portion of sentence 10 (reproduced below)?

But if that album was buried somewhere in my aunt's closet full of dusty records, she never knew it.

(A) records, they would never know it.
(B) records; they would never know.
(C) records, who would know that?
(D) records, my aunt will never know.
(E) Records, they never knew it.

!

50. In context, which of the following is the best version of sentence 11 (reproduced below)?

Long before she learned it, she had thrown them out.

(A) (As it is now)
(B) Long before she learned that the records could be valuable, she had thrown them out.
(C) Long before she has learned about the records, she throws them out.
(D) It was long before she learned about the records that she threw them out.
(E) She throws the records out long before she hears about them

STOP

this is the end of the exercise

SAT Writing Exercise #16

50 Questions

!

!

1. Having <u>methodically examined</u> the building
       A   B
and its entrances, the fire inspector concluded

<u>that</u> the landlord had <u>complied with</u> all
 C   D
regulations. <u>No error</u>
             E

2. The twins wanted to be <u>a member</u> of the team,
                              A
<u>but</u> the captain <u>had already made</u>
 B   C
her selections. <u>No error</u>
 D   E

3. Mary Philbrook <u>began</u> her crusade for the
                      A
Equal Rights Amendment in 1923; today,

<u>more than</u> twenty years <u>after</u> her death, the
 B   C
crusade still <u>continues</u>. <u>No error</u>
              D   E

4. <u>Revered as</u> one of the world's most versatile
       A
geniuses, Leonardo da Vinci excelled <u>in every</u>
                                      B
endeavor he attempted and <u>serving</u> as <u>a</u>
                           C
<u>prototype</u> for the Renaissance man. <u>No error</u>
 D   E

5. <u>Of</u> the nominees <u>for</u> the Nobel Prize in
       A   B
literature this year, <u>few</u> are <u>as qualitifed as</u> the
                       C   D
English novelist Anthony Powell. <u>No error</u>
                                  E

6. The recent production <u>of</u> Arthur Miller's *A*
                             A
View From the Bridge exemplifies the strength

of this unsung masterpiece <u>and demonstrates</u>
                            B
that the work <u>has been</u> ignored <u>unjust</u>.
               C   D
<u>No error</u>
 E

GO ON TO THE NEXT PAGE →

7. Yoga is <u>more than</u> simply a <u>series of</u> stretches
　　　　　　　A　　　　　　　　　B
and poses; it is a means of centering oneself

spiritually and <u>focus</u> in such a way <u>as to</u> put
　　　　　　　　C　　　　　　　　　D
one's life in order. <u>No error</u>
　　　　　　　　　　　E

8. <u>Prior to</u> the Industrial Revolution, children and
　　　A
parents <u>spend</u> a great deal <u>of time</u> working
　　　　　B　　　　　　　　C
together to meet the needs <u>of the family</u>.
　　　　　　　　　　　　　　D
<u>No error</u>
　　E

9. The fund-raising campaigns <u>of many</u> public
　　　　　　　　　　　　　　　A
radio and television <u>are</u> often <u>viewed by</u>
　　　　　　　　　B　　　　　C
subscribers as a necessary, <u>albeit</u> undesirable
　　　　　　　　　　　　　　D
evil. <u>No error</u>
　　　　E

10. <u>It's</u> a good thing that the folks in the cast live
　　　A
<u>close by</u>, so <u>they</u> won't have to travel <u>very far</u>
　　B　　　　C　　　　　　　　　　D
to get home after the show. <u>No error</u>
　　　　　　　　　　　　　E

11. Neither the president <u>nor</u> the CEO of the
　　　　　　　　　　　A
three sister companies <u>was</u> able to determine
　　　　　　　　　　B
why the last quarter's financial reports <u>were</u> so
　　　　　　　　　　　　　　　　　　C
inconsistent with previous <u>years</u>. <u>No error</u>
　　　　　　　　　　　　D　　　E

12. If one is interested <u>in</u> learning more about
　　　　　　　　　　　A
Jacob Lawrence, <u>you should</u> visit the
　　　　　　　　　B
Metropolitan Museum of Art when next <u>his</u>
　　　　　　　　　　　　　　　　　　C
work <u>is exhibited</u>. <u>No error</u>
　　　　D　　　　E

13. In many colleges in the Northeast, it is

<u>necessarily</u> for students <u>to wear</u> snowshoes to
　　A　　　　　　　　　B
get from the dormitory to <u>their</u> classes <u>during</u>
　　　　　　　　　　　　C　　　　　D
the winter months. <u>No error</u>
　　　　　　　　　E

14. <u>Just as</u> parents vary in their readiness to have
　　　A
their babies learn <u>to</u> walk, babies vary in <u>their</u>
　　　　　　　　　B　　　　　　　　　C
readiness to take <u>his or her</u> first step. <u>No error</u>
　　　　　　　D　　　　　　　　　E

GO ON TO THE NEXT PAGE

15. While in training, each member of the team

were required to focus exclusively on the tasks
A
associated with her position, and therefore had
B   C
little sense of the functioning of the team

as a whole. No error
D   E

16. The gift that Karen and Mary ultimately

purchased for her mother was much less
A   B   C
expensive than the gift they originally intended

to purchase. No error
D   E

17. Thomas Pynchon's novel *The Crying of Lot 49*

has been lauded for it's satirical prose and
A   B
favorably described as akin to Joyce's *Ulysses*.
C   D
No error
E

18. John knew he should've went home on the
A
team's bus when he had the chance instead of
B   C
waiting for the bus to return to bring home the
D
spectators. No error
E

19. Many students find Shakespeare's *Richard III*
A
impossible to understand; yet, when proper
B   C
conveyed, students can often learn from the

familial turmoil and inner conflict that occurs
D
in the play. No error
E

20. When Ms. Ruiz arrived at the holiday sale, she
A
realized that she had left her wallet at home
B   C
and must go back to get it. No error
D   E

21. Many scholars agree that there has been no
A   B
greater contributor to the advancement

of architecture in the twentieth century than
C
that of Frank Lloyd Wright. No error
D   E

22. Constructing a fence ought not to be seen as
A
an insurmountable task; rather, it should be
B
viewed as a challenged that can be
C
accomplished by a combination of
D
perseverance and patience. No error
E

GO ON TO THE NEXT PAGE

23. If America <u>were</u> invaded by foreign forces, <u>all</u>
           A   B

able-bodied men <u>would,</u> <u>without hardly</u> a
                 C   D

doubt, enlist at the nearest armed services

recruitment center. <u>No error</u>
                    E

24. The pilot's carelessness, <u>as well as</u> her
                                A

equipment's malfunctioning, <u>was</u>
                           B

<u>responsible for</u> the <u>near-disaster</u> at Kennedy
     C   D

Airport. <u>No error</u>
        E

25. <u>Instead of</u> concentrating <u>on doing their</u>
        A   B

homework <u>as</u> they should, many teenagers
              C

watch television, talk on the phone, and

<u>they listen to the radio.</u> <u>No error</u>
            D   E

26. Vocalists <u>are</u> often able <u>to sing</u> oratories in
             A   B

flawless Latin, even if none of them <u>have</u> ever
                              C

<u>studied</u> Latin in school. <u>No error</u>
  D   E

GO ON TO THE NEXT PAGE

DIRECTIONS

Thes following sentences test your ability to express ideas in writing effectively and efficiently. Each sentence is either partially or completely underlined. The first of the five choices given will repeat the original wording and the other four choices will contain alternative wording. Choose the change that best improves the senetence or choose A if the original is superior to any of the other choices given.

In making your choice keep in mind the standards of proper written English. Among other things, pay close attention to grammar, word choice, punctuation, precision, and correct usage of tenses. Avoid awkward and ambiguous construction.

EXAMPLE:

I want your love, and I want your revenge; you and me can write a bad romance.

(A) you and me can write
(B) you and me could write
(C) you and me writing
(D) you and I can write
(E) me and you can write

27. The company, once close to filing for bankruptcy, is now a self-sufficient, competitive firm.

(A) The company, once close to filing for bankruptcy, is
(B) The company was once close to filing for bankruptcy, it is
(C) The company that once having been close to filing for bankruptcy is
(D) The company, because it was once close to filing for bankruptcy, is
(E) The company was once close to filing for bankruptcy, and it is

28. Dante Alighieri absorbed the sights and sounds of Florence, his native city, and these are impressions that are included in his best-known writing.

(A) these are impressions that are included
(B) the inclusion of these impressions is
(C) these impressions having been included
(D) his inclusion of these impressions
(E) included these impressions

29. One of the families of North American languages, Na-Dene, was once thought to be related with language families of the Eastern Hemisphere, including Sino-Tibetan, Basque, and Sumerian.

(A) to be related with language families of the Eastern Hemisphere, including
(B) to be related with the language families of the Easter Hemisphere, they include
(C) to be, in its relationship, including the language families of the Eastern Hemisphere
(D) related to language families of the Eastern Hemisphere and include
(E) to be related to language families of the Eastern Hemisphere that include

30. Neither Frances nor her sister appears like they are extroverts.

(A) like they are extroverts
(B) to be extroverts
(C) to be an extrovert
(D) like extroverts
(E) like an extrovert

GO ON TO THE NEXT PAGE

31. According to 1974 census reports, <u>the population of Tokyo was larger than that of any other city in the world except New York</u>.

  (A) the population of Tokyo was larger than that of any other city in the world except New York

  (B) the population of Tokyo was larger than that of any other cities in the world except that of New York

  (C) the population of Tokyo was larger than the population of any city in the world except for New York's

  (D) Tokyo had the largest population of any of the world's other cities except New York

  (E) Tokyo had the largest population of any city in the world except that of New York's

32. Since their readers often assume that journalists are objective and truthful, do journalists have a responsibility <u>that other writers do not</u>?

  (A) that other writers do not

  (B) that writers lack who are not journalists

  (C) lacking in others who are also writing

  (D) not had by those who write differently

  (E) when other writers have not

33. The composer, turning out countless jingles for TV <u>commercials, and tormented by</u> her sense of isolation from serious music.

  (A) commercials, and tormented by

  (B) commercials, tormented by

  (C) commercials, was tormented by

  (D) commercials; she found torment in

  (E) commercials; she was tormented by

34. In 1922, African American educator Anna Julia Cooper earned a doctorate at sixty-six, <u>and this is when most people consider retirement.</u>

  (A) and this is when most people Consider retirement

  (B) an age at which most people consider retirement

  (C) and by then most people consider retirement

  (D) considered by most people for being an age for retirement

  (E) which is considered retirement by most people

35. The earliest known encyclopedia still in existence <u>being the work of one person: Pliny the Elder, a Roman who</u> lived almost two thousand years ago.

  (A) being the work of one person: Pliny the Elder, a Roman who

  (B) being the work of one person, Pliny the Elder, a Roman and he

  (C) is the work of Pliny the Elder, the one person who

  (D) is the work of one person, Pliny the Elder, a Roman who

  (E) is the work of one person, Pliny the Elder, a Roman and that

GO ON TO THE NEXT PAGE

36. As a pediatrician with many years of experience, <u>advocating better nutrition for children, the doctor believes, should be the primary focus of physicians.</u>

(A) advocating better nutrition for children, the doctor believes, should be the primary focus of physicians

(B) the primary focus of physicians, the doctor believes, should be advocating better nutrition for children

(C) the doctor believes that advocating better nutrition for children should be the primary focus of physicians

(D) advocating better nutrition for children, which the doctor believes should be the primary focus of physicians

(E) the doctor has believed, advocating better nutrition for children should be the primary focus of physicians

37. If you desire something badly enough, <u>a person will probably attempt with all your might to acquire it.</u>

(A) a person will probably attempt with all your might to acquire it

(B) a determined attempt will probably be made to acquire it

(C) one will probably have attempted to acquire it with all his or her might

(D) you will probably attempt with all your might to acquire it

(E) you will probably have attempted with all your might to have acquired it

38. <u>If you cannot play Mozart, you cannot play Spanish music or any music, this is the opinion of Alicia de Larrocba.</u>

(A) If you cannot play Mozart, you cannot play Spanish music or any music, this is the opinion of Alicia de Larrocha

(B) Alicia de Larrocha's opinion is if you cannot play Mozart; one cannot play Spanish music or any music

(C) Accordfug to Alicia de Larrocha, not to be abie to play Mozart means you cannot play Spanish or any other music

(D) According to Alicia de Larrocha, if you cannot play Mozart, you cannot play Spanish music or any other music

(E) If a person cannot play Mozart, in Alicia de Larrocha's opinion, you cannot play Spanish music or any other music

39. <u>Opposite to what has always been taught to us,</u> a tourniquet should be applied only when heavy bleeding cannot be controlled.

(A) Opposite to what has always been taught to us

(B) Against that which has always been taught to us

(C) Contrary to that which bas always been taught us

(D) Against what we have always been taught

(E) Contrary to what we have always been taught

GO ON TO THE NEXT PAGE

40. He testified <u>as to its being hypocritical for a state supporting</u> its own state lottery while stamping out other forms of gambling.

(A) as to its being hypocritical for a state supporting
(B) about the hypocrisy there is for a state that supports
(C) that it is hypocritical for a state to support
(D) as regarding the hypocrisy of a state supporting
(E) about a state's hypocrisy when they support

41. People today <u>would be healthier if they have eaten</u> the lean meat, grains, nuts, and fruits that formed the diet of Stone Age hunters and gatherers.

(A) would be healthier if they have eaten
(B) would have healthier if they ate
(C) would be healthier if they are to eat
(D) would be healthy if they would have eaten
(E) would be healthier if they ate

42. <u>The soles of the feet of most bear species are bare, the soles</u> of polar bears have hair, which helps provide traction as they walk on ice.

(A) The soles of the feet of most bear species are bare, the soles
(B) The soles of the feet of most species of bear are bare, but the soles
(C) Whereas the soles of the feet of most species of bear are bare, but the soles
(D) Most species of bear have bare soles on their feet, and the soles
(E) Although the soles of the feet of most species of bear are bare, but the soles

43. Neither the opposition of some key Republicans <u>nor risking secession by the southern states were</u> sufficient to stop Lincoln from campaigning on the platform that slavery would not be expanded.

(A) nor risking secession by the southern states were
(B) nor the risk of secession by the southern states was
(C) nor risking that the southern states would secede was
(D) or the risk that the southern states would be seceding was
(E) or the risk of secession by the southern states were

44. Although Samarkand had been sacked by Alexander the Great, conquered by Arabs and Turks, and devastated by Genghis Khan, <u>Tamerlane, too, chose the ruined oasis city for his capital, and it was rebuilt.</u>

(A) Tamerlane, too, chose the ruined oasis city for his capital, and it was rebuilt
(B) the ruined oasis city was chosen by Tamerlane for his capital, whereupon he rebuilt it
(C) the ruined oasis city was chosen for his capital and rebuilt by Tamerlane
(D) the ruined oasis city was chosen by Tamerlane for his capital and rebuilt by him
(E) Tamerlane chose the ruined oasis city for his capital and had it rebuilt

GO ON TO THE NEXT PAGE

Questions 45-50 are based on the following passage.

[1] In the last fifty years, computers in many forms have become increasingly accessible. [2] For example, today the calculator is regarded as an essential tool for basic calculations by students and businesspeople. [3] The word processor, is considered indispensable by most writers, researchers, and office workers. [4] In addition, many families use computers to organize information, to balance budgets, and to provide entertainment.

[5] In spite of the growing popularity of computers, some people are genuinely afraid of these machines. [6] They fear that computers have intelligence and that they will take control over people and things. [7] Because of this fear, people lack the confidence to try the new technology.

[8] This is unfortunate. [9] Computers perform many important functions. [10] What would happen if we did not have any computers? [11] Not only would the cost of communications increase, and many processes would require more time than before to carry out. [12] Further, technological achievements such as space programs and scientific discoveries would probably slow down. [13] Computers have become an integral and important part of daily life. [14] To those of you who are afraid, we should remember that computers are simply advanced adding machines and typewriters!

45. Which of the following would be the most suitable sentence to insert immediately after sentence 1?
(A) The race is on to produce the "ultimate" computer.
(B) I have found the computer somewhat difficult to learn to operate.
(C) Many people are understandably intimidated by computers.
(D) They are now so common that they have a profound effect on daily life.
(E) Modern telephones belong to the family of computers.

46. To best connect sentence 3 to the rest of the first paragraph, which is the best word or phrase to insert after "*The word processor,*" in sentence 3 (reproduced below)?

The word processor, is considered indispensable by most writers, researchers, and office workers.

(A) surely,
(B) however,
(C) another form of computer,
(D) you see,
(E) contrastingly,

47. In context, sentence 8 could be made more precise by adding which of the following words after "*This*"?

(A) Technology
(B) Confidence
(C) Example
(D) Computer
(E) Situation

GO ON TO THE NEXT PAGE

48. The function of sentence 10 is to

(A) set up a hypothetical circumstance
(B) raise doubt in the reader's mind about the usefulness of computers
(C) allow the writer to take on a pose of humility
(D) contest a common assertion about computers
(E) show the writer's bewilderment about some aspect of computers

49. Which of following is the best revision of the underlined portion of sentence 11 (reproduced below)?

Not only would the cost of communications increase, and many processes would require more time than before to carry out.

(A) but so would the many processes require more time to carry out
(B) and also many processes require more time to carry out
(C) but they would require more time to carry out the process
(D) as well as to require more time for many processes to be carried out
(E) but so would the time required to carry out many processes

50. Which of the following versions of the underlined portion of sentence 14 (reproduced below) best suits the context?

To those of you who are afraid, we should remember that computers are simply advanced adding machines and typewriters!

(A) (As it is now)
(B) You who are fearing it should remember that computers
(C) But remember, you may be afraid that computers
(D) Those who are fearful should remember that computers
(E) What we fear about computers is that we see that they

STOP

this is the end of the exercise

Mathematics
16 practice exercises

SAT Math Exercise #01
34 questions

Reference Information

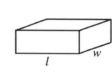

$A = \pi r^2$
$C = 2\pi r$
$A = lw$
$A = \frac{1}{2}bh$
$V = lwh$
$V = \pi r^2 h$
Special Right Triangles

The number of degrees in a circle is 360°
The angles of a triangle measured in degrees have a sum of 180°

1. $0.2 \times 0.02 \times 0.002 =$

(A) .08
(B) .008
(C) .0008
(D) .00008
(E) .000008

2. If it costs \$1.30 a square foot to lay linoleum, what will be the cost of laying 20 square yards of linoleum? (3 ft. = 1yd)

(A) \$47.50
(B) \$49.50
(C) \$150.95
(D) \$249.00
(E) \$234.00

3. In a family of five, the heights of the members are 5 feet 1 inch, 5 feet 7 inches, 5 feet 2 inches, 5 feet, and 4 feet 7 inches. The average height is
(A) 4 feet $4\frac{1}{5}$ inches.
(B)
(C) 5 feet
(D) 5 feet 1 inch
(E) 5 feet 2 inches
(F) 5 feet 3 inches

4. Three times the first of three consecutive odd integers is 3 more than twice the third. Find the third integer.

(A) 7
(B) 9
(C) 11
(D) 13
(E) 15

GO ON TO THE NEXT PAGE

5. In the figure below, the largest possible circle is cut out of a square piece of tin. The area, in square inches, of the remaining pieces of tin is approximately

(A) .14
(B) .75
(C) .86
(D) 1.0
(E) 3.14

6. The figure above shows on square inside another and a rectangle of diagonal T. The best approximation to the value of T, in inches, is given by which of the following inequalities?

(A) $8 < T < 9$
(B) $9 < T < 10$
(C) $10 < T < 11$
(D) $11 < T < 12$
(E) $12 < T < 13$

7. If nails are brought at 35 cents per dozen and sold at 3 for 10 cents, the total profits on $5\frac{1}{2}$ is

(A) 25 cents

(B) $27\frac{1}{2}$ cents

(C) $28\frac{1}{2}$ cents

(D) $31\frac{1}{2}$ cents

(E) 35 cents

8. The total number of eights in $2\frac{3}{4}$ is

(A) 11
(B) 14
(C) 19
(D) 22
(E) 24

9. What is the difference when $-x - y$ is subtracted from $-x^2 + 2y$?
(A) $x^2 - x - 3y$
(B) $-3x + y$
(C) $x^2 + 3y$
(D) $-x^2 + x - 3y$
(E) $x^2 + x + 3y$

GO ON TO THE NEXT PAGE

10. If $2^m = 4x$ and $2^w = 8x$, what is m in terms of w?

   (A) $w - 1$
   (B) $w + 1$
   (C) $2w - 1$
   (D) $2w + 1$
   (E) w^2

11. $1\frac{1}{4}$ subtracted from its reciprocal is

   (A) $\frac{9}{20}$

   (B) $\frac{1}{5}$

   (C) $-\frac{1}{20}$

   (D) $-\frac{1}{5}$

   (E) $-\frac{9}{20}$

12. The total number of feet in x yards, y feet, and z inches is

   (A) $3x + y + \frac{z}{12}$

   (B) $12(x + y + z)$

   (C) $x + y + z$

   (D) $\frac{x}{36} + \frac{y}{12} + z$

   (E) $x + 3y + 36z$

13. If five triangles are constructed having sides of the lengths indicated below, the triangle that will not be a right triangle is

   (A) 5, 12, 13
   (B) 3, 4, 5
   (C) 8, 15, 17
   (D) 9, 40, 41
   (E) 12, 15, 18

14. Of the following, the one that may be used correctly to compared to compute $26 \times 3\frac{1}{2}$ is

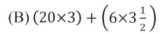

   (A) $(26 \times 30) + \left(26 \times \frac{1}{2}\right)$

   (B) $(20 \times 3) + \left(6 \times 3\frac{1}{2}\right)$

   (C) $\left(20 \times 3\frac{1}{2}\right) + (6 \times 3)$

   (D) $(20 \times 3) + \left(26 \times \frac{1}{2}\right) + \left(6 \times 3\frac{1}{2}\right)$

   (E) $\left(26 \times \frac{1}{2}\right) + (20 \times 3) + (6 \times 3)$

GO ON TO THE NEXT PAGE

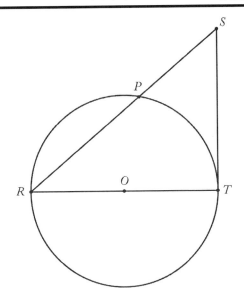

15. In the figure, ST is tangent to the circle at T.
RT is a diameter. If $RS = 12$, and $ST = 8$,
what is the area of the circle?

(A) 5π
(B) 8π
(C) 9π
(D) 20π
(E) 40π

16. What would be the marked price of an article
if the cost was $12.60 and the gain was 10%
of the selling price?

(A) $11.34
(B) $12.48
(C) $13.66
(D) $13.86
(E) $14.00

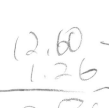

17. If the average weight of boys who are John's
age and height is 105 lbs, and if John weighs
110% of the average, then how many pounds
does John weigh?

(A) 110
(B) 110.5
(C) 112
(D) 114.5
(E) 115.5

18. The radius of a circle that has a circumference
equal to the perimeter of a hexagon whose
sides are 22 inches long is closest in length to
which of the following?

(A) 7
(B) 14
(C) 21
(D) 24
(E) 28

19. The average temperatures for five days were
$82°, 86°, 91, 79°, 91°$. What is the mode for
these temperatures?

91

GO ON TO THE NEXT PAGE

20. If $-2x + 5 = 2 - (5 - 2x)$, what is the value of x

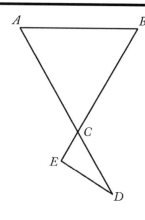

22. In the figure below, $AC = BC$. If $\angle B = 50°$, what is the measure of $\angle ECD$? (Do not use the degree symbol when gridding)

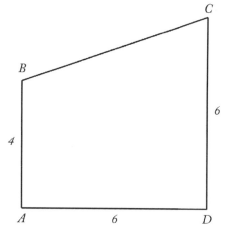

21. In the figure below, $BA \perp AD$ and $CD \perp AD$. Using the values indicated in the figure, what is the area of polygon $ABCD$?

23. What is the value of $-m^2n^3$, when $m = -2$ and $n = -1$?

24. Given a square, a rectangle, a trapezoid, and a circle, if one of these figures is selected at random, what is the probability that the figure has four right angles?

GO ON TO THE NEXT PAGE

25. Given the concentric circles above, if radius JN is 3 times JU, then the ratio of the shaded area to the area of sector NJL is $1:b$. What is the value of b?

26. In a three-hour examination of 350 questions, there are 50 mathematical problems. If twice as much time should be allowed for each problem as for each of the other questions, how many minutes should be spent

27. In the first year of the United States Stickball League, the Bayonne Bombers won 50% of their games. During the second season of the league the Bombers won 65% o their games. If there were twice as many games played in the second season as in the first, what percentage of the games did the Bombers win in the first two years of the league

   (A) 115%
   (B) 60%
   (C) 57.5%
   (D) 55%
   (E) It cannot be determined from the information given.

28. If the total weight of an apple is $\frac{4}{5}$ of its weight plus $\frac{4}{5}$ of an ounce, what is the weight in ounces

   (A) $1\frac{3}{5}$

   (B) $3\frac{1}{2}$

   (C) 4

   (D) $4\frac{1}{2}$

   (E) 5

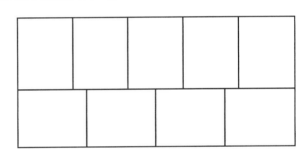

29. Nine playing cards from the same deck are placed as shown in the figure below to form a large rectangle of area 180 sq.in. How many inches are there in the perimeter of this large rectangle?

   (A) 29
   (B) 58
   (C) 64
   (D) 116
   (E) 210

GO ON TO THE NEXT PAGE

30. If each dimension of a rectangle is increased 10%, the area is increased

(A) 100%
(B) 200%
(C) 300%
(D) 400%
(E) 500%

31. A recipe for a cake calls for $2\frac{1}{2}$ cups of milk and 3 cups of flour. With this recipe, a cake was baked using 14 cups of flour. How many cups of milk were required?

(A) $10\frac{1}{3}$

(B) $10\frac{3}{4}$

(C) 11

(D) $11\frac{3}{5}$

(E) $11\frac{2}{3}$

32. In the figure below, M and N are midpoints of the sides PR and PQ, respectively of ΔPQR. What is the ration of the area of ΔMNS to that of ΔPQR?

(A) 2 : 5
(B) 2 : 9
(C) 1 : 4
(D) 1 : 8
(E) 1 : 12

33. What is 10% of $\frac{1}{3}x$ if $\frac{2}{3}x$ is 105 if 60?

(A) . 1
(B) . 2
(C) . 3
(D) . 4
(E) . 5

34. The front wheels of a wagon are 7 feet in circumference and the back wheels are 9 feet in circumference. When the front wheels have made 10 more revolutions than the back wheels, what distance in feet has the wagon gone?

(A) 126
(B) 180
(C) 189
(D) 315
(E) 630

STOP

this is the end of the exercise

SAT Math Exercise #02

34 questions

Reference Information

   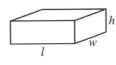

$A = \pi r^2$
$C = 2\pi r$ $\quad A = lw \quad\quad A = \frac{1}{2}bh \quad\quad V = lwh \quad\quad V = \pi r^2 h \quad$ *Special Right Triangles*

The number of degrees in a circle is 360°
The angles of a triangle measured in degrees have a sum of 180°

---

1. The total savings in purchasing thirty 13-cent lollipops for a class party for a class party at a reduced rate of $1.38 per dozen is

   (A) $0.35
   (B) $0.38
   (C) $0.40
   (D) $0.45
   (E) $0.50

---

2. A gallon of water is equal to 231 cubic inches. How many gallons of water are needed to fill a fish tank that measures 11" high, 14" long, and 9" wide?

   (A) 6
   (B) 8
   (C) 9
   (D) 14
   (E) 16

---

3. The area of a right triangle is 12 square inches. The ratio of its legs is 2:3. Find the number of inches in the hypotenuse of this triangle

   (A) $\sqrt{13}$
   (B) $\sqrt{26}$
   (C) $3\sqrt{13}$
   (D) $\sqrt{52}$
   (E) $4\sqrt{13}$

---

4. A rectangular block of metal weighs 3 ounces. How many pounds will a similar block of the same metal weigh if the edges are twice as large?

   (A) $\frac{3}{8}$
   (B) $\frac{3}{4}$
   (C) $1\frac{1}{2}$
   (D) 3
   (E) 24

GO ON TO THE NEXT PAGE

5. A college graduate goes to work for x dollars per week. After several months the company gives all the employees a 10% pay cut. A few months later the company gives all the employees as 10% raise. What is the college graduate's new salary?

(A). $90x$
(B). $99x$
(C) x
(D) $1.01x$
(E) $1.11x$

6. What is the next among of a bill of $428.00 after a discount of 6% has been allowed

(A) $432.62
(B) $430.88
(C) $414.85
(D) 412.19
(E) 402.32

7. A certain type of boar is sold only in length of multiples of 2 feet, from 6 feet, to 24 feet. A builder needs a large quantity of this type of board in $5\frac{1}{2}$ foot lengths. For minimum waste, the lengths in feet to be ordered should be

(A) 6
(B) 12
(C) 18
(D) 22
(E) 24

8. A cube has an edge which if four inches long. If the edge is increased by 25%, then the volume is increased by approximately.

(A) 25%
(B) 48%
(C) 73%
(D) 95%
(E) 122%

9. The ratio of $\frac{1}{4}$ to $\frac{3}{5}$ is

(A) 1 to 3
(B) 3 to 20
(C) 5 to 12
(D) 3 to 4
(E) 5 to 4

10. Which of the following numbers is the smallest?

(A) $\sqrt{3}$
(B) $\frac{1}{\sqrt{3}}$
(C) $\frac{\sqrt{3}}{3}$
(D) $\frac{1}{3}$
(E) $\frac{1}{3\sqrt{3}}$

GO ON TO THE NEXT PAGE

11. One angle of a triangle is 82°. The other two angles are in the ratio 2:5. Find the number of degrees in the smallest angle of the triangle.

(A) 14
(B) 25
(C) 28
(D) 38
(E) 82

12. Village A has a population of 6,800, which is decreasing at a rate of 120 per year. Village B has a population of 4,200, which is increasing at a rate of 80 per year. In how many years will the population of the two villages be equal?

(A) 9
(B) 11
(C) 13
(D) 14
(E) 16

13. If $* x$ is defined such that $* x = x^2 - 2x$, the value of $* 2 - * 1 =$

(A) -1
(B) 0
(C) 1
(D) 2
(E) 4

14. In a right triangle, the ratio of the legs is 1:2. If the area of the triangle is 25 square units, what is the length of the hypotenuse?

(A) $\sqrt{5}$
(B) $5\sqrt{5}$
(C) $5\sqrt{3}$
(D) $10\sqrt{3}$
(E) $25\sqrt{5}$

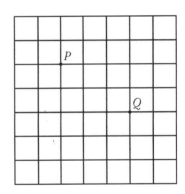

15. In the graph above, the axes and the origin are not shown. If point P has coordinates $(3,7)$, what are the coordinates of point Q, assuming each box is one unit?

(A) (5,6)
(B) (1,10)
(C) (6,9)
(D) (6,5)
(E) (5,10)

GO ON TO THE NEXT PAGE

16. If $r = 5x$, how many tenths of
r does $\frac{1}{2}$ of x equal?

(A) 1
(B) 2
(C) 3
(D) 4
(E) 5

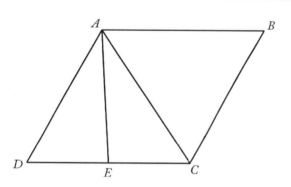

17. $ABCD$ is a parallelogram, and $DE = EC$.
What is the ratio of the triangle ADE to the
area of the parallelogram?

(A) 2:5
(B) 1:2
(C) 1:3
(D) 1:4
(E) Cannot be determined from the
information given.

18. In any square, the length of one side is

(A) One-half the diagonal of the square
(B) The square root of the perimeter of the
square
(C) About .7 the length of the diagonal of the
square
(D) The square root of the diagonal
(E) One-fourth the area

19. $\left(\sqrt{18} - \sqrt{18}\right)^2 =$

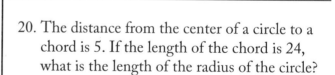

20. The distance from the center of a circle to a
chord is 5. If the length of the chord is 24,
what is the length of the radius of the circle?

GO ON TO THE NEXT PAGE

21. If the cost of a party is to be split equally among 11 friends, each would pay $15.00. if 20 persons equally split the same cost, how much would each person pay?

5.25

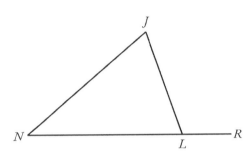

22. In the figure, $m\angle N = (9x + 40)^\circ$ and $m\angle JLR = (8x = 40)^\circ$. What is the measure of $\angle J$?

79°

23. $\frac{2^3 + 3^2}{5^2} + \frac{1}{10} =$ 0.62

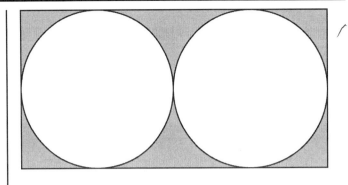

24. In the figure above two circles are tangent to each other and each is tangent to three sides of the rectangle. If the radius of each circle is 3, then the area of the shaded portion is $a - b\pi$. What is the value of a and b?

a=72
b=18

25. The measures of the angles of a triangle are in the ratio of 3:5:7. What is the measure, in degrees, of the smallest angle?

36

GO ON TO THE NEXT PAGE

26. The length of the line segment whose end points are $(3, -2)$ and $(-4, 5)$ is $b\sqrt{2}$ what is the value of b?

$b = 7$

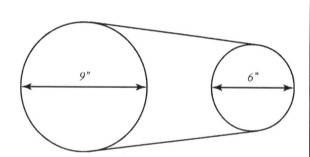

27. A pulley having a 9-inch diameter is belted to a pulley having a 6-inch diameter, as shown in the figure. If the large pulley runs at 120 rpm, how fast does the small pulley run, in revolutions per minute?

(A) 80
(B) 100
(C) 160
(D) 180
(E) 240

28. The number of degrees through which the hour hand of a clock moves in 2 hours and 12 minutes is?

(A) 66
(B) 72
(C) 126
(D) 732
(E) 792

29. The average of 8 numbers is 6; the average of 6 other numbers is 8. What is the average of all 14 numbers?

(A) 6
(B) $6\frac{6}{7}$
(C) $6\frac{6}{7}$
(D) $7\frac{2}{7}$
(E) $8\frac{6}{7}$

30. If x is between 0 and 1, which of the following increases as x increases?

I. $1 - x^2$
II. $x - 1$
III. $\frac{1}{x^2}$

(A) I and II
(B) II and III
(C) I and III
(D) II only
(E) I only

GO ON TO THE NEXT PAGE

31. In the series 3, 7, 12, 18, 25, ... the 9th term is

   (A) 50
   (B) 63
   (C) 75
   (D) 86
   (E) 88

32. Simplify $\frac{x^2-y^2}{x-y}$

   (A) $\frac{xy}{x+y}$

   (B) $\frac{x+y}{xy}$

   (C) $x + y$
   (D) x
   (E) $x^2 + y^2 - 1$

33. A rectangular flowerbed, dimensions 16 yards by 12 yards, is surrounded by a wall 3 yards wide. The area of the walk in square yards is

   (A) 78
   (B) 93
   (C) 132
   (D) 204
   (E) 396

34. Doreen can wash her car in 15 minutes, while her younger brother Dave takes twice as long to do the same job. If they work together, how many minutes will the job take them?

   (A) 5

   (B) $7\frac{1}{2}$

   (C) 10

   (D) $22\frac{1}{2}$

   (E) 30

STOP

this is the end of the exercise

SAT Math Exercise #03
34 questions

1. A circle inscribed in a given square and another circle is circumscribed about the same square. What is the ratio of the area of the inscribed to the circumscribed circle?

   (A) 1 : 4
   (B) 4 : 9
   (C) 1 : 2
   (D) 2 : 3
   (E) 3 : 4

2. If $\frac{3}{7}$ of a bucket can be filled in 1 minute, how many minutes will it take to fill the rest of the bucket?

   (A) $\frac{7}{3}$

   (B) $\frac{4}{3}$

   (C) 1

   (D) $\frac{3}{4}$

   (E) $\frac{4}{7}$

   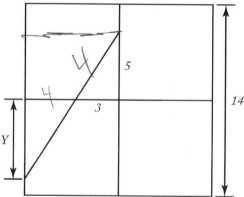

3. In the figure above, the side of the large square is 14. The four smaller squares are formed by joining the midpoints of opposite sides. Find the value of Y.

   (A) 5
   (B) 6
   (C) $6\frac{5}{8}$
   (D) $6\frac{2}{3}$
   (E) 6.8

GO ON TO THE NEXT PAGE

4. If the base of a rectangle is increased by 30% and the altitude is decreased by 20%, the area is increased by

(A) 4%
(B) 5%
(C) 10%
(D) 25%
(E) 104%

5. Using 9×12-inch sheet of paper lengthwise a typist leaves a 1-inch margin on each side and a $1\frac{1}{2}$ inch margin on top and bottom. What fractional part of the page is used for typing?

(A) $\frac{5}{12}$

(B) $\frac{7}{12}$

(C) $\frac{5}{9}$

(D) $\frac{3}{4}$

(E) $\frac{21}{22}$

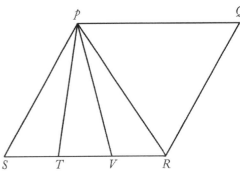

6. In the figure, $PQRS$ is a parallelogram, and $ST = TV = VR$. What is the ratio of the area of the triangle SPT to the area of the parallelogram?

(A) $\frac{1}{6}$

(B) $\frac{1}{5}$

(C) $\frac{2}{7}$

(D) $\frac{1}{3}$

(E) It cannot be determined from the information given

7. Which of the following quantities has the lowest numerical value?

(A) $\frac{4}{5}$

(B) $\frac{7}{9}$

(C) $.76$

(D) $\frac{5}{7}$

(E) $\frac{9}{11}$

GO ON TO THE NEXT PAGE

8. A salesperson earns twice as much in December as in each of the other months of a year. What part of this salesperson's entire year's earnings are earned in December?

(A) $\frac{1}{7}$

(B) $\frac{2}{13}$

(C) $\frac{1}{6}$

(D) $\frac{2}{11}$

(E) $\frac{3}{14}$

9. If $x = -1$, then $3x^3 + 2x^2 + x + 1 =$

(A) -5

(B) -1

(C) 1

(D) 2

(E) 5

10. $.03\% \times 2.1$

(A) .63

(B) .063

(C) .0063

(D) .00063

(E) .000063

11. An equilateral triangle 3 inches on a side is cut up into smaller equilateral triangles one inch on a side. What is the greatest number of such triangles that can be formed?

(A) 3

(B) 6

(C) 9

(D) 12

(E) 15

12. A square 5 units on a side has one vertex at the point (1,1). Which one of the following points *cannot* be diagonally opposite that vertex?

(A) (6,6)

(B) (−4,6)

(C) (−4, −4)

(D) (6, −4)

(E) (4, −6)

13. Five equal squares are placed side by side to make a single rectangle whose perimeter is 372 inches. Find the number of square inches in the area of one of these squares.

(A) 72

(B) 324

(C) 900

(D) 961

(E) 984

GO ON TO THE NEXT PAGE

14. The water level of a swimming pool 75 feet by 42 feet, is to be raised four inches. How many gallons of water must be added to accomplish this?

(7.48 gal = 1 cubic ft.)

(A) 140
(B) 7,854
(C) 31,500
(D) 94,500
(E) 727,650

15. What part of the total quantity is represented by a 24-degree sector of a circle graph?

(A) $6\frac{2}{3}$%

(B) 12%

(C) $13\frac{1}{3}$%

(D) 15%
(E) 24%

16. The square of a fraction between 0 and 1 is

(A) Less than the original fraction
(B) Greater than the original fraction
(C) Twice the original fraction
(D) Less than the cube of the fraction
(E) Not necessarily any of the preceding

17. If $2y = \frac{1}{3}$, then $\frac{1}{4y} =$

(A) $\frac{3}{2}$

(B) $\frac{3}{4}$

(C) $\frac{2}{5}$

(D) $\frac{1}{5}$

(E) $\frac{4}{3}$

18. Pieces of wire are soldered together so as to form the edges of a cube, whose volume is 64 cubic inches. The number of inches of wire used is

(A) 24
(B) 48
(C) 64
(D) 96
(E) 120

19. Jessica caught five fish with an average weight of 10 pounds. If three of the fish weigh 9, 9, and 10 pounds, respectively, what is the average (arithmetic mean) weight of the other two fish?

GO ON TO THE NEXT PAGE

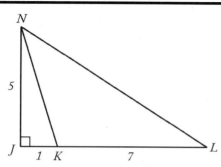

20. In the figure above, what is the area of ΔNKL?

21. The average of 8 numbers is 6; the average of 6 other numbers is 8. What is the average of all 14 numbers?

22. If $3a + 5b = 10$, and $a - b = 6$, find the value of $7a + 7b$

23. $a - b = b - c = c - a$. What is the value of $\frac{2a+3b}{c}$?

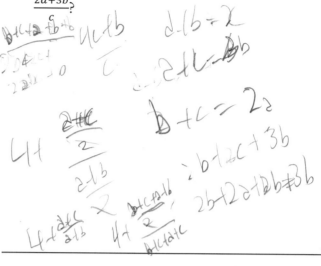

24. If $\frac{4}{3}$ is subtracted from its reciprocal, the result is

25. If the ratio of $a:b$ is 1:5 and the ratio pf $b:c$ is 3:2. Then the ratio of $(a + c):c$ is

GO ON TO THE NEXT PAGE

26. If $4x - 9 = 27$, what is x^3?

27. If a box of notepaper costs \$4.20 after a 40% discount, what was its original price?

(A) \$2.52
(B) \$4.60
(C) \$5.33
(D) \$7.00
(E) \$10.50

28. A is 15 ears old. B is one-third older. How many years ago was B twice as old as A?

(A) 3
(B) 5
(C) 7.5
(D) 8
(E) 10

29. The distance s, in feet that an object falls in t seconds when dropped from a height is obtained by use of the formula $s = 16t^2$. How many feet will an object fall in 8 seconds?

(A) 256
(B) 1,024
(C) 2,048
(D) 15,384
(E) 16,000

30. Three circles are tangent externally to each other and have radii of 2 inches, 3 inches, and 4 inches, respectively. How many inches are in the perimeter of the triangle formed by joining centers of the three circles?

(A) 9
(B) 12
(C) 15
(D) 18
(E) 21

31. One-tenth is what part of three-fourths?

(A) $\frac{3}{40}$
(B) $\frac{1}{18}$
(C) $\frac{2}{15}$
(D) $\frac{15}{2}$
(E) $\frac{40}{3}$

GO ON TO THE NEXT PAGE

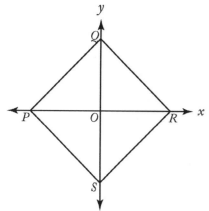

32. The area of square $PQRS$ is 49. What are the coordinates of Q?

(A) $\left(\frac{7}{2}\sqrt{2}, 0\right)$

(B) $\left(0, \frac{7}{2}\sqrt{2}\right)$

(C) $(0,7)$

(D) $(7,0)$

(E) $\left(0, \frac{7}{2}\sqrt{2}\right)$

---

33. If $9x + 5 = 23$, what is the numerical value of $18x + 5$?

(A) 46

(B) 41

(C) 36

(D) 32

(E) It cannot be determined from the information given.

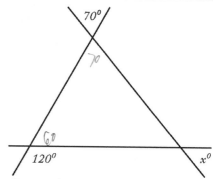

34. In the figure above, $x =$

(A) 35

(B) 50

(C) 70

(D) 90

(E) 110

STOP

this is the end of the exercise

SAT Math Exercise #04

34 questions

Reference Information

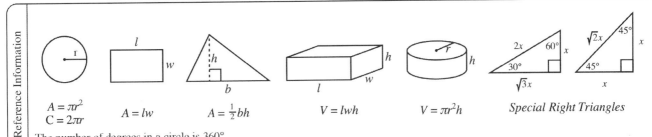

$A = \pi r^2$
$C = 2\pi r$

$A = lw$

$A = \frac{1}{2}bh$

$V = lwh$

$V = \pi r^2 h$

Special Right Triangles

The number of degrees in a circle is 360°
The angles of a triangle measured in degrees have a sum of 180°

1. If one-half of the female students in a certain college eat in the cafeteria and one-third of the male students eat there, what fractional part of the student body eats in the cafeteria?

    (A) $\frac{5}{12}$

    (B) $\frac{5}{12}$

    (C) $\frac{5}{12}$

    (D) $\frac{5}{12}$

    (E) It cannot be determined from the information given.

2. A recent report states that if you were to eat each meal in a different restaurant in New York City, it would take you more than 19 years to cover all of New York City's eating places, assuming that you eat three meals a day. On the basis of this information, the number of restaurants in New York City

    (A) Exceeds 20,500
    (B) Is closer to 20,000 than 21,00
    (C) Exceeds 21,000
    (D) Exceeds 21,000 but does not exceed 21,500
    (E) Is less than 20,500

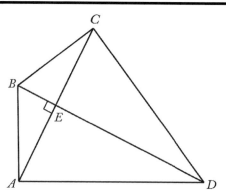

3. In the figure below, $AB = BC$ and angle BEA is a right angle. If the length of DE is four times the length of BE

(A) 1 : 4
(B) 1 : 2
(C) 2 : 1
(D) 4 : 1
(E) It cannot be determined from the information given

4. A pound of water is evaporated from 6 pounds to seawater containing 4% salt. The percentage of salt in the remaining solution is

(A) 3.6%
(B) 4%
(C) 4.8%
(D) 5.2%
(E) 6%

5. The product of 75^3 and 75^7 is

(A) $(75)^5$
(B) $(75)^{10}$
(C) $(150)^{10}$
(D) $(5626)^{10}$
(E) $(75)^{21}$

6. The distance from City A to City B is 150 miles and the distance from City A and City C is 90 miles. Therefore, it is necessarily true that

(A) the distance between B and C is 60 miles.
(B) six times the distance from A to B equals 10 times the distance from A and C.
(C) the distance from B and C is 240 miles.
(D) the distance from A and C exceeds by 30 miles twice the distance from A to C.
(E) three times the distance from A to C exceeds by 30 miles twice the distance from A to B.

7. If $a + b = 3$ and $ab = 4$, then $\frac{1}{a} + \frac{1}{b} =$

(A) $\frac{3}{4}$
(B) $\frac{3}{7}$
(C) $\frac{4}{7}$
(D) $\frac{1}{7}$
(E) $\frac{1}{12}$

8. $(x)^6 + (2x^2)^2 + (3x^3)^2 =$

(A) $5x^5 + x^6$
(B) $17x^5 + x^6$
(C) $6x^6$
(D) $18x^6$
(E) $6x^{18}$

GO ON TO THE NEXT PAGE

9. The scale of a map is $\frac{3}{4}$ inch = 10 miles. If the distance on the map between two towns is 6 inches, the actual distance in miles is

(A) 45
(B) 60
(C) 75
(D) 80
(E) 90

10. If $d = m - \frac{50}{m}$, and m is a positive number, then as m increases in value, d

(A) Increases in value
(B) Decreases in value
(C) Remains unchanged
(D) Increases, then decreases
(E) Decreases, then increases

11. If a cubic inch of metal weighs 2 pounds, a cubic foot of the same metal weighs how many pounds?

(A) 8
(B) 24
(C) 96
(D) 288
(E) 3,456

12. If the number of square inches in the area of a circle is equal to the number of inches in its circumference, the diameter of the circle in inches is

(A) 4
(B) π
(C) 2
(D) $\frac{\pi}{2}$
(E) 1

13. John is now three times Pat's age. Four years from now John will be x years old. In terms of x, how old is Pat now?

(A) $\frac{x+4}{3}$
(B) $3x$
(C) $x + 4$
(D) $x - 4$
(E) $\frac{x-4}{3}$

14. In the figure, what percent of the area of rectangle $PQRS$ is shaded?

(A) 20
(B) 25
(C) 30
(D) $33\frac{1}{3}$
(E) 35

GO ON TO THE NEXT PAGE

15. One wheel has a diameter of 30 inches and a second wheel has a diameter of 20 inches. The first wheel traveled a certain distance in 240 revolutions. In how many revolutions did the second wheel travel the same distance?

   (A) 120
   (B) 160
   (C) 360
   (D) 420
   (E) 480

16. The one of the following to which 1.86×10^5 is equivalent is

   (A) 18,600
   (B) 186,000
   (C) 18,600,000
   (D) $186 \times 500,000$
   (E) 1,860,000

17. How many of the numbers between 100 and 300 begin or end with 2?

   (A) 20
   (B) 40
   (C) 100
   (D) 110
   (E) 180

18. The area of a square is $49x^2$. What is the length of a diagonal of the square?

   (A) $7x$
   (B) $7x\sqrt{2}$
   (C) $1\frac{1}{8}$
   (D) $1\frac{1}{4}$
   (E) $1\frac{1}{2}$

19. Joshua bought two dozen apples for 3 dollars. At this rate, how much will 18 apples cost? (Do not grid the dollar sign)

20. What is $\frac{1}{10}$% of $\frac{1}{10}$ of 10?

GO ON TO THE NEXT PAGE

21. $\dfrac{-\frac{1}{3}}{3} - \dfrac{3}{-\frac{1}{3}} =$

22. Dawn's average for four math tests is 80. What score must she receive on her next exam to increase her average by three points?

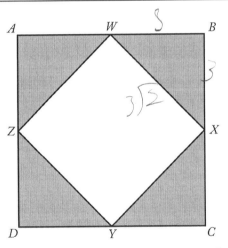

23. In the figure below, square $WXYZ$ is formed by connecting the midpoints of sides of square $ABCD$. If the length of $AB = 6$, what is the area of the shaded region?

24. Thirty thousand two hundred and forty minutes is equivalent to how many weeks?

25. In the figure below, line L_1 is parallel to L_2. Transversals t_1 and t_2 are drawn. What is the value of $a + b + c + d$? (Do not grid the degree symbol.)

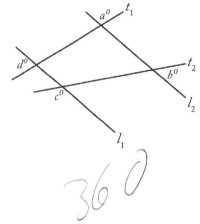

26. A car traveled from town A to town B, a distance of 360 miles, in 9 hours. How many hours would the same trip have taken had the car travelled 5 mph faster?

GO ON TO THE NEXT PAGE

27. If shipping charges to a certain point are 62 cents for the first five ounces and 8 cents for each additional ounce, the weight of the a package, in pounds, for which the charges are $1.66 is

(A) $\frac{7}{8}$

(B) 1

(C) $1\frac{1}{8}$

(D) $1\frac{1}{4}$

(E) $1\frac{1}{2}$

28. If 15 cans of food are needed for seven adults for two days, the number of cans needed to feed four adults for seven days is

(A) 15
(B) 20
(C) 25
(D) 30
(E) 35

29. A rectangle sign is cut down by 10% of its height and 30% of its width. What percent of the original area remains?

(A) 30
(B) 37
(C) 57
(D) 63
(E) 70

30. If the average (arithmetic mean) of a series of numbers is 20 and their sum is 160, how many numbers are in the series?

(A) 8
(B) 16
(C) 32
(D) 48
(E) 80

31. If the result of squaring a number is less than the number, the number is

(A) Negative and greater than -1
(B) Negative and less than -1
(C) A positive fraction greater than 1
(D) Positive and less than 1
(E) 1 and only 1

32. If for all real numbers (a.b.c. − d.e.f.) = (a − d) × (b − e) × (c − f), then (4.5.6 − 1.2.3.) =

(A) -27
(B) 0
(C) 27
(D) 54
(E) 108

GO ON TO THE NEXT PAGE

33. The sum of an odd number and an even number is

    (A) Sometimes an even number
    (B) Always divisible by 3 or 5 or 7
    (C) Always an odd number
    (D) Always a prime number (not divisible)
    (E) Always divisible by 2

34. If $6x + 12 = 9$, $x^2 =$

    (A) $\frac{21}{6}$
    (B) $-\frac{1}{2}$
    (C) $\frac{9}{12}$
    (D) $\frac{1}{4}$
    (E) $\frac{9}{6}$

STOP

this is the end of the exercise

SAT Math Exercise #05

34 questions

Reference Information

   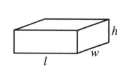

$A = \pi r^2$
$C = 2\pi r$ $A = lw$ $A = \frac{1}{2}bh$ $V = lwh$ $V = \pi r^2 h$ *Special Right Triangles*

The number of degrees in a circle is 360°
The angles of a triangle measured in degrees have a sum of 180°

---

1. Under certain conditions, sound travels at about 1,100 ft. per second. If 88 ft. per second is approximately equivalent to 60 miles per hour, the speed of sound in miles per hour under the above conditions is closest to

    (A) 730
    (B) 740
    (C) 750
    (D) 760
    (E) 780

2. If on a blueprint $\frac{1}{4}$ inch equals 12 inches, what is the actual length in feet of a steel bar that is represented on the blueprint by a line $3\frac{3}{8}$ inches long?

    (A) $2\frac{1}{2}$

    (B) $3\frac{3}{8}$

    (C) $6\frac{3}{4}$

    (D) 9

    (E) $13\frac{1}{2}$

GO ON TO THE NEXT PAGE

3. If one angle of a triangle is three times a second angle and the third angle is 20 degrees more than the second angle, the second angle, in degrees, is

(A) 64
(B) 50
(C) 40
(D) 34
(E) 32

4. If $x = \frac{3}{2}$ and $y = 2$, then $x + y^2 - \frac{1}{2} =$

(A) 5
(B) 10
(C) $11\frac{1}{2}$
(D) $9\frac{1}{2}$
(E) $\frac{6}{2}$

5. A math class has 27 students in it. Of those students, 14 are also enrolled in history and 17 are enrolled in English. What is the minimum percentage of the students in math class who also enrolled in history *and* English?

(A) 15%
(B) 22%
(C) 49%
(D) 63%
(E) 91%

6. A cylindrical container has a diameter of 14 inches and a height of 6 inches. Since one gallon equals 231 cubic inches, the capacity of the tank in gallons is approximately

(A) $\frac{2}{3}$
(B) $1\frac{1}{7}$
(C) $2\frac{2}{7}$
(D) $2\frac{2}{3}$
(E) 4

7. If $\frac{1}{x+y} = 6$ and $x = 2$, then $y =$

(A) $-\frac{11}{6}$
(B) $-\frac{9}{4}$
(C) -2
(D) -1
(E) 4

8. The number of grams in one ounce is 28.35. The number of grams in a kilometer is 1,000. Therefore the number of kilograms in one pound is approximately

(A) 0.045
(B) 0.45
(C) 1.0
(D) 2.2
(E) 4.5

GO ON TO THE NEXT PAGE

9. Which of the following numbers is not the square of a rational number?

   (A) .0016
   (B) .16
   (C) 1.6
   (D) 16
   (E) 1,600

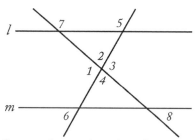

10. In the figure above, line l and m are parallel. Which of the following must be equal to 180 degrees?
   I.   1 plus 3
   II.   2 plus 4
   III. 5 plus 6
   IV.   7 plus 8
   V.   8 plus 6

   (A) I and II only
   (B) III and IV only
   (C) V only
   (D) I, II, III, IV only
   (E) I, II, III, IV, V

11. If x is a fraction which ranges from $\frac{1}{4}$ to $\frac{1}{2}$ and y is a fraction which ranges from $\frac{3}{4}$ to $\frac{11}{12}$, what is the maximum value for $\frac{x}{y}$?

   (A) $\frac{3}{16}$
   (B) $\frac{11}{48}$
   (C) $\frac{3}{8}$
   (D) $\frac{11}{24}$
   (E) $\frac{2}{3}$

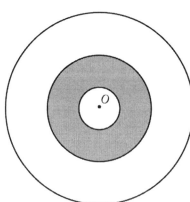

12. These circles share a common center, point 0. The smallest circle has a radius of 2, the next circle a radius of 5, and the largest circle a radius of 9. What fraction of the area of the largest circle is the area of the shaded region?

   (A) $\frac{7}{27}$
   (B) $\frac{25}{81}$
   (C) $\frac{1}{3}$
   (D) $\frac{7}{11}$
   (E) $\frac{12}{17}$

GO ON TO THE NEXT PAGE

13. If n and d represent positive whole numbers (n > d > 1), the fractions

   I. $\frac{d}{n}$

   II. $\frac{d+1}{n+1}$

   III. $\frac{d-1}{n-1}$

   IV. $\frac{n}{d}$

   V. $\frac{n-1}{d-1}$

arranged in ascending order of magnitude are represented correctly by

(A) III, II, I, V, IV
(B) IV, V, III, I, II
(C) II, I, IV, III, V
(D) III, V, IV, I, II
(E) III, I, II, IV, V

14. A train running between two towns arrives at its destination 10 minutes late when it goes 40 miles per hour and 16 minutes late when it goes 30 miles per hour. The distance in miles between the towns is

(A) $8\frac{6}{7}$
(B) 12
(C) 192
(D) 560
(E) 720

15. A square has a diagonal of x units. If the diagonal is increased by 2 units, what is the length of the side of the new square?

(A) $x + 2$
(B) $(x + 2)\sqrt{2}$
(C) $\frac{(x+2)\sqrt{2}}{2}$
(D) $(x + 2)2$
(E) $\frac{(x+2)\sqrt{2}}{4}$

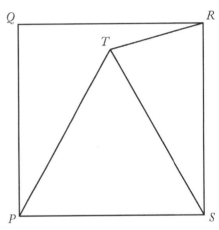

16. $PQRS$ is a square and PTS is an equilateral triangle. How many degrees are there in angle TRS?

(A) 60
(B) 75
(C) 80
(D) 90
(E) It cannot be determined from the information given.

GO ON TO THE NEXT PAGE

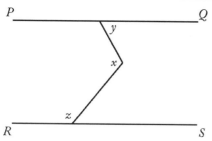

17. In the figure above, line PQ is parallel to line RS, angle $y = 60^0$, and angle $z = 130^0$. How many degrees are there in angle x?

(A) 90°
(B) 100°
(C) 110°
(D) 120°
(E) 130°

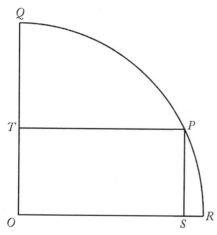

18. In the figure above, QOR is a quadrant of a circle. $PS = 6$ and $PT = 8$. What is the length of arc QR?

(A) 5π
(B) 10π
(C) 20π
(D) 24π
(E) It cannot be determined from the information given.

19. What is the ratio of 6 minutes to 6 hours?

1:60

20. At Ungerville High School, the ratio of girls to boys is 2:1. If $\frac{3}{5}$ of the boys are on a team and the remaining 40 boys are not, how many girls are in the school?

200

21. Jerry grew 5 inches in 1993, and 2 inches more in 1994 before reaching his final height of 5 feet 10 inches. What percentage of his final height did his 1993-1994 growth represent?

10%

GO ON TO THE NEXT PAGE

22. If $p = 2r = 3s = 4t$, then $\dfrac{pr}{st} =$

23. $\sqrt{7 + 9 + 7 + 9 + 7 + 9 + 7 + 9} =$

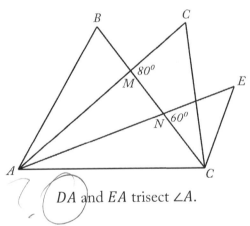

DA and EA trisect ∠A.

24. If $\angle DMC = 80°$ and $\angle ENC = 60°$, then
$\angle A =$

25. $\dfrac{\frac{7}{8} + \frac{7}{8} + \frac{7}{8}}{\frac{8}{7} + \frac{8}{7} + \frac{8}{7}}$

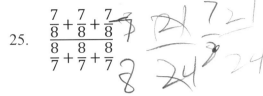

26. If the ratio of 4a to 3b is 8 to 9, what is the
ratio of 3a to 4b?

27. The ice compartment in a refrigerator is 8
inches deep, 5 inches high, and 4 inches wide.
How many ice cubes will it hold if each cube
is 2 inches on each edge?

(A) 16
(B) 20
(C) 24
(D) 80
(E) 160

GO ON TO THE NEXT PAGE

28. If Paul can paint a fence in 2 hours and Fred can paint the same fence in 3 hours, Paul and Fred working together can paint the fence in how many hours?

(A) 2.5

(B) $\frac{5}{6}$

(C) 5

(D) 1

(E) 1.2

29. If one-third of the liquid contents of a can evaporates on the first day and the three-fourths of the remainder evaporates on the second day, the fractional part of the original contents remaining at the close of the second day is

(A) $\frac{1}{6}$

(B) $\frac{1}{4}$

(C) $\frac{5}{12}$

(D) $\frac{1}{2}$

(E) $\frac{7}{12}$

30. A motorist drives 60 miles to her destination at an average speed of 40 miles per hour and makes the return trip at an average rate of 30 miles per hour. Her average speed in miles per hour for the entire trip is

(A) 17

(B) $34\frac{2}{7}$

(C) 35

(D) $43\frac{1}{3}$

(E) 70

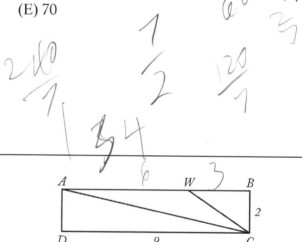

31. In the figure above, BW is one third the length of AB. What is the area of triangle ACW?

(A) 4

(B) 5

(C) 6

(D) 8

(E) 9

GO ON TO THE NEXT PAGE

32. Of the following, the one that is not equivalent to 376 is

   (A) $(3\times100) + (6\times10) + 16$
   (B) $(2\times100) + (17\times10) + 6$
   (C) $(3\times100) + (7\times10) + 6$
   (D) $(2\times100) + (16\times10) + 6$
   (E) $(2\times100) + (7\times10) + 106$

33. Emily can pack 6 cartons in h days. At this rate she can pack $3h$ cartons in how many days?

   (A) 18
   (B) 2h
   (C) h^2
   (D) $\dfrac{h^2}{2}$
   (E) $2h^2$

34. What is the total length of fencing needed to enclose a rectangular area 46 feet by 34 feet (3ft=1yd.)?

   (A) 26 yards 1 foot
   (B) $26\frac{2}{3}$ yards
   (C) 52 yards 2 feet
   (D) $53\frac{1}{3}$ yards
   (E) $37\frac{2}{3}$ yards

STOP

this is the end of the exercise

SAT Math Exercise #06

34 questions

Reference Information

   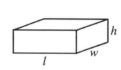

$A = \pi r^2$
$C = 2\pi r$

$A = lw$

$A = \frac{1}{2}bh$

$V = lwh$

$V = \pi r^2 h$

Special Right Triangles

The number of degrees in a circle is 360°
The angles of a triangle measured in degrees have a sum of 180°

1. On an income of \$15,000 a year, a clerk pays 15% in federal taxes and 10% of the remainder in state taxes. How much is left?

   (A) \$9,750
   (B) \$11,475
   (C) \$12,750
   (D) \$13,500
   (E) \$14,125

2. $(x^a)^b =$

   (A) $x \cdot a \cdot b$
   (B) x^{a+b}
   (C) x^{ab}
   (D) $(ax)^b$
   (E) b^{xa}

3. A is 300 miles from B. The path of all points equidistant from A and B can best be described as

   (A) a line ∥ to AB and 150 miles north of AB
   (B) a transverse segment cutting through AB at a 45° angle
   (C) a circle with AB as its diameter
   (D) the perpendicular bisector AB
   (E) the line AB

4. If $y = x^2 \cdot z = x^3$, and $w = xy$ then $y^2 + z^2 + w^2 =$

   (A) $x^4 + x^6 + x^{10}$
   (B) $x^4 + 2x^5$
   (C) $x^4 + 2x^6$
   (D) $2x^9$
   (E) $2x^{10}$

GO ON TO THE NEXT PAGE

5. The number missing in the series 2, 6, 12, 20, ?, 42, 56, 72 is

(A) 24
(B) 30
(C) 36
(D) 38
(E) 40

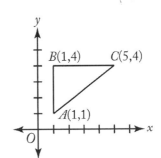

6. The square and the equilateral triangle in the above drawing both have a side of 6. If the triangle is placed inside the square with one side of the triangle directly on one side of the square, what is the area of the shaded region?

(A) $36 - 18\sqrt{3}$
(B) $36 - 9\sqrt{3}$
(C) $36 - 6\sqrt{3}$
(D) $36 + 6\sqrt{3}$
(E) $36 + 9\sqrt{3}$

7. If $3x + 2 > 2x + 7$, then x is

(A) 5
(B) < 5
(C) > 5
(D) < 1
(E) < -1

8. If $x \neq \frac{2}{3}$, the $\frac{6x^2 - 13x + 6}{3x - 2}$

(A) $3x - 2$
(B) $3x - 3$
(C) $2x - 6$
(D) $2x - 3$
(E) $2x^2 - 3x - 3$

9. What is the length of side AC?

(A) $2\frac{1}{2}$
(B) 5
(C) 7
(D) 11
(E) 25

GO ON TO THE NEXT PAGE

10. If 3! means $3 \times 2 \times 1$ and 4! means $4 \times 3 \times 2 \times 1$, then what does $\frac{8!}{9!}$ equal?

   (A) 9

   (B) $\frac{8}{9}$

   (C) $\frac{1}{9}$

   (D) $\frac{1}{89}$

   (E) 0

11. If a distance estimated at 150 feet is really 140 feet, the percent of error in this estimate is

   (A) 10%

   (B) $7\frac{1}{7}\%$

   (C) $6\frac{2}{3}\%$

   (D) 1%

   (E) 0.71%

12. There are x cookies in a cookie jar. One child eats $\frac{1}{4}$ of all the cookies. A second child eats $\frac{1}{3}$ of the remaining cookies. If the remaining cookies are distributed among four other children, what fraction of the original number of cookies did each of the four children receive?

   (A) $\frac{7}{12}$

   (B) $\frac{1}{2}$

   (C) $\frac{5}{12}$

   (D) $\frac{1}{6}$

   (E) $\frac{1}{8}$

13. If $|2y - 4| = 6$, the $y =$

   (A) -5 or 1
   (B) -8
   (C) -4 or 3
   (D) 5 or -1
   (E) 0

14. Given the system of equations $3x + 2y = 4$ and $6x - 3y = 6$, what does y equal?

   (A) 14

   (B) $\frac{14}{6}$

   (C) 2

   (D) $\frac{11}{7}$

   (E) $\frac{2}{7}$

15. If the radius of a circle is diminished by 20%, the area is diminished by

   (A) 20%
   (B) 36%
   (C) 40%
   (D) 64%
   (E) 400%

GO ON TO THE NEXT PAGE

16. If $x - y = 10$ and $x + y = 20$ then what the value of $x^2 - y^2$?

   (A) 400
   (B) 200
   (C) 100
   (D) 30
   (E) It cannot be determined from the information given.

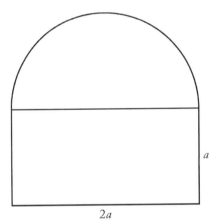

2a

17. A semicircle surmounts a rectangle whose length a $2a$ and whose width is a. As shown in the diagram. A formula for finding the area of the whole figure is

   (A) $2a^2 + \frac{\pi a^2}{2}$
   (B) $2\pi a^2$
   (C) $3\pi a^2$
   (D) $2a^2 + \pi a^2$
   (E) $2a^2 + 2\pi a^2$

18. An airplane flies 550 yards in 3 seconds. What is the speed of the airplane, expressed in miles per hour? (5,280 ft. = 1 mi.)

   (A) 1,125
   (B) 375
   (C) 300
   (D) 125
   (E) 90

19. Let the "JOSH" of a number be defined as three less than three times the number. What number is equal to its "JOSH"?

$$3x - 3 = x$$
$$2x = -3$$
$$-3$$
$$2$$

20. Machine A produces flue covers at a uniform rate of 2,000 per hour. Machine B produces flue covers at a uniform rate of 5,000 in $2\frac{1}{2}$ hours. After $7\frac{1}{2}$ hours. Machine A has produced how many more flue covers than Machine B?

21. .01 is the ratio of .1 to what number?

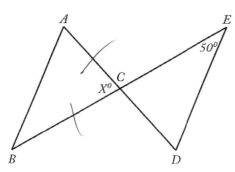

22. In the figure above, AB is parallel to ED and $AC = BC$. If angle E is 50^0, then $x=$

23. At NJL High School, $\frac{1}{4}$ of the school population are seniors, $\frac{1}{5}$ are juniors and $\frac{1}{3}$ are sophomores. If there are 390 freshmen, what is the total school population?

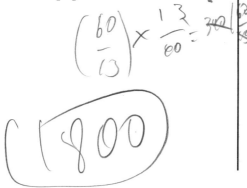

24. From the town Williston Park to Albertson there are 3 different roads. From the town of Albertson to Mineola there are 5 routes. How many different paths are there to go from Williston Park to Mineola through Albertson?

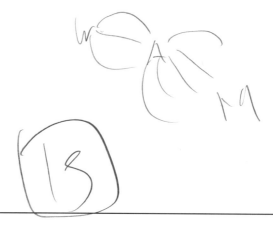

25. If 12 candles cost $1.70, how many of these candies can be bought for $10.20?

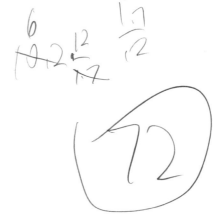

26. Two roads intersect at right angles. A pole is 30 meters from one road and 40 meters from the other road. How far (in meters) is the pole from the point where the roads intersect?

GO ON TO THE NEXT PAGE

27. Given that 1 meter = 3.28 ft., the distance run in a 100-meter race approximates most closely

    (A) 100 yards
    (B) 90 yards
    (C) 105 yards
    (D) 110 yards
    (E) 103 yards

28. Of the following sets of fractions, the set that is arranged in increasing order is

    (A) $\frac{7}{12}, \frac{6}{11}, \frac{3}{5}, \frac{5}{8}$

    (B) $\frac{6}{11}, \frac{7}{12}, \frac{5}{8}, \frac{3}{5}$

    (C) $\frac{6}{11}, \frac{7}{12}, \frac{3}{5}, \frac{5}{8}$

    (D) $\frac{3}{5}, \frac{5}{8}, \frac{6}{11}, \frac{7}{12}$

    (E) $\frac{7}{12}, \frac{6}{11}, \frac{5}{8}, \frac{3}{5}$

29. If one pipe can fill a tank in $1\frac{1}{2}$ hours and another can fill the same tank in 45 minutes, then how many hours will it take the two pipes to fill the tank if they are working together?

    (A) $\frac{1}{3}$

    (B) $\frac{1}{2}$

    (C) $\frac{5}{6}$

    (D) 1

    (E) $1\frac{1}{2}$

30. If the sum of the edges of a cube is 48 inches, the volume of the cube in cubic inches is

    (A) 64
    (B) 96
    (C) 149
    (D) 512
    (E) 1,72

31. If the length of each side of a square is $\frac{2x}{3} + 1$, the perimeter of the square is

    (A) $\frac{8x+4}{3}$

    (B) $\frac{8x+12}{3}$

    (C) $\frac{2x}{3} + 4$

    (D) $\frac{2x}{3} + 16$

    (E) $\frac{4x}{3} + 2$

GO ON TO THE NEXT PAGE

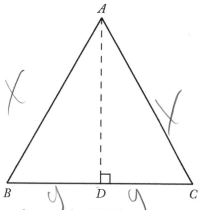

32. Equilateral triangle *ABC* has a perpendicular line drawn from *A* to point *D*. If the triangle is "folded over" on the perimeter of the new triangle is approximately what percent of the perimeter of the triangle before the fold?

(A) 100%
(B) 78%
(C) 50%
(D) 32%
(E) It cannot be determined from the information given.

33. To find the radius of a circle whose circumference is 60 inches

(A) multiply 60 by π
(B) divide 60 by 2π
(C) divide 30 by 2π
(D) divide 60 by π and extract the square root of the result.
(E) multiply 60 by $\frac{\pi}{2}$

34. If the outer diameter of a metal pipe is 2.84 inches and the inner diameter is 1.94 inches, the thickness of the metal in inches is

(A) .45
(B) .90
(C) 1.42
(D) 1.94
(E) 2.39

SAT Math Exercise #07

34 questions

Reference Information

    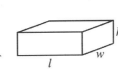 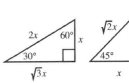

$A = \pi r^2$
$C = 2\pi r$
$A = lw$
$A = \frac{1}{2}bh$
$V = lwh$
$V = \pi r^2 h$
Special Right Triangles

The number of degrees in a circle is 360°
The angles of a triangle measured in degrees have a sum of 180°

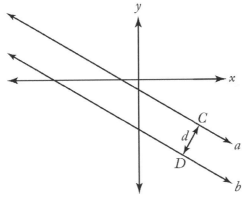

1. Line a‖b, while d is the distance between a and b at point C and D. The length of segment d

    (A) steadily increases as it is moved along lines a and b to the right
    (B) steadily decreases as it is moved towards the left
    (C) fluctuates in both directions
    (D) Remains constant
    (E) none of the above

2. $(x + 9)(x + 2) =$

    (A) $x^2 + 18$
    (B) $11x$
    (C) $x^2 + 11$
    (D) $x^2 + 11x + 18$
    (E) $9(x + 2) + 2(x + 9)$

3. The points $(3, 1)$ and $(5, y)$ are $\sqrt{13}$ units apart. What does y equal?

    (A) -3
    (B) 4
    (C) $\sqrt{17}$
    (D) 10
    (E) 17

GO ON TO THE NEXT PAGE

4. In a baseball game, a pitcher needs to throw nine strikes to complete an inning. If a pitcher is able to throw strikes on 85% of his pitches, how many pitches to the nearest whole number would it take for him to throw the necessary number of strikes for a nine-inning game?

(A) 95
(B) 97
(C) 103
(D) 105
(E) 111

6. If a triangle of base 7 is equal in area to a circle of radius 7, what is the altitude of the triangle?

(A) 8 π
(B) 10 π
(C) 12 π
(D) 14 π
(E) It cannot be determined from the information given.

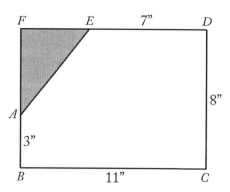

5. Corner AFE is cut from the rectangle as shown in the figure below. The area of the remaining polygon ABCDE in square inches is

(A) 29
(B) 68
(C) 78
(D) 88
(E) 98

7. If the following numbers are arranged in order from the smallest to the largest, what will be their correct order?

I. $\frac{9}{13}$

II. $\frac{13}{8}$

III. 70%

IV. $\frac{1}{.70}$

(A) II, I, III, IV
(B) III, II, I, IV
(C) III, IV, I, II
(D) II, IV, III, I
(E) I, III, IV, II

GO ON TO THE NEXT PAGE

8. The coordinates of the vertices of the quadrilateral $PQRS$ are $P(0,0)$, $Q(9,0)$, $R(10,3)$, and $S(1,3)$, repectively. What is the area of $PQRS$?

(A) $9\sqrt{10}$

(B) $\frac{9}{2}\sqrt{10}$

(C) $\frac{27}{2}$

(D) 27

(E) It cannot be determined from the information given.

9. If $8x + 4 = 64$, then $2x + 1 =$

(A) 12
(B) 13
(C) 16
(D) 24
(E) 60

10. A circle whose radius is 7 has its center at the origin. Which of the following points are outside the circle?

  I. $(4,4)$
  II. $(5,5)$
  III. $(4,5)$
  IV. $(4,6)$

(A) I and II only
(B) II and III only
(C) II, III, and IV only
(D) II and IV only
(E) III and IV only

11. What is the difference in surface area between a square with side 9 and a cube with edge 3?

(A) 516
(B) 432
(C) 72
(D) 27
(E) 18

12. A set of numbers is "quarked" if the sum of all the numbers in the set is evenly divisible by each of the numbers in the set. Which of the following sets is "quarked"?

(A) $(1, 3, 5, 7)$
(B) $(4, 6, 8)$
(C) $(6, 7, 8, 9)$
(D) $(2, 4, 6)$
(E) $(5, 10, 15, 20)$

13. If $x \neq -2$, $\frac{3(x^2-4)}{x+2} =$

(A) $3x^2 + 4$
(B) $3x - 2$
(C) $x - 2$
(D) $3x - 6$
(E) $3x + 6$

GO ON TO THE NEXT PAGE

14. An ice-cream truck runs down a certain street 4 times a week. This truck runs down a certain street 4 times a week. This truck carries 5 different flavors of ice-cream bars, each of which comes in 2 different designs. Considering that the truck runs Monday through Thursday, and Monday was the first day of the month, by what day of the month could a person, buying one ice-cream bar each truck-run, purchase all the different varieties of ice-cream bars?

(A) 11ᵗʰ
(B) 16ᵗʰ
(C) 21ˢᵗ
(D) 24ᵗʰ
(E) 30ᵗʰ

15. If $N! = N(N-1)(N-2) \ldots [N-(N-1)]$, what does $\frac{N!}{(N-2)!}$ equal?

(A) $N^2 - N$
(B) $N^5 + N^3 - N^2 + \frac{N}{N^2}$
(C) $N + 1$
(D) 1
(E) 6

16. If $\frac{2}{3} + \frac{3}{4} + \frac{5}{6} + p = 3$, then $p =$

(A) $\frac{4}{3}$
(B) $\frac{3}{4}$
(C) $\frac{2}{3}$
(D) $\frac{1}{2}$
(E) $\frac{1}{3}$

17. In the figure above, x + y=

(A) 360
(B) 180
(C) 130
(D) 50
(E) It cannot be determined from the information given.

18. If $P = QR$ and $Q = S + 2$, then which of the following is equal to $\frac{P}{R}$?

(A) $S + 2$
(B) S
(C) $S - 2$
(D) $Q(S + 2)$
(E) SQ

19. Two adjacent sides of a rectangle measure 4 and 7. What is the perimeter of the rectangle?

Measure	Frequency
70	4
85	3
90	2
95	1

20. Based on the table above, what is the median for the set of data?

23. The expression $\frac{6}{\frac{1}{2}+\frac{1}{3}}=$

24. In the figure below, if $\angle AOC$ is a central angle and the measure of $\angle AOC$ is 70^0, what is the measure of $\angle ABC$? (Do not grid the degree symbol)

21. Let $(x) = x - 1$ and $[x] = 2x$.
   $(-1) + [1] =$

22. What is the value of $x + y^2 - z$, if $x = y = z = -1$?

25. In the junior class at Dawnville High School, 44 of 70 juniors take pre-calculus and 46 take chemistry. If 10 take neither course, how many take both pre-calculus and chemistry?

GO ON TO THE NEXT PAGE

26. If a student's average (arithmetic mean) for five exams is 70 and two lowest test grades for 50 and 30 are disregarded, what is the student's average for the remaining exams?

27. If $x = -\frac{1}{2}$, then which of the following is the greatest?

(A) x^5
(B) x^4
(C) x^3
(D) x^2
(E) x

28. A man runs 5 miles per hour for one and one-half hours. If a women runs the same direction in one hour, what is the women's average speed in miles per hour?

(A) 10

(B) $9\frac{1}{2}$

(C) $7\frac{1}{2}$

(D) 5

(E) $4\frac{1}{2}$

29. What is the sum of four integers whose average is 11?

(A) 36
(B) 38
(C) 40
(D) 42
(E) 44

30. In a basket containing 180 pears, 9 are spoiled. What percent of the pears in the basket are not spoiled?

(A) 95%
(B) 90%
(C) 50%
(D) 25%
(E) 20%

31. A number r is tripled, the new number is decreased by three, and that number is then divided by three. Which of the following reflects the above statements?

(A) $3(r - 3)$
(B) $9r$
(C) $r - 3$
(D) r
(E) $r - 1$

GO ON TO THE NEXT PAGE

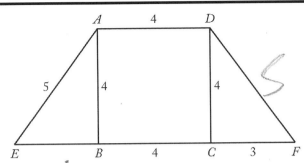

32. If $ABCD$ is a square with a side of 4, then what is the sum of the perimeter of $\triangle ABE$ and $\triangle DCF$?

(A) 48
(B) 36
(C) 24
(D) 12
(E) 6

33. $\sqrt{\frac{3}{4} - \frac{3}{16}} =$

(A) $\frac{4}{3}$

(B) $\frac{3}{4}$

(C) $\frac{9}{16}$

(D) $\frac{1}{3}$

(E) $\frac{1}{4}$

34. If $\{w, x, y, z\} = z(w + x + y)$, so that $\{1, 2, 3, 4\} = 4(1 + 2 + 3) = 24$, then all of the following are equal *except*

(A) $\{2, 3, 4, 6\}$
(B) $\{4, 3, 2, 6\}$
(C) $\{3, 5, 1, 6\}$
(D) $\{4, 1, 5, 6\}$
(E) $\{1, 5, 3, 6\}$

SAT Math Exercise #08
34 questions

Notes

1. The use of calculators is allowed.
2. All numbers are real numbers.
3. Figures that accompany problems in this test are intended to provide information useful in solving the problems. They are drawn as accurately as possible EXCEPT when it is stated in a specific problem that the figure is not drawn to scale. All figures lie in a plane unless otherwise indicated.
4. The domain of any function $f(x)$ is assumed to be all real numbers unless otherwise indicated.

Reference Information

   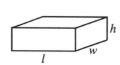 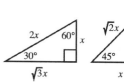

$A = \pi r^2$
$C = 2\pi r$
$A = lw$
$A = \frac{1}{2}bh$
$V = lwh$
$V = \pi r^2 h$
Special Right Triangles

The number of degrees in a circle is 360°
The angles of a triangle measured in degrees have a sum of 180°

---

1. If a pound contains 16 ounces, 16.4 ounces would be how many pounds?

   (A) 1.75
   (B) 1.5
   (C) 1.25
   (D) 1.025
   (E) 1.0025

2. If a certain circle has a circumference of x, then which of the following is the radius of the circle?

   (A) $\frac{x}{2\pi}$
   (B) $\frac{x}{\pi}$
   (C) $\frac{2x}{\pi}$
   (D) $2 \times \pi$
   (E) $4 \times \pi$

3. If $(x + 1)(x - 2)$ is positive, then

   (A) $x < -1$ or $x > 2$
   (B) $x > -1$ or $x < 2$
   (C) $-1 < x < 2$
   (D) $-2 < x < 1$
   (E) $x = -1$ or $x = 2$

4. Rectangle $ABCD$ has length of 12 and a width of 8. Point E is a point on side BC. What is the ratio of the area of $\triangle AED$ to the area of rectangle $ABCD$?

   (A) 1 : 6
   (B) 1 : 4
   (C) 2 : 5
   (D) 3 : 7
   (E) 1 : 2

GO ON TO THE NEXT PAGE

5. A "full" number is one that is the sum of all the other numbers beside itself by which it can be divided without leaving a remainder. Which of the following is a "full" number?

    I.   6
    II. 12
    III. 28
    IV. 32

    (A) I only
    (B) I and II only
    (C) I and III only
    (D) III and IV only
    (E) I, III, and IV only

Annual Sale of Cassettes
ABC Sound Stores

Year	Number Sold
1985	7,000
1986	9,000
1987	12,000
1988	16,000
1989	20,000
1990	24,000

6. In the above table, which yearly period had the smallest percent increase in sales?

    (A) 1985-86
    (B) 1986-87
    (C) 1987-88
    (D) 1988-89
    (E) 1989-90

7. A student scored 70, 75, and 80 on three tests. If the student scored y on the fourth test, what is the average (arithmetic mean) of the four tests?

    (A) $\frac{225+y}{4}$

    (B) $\frac{225+y}{3}$

    (C) $\frac{75+y}{4}$

    (D) $\frac{75+y}{2}$

    (E) y

8. Two snails are three feet apart and directly facing each other. If one snail moves forward continuously at .04 inches per second and the other moves forward continuously at .05 inches per second, how many minutes will it take for the snails to touch?

    (A) $3\frac{1}{3}$ minutes
    (B) $6\frac{2}{3}$ minutes
    (C) 9 minutes
    (D) $12\frac{1}{2}$ minutes
    (E) 18 minutes

9. A person is hired for a job that pays $500 per month and receives a 10% raise in each following month. IN the fourth month, how much will that person earn?
    (A) $550
    (B) $600.50
    (C) $650.50
    (D) $665.50
    (E) $700

GO ON TO THE NEXT PAGE

10. If $a^2 - 2ab + b^2 = 36$ and $a^2 - 3ab + b^2 = 22$, what is the value of ab?

(A) 6
(B) 8
(C) 12
(D) 14
(E) It cannot be determined from the information given.

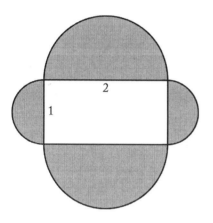

11. In the figure above, four semicircles are drawn on the four sides of a rectangle. What is the total area of the shaded portion?

(A) 5π
(B) $\frac{5\pi}{2}$
(C) $\frac{5\pi}{4}$
(D) $\frac{5\pi}{8}$
(E) $\frac{5\pi}{16}$

12. John is now four times as old as Anne was six years ago. How old is Anne today if John is 20 years old?

(A) 8
(B) 11
(C) 12
(D) 14
(E) 15

13. $P = \frac{1}{2} + \frac{1}{3}$ and $Q = P^2$, what is $Q - P$?

(A) 1
(B) $\frac{5}{36}$
(C) 0
(D) $-\frac{5}{36}$
(E) $-\frac{25}{36}$

14. Which of the following is a multiple of 2 and 4 but not 6?

(A) 8
(B) 12
(C) 24
(D) 28
(E) 36

GO ON TO THE NEXT PAGE

15. Which of the following is smaller than $-\frac{1}{2}$?

(A) $-\frac{3}{5}$

(B) $-\frac{3}{7}$

(C) $-\frac{2}{5}$

(D) $-\frac{1}{3}$

(E) $-\frac{1}{4}$

16. Two-thirds of a certain number is 6 more than $\frac{1}{2}$ of the same number. What is the number?

(A) 48
(B) 36
(C) 30
(D) 24
(E) 12

17. What percent is 10 of 2?

(A) 20%
(B) 50%
(C) 200%
(D) 400%
(E) 500%

18. A quart of oil usually sells for $1.39. During a sale, the price is reduced to 59 cents. If a customer buys a six quarts at the sale price, how much is she saving off the regular price?

(A) $8.34
(B) $6.40
(C) $4.80
(D) $3.54
(E) $2.88

19. What is the value of $(2a^2 - a^3)^2$ when $a = -1$?

$2 + 1$

9

20. A jar contains 2 red marbles, 3 green marbles, and 4 oranges marbles. If a marble is picked at random, what is the probability that the marble is not orange?

$\frac{5}{9}$

GO ON TO THE NEXT PAGE

21. In the country of Glup, 1 glop is 3 glips and 4 glips are 5 globs. How many globs are 2 glops?

7.5

22. Solve for k: $\frac{k}{3} + \frac{k}{4} = 1$

$\frac{7k}{12} = 1$

$k = \frac{12}{7}$

23. If the area of a square of side x is 5 . what is the area of a square of side $3x$?

45

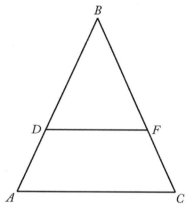

24. In the diagram above, $\triangle ABC$ is similar to $\triangle DBF$. If $DF = 3$, $BD = BF = 6$, and $AC = 4$, what is the perimeter of $\triangle ABC$?

12

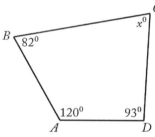

25. In quadrilateral $ABCD$ above, the measure of $<A = 120°$, the measure of $< B = 82°$, and the measure of $<D = 93°$. What is the value of x?

36

GO ON TO THE NEXT PAGE

26. If $2x + 2y = 6$ and $3x - 3y = 9$, what is the value of $x^2 - y^2$?

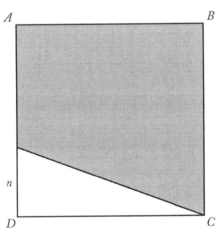

27. If square $ABCD$ has a side of m, then which of the following represents the shaded area?

(A) $m^2 - \frac{mn}{2}$

(B) $m^2 + \frac{mn}{2}$

(C) $mn + m^2$

(D) $m^2 - mn$

(E) $m^2 - 2n$

28. John is 6 inches taller than Henry, who is $\frac{3}{4}$ as Mark. Which of the following could be the heights of the boys?

 I. Mark=4' John=$3\frac{1}{2}$' Henry=3'

 II. Mark=6' John=$5\frac{1}{2}$' Henry= $4\frac{1}{2}$'

 III. Mark=$5\frac{1}{2}$' John=$4\frac{1}{2}$' Henry=4'

(A) I only
(B) I and II only
(C) II and III only
(D) I and III only
(E) None of the above

29. What is the average of $\frac{2}{3}$, $\frac{3}{4}$, and $\frac{5}{6}$?

(A) $\frac{7}{9}$

(B) $\frac{3}{4}$

(C) $\frac{2}{3}$

(D) $\frac{5}{12}$

(E) $\frac{5}{24}$

30. If $k = \frac{3}{4}j$ and both j and k are positive integers, k could be any of the following except

(A) 9
(B) 12
(C) 15
(D) 18
(E) 20

GO ON TO THE NEXT PAGE

31. If r is an even integer greater than 2, then which of the following must be also be even?

(A) $(r-1)^2$
(B) $(r+1)^2$
(C) $\frac{r}{2}+1$
(D) $2r+1$
(E) r^2+r

33. $.2 \times .02 \times .002 =$

(A) $.000008$
(B) $.00008$
(C) $.0008$
(D) $.008$
(E) $.08$

A   B   C   D

32. Segment AB is three times longer than segment BC, which is two times as long as segment CD. If segment BC is removed from the line and the other two segments are joined to form one line, then what is the ratio of the original line AD to the new line AD?

(A) 3:2
(B) 9:7
(C) 5:4
(D) 7:6
(E) 11:10

34. If $\frac{p}{q} = 6$ and $q = -3$, then $\frac{p+q}{q} =$

(A) -21
(B) -14
(C) -7
(D) 1
(E) 7

STOP

this is the end of the exercise

SAT Math Exercise #09

34 questions

Reference Information

   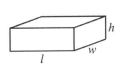

$A = \pi r^2$
$C = 2\pi r$　　　$A = lw$　　　$A = \frac{1}{2}bh$　　　$V = lwh$　　　$V = \pi r^2 h$　　　*Special Right Triangles*

The number of degrees in a circle is 360°
The angles of a triangle measured in degrees have a sum of 180°

1. If s, t, and u are different positive integers and $\frac{s}{t}$ and $\frac{t}{u}$ are also positive integers, which of the following cannot be a positive integers?

   (A) $5u$
   (B) $s \cdot t$
   (C) $\frac{u}{s}$
   (D) $(s + t)u$
   (E) $(s - u)t$

2. Of the people attending a concert, $\frac{3}{4}$ are seated in the auditorium and the remaining $\frac{1}{4}$ are in the lobby. If $\frac{1}{2}$ of those in the lobby move to seats in the auditorium, then what is the ratio of those seated in the auditorium to those in the lobby?

   (A) 16:1
   (B) 12:1
   (C) 9:1
   (D) 7:1
   (E) 6:1

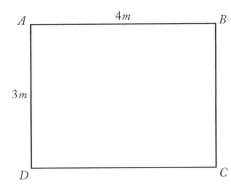

3. If the perimeter of the rectangle below is 42, then what is the area of the rectangle?

   (A) 21
   (B) 42
   (C) 84
   (D) 108
   (E) 216

4. $390 is 13% of the total sum of money in a bank account. How much money is in the bank account?

   (A) $6,000
   (B) $3,000
   (C) $1,057
   (D) $557
   (E) $50.57

5. If $n(q + 5) = s$ and $q(n + 4) = s$, and n, q and s are positive integers, then which of the following statements must be true?

   I. $n(q + 5) = q(n + 4)$

   II. $\frac{n(q+5)}{q(n+4)} = 1$

   III. $q > n$

   (A) I only
   (B) II Only
   (C) III Only
   (D) I and III Only
   (E) I, II and III

6. $\frac{\frac{2}{3}(x^2y^3)^4}{\frac{3}{4}(x^4y^3)^2} =$

   (A) $\frac{8y^6}{9}$

   (B) $\frac{9y^6}{8}$

   (C) $\frac{3}{4}xy$

   (D) $\frac{2y^6}{3}$

   (E) $\frac{8}{9y^6}$

7. Jane has walked m miles. After a rest she walks n miles. If Jane always walked s steps per mile, then how many steps did Jane take?

   (A) $s + m + n$

   (B) $\frac{sm}{n}$

   (C) $\frac{m}{sn}$

   (D) $(s + m)n$

   (E) $s(m + n)$

8. Tim can fold a certain number of brochures in 20 minutes. John can fold the same number in 15 minutes. If Tim and John work together for 3 hours and during that time John folds x brochures, how many brochures will Tim fold?

   (A) $\frac{4x}{3}$

   (B) $\frac{5x}{4}$

   (C) $\frac{3x}{4}$

   (D) $\frac{2x}{4}$

   (E) $\frac{x}{2}$

GO ON TO THE NEXT PAGE

For questions 13 and 14, refer to the table below.

Mathematics Score

Score	No. of students
40-52	5
53-64	11
65-76	7
77-88	32
89-100	40

9. If the lowest passing grade is 65, then, to the nearest percent, what percent of the students failed the test?

(A) 5%
(B) 7%
(C) 11%
(D) 17%
(E) 52%

10. If 9 students scored 100, how many scored from 77 to 99?

(A) 72
(B) 63
(C) 51
(D) 40
(E) 31

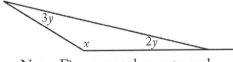

Note: Figure not drawn to scale.

11. In the figure below, which of the following is x necessarily equal to?

(A) $180 - 5y$
(B) $180 + 5y$
(C) $90 - 5y$
(D) $190 + 5y$
(E) $5y$

12. For which values of x will $x(x + 2)(x - 3)(x + 4)$ be equal to 0?

(A) 0
(B) 2, -3, and 4
(C) 0 and -2
(D) -2, 3, and -4
(E) 0, -2, 3, and -4

For questions 13 and 14 let $a \square b = a^b + b^4$

13. What is the value of $2 \square 3$?

(A) 5
(B) 6
(C) 13
(D) 17
(E) 19

14. If a and b are different positive integers, then which of the following statements must be false?

(A) The smallest value for $a \square b$ is 3.
(B) $a^b \cdot b^a = b^a \cdot a^b$
(C) a^b is never equal to b^a
(D) $a \square b$ can be equal 0
(E) $a \square b = b \square a$

15. A pool is filled to $\frac{3}{4}$ of its capacity. $\frac{1}{9}$ of the water in the pool evaporates. If the pool can hold 24,000 gallons when its full, how many gallons of water will have to be added in order to fill the pool?

(A) 6,000
(B) 8,000
(C) 12,000
(D) 16,000
(E) 18,000

16. If $\frac{12m}{7}$ is an integer, m could be any of the following *except*

(A) 63
(B) 49
(C) 21
(D) 15
(E) 7

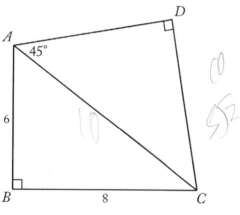

17. What is side AD+ side DC?

(A) $18\sqrt{2}$
(B) $8\sqrt{2}$
(C) $10\sqrt{2}$
(D) 10
(E) $6\sqrt{2}$

18. Four "*ABCD*" equals three "*EFGH*." Four "*EFGH*" equals five "*IJKL*." How many "*ABCD*" are equal to fifteen "*IJKL*"?

(A) 4
(B) 8
(C) 12
(D) 16
(E) 20

19. Let d be the least integer greater than 96,666 such that four of $d's$ digits are identical. Find the value of $d - 96,666$

20. Find 25 percent of 25 percent of 2

GO ON TO THE NEXT PAGE

21. One-half of the contents of a container evaporates in one week, and three-fourths of the remainder evaporates in the following week. At the end of two weeks, what fractional part of the original contents remains? Express your answer in lowest terms.

22. The distance from the center of a circle to the midpoint of a chord is 3. If the length of the chord is 8, what is the length of the radius of the circle?

23. Three friends decide to split the cost of a pizza, with each chipping in $3.25. If two friends join them, and each pays an equal share, how much less will each of the three friends have to pay?

24. Given $r = a + b$ and $s = b - a$. When $a = 5$ and $b = 4$, find the value of $r - s$.

25. A bag contains exactly 4 blue marbles, 7 green marbles, and 8 yellow marbles. Fred draws marbles at rando m from the bag without replacement, one by one. If he does not look at the marble he draws out, how many marbles will he have draw out before he knows for sure his *next* draw he will have 1 marble for every colors?

26. In a three-hour examination of 350 questions, there are 50 mathematical problems. If twice as much time should be allowed for each problem as for each of the other questions, how many minutes should be spent

GO ON TO THE NEXT PAGE

j	k
1	$\frac{2}{3}$
2	$\frac{4}{3}$
3	2
4	$\frac{8}{3}$

27. According to the above chart, $k =$

(A) $\frac{2}{3}j$

(B) $j - \frac{1}{3}$

(C) $\frac{3}{2}j$

(D) $\frac{j}{2}$

(E) $\frac{j}{3}$

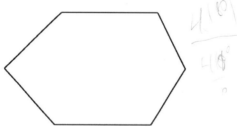

28. In the figure, what is the sum of the six angles divided by the average of the six angles?

(A) 72
(B) 36
(C) 12
(D) 6
(E) It cannot be determined from the information given.

29. An investor bought 1,200 shares of stock at $\$22\frac{5}{8}$ and sold the same 1,200 shares at $\$23\frac{1}{2}$. What is the profit not counting commissions or taxes?

(A) $4,050
(B) $3,050
(C) $2,050
(D) $1,050
(E) $550

30. A certain neon sign flashes every 2 seconds, another sign flashes every 3 seconds, and a third flashes every 5 seconds. If the all start flashing together, how many seconds will pass before they all flash simultaneously again?

(A) 45 seconds
(B) 30 seconds
(C) 20 seconds
(D) 15 seconds
(E) 10 seconds

31. Marianne can read at a rate of 300 words per minute. While taking a speed reading course, Marianne increases her speed by $\frac{1}{3}$. After finishing the course, Marianne's speed drops by 100 words per minute. What percent of her original speed in her current speed?

(A) 200%
(B) 100%
(C) 50%
(D) 205
(E) 0%

GO ON TO THE NEXT PAGE

32. Which of the following is less than $\frac{1}{2}$?

(A) $\frac{9}{16}$

(B) $\frac{11}{21}$

(C) $\frac{8}{17}$

(D) $\frac{14}{27}$

(E) $\frac{6}{11}$

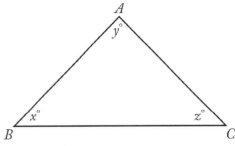

34. If the triangle below is distorted so that angle y is doubled and the angle z is tripled, then angle x will become a right angle. Which of the following is a possible value for angle y?

(A) 90
(B) 75
(C) 60
(D) 45
(E) 30

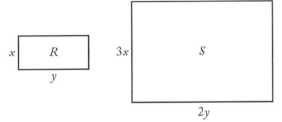

33. Rectangle R has sides of x and y. Rectangle S has sides of $3x$ and $2y$. What is the area of S minus the area of R?

(A) $12xy$
(B) $9xy$
(C) $6xy$
(D) $5xy$
(E) $4xy$

STOP
this is the end of the exercise

SAT Math Exercise #10
34 questions

Reference Information

      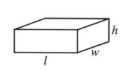 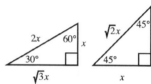

$A = \pi r^2$
$C = 2\pi r$
$A = lw$
$A = \frac{1}{2}bh$
$V = lwh$
$V = \pi r^2 h$
Special Right Triangles

The number of degrees in a circle is 360°
The angles of a triangle measured in degrees have a sum of 180°

1. If $3x + 3$ is 6 more than $3y + 3$, then $x - y =$

(A) 0
(B) 2
(C) 4
(D) 6
(E) 9

2. Jim's average score for three bowling games was 162. In the second game, Jim scored 10 less than in the first game. In the third game, he scored 13 less than in the second game. What was his score in the first game?

(A) 189
(B) 179
(C) 173
(D) 173
(E) 168

3. $3 \times 10^3 \times 2 \times 10^2$

(A) 6,000,000
(B) 600,000
(C) 60,000
(D) 6,000
(E) 600

4. A certain machine makes a widget every 2.5 seconds. How many widgets does machine make in 40 minutes?

(A) 12,600
(B) 9,600
(C) 4,800
(D) 1,200
(E) 960

GO ON TO THE NEXT PAGE

5. A cassette tape has two sides and each side can record for 45 minutes. A student brings 3 tapes in order to record a three-hour lecture. If the time spent loading and unloading the tapes is negligible, what percent of the total available tape will not be used to record the lecture?

(A) 75%
(B) 50%
(C) $33\frac{1}{3}$%
(D) 25%
(E) 20%

6. If $\frac{(a+b)}{(c+d)} = 5$ and $\frac{(e+f)}{(g+h)} = 6$, then what is the value of $\frac{(a+b)}{(g+h)} \cdot \frac{(e+f)}{(c+d)}$?

(A) 0
(B) 1
(C) 11
(D) 30
(E) It cannot be determined from the information given.

7. The fraction $\frac{2}{7}$ is represented by the decimal .285714 repeated.
$\frac{2}{7} = .285714\ 285714\ 285714\ ....$ What is the 753rd decimal digit?

(A) 2
(B) 8
(C) 5
(D) 7
(E) 1

8. $0.1 \times 0.01 \times 0.001 =$

(A) .01
(B) .03
(C) .003
(D) .0001
(E) .000001

9. The average height of the four-member gymnastics squad is 5 feet. Three of the girls are 4 feet 10 inches tall. How tall is the fourth member?

(A) 5 feet
(B) 5 feet 2 inches
(C) 5 feet 4 inches
(D) 5 feet 6 inches
(E) It cannot be determined from the information given.

10. $\frac{1}{5}$ times its reciprocal is

(A) $\frac{2}{5}$
(B) $\frac{1}{25}$
(C) 1
(D) 5
(E) 25

GO ON TO THE NEXT PAGE

11. How many sixteenths are in $5\frac{1}{4}$?

(A) 17
(B) 20
(C) 80
(D) 81
(E) 84

12. Whenever a particular organism reproduces, it doubles in number each hour. If you start with one organism at 3:00, how many will you have by 6:00?

(A) 4
(B) 6
(C) 8
(D) 24
(E) 120

13. If $x = \frac{1}{4}y$, what is the value of $\frac{x}{4}$?

(A) 16
(B) $\frac{y}{16}$
(C) $\frac{y}{4}$
(D) y
(E) $4y$

14. If the sides of a square are tripled, what always happens to its perimeter?

(A) It remains the same.
(B) It is cubed.
(C) It increases by 100%
(D) It is tripled.
(E) It increased by 900%.

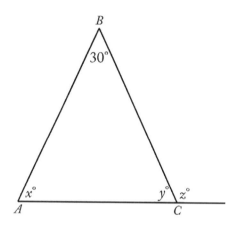

15. If $\triangle ABC$ is an isosceles triangle, what is the value of z?

(A) 60
(B) 90
(C) $2y$
(D) 100
(E) 105

16. Leo is 67. His son Robert is 29. In how many years will Robert be exactly half his father's age?

(A) 2
(B) 5
(C) 7
(D) 9
(E) 12

GO ON TO THE NEXT PAGE

17. When the number $\frac{1}{4}$, $\frac{3}{10}$, 0.23, and $\frac{4}{15}$ are arranged in ascending order of size, the result is

(A) $0.23, \frac{3}{10}, \frac{1}{4}, \frac{4}{15}$

(B) $\frac{1}{4}, 0.23, \frac{3}{10}, \frac{4}{15}$

(C) $0.23, \frac{1}{4}, \frac{3}{10}, \frac{4}{15}$

(D) $\frac{4}{15}, \frac{3}{10}, \frac{1}{4}, 0.23$

(E) $0.23, \frac{1}{4}, \frac{4}{15}, \frac{3}{10}$

18. If $a + b = 12$ and $\frac{b}{a} = 3$, then

(A) $a = 9$
(B) $b = \frac{a}{3}$
(C) $12 = 3b$
(D) $b - a = 9$
(E) $ab = 27$

19. If $\frac{1}{4} < x < \frac{1}{3}$ find one value of x.

20. Given $3x + y = 17$ and $x + 3y = -1$, find the value of $3x + 3y$.

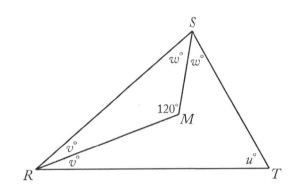

21. If $\angle RST = 80^0$, find u.

22. There are 22 people on an island. A tram can carry at most 4 people at a time. What is the least number of trips that the tram must make to the mainland to get all the people to the mainland?

GO ON TO THE NEXT PAGE

23. Let us define the operation $\odot$ as
$a \odot b = (a + b)^2 - (a - b)^2$
Find the value of $\sqrt{18} \odot \sqrt{2}$.

_____

24. How many ordered pairs of *integers* (x, y) satisfy $x^2 + y^2 < 9$?

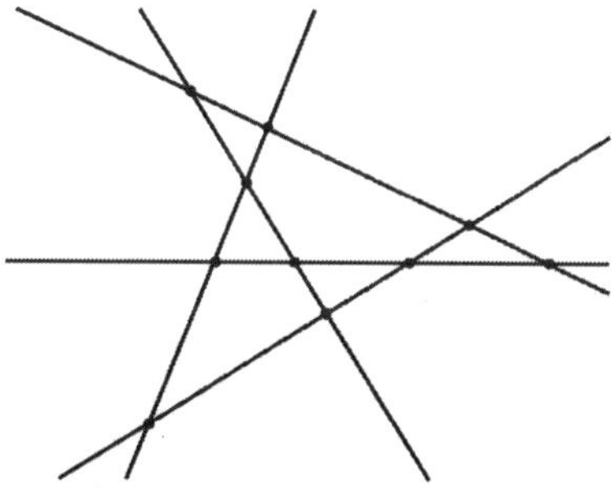

_____

25. The figure above demonstrates that 5 straight lines can have 10 points of intersection. What is the maximum number of points of intersection of 4 straight lines?

26. A boy planned to buy some chocolate bars at 50 cents each but instead decided to purchase 30-cent chocolate bars. If he originally had enough money to buy 21 of the 50-cent bars, how many of the less expensive ones did he buy?

_____

27. The side of a square forms the radius of a circle with a circumference of 10. What is the perimeter of the square?

(A) $\frac{5}{\pi}$

(B) $\frac{10}{\pi}$

(C) $\frac{20}{\pi}$

(D) 4π

(E) 100π

_____

28. Station *KBAZ* is on the air 24 hours a day. Yesterday it sold ads and took in money at this rate: 20% from drive-time ads at \$20/minute, 50% from daytime ads at \$10/minute, and 30% from nighttime ads at \$5/minute. If the station made \$500 yesterday, how much air time was dedicated to ads?

(A) 30 minutes
(B) 1 hour
(C) 2 hours
(D) 3 hours
(E) 3 hours, 30 minutes

GO ON TO THE NEXT PAGE

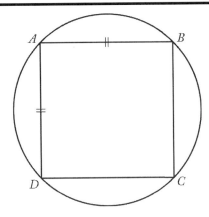

29. In the figure above, the area of the circle is equivalent to

(A) $\frac{AB}{\pi}$

(B) AB

(C) πAB

(D) $\pi \left(\frac{AC}{2}\right)^2$

(E) πAC^2

30. A motorist drives 90 miles at an average speed of 50 miles per hour and returns at an average speed of 60 miles per hour. What is her average speed in miles per hour for the entire trip?

(A) 53
(B) 54.5
(C) 56.5
(D) 58
(E) It cannot be determined from the information above.

31. If $17x - 32 = 308$, what is $\frac{x}{4}$?

(A) 5
(B) 10
(C) 20
(D) 50
(E) 85

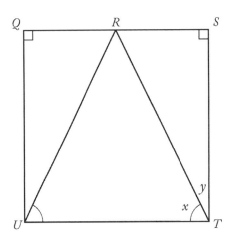

32. In the square above, ΔUQR and ΔRST are equal in area. If $QR = 2$, what is the area of triangle RUT?

(A) 2
(B) 4
(C) 8
(D) 12
(E) 16

GO ON TO THE NEXT PAGE

33. If the radius of a circle is increased by 10%, the area of the circle is increased by

(A) 10%
(B) 21%
(C) 100%
(D) 110%
(E) 121%

34. Where $a \neq 1$, $\dfrac{a^7 - a^6}{a - 1} =$

(A) $\dfrac{a}{a-1}$

(B) $\dfrac{1}{a-1}$

(C) $a^6 - a^5$
(D) a^5
(E) a^6

STOP

this is the end of the exercise

SAT Math Exercise #11

34 questions

Reference Information

    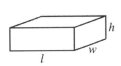

$A = \pi r^2$
$C = 2\pi r$ $A = lw$ $A = \frac{1}{2}bh$ $V = lwh$ $V = \pi r^2 h$ *Special Right Triangles*

The number of degrees in a circle is 360°
The angles of a triangle measured in degrees have a sum of 180°

1. Sarah is twice as old as John. Six years ago, Sarah was 4 times as old as John was then. How old is John now?

   (A) 3
   (B) 9
   (C) 18
   (D) 20
   (E) Cannot be determined.

2. 200 is what percent of 20?

   (A) $\frac{1}{10}$
   (B) 10
   (C) 100
   (D) 1,000
   (E) 10,000

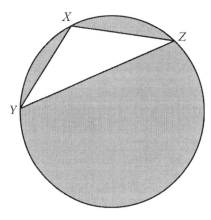

3. In the diagram above, ΔXYZ has been inscribed in a circle. If the circle encloses an area of 64, and the area of ΔXYZ is 15, then what is the area of the shaded region?

   (A) 25
   (B) 36
   (C) 49
   (D) 79
   (E) Cannot be determined.

GO ON TO THE NEXT PAGE

4. $66^2 + 2(34)(66) + 34^2 =$

    (A) 4,730
    (B) 5,000
    (C) 9,860
    (D) 9,950
    (E) 10,000

5. The average height of three students is 68 inches. If two of the students have heights of 70 inches and 72 inches respectively, then what is the height (in inches) of the third student?

    (A) 60
    (B) 62
    (C) 64
    (D) 65
    (E) 66

6. If $0 < x < 1$, then which of the following must be true?
    I. $2x < 2$
    II. $x - 1 < 0$
    III. $x^2 < x$

    (A) I only
    (B) II only
    (C) I and II only
    (D) II and III only
    (E) I, II, and III

7. The sum of the cubes of any two consecutive positive integers is always

    (A) An odd integer
    (B) An even integer
    (C) The cube of an integer.
    (D) The square of an integer.
    (E) The product of an integer and 3

8. If p is a positive integers, which *could* be an odd integer?

    (A) $2p + 2$
    (B) $p^3 - p$
    (C) $p^2 + p$
    (D) $p^2 - p$
    (E) $7p - 3$

A _____ l

9. In the figure above, two points, B and C, are placed to the right of point A such that $4AB = 3AC$. The value of BC/AB?

    (A) equals $\frac{1}{3}$

    (B) equals $\frac{2}{3}$

    (C) equals $\frac{3}{2}$

    (D) equals 3
    (E) Cannot be determined.

GO ON TO THE NEXT PAGE

10. If 12 is the average (arithmetic mean) of 5 different integers, each integer > 0, then what is the greatest that any one of the integers could be?

234

11. A classroom has 12 seated students, 5 students at the board and 7 empty seats. If 3 students leave the room, 2 enter and all sit down, how many empty seats will there be?

12. How many different *pairs* of parallel edges are there in a rectangular solid?

13. In the sum of $2r$ and $2r + 3$ is less than 11, find a possible value of r?

1

14. Given the sum of two angles of a quadrilateral is 90^0, find the average (arithmetic mean) of the measures of the other two angles. (Disregard the angle sign when gridding in your answer.)

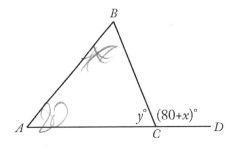

15. If AD is a straight line segment in the figure above, find the value of $x + y$.

100

GO ON TO THE NEXT PAGE

16. If $x^2 + 2xy + y^2 = 25$, $x + y > 0$ and $x - y = 1$, then $x =$

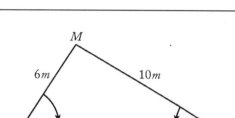

17. In the figure above, if sides LM and NM are cut apart from each other at point M creating 2 free swinging segments and each is folded down to LN in the directions shown by the arrows, what will be the length, in meters, of the overlap of 2 segments?(Disregard the thickness of the segment.)

18. A man rode bicycle a straight distance at a speed of 10 miles per hour. He came back the same way, traveling the same distance at a speed of 20 miles per hour. What was the man's total number of miles for the trip back and forth if his total traveling time was one hour?

(A) 15

(B) $13\frac{1}{3}$

(C) $7\frac{1}{2}$

(D) $6\frac{2}{3}$

(E) $6\frac{1}{3}$

19. If the symbol ♦ is defined by the equation $a ♦ b = a - b - ab$ for all a and b, then
$$\left(-\frac{1}{3}\right) ♦ (-3) =$$

(A) $\frac{5}{3}$

(B) $\frac{11}{3}$

(C) $-\frac{13}{5}$

(D) -4

(E) -5

20. If $y^8 = 4$ and $y^7 = \frac{3}{x}$, what is the value of y in terms of x?

(A) $\frac{4x}{3}$

(B) $\frac{3x}{4}$

(C) $\frac{4}{x}$

(D) $\frac{x}{4}$

(E) $\frac{12}{x}$

21. If $4x + 5y = 10$ and $x + 3y = 8$, then $\frac{5x+8y}{3} =$

(A) 18

(B) 15

(C) 12

(D) 9

(E) 6

GO ON TO THE NEXT PAGE

22. The size of a television screen is given as the length of the screen's diagonal. If the screens were flat, then the area of a square 21-inch screen would be how many square inches greater than the area of a square 19-inch screen?

(A) 2
(B) 4
(C) 16
(D) 38
(E) 40

23. If the average (arithmetic mean) of x and y is 60 and the average (arithmetic mean) of y and z is 80, what is the value of $z - x$?

(A) 70
(B) 40
(C) 20
(D) 10
(E) It cannot be determined from the information given.

24. If 3 and 8 are the lengths of two sides of a triangular region, which of the following can be the length of the third side?

I.   5
II. 8
III. 11

(A) II only
(B) III only
(C) I and II only
(D) II and III only
(E) I, II, and III

25. One night a certain motel rented $\frac{3}{4}$ of its rooms, including $\frac{2}{3}$ of its air-conditioned rooms. If $\frac{3}{5}$ of its rooms were air-conditioned, what percent of the rooms that were <u>not</u> rented were air-conditioned?

(A) 20%
(B) $33\frac{1}{3}$%
(C) 35%
(D) 40%
(E) 80%

26. A certain electronic component is sold in boxes of 54 for $16.20 and in boxes of 27 for $13.20. A customer who needed only 54 components for a project had to buy 2 boxes of 27 because boxes of 54 were unavailable. Approximately how much more did the customer pay for each component due to the unavailability of the larger boxes?

(A) $0.33
(B) $0.19
(C) $0.11
(D) $0.06
(E) $0.03

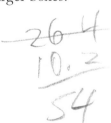

GO ON TO THE NEXT PAGE

27. On a certain street, there is an odd number of houses in a row. The houses in the row are painted alternately white and green, with the first house painted white. If n is the total number of houses in the row, how many of the houses are painted white?

   (A) $\frac{n+1}{2}$

   (B) $\frac{n-1}{2}$

   (C) $\frac{n}{2} + 1$

   (D) $\frac{n}{2} - 1$

   (E) $\frac{n}{2}$

28. Which of the following fractions is equal to the decimal 0.0625?

   (A) $\frac{5}{8}$

   (B) $\frac{3}{8}$

   (C) $\frac{1}{16}$

   (D) $\frac{1}{18}$

   (E) $\frac{3}{80}$

29. The regular price of a can of soup is $0.40, and every 3 cans is sold for $1.00. The price is reduced at a sale and each can is $0.30 and every 3 cans is sold for $0.75. If 14 cans are bought at this sale, how much money is saved?

   (A) $1.00
   (B) $1.20
   (C) $1.50
   (D) $2.20
   (E) $2.50

30. If Jim and Tom go on a fishing trip and catch 10 trout, 15 bass, and 15 yellowtails, what percent of the catch were the trout?

   (A) 25%

   (B) $33\frac{1}{3}\%$

   (C) $37\frac{1}{2}\%$

   (D) 40%

   (E) $42\frac{1}{2}\%$

31. $\frac{(0.3)^5}{(0.3)^3} =$

   (A) 0.001
   (B) 0.01
   (C) 0.09
   (D) 0.9
   (E) 1.0

GO ON TO THE NEXT PAGE

32. The cost to rent a small bus for a trip is x dollars, which is to be shared equally among the people taking the trip. If 10 people take the trip rather than 16, how many more dollars, in terms of x, will it cost per person?

(A) $\frac{x}{6}$

(B) $\frac{x}{10}$

(C) $\frac{x}{16}$

(D) $\frac{3x}{40}$

(E) $\frac{3x}{80}$

34. An optometrist charges \$150 per pair for soft contact lenses and \$85 per pair for hard contact lenses. Last week she sold 5 more pairs of soft lenses than hard lenses. If her total sales for pairs of contact lenses last week were \$1,690, what was the total number of pairs of contact lenses that she sold?

(A) 11

(B) 13

(C) 15

(D) 17

(E) 19

33. If x is an integer and $y = 3x + 2$, which of the following CANNOT be a divisor of y?

(A) 4

(B) 5

(C) 6

(D) 7

(E) 8

STOP

this is the end of the exercise

SAT Math Exercise #12

34 questions

Reference Information

     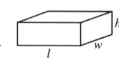

$A = \pi r^2$
$C = 2\pi r$

$A = lw$

$A = \frac{1}{2}bh$

$V = lwh$

$V = \pi r^2 h$

Special Right Triangles

The number of degrees in a circle is 360°
The angles of a triangle measured in degrees have a sum of 180°

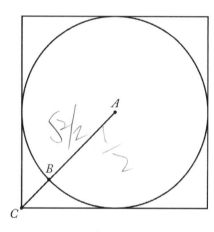

1. The circle with center A and radius AB is inscribed in the square here. AB is extended to C. What is the ratio of AB to AC?

    -Figure

    (A) $\sqrt{2}$

    (B) $\frac{\sqrt{2}}{4}$

    (C) $\frac{\sqrt{2}-1}{2}$

    (D) $\frac{\sqrt{2}}{2}$

    (E) None of these.

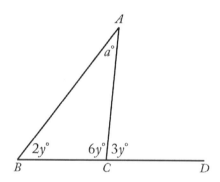

2. In the figure above, side BC of triangle ABC is extended to D. What is the value of a?

    (A) 15
    (B) 17
    (C) 20
    (D) 24
    (E) 30

GO ON TO THE NEXT PAGE

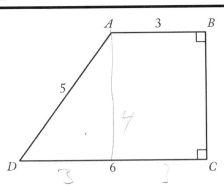

3. What is the perimeter of the figure above if B and C are right angles?

(A) 14
(B) 16
(C) 18
(D) 20
(E) Cannot be determined.

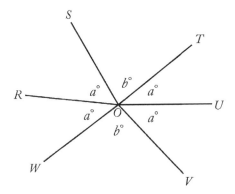

4. Which of the angles below has a degree measure that can be determined?

(A) $\angle WOS$
(B) $\angle SOU$
(C) $\angle WOT$
(D) $\angle ROV$
(E) $\angle WOV$

5. If $y^8 = 4$ and $y^7 = \frac{3}{x}$, what is the value of y in terms of x?

(A) $\frac{4x}{3}$
(B) $\frac{3x}{4}$
(C) $\frac{4}{x}$
(D) $\frac{x}{4}$
(E) $\frac{12}{x}$

6. If $y + 2q = 15, q + 2p = 5,$ and $p + 2y = 7$, then $p + q + y =$

(A) 6
(B) 7
(C) 8
(D) 9
(E) 10

7. Sarah is twice as old as John. Six years ago Sarah was 4 times as old as John was then. How old is John now?

(A) 3
(B) 18
(C) 20
(D) 9
(E) Cannot be determined.

GO ON TO THE NEXT PAGE

8. If $x + y = 7$ and $xy = 4$, then $x^2 + y^2 =$

(A) 38
(B) 39
(C) 40
(D) 41
(E) 42

x	$f(x)$
0	3
1	4
2	2
3	5
4	8

11. According to the table above, for what value of x does $f(x) = x + 2$?

(A) 0
(B) 1
(C) 2
(D) 3
(E) 4

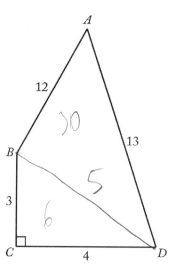

9. The area of the above figure $ABCD$

(A) is 36
(B) is 108
(C) is 156
(D) is 1872
(E) Cannot be determined.

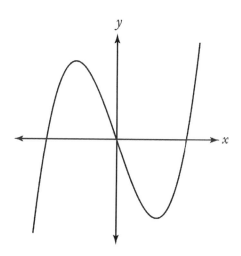

10. On a street with 25 houses, 10 houses have fewer than 6 *rooms,* 10 houses have *more than 8 rooms.* What is the total number of houses on the street that are *either* 6-, 7-. or 8-room houses?

(A) 5
(B) 9
(C) 11
(D) 14
(E) 15

12. Which of the equation could represent the graph above?

(A) $y = x^3 + 2$
(B) $y = x^3 + 2x + 4$
(C) $y = x^2$
(D) $y = x^3 - x$
(E) $y = x^3 + x^2 - x - 1$

GO ON TO THE NEXT PAGE

13. The degree measures of the four angles of a quadrilateral are $w, x, y,$ and respectively. If w is the average (arithmetic mean) of $x, y,$ and $z,$ then $x + y + z =$

    (A) 45°
    (B) 90°
    (C) 120°
    (D) 180°
    (E) 270°

14. If the numerical value of the binomial coefficient $\binom{n}{2}$ is given by formula $\frac{n(n-1)}{2}$, then what is the numerical value of $\binom{15}{2}$?

15. The letters r and s represent numbers satisfying $r^2 = 9$ and $s^2 = 25$. What is the difference between the greatest possible values of $s - r$ and $r - s$?

$$
\begin{array}{r}
N\ 5 \\
\times\ L\ M \\
\hline
3\ 8\ 5 \\
3\ 8\ 5 \\
\hline
4\ 2\ 3\ 5
\end{array}
$$

16. In the multiplication problem above, L, M, and N each represent one of the digits 0 through 9. If the problem is computed correctly, find N.

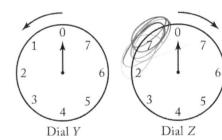

Dial Y   Dial Z

17. In the figure above, the hand of dial Z moves in a clockwise direction. When its hand makes one complete revolution, it causes the hand of dial Y to move 1 number in the counterclockwise direction. How many complete revolution of the hand of dial Z are needed to move the hand of dial Z are needed to move the hand of dial Y 3 complete revolution?

GO ON TO THE NEXT PAGE

18. According to the graph, what percent of the people in the group had brown eyes?
-Graph

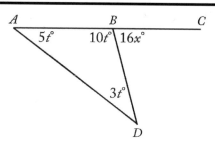

21. In the figure above, *ABC* is a line segment. What is the value of x?

19. To make enough paste to hang 6 rolls of wallpaper. A $\frac{1}{4}$ – pound package of powder is mixed with $2\frac{1}{2}$ quarts of water. How many pounds of powder are needed to make enough of the same mixture of the paste to hang 21 rolls of paper?

22. An athlete runs 90 laps in 6 hours. This is the same as how many laps per minute?

(A) $\frac{1}{15}$

(B) $\frac{1}{9}$

(C) $\frac{1}{4}$

(D) $\frac{1}{2}$

(E) 1

20. On a mathematic test, the average score for a certain class was 90. If 40 percent of the class scored 100 and 10 percent scored 80, what was the average score for the remainder of the class?

23. If $x = 16, x^{-3/4} =$

(A) $\frac{1}{2}$

(B) $\frac{1}{4}$

(C) $\frac{1}{8}$

(D) $\frac{1}{16}$

(E) $\frac{1}{32}$

GO ON TO THE NEXT PAGE

24. If for x, real, $f(x) = (x - 1)^2 + (x - 2)^2 + (x - 3)^2$, $f(x + 2) =$

    (A) $3x^2 + 4x + 2$
    (B) $3x$
    (C) $(x + 2)^2 + x^2 + (x - 2)^2$
    (D) $3x^2 + 2$
    (E) $4x^2 + 4$

25. If r and s are negative numbers, then all of the following must be positive *except*

    (A) $\frac{r}{s}$
    (B) rs
    (C) $(rs)^2$
    (D) $r + s$
    (E) $-r - s$

26. If $f(x) = x^2 + 2x + 1$, $f(x - 1) =$

    (A) $x^2 + 2x$
    (B) 0
    (C) 1
    (D) x^2
    (E) $2x + 1$

27. Which of the following is a graph of $y = 2x - 4$?

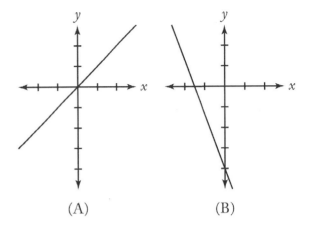

    (A)   (B)

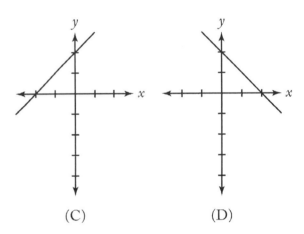

    (C)   (D)

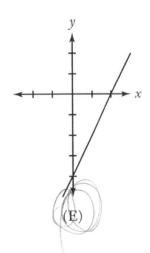

    (E)

GO ON TO THE NEXT PAGE

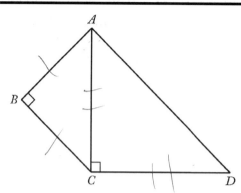

28. In the figure above, $AB = BC$ and $AC = CD$.
How many of the angles have a measure of 45 degrees?

(A) none
(B) two
(C) three
(D) four
(E) five

---

29. The organizers of a fair projected a 25 percent increase in attendance this year over that of last year, but attendance this year actually decreased by 20 percent. What percent of the projected attendance was the actual attendance?

(A) 45%
(B) 56%
(C) 64%
(D) 75%
(E) 80%

30. Which of the rectangles below has a length of $\frac{4}{3}$, if each has an area of 4?

(A)
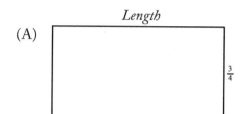

(B)
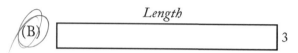

(C)
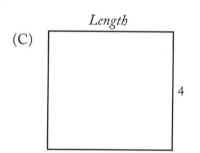

(D)
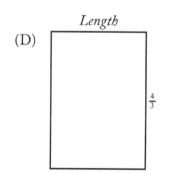

(E)
Length
$\frac{1}{4}$

GO ON TO THE NEXT PAGE

31. The ratio of two quantities is 3 to 4. If each of the quantities is increased by 5, what is the ratio of these two new quantities?

   (A) $\frac{3}{4}$

   (B) $\frac{8}{9}$

   (C) $\frac{18}{19}$

   (D) $\frac{23}{24}$

   (E) It cannot be determined from the information given.

32. In 1986 the book value of a certain car was $\frac{2}{3}$ of the original purchase price, and in 1988 its book value was $\frac{1}{2}$ of the original purchase price. By what percent did the book value of this car decrease from 1986 to 1988?

   (A) $16\frac{2}{3}\%$

   (B) 25%

   (C) $33\frac{1}{3}\%$

   (D) 50%

   (E) 75%

33. An automobile's gasoline mileage varies, depending on the sped of the automobile, between 18.0 and 22.4 miles per gallon, inclusive. What is the maximum distance, in miles, that the automobile could be driven on 15 gallons of gasoline?

   (A) 336
   (B) 320
   (C) 303
   (D) 284
   (E) 270

34. In a horticultural experiment, 200 seeds were planted in plot I and 300 were planted in plot II. If 57 percent of the seeds in plot I germinated and 42 percent of the seeds in plot II germinated, what percent of the total number of planted seeds germinated?

   (A) 45.5%
   (B) 46.5%
   (C) 48.0%
   (D) 49.5%
   (E) 51.0%

STOP

this is the end of the exercise

SAT Math Exercise #13

34 questions

Reference Information

    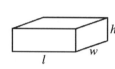   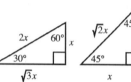

$A = \pi r^2$
$C = 2\pi r$

$A = lw$

$A = \frac{1}{2}bh$

$V = lwh$

$V = \pi r^2 h$

Special Right Triangles

The number of degrees in a circle is 360°
The angles of a triangle measured in degrees have a sum of 180°

1. What fraction of 1 week is 24 min?

(A) $\frac{1}{60}$

(B) $\frac{1}{168}$

(C) $\frac{1}{420}$

(D) $\frac{1}{1440}$

(E) $\frac{1}{10080}$

2. $2 \times 10^{-5} \times 8 \times 10^2 \times 5 \times 10^2 =$

(A) .00008
(B) .008
(C) .08
(D) 8
(E) 800

3. Johnny spent $\frac{2}{5}$ of his allowance on candy and $\frac{5}{6}$ of the remainder on ice cream. If his allowance is $30, how much money did he have left after buying the candy and ice cream?

(A) $1
(B) $2
(C) $3
(D) $5
(E) $10

GO ON TO THE NEXT PAGE

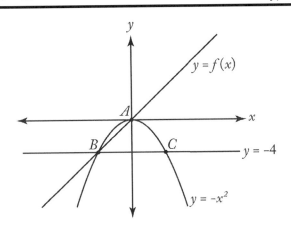

4. The x-coordinate of point B is

   (A) -2
   (B) -3
   (C) -4
   (D) -5
   (E) -6

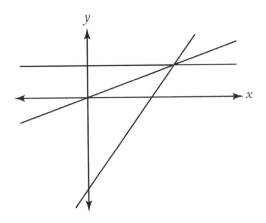

5. Which of the following equations could *not* represent any of the above graphs?

   (A) $2y = x$
   (B) $y = 2$
   (C) $y = 2x - 6$
   (D) $y = 2x + 4$
   (E) $y = 4$

6. The graph of the equation $y = f(x)$ is of the form $y = mx + b$ where b is

   (A) 0
   (B) 1
   (C) 2
   (D) 3
   (E) 4

7. If $f(x) = |x| - x$, which of the following is true?

   (A) $f(x) = f(-x)$
   (B) $f(2x) = 2f(x)$
   (C) $f(x + y) = f(x) + f(y)$
   (D) $f(x) = -f(-x)$
   (E) $f(x - y) = 0$

8. At how many points does the graph of the equation $y = x^4 + x^3$ intersect the x-axis?

   (A) 0
   (B) 1
   (C) 2
   (D) 3
   (E) 4

GO ON TO THE NEXT PAGE

9. If a and b are positive integers and $ab = 64$, what is the smallest possible value of $a + b$?

(A) 65
(B) 34
(C) 20
(D) 16
(E) 8

10. Find the value of $x + x^3 + x^5 + x^6$ if $x = -1$

(A) -4
(B) -2
(C) 1
(D) 2
(E) 4

$$\begin{array}{r} A\ \ B \\ +\ B\ \ A \\ \hline 6\ \ 6 \end{array}$$

11. If $0 < A < 6$ and $0 < B < 6$ in the addition problem above, how many different integer values of A are possible?

(A) Two
(B) Three
(C) Four
(D) Five
(E) Six

12. At 8:00 A.M. the outside temperature was $-15°F$. At 11:00 A.M. the temperature was $0°F$. If the temperature continues to rise at the same uniform rate, what will the temperature be at 5:00 P.M. on the same day?

(A) $-15°F$
(B) $-5°F$
(C) $0°F$
(D) $15°F$
(E) $30°F$

Number of Shirts	Total Price
1	$12.00
Box of 3	$22.50
Box of 6	$43.40

13. Which of the following is the closest approximation of the lowest cost per shirt, when a box of shirts is purchased?

(A) $7.10
(B) $7.20
(C) $7.30
(D) $7.40
(E) $7.50

14. If exactly 11 shirts are to be purchased, what is the minimum amount of money that must be spent?

(A) $65.90
(B) $89.90
(C) $91.50
(D) $103.40
(E) $132.00

GO ON TO THE NEXT PAGE

15. If $5x^2 - 15x = 0$ and $x \neq 0$, find the value of x.

(A) -10
(B) -3
(C) 10
(D) 5
(E) 3

16. The chickens on a certain farm consumed 600 pounds of feed in half a year. During that time the total number of eggs laid was 5,000. If the feed cost \$1.25 per pound, then the feed cost per egg was

(A) \$0.0750
(B) \$0.1250
(C) \$0.15
(D) \$0.25
(E) \$0.3333

17. If 55,555 $= y + 50,505$ find the value of $50,505 - 10y$.

(A) -5.05
(B) 0
(C) 5
(D) 5.05
(E) 50.5

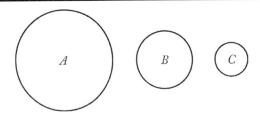

18. In the figure above, there are three circles, $A, B,$ and C. The area of A is three times that of B, and the area of B is three times that of C. If the area of B is 1, find the sum of areas of $A, B,$ and C.

(A) 3
(B) $3\frac{1}{2}$
(C) $4\frac{1}{3}$
(D) 5
(E) $6\frac{1}{3}$

19. If $m = 94$ and $n = 6$, then find the value of $23m + 23n$

20. A horizontal line has a length of 100 yards. A vertical line is drawn at one of its ends. If lines are drawn every ten yards thereafter, until the other end is reached, how many vertical lines are finally drawn?

GO ON TO THE NEXT PAGE

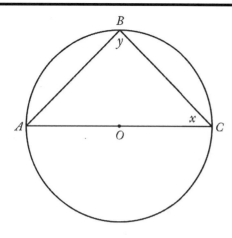

21. In the circle above with center O, diameter AC, and AB=BC, find the value of $x + y$.

24. Given the circle above, with center P, what is the length of its radius?

22. In a certain class containing 60 students, the average (arithmetic mean) age is 20. In another class containing 20 students, the average age is 40. Find the average age of all 80 students.

25. A lawn covers 108.6 square feet. Russ mowed all of the lawn in three evenings. He mowed $\frac{2}{9}$ of the lawn during the first evening. He mowed twice that amount on the second evening. On the third and final evening he moved the remaining lawn. How many square feet were mowed on the third evening?

23. In the addition problem shown below, if □ is a constant, where must □ equal in equal in order for the answer to be correct?

$$\square \, 1$$
$$6 \, \square$$
$$\square \, 9$$
$$\overline{15 \, \square}$$

26. If $\frac{5}{8}$ of a number is 3 less than $\frac{3}{4}$ of the number, what is the number?

GO ON TO THE NEXT PAGE

27. $[(3a^3b^2)^3]^2 =$

   (A) $27a^9b^6$
   (B) $54a^9b^6$
   (C) $729a^9b^6$
   (D) $729a^{18}b^{12}$
   (E) $729a^{54}b^{16}$

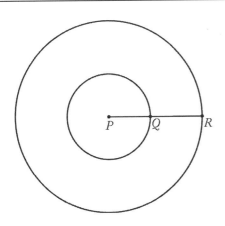

28. In the figure above, two concentric circles with center P are shown. PQS, a radius of the larger circle, equals 9. PQ, a radius of the smaller circle, equals 4. If a circle L (not shown) is drawn with center at R and Q on its circumference, find the radius of circle L.

   (A) 13
   (B) 5
   (C) 4
   (D) 2
   (E) It cannot be determined from the information given.

29. Given that $\left(\frac{3}{10}\right)^2$ is equal to p hundredth, find the value of p.

   (A) 5
   (B) 6
   (C) 9
   (D) 12
   (E) 32

30. Find the circumference of a circle that has the same area as a square that has perimeter 2π.

   (A) $2\sqrt{2}$
   (B) $\pi\sqrt{\pi}$
   (C) $\frac{\pi}{2}$
   (D) $\frac{\sqrt{2}}{\pi}$
   (E) 2

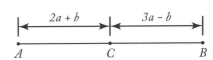

31. Given ACB is a straight line segment, and C is the midpoint of AB. If the two segments have the lengths shown above, then
   (A) $a = -2b$
   (B) $a = -\frac{2}{5}b$
   (C) $a = \frac{2}{5}b$
   (D) $a = b$
   (E) $a = 2b$

GO ON TO THE NEXT PAGE

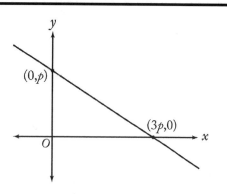

32. What is the slope of line l in the above figure?

(A) -3

(B) $-\frac{1}{3}$

(C) 0

(D) $\frac{1}{3}$

(E) 3

33. Bus A averages 40 kilometers per gallon of fuel. Bus B averages 50 kilometers per gallon of fuel. If the price of fuel is $3 per gallon, how much less would an 800-kilometer trip cost for Bus B than for Bus A?

(A) $18
(B) $16
(C) $14
(D) $12
(E) $10

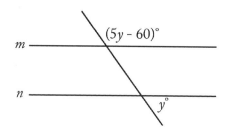

34. $m \parallel n$ in the figure above. Find y.

(A) 10
(B) 20
(C) 40
(D) 65
(E) 175

STOP

this is the end of the exercise

SAT Math Exercise #14

34 questions

Reference Information

   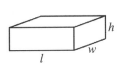

$A = \pi r^2$
$C = 2\pi r$ $A = lw$ $A = \frac{1}{2}bh$ $V = lwh$ $V = \pi r^2 h$ *Special Right Triangles*

The number of degrees in a circle is 360°
The angles of a triangle measured in degrees have a sum of 180°

1. Given the percent of $(2a + b)$ is 18 and a is a positive integer. What is the *greatest* possible value of b?

   (A) $19\frac{4}{9}°$
   (B) $31°$
   (C) $51°$
   (D) $63°$
   (E) $82°$

2. A square has an area of R^2. An equilateral triangle has a perimeter of E. If r is the perimeter of the square and e is a side of the equilateral triangle, then, in terms of R and E, $e + r =$

   (A) $\frac{E+R}{7}$
   (B) $\frac{4R+3E}{3}$
   (C) $\frac{3E+4R}{12}$
   (D) $\frac{12E+R}{3}$
   (E) $\frac{E+12R}{3}$

3. Using the formula $C = \frac{5}{9}(F - 32)$, if the Celsius (C) temperature increased 35°, by how many degrees would the Fahrenheit (F) temperature be increased?

   (A) $19\frac{4}{9}°$
   (B) $31°$
   (C) $51°$
   (D) $63°$
   (E) $82°$

GO ON TO THE NEXT PAGE

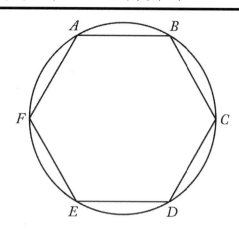

4. Equilateral polygon $ABCDEF$ is inscribed in the circle. If the length of arc BAF is 14π, find the length of the diameter of the circle.

(A) 7
(B) 14
(C) 7π
(D) 21
(E) 42

5. If $\frac{a}{b} = \frac{1}{4}$, where a is positive integer, which of the following is a possible value of $\frac{a^2}{b}$?

    I. $\frac{1}{4}$
    II. $\frac{1}{2}$
    III. 1

(A) None
(B) I only
(C) I and II only
(D) I and III only
(E) I, II, and III

6. A plane left airport A and has traveled x kilometers per hour for y hour. In terms of x and y, how many kilometers from airport A had the plane traveled $\frac{2}{3}y$ hours ago?

(A) $\frac{xy}{6}$
(B) $\frac{xy}{3}$
(C) xy
(D) $\frac{3xy}{2}$
(E) $\frac{xy}{12}$

7. The average (arithmetic mean) of k scores is 20. The average of 10 of these scores is 15. Find the average of the remaining scores in terms of k?

(A) $\frac{20k+150}{10}$
(B) $\frac{20k-150}{10}$
(C) $\frac{150-20k}{10}$
(D) $\frac{150-20k}{k-10}$
(E) $\frac{20k-150}{k-10}$

GO ON TO THE NEXT PAGE

8. If $\sqrt{x}$ is an odd integer, which of the following *MUST* be even?

(A) x
(B) $3\sqrt{x}$
(C) $\sqrt{2x}$
(D) $2\sqrt{x}$
(E) x^2

9. If a rectangle is drawn on the grid above with line *MN* as one of its diagonals, which of the following could be the coordinates of another vertex of the rectangle?

(A) $(1 , 0)$
(B) $(2 , 0)$
(C) $(3 , 3)$
(D) $(4 , 3)$
(E) $(5 , 2)$

10. The degree measures of the four angles of a quadrilateral are $w, x, y,$ and z respectively. If w is the average (arithmetic mean) of $x, y,$ and z, then $x + y + z =$

(A) $45°$
(B) $90°$
(C) $120°$
(D) $180°$
(E) $270°$

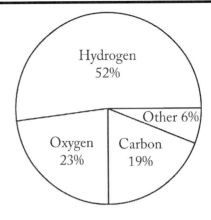

11. A certain mixture contains carbon, oxygen, hydrogen, and other elements in the percentages shown in the graph below. If the total mixture weighs 24 pounds, which number represents the closest number of pounds of carbon that is contained in the mixture?

(A) 5.2
(B) 4.6
(C) 2.1
(D) 1.2
(E) 0.5

12. If p is the average of x and y, and if q is the average of y and z, and if r is the average of x and z, then what is the average of $x, y,$ and z?

(A) $\frac{p+q+r}{3}$

(B) $\frac{p+q+r}{2}$

(C) $\frac{2}{3}(p + q + r)$

(D) $p + q + r$

(E) $\frac{3}{2}(p + q + r)$

GO ON TO THE NEXT PAGE

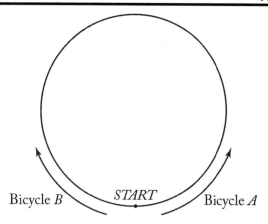

Bicycle B   START   Bicycle A

13. In the figure above, two bicycles are being pedaled in opposite directions around a circular race track of circumference = 120 feet. Bicycle A is traveling at 5 feet/second in the counterclockwise direction, and Bicycle B is traveling at 8 feet/second in clockwise direction. When Bicycle B has completed exactly 600 revolutions, how many complete revolutions will Bicycle A have made?

(A) 180
(B) 375
(C) 475
(D) 960
(E) It cannot be determined from the given information.

14. At Jones College, there are total of 100 students. If 30 of the students have cars on campus and 50 have bicycles, and 20 have both cars and bicycles, then how many students have neither a car nor a bicycle on campus?

(A) 80
(B) 60
(C) 40
(D) 20
(E) 0

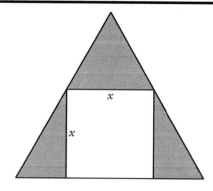

15. A square of side x is inscribed inside an equilateral triangle of area $x^2\sqrt{3}$. If a rectangle with width x has the same area as the shaded region shown in the figure above, what is the length of the rectangle in terms of x?

(A) $\sqrt{3}x - 1$
(B) $x\sqrt{3}$
(C) $\sqrt{3} - x$
(D) $x(\sqrt{3} - 1)$
(E) $x^2\sqrt{3} - x^2$

16. Tommy and Bobby like to watch their school's baseball team play. Tommy watched $\frac{2}{3}$ of all the games the team played last season. Bobby watched 28 games. If Tommy watched more games than Bobby did last season, which of the following could be the number of games the team played last season?

(A) 33
(B) 36
(C) 39
(D) 42
(E) 45

GO ON TO THE NEXT PAGE

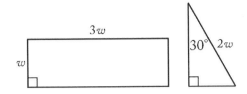

17. The length and width of a rectangle are $3w$ and w respectively. The length of hypotenuse of a right triangle, one of whose acute angles is 30°, is $2w$. What is the ratio of the area of the rectangle to that of the triangle?

(A) $2\sqrt{3}:1$
(B) $\sqrt{3}:1$
(C) $1:\sqrt{3}$
(D) $1:2\sqrt{3}$
(E) $1:6$

18. At a certain college, the number of freshmen is three times the number of seniors. If $\frac{1}{4}$ of the freshmen and $\frac{1}{3}$ of the seniors attend a football game, what fraction of total number of freshman and seniors attends the game?

(A) $\frac{5}{24}$
(B) $\frac{13}{48}$
(C) $\frac{17}{48}$
(D) $\frac{11}{24}$
(E) $\frac{23}{48}$

19. Let Δn represent the greatest even integer less than n that divides n, for any positive integer n. For example, $\Delta24=12$. Find the value of $\Delta20$

20. At a certain picnic, each of the guests was served either a single scoop or a double scoop of ice cream. At the picnic, 60 percent of the guests were served a double scoop of ice cream and a total of 120 scoops of ice cream were served to all the guests at the picnic.
How many of the guests were served a double scoop of ice cream?

21. By what percent was the price of a certain candy bar increased if the price of the candy bar was increased by 5 cents and the price after the increase was 45 cents?

GO ON TO THE NEXT PAGE

22. A certain bakery sells rye bread in 16-ounce loaves and 24-ounce loaves, and all loaves of the same size sell for the same price per loaf regardless of the number of loaves purchased. What is the price of a 24-ounce loaf of rye bread in this bakery if the total price of a 16-ounce loaf and a 24-ounce loaf of this bread is $2.40 and the total price of two 16-ounce loaves and one 24-ounce loaf of this bread is $3.40?

23. If a certain company hires 3 employees and all of the present employees remain, there will be at least 20 employees in the company. If no additional employees are hired by the company and 3 of the present employees resign, there will be fewer than 15 employees in the company. How many employees are currently in the company?

24. If a, b, and c are integers, and b is negative and c is positive, is $a-b+c$ greater than $a+b-c$?

25. If x and y are positive, and $x = 3.927y$ and $y = 2.279$, what is the value of x to the nearest thousandth?

26. Carlotta can drive from her home to her office by one of two possible routes. When she drives from her home to her office by the shorter route and returns by the longer route she drives a total of 42 kilometers. When she drives to the office and back by the longer route, she drives a total of 46 kilometers. What is the distance of the shorter route?

GO ON TO THE NEXT PAGE

27. $3x(4x + 2y) =$

(A) $7x + 5xy$
(B) $12x + 6xy$
(C) $12x^2 + 2y$
(D) $12x^2 + 6xy$
(E) $12x^2 + 6x$

Box Number	Height of Box (in millimeters)
A	1700
B	2450
C	2735
D	1928
E	2130

28. Exactly how many of the boxes listed in the table above are more than 20 decimeters high? (1 decimeter = 100 millimeters)

(A) Zero
(B) One
(C) Two
(D) Three
(E) Four

29. If $a - 3 = 7$, then $2a - 14 =$

(A) -6
(B) -4
(C) 2
(D) 4
(E) 6

30. An athlete runs 90 laps in 6 hours. This is the same as how many laps per minute?

(A) $\frac{1}{15}$

(B) $\frac{1}{9}$

(C) $\frac{1}{4}$

(D) $\frac{1}{2}$

(E) 1

31. $\frac{7}{10} + \frac{7}{100} + \frac{77}{1000} =$

(A) .0091
(B) .7777
(C) .784
(D) .847
(E) .854

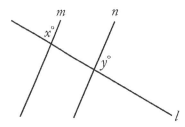

32. Parallel lines m and n are intersected by line l as shown. Find the value of $x + y$.

(A) 180
(B) 150
(C) 120
(D) 90
(E) It cannot be determined form the information given.

GO ON TO THE NEXT PAGE

Item	Value
1	P
2	$P \times 3$
3	$(P \times 3) \div 2$
4	$[(P \times 3) \div 2] + 12$
5	$[(P \times 3) \div 2] + 12 - 1$

33. According to the table above, which item has the greatest value when $P = 12$?

(A) 1
(B) 2
(C) 3
(D) 4
(E) 5

34. If $\frac{3x}{4} = 9$, find $6x$

(A) 12
(B) 18
(C) 27
(D) 36
(E) 72

STOP

this is the end of the exercise

SAT Math Exercise #15

34 questions

Reference Information

    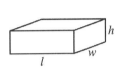

$A = \pi r^2$
$C = 2\pi r$ $A = lw$ $A = \frac{1}{2}bh$ $V = lwh$ $V = \pi r^2 h$ *Special Right Triangles*

The number of degrees in a circle is 360°
The angles of a triangle measured in degrees have a sum of 180°

1. If 8 people share a winning lottery ticket and divide the cash prize equally, what percent of the prize do 2 of them together receive?

   (A) 8%
   (B) 10%
   (C) 20%
   (D) 25%
   (E) 40%

2. Given $8r + 3s = 12$ and $7r + 2s = 9$, find the value of $5(r + s)$.

   (A) 5
   (B) 10
   (C) 15
   (D) 20
   (E) 25

3. Paul's average (arithmetic mean) for 3 tests was 85. The average of his score for the first two tests was also 85. What was his score for the third test?

   (A) 80
   (B) 85
   (C) 90
   (D) 95
   (E) It cannot be determined from the information given.

GO ON TO THE NEXT PAGE

4. The operation ⊙ is defined for all numbers x and y by the following: $x \odot y = 3 + xy$. For example, $2 \odot 7 = 3 + 2(7) = 17$. If $y \neq 0$ and x is a number such that $x \odot y = 3$, then find x.

(A) 0

(B) $-\dfrac{3}{y}$

(C) $-y + 3$

(D) $\dfrac{3}{y}$

(E) $y + 3$

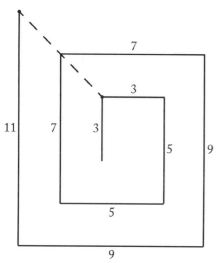

5. In the figure above, each pair of intersecting segments is perpendicular with lengths as shown. Find the length of the dash line segment.

(A) 7
(B) $6\sqrt{3}$
(C) $4\sqrt{2}$
(D) $\sqrt{46}$
(E) $\sqrt{59}$

6. For how many two-digit positive numbers tripling the tens digit give us a two-digit number that is triple the original number?

(A) None
(B) One
(C) Two
(D) Three
(E) Four

7. If A is the least positive 5-digit integer with *nonzero* digits, none of which is repeated, and B is the greatest of such positive integers, then $B - A =$

(A) 2,468
(B) 66,666
(C) 86,420
(D) 86,424
(E) 89,999

8. At one instant, two meteors are 2,500 kilometers apart and traveling toward each other in straight paths along the imaginary line joining them. One meteor has a velocity of 300 meters per second while the other travels at 700 meters per second. Assuming that their velocities are constant and that they continue along the same paths, how many seconds elapse from the first instant to the time of their collision (1 kilometer = 1000 meters)

(A) 250
(B) 500
(C) 1,250
(D) 2,500
(E) 5,000

GO ON TO THE NEXT PAGE

9. Let $x = \sqrt{\dfrac{1}{9} + \left(\dfrac{1}{3} + \dfrac{1}{9} + \dfrac{1}{27} + \dfrac{1}{81}\right)}$

   An equivalent expression for x is

   (A) $\dfrac{1}{9}$

   (B) $\dfrac{\sqrt{3}}{3}$

   (C) $\dfrac{1}{81}$

   (D) $\dfrac{1}{3\sqrt{3}}$

   (E) $\dfrac{7}{9}$

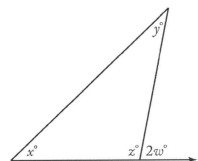

10. In the figure above, one side of a triangle has been extended. What is the value of $w + x + y$?

    (A) $3w$
    (B) $3z$
    (C) $2x + y$
    (D) $2x + 2y$
    (E) $2w + z$

Questions $11 - 12$ refer to the following game. A computer generates numbers. Points are assigned as described in the following table each time any of the four number pairs given appears in a number.

Number Pair	Number of Points
"33"	11
"34"	6
"43"	4
"44"	3

11. As an example, the number 4,347 is assigned 4 points for "43" and 6 points more for "34", giving a total of 10 points. Which of the following numbers would be assigned the most points?

    (A) 934,432
    (B) 464,457
    (C) 834,415
    (D) 437,934
    (E) 336,283

12. If a certain number has 13 points assigned to it, which of the following statements must be true?

    I.　　33 is not in the number.
    II.　　34 and 43 are both in the number.
    III.　　43 is in the number.

    (A) I only
    (B) II only
    (C) III only
    (D) I and III only
    (E) I, II, and III

GO ON TO THE NEXT PAGE

13. Given the volume of a cube is 8 cubic meters. Find the distance from any vertex to the center point inside the cube.

(A) $1m$
(B) $\sqrt{2}m$
(C) $2\sqrt{2}m$
(D) $2\sqrt{3}m$
(E) $\sqrt{3}m$

14. The ratio of Sue's age to Bob's age is 3 to 7. The ratio of Sue's age to Joe's is 4 to 9. The ratio of Bob's age to Joe's is

(A) 28 to 27
(B) 7 to 9
(C) 27 to 28
(D) 10 to 13
(E) 13 to 10

15. The sum of r consecutive positive integers will always be divisible by 2 if r is a multiple of

(A) 6
(B) 5
(C) 4
(D) 3
(E) 2

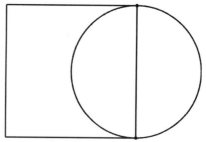

16. The square in the figure above the two sides tangent to the circle. If the area of the circle is $9a^2\pi^2$ find the area of the square.

(A) $12a^2\pi^2$
(B) $36a^2\pi$
(C) $36a^2\pi^2$
(D) $18a^4\pi^2$
(E) It cannot be determined from the informative given.

17. Given that $500w = 3 \times 700$, find the value of w.

(A) $\frac{5}{21}$
(B) 2
(C) $\frac{11}{5}$
(D) $\frac{21}{5}$
(E) 7

18. If $\frac{3+y}{y} = 7$, then $y =$

(A) 4
(B) 3
(C) 2
(D) 1
(E) $\frac{1}{2}$

GO ON TO THE NEXT PAGE

19. The total cost of the gasoline used by the car for an 180-mile trip was $12.00. The cost of the gasoline used by the car for the trip was $1.20 per gallon. What was the average number of miles per gallon of gasoline for a car during this trip?

20. The only contents of a parcel are 25 photographs and 30 negatives. If the weight of each photograph is 3 times the weight of each negative and the weight of 1 of the photographs and 2 of the negatives is $\frac{1}{3}$ ounce, what is the total weight, in ounces, of the parcel's contents?

21. If x, y, and z are three integers and $z - x = 2$ and $x < y < z$, are they consecutive integers?

22. The regular price for canned soup was reduced during a sale. The regular price for the 7-ounce cans was 3 for a dollar. The reduced price for the 7-ounce cans was 4 for a dollar. How much money could one have saved by purchasing a dozen 6-ounce cans of soup at the reduced price rather than at the regular price?

23. If r and s are integers and s is divisible by 3 and r is divisible by 3, is $r + s$ divisible by 3?

24. From May 1, 1960 to May 1, 1975, the closing price of a share of stock X doubled. From May 1, 1975 to May 1, 1984, the closing price of a share of stock X doubled, increasing by $4.50. What was the closing price of a share of stock X on May 1, 1960?

GO ON TO THE NEXT PAGE

25. One of an integer Q's digits is 3 more than the other and the sum of its digits is 9. If $Q < 50$ and Q is between 10 and 100, what is the value of Q?

26. Committee member W wants to schedule a one-hour meeting on Thursday for himself and three other committee members, X, Y, and Z. On Thursday W and X have an open period from 9:00 a.m. to 12:00 noon. On Thursday Y has an open period from 10:00 a.m. to 1:00 p.m. and Z has an open period from 8:00 a.m. to 11:00 a.m. What is the one-hour period that is open for all four members?

27. The positive integer x is a multiple of 9 and also a multiple of 12. The smallest possible value of x is

(A) 3
(B) 12
(C) 21
(D) 36
(E) 72

28. Find $(r - s)(t - s) + (s - r)(s - t)$ for all numbers r, s, and t.

(A) 0
(B) 2
(C) $2rt$
(D) $2(s - r)(t - s)$
(E) $2(r - s)(t - s)$

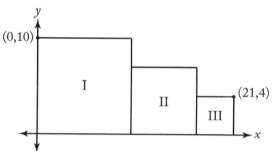

29. In the figure above, squares I, II, and III are situated along the x-axis as shown. Find the area of square II.

(A) 16
(B) 25
(C) 49
(D) 100
(E) 121

30. A certain cup holds 100 grams of butter. If a cake requires 75 grams of butter and a pie requires 225 grams of butter, then 4 cups of butter is *not* enough for any of the following *except*

(A) 6 cakes
(B) 2 pies
(C) 3 cakes and 1 pie
(D) 2 cakes and 2pie
(E) 2 cakes and 1 pie

GO ON TO THE NEXT PAGE

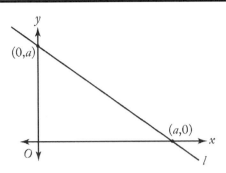

31. Which of the following is true about line l above?

I. The slope is -1
II. The distance of point $(0, a)$ to point $(a, 0)$ is equal to $a\sqrt{2}$
III. The acute angle that the line l makes with the $x-$axis is 45°

(A) I only
(B) II only
(C) III only
(D) II and III only
(E) I, II, and III

32. If 3 added to a number and this sum is divided by 4, the result is 6. What is the number?

(A) 5
(B) 7
(C) 12
(D) 21
(E) 27

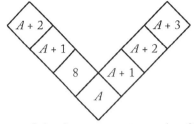

33. If the sum of the four terms in each of the diagonal rows is the same, then $A =$

(A) 4
(B) 5
(C) 6
(D) 7
(E) 8

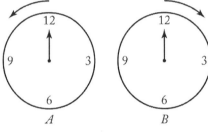

34. The dials shown above operate simultaneously in the following manner: The hand A turns *counterclockwise* while the hand in B turns *clockwise*. The hand of A moves to 9 at exactly the same moment that the hand B moves to 3. Then the hand of A moves to 6 at exactly the same moment that the hand of B moves to 6, and so on. If each hand starts at 12, where will each hand be at the end of 17 moves?

(A) Both at 12
(B) Both at 9
(C) A at 3 and B at 12
(D) A at 3 and B at 9
(E) A at 9 and B at 3

STOP

this is the end of the exercise

SAT Math Exercise #16
34 questions

Reference Information

     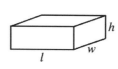

$A = \pi r^2$
$C = 2\pi r$ $A = lw$ $A = \frac{1}{2}bh$ $V = lwh$ $V = \pi r^2 h$ *Special Right Triangles*

The number of degrees in a circle is 360°
The angles of a triangle measured in degrees have a sum of 180°

1. Given that $w = 7r + 6r + 5r + 4r + 3r$, which of the terms listed below may be added to w, so that the resulting sum will be divisible by 7 for every positive integer r?

   (A) $7r$
   (B) $6r$
   (C) $5r$
   (D) $4r$
   (E) $3r$

2. If the perimeter of a square is 20 meters, how many square meters are contained in its area?

   (A) 100
   (B) 25
   (C) 20
   (D) 10
   (E) 5

3. Given that $80 + a = -32 + b$, find the value if $b - a$.

   (A) -112
   (B) -48
   (C) 2.5
   (D) 48
   (E) 112

4. If x is a positive integer, which of the following must be an even integer?

   (A) $x + 2$
   (B) $2x + 1$
   (C) $3x + 1$
   (D) $x^2 + x + 1$
   (E) $x^2 + x + 2$

GO ON TO THE NEXT PAGE

5. Given that $\frac{3}{4} < x < \frac{4}{5}$, which of the following is a possible value of x?

   (A) $\frac{7}{16}$

   (B) $\frac{13}{20}$

   (C) $\frac{31}{40}$

   (D) $\frac{16}{20}$

   (E) $\frac{6}{7}$

6. A painter earns \$10 an hour for all hours spent on a job. For a certain job, he worked from 7:00 A.M. until 5:00 P.M. On Monday, Tuesday, and Thursday and from 1:00 P.M. until 7:00 P.M. on Wednesday, Friday, and Saturday. How much did he earn for the entire job?

   (A) \$420
   (B) \$450
   (C) \$480
   (D) \$510
   (E) \$540

7. If $(a)(b) = \frac{a+1}{b-1}$, where a and b are positive integers and $b > 1$, which of the following is largest?

   (A) $(2)(3)$
   (B) $(3)(3)$
   (C) $(3)(5)$
   (D) $(4)(5)$
   (E) $(5)(3)$

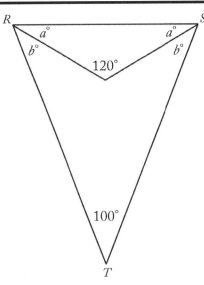

8. Given $\triangle RST$ above, what is the value of b?

   (A) 50
   (B) 40
   (C) 30
   (D) 20
   (E) 10

9. A rectangle solid has dimensions of 2 feet × 1 foot. If it is sliced in small cubes, each of edge, 1 foot, what is the maximum number of such cubes that can be formed?

   (A) 40
   (B) 500
   (C) 1,000
   (D) 2,000
   (E) 4,000

GO ON TO THE NEXT PAGE

Questions 8-9 refer to the graph below.

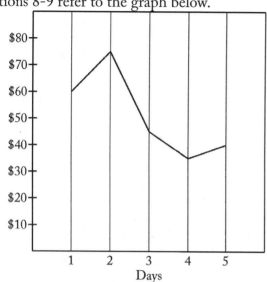

10. John works for 5 days. His daily earnings are displayed on the above graph. What is John's average daily wage during the 5 days?

(A) $75
(B) $35
(C) $50
(D) $51
(E) $39

11. If John earned $35 on the sixth day, what would be the difference between the median and the mode of the wages during the six days?

(A) 5.5
(B) 6.5
(C) 7.5
(D) 8.5
(E) 9.5

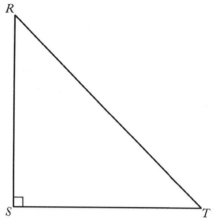

12. In $\triangle RST$ above, RS and ST have lengths equal to the same integers. All of the following could be the area if triangle RST except

(A) $\frac{1}{2}$
(B) 2
(C) $4\frac{1}{2}$
(D) $12\frac{1}{2}$
(E) 20

13. A circle is inscribed in a square. If the perimeter of the square is 40, what is the area of the circle?

(A) $100\,\pi$
(B) $50\,\pi$
(C) $40\,\pi$
(D) $25\,\pi$
(E) $5\,\pi$

GO ON TO THE NEXT PAGE

14. In the figure above, AC is a straight line, Line segments are drawn from B to $D, E, F, G, H, I, J,$ and K, respectively. Which of the following angles has a degree measure that can be found?

(A) $\angle FBG$
(B) $\angle EBG$
(C) $\angle DBG$
(D) $\angle GBI$
(E) $\angle GBJ$

15. If $ax = r$ and $by = r - 1$, then which of the following is correct expression for x?

(A) $\dfrac{by+1}{a}$

(B) $\dfrac{by-1}{a}$

(C) $\dfrac{by+r}{a}$

(D) $by + ar$
(E) $ab + ry$

16. If a, b are odd numbers, and c is even, which of the following is an even number?

(A) $ab + c$
(B) $a(b + c)$
(C) $(a + b) + (b + c)$
(D) $(a + b) - c$
(E) $a + bc$

Distribution of Stamps in Harry's Collection

English	22%
French	18%
South American	25%
U.S.	35%

Distribution of U.S. Stamps in Harry's Collection

Commemoratives	52%
Special Delivery	10%
Postage Due	15%
Air Mail	23%

17. According to the table above, of Harry's collection, U.S. air mail stamps make up

(A) 4.00%
(B) 8.05%
(C) 15.50%
(D) 16.00%
(E) 21.35%

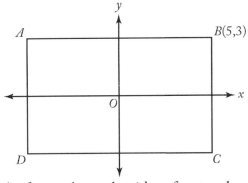

18. In the figure above, the sides of rectangle $ABCD$ are parallel to the y-axis and x-axis are shown. If the rectangle is rotated clockwise about the origin through $90°$, what was the new coordinates of B?

(A) $(3, -5)$
(B) $(-3, 5)$
(C) $(-3, -5)$
(D) $(5, -3)$
(E) $(-5, 3)$

GO ON TO THE NEXT PAGE

19. What is the value of the positive integer n if $n^4 < 25$ and $n \neq n^2$?

20. If x and y are positive integers, $x = 2$ and $x^y = x^{2y-3}$, what is the value of x^y?

21. If k and n are integers, $n - 3 = 2k$ and $2k - 4$ is divisible by 7, is n divisible by 7?

22. If $\frac{1}{2}$ of the money in a certain trust fund was invested in stocks, $\frac{1}{4}$ in bonds, and $\frac{1}{5}$ in a mutual fund, and the remaining $10,000 in a government certificate, what was the total amount of the trust fund?

23. P and Q are each circular regions and the area of P plus the area of Q is equal to 90. The larger circular region has a radius that is 3 times the radius of the smaller circular region. What is the radius of the larger of these regions?

24. If $xy > 0$, $yz < 0$, and $x > 0$, is z less than 0?

GO ON TO THE NEXT PAGE

25. A town T has 20,000 residents, 60 percent of whom are female. The number of female residents who were born in Town T is twice the number of male residents who were <u>not</u> born in Town T. The number of female residents who were <u>not</u> born in Town T is twice the number of female residents who were born in Town T. What percent of the residents were born in Town T?

26. A certain amount of money was donated to a certain charity. Of the amount donated, 40 percent came from corporate donations and $1.5 million came from noncorporate donations. What was the total amount of money donated?

27. The half-life of a certain radioactive substance is 6 hours. In other words, if you start with 8 grams of the substance, 6 hours later you will have 4 grams. If a sample of this substance contains x grams, how many grams remain after 24 hours?

(A) $\frac{x}{32}$

(B) $\frac{x}{16}$

(C) $\frac{x}{8}$

(D) $2x$

(E) $4x$

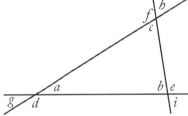

28. In the figure above, what is the sum of the degree measures of the marked angles?

(A) 360^0
(B) 720^0
(C) 900^0
(D) 1080^0
(E) The answer cannot be determined from the information given.

GO ON TO THE NEXT PAGE

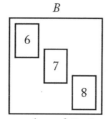

29. Box A contains 3 cards, numbered 3, 4, and 5. Box B contains 3 cards, numbered 6, 7, and 8. If one card is drawn from each box and their sum is calculated, how many different sums are possible?

(A) Eight
(B) Seven
(C) Six
(D) Five
(E) Four

30. Points $A, B,$ and C are on line m, as shown above, such that $AC = \frac{4}{3}AB$. What is the ratio of BC to AB?

(A) $\frac{1}{4}$

(B) $\frac{1}{3}$

(C) $\frac{1}{2}$

(D) $\frac{2}{3}$

(E) The answer cannot be determined from the given information.

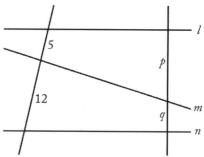

31. Line l and n are parallel to each other, but line m is parallel to neither of the other two. Find $\frac{p}{q}$ if $p + q = 13$.

(A) $\frac{13}{5}$

(B) $\frac{12}{5}$

(C) $\frac{7}{6}$

(D) $\frac{1}{5}$

(E) The answer cannot be determined from the information given.

32. Ross wants to make up 3 letter combinations. He wants each combination to have exactly 3 of the following letters: $A, B, C,$ and D. No letter can be used more than once. For example, "AAB" is not acceptable. What is the maximum number of such triplets that Ross can make up? (The order of the letters must be considered. Example: "ABC" and "CHA" are acceptable triplets.)

(A) 6
(B) 9
(C) 24
(D) 27
(E) 64

GO ON TO THE NEXT PAGE

33. If $x + y + z = 3(a + b)$, which of the following is the average (arithmetic mean) of x, y, z, a, and b in terms of a and b?

(A) $\frac{a+b}{5}$

(B) $\frac{4(a+b)}{15}$

(C) $\frac{a+b}{2}$

(D) $\frac{4(a+b)}{5}$

(E) $(a + b)$

34. A certain number is divided by 3, but its value remains the same. What is this number?

(A) -1

(B) $-\frac{1}{2}$

(C) 0

(D) $\frac{1}{2}$

(E) 1

STOP

this is the end of the exercise